THE COOL MOOSE

ROBERT J. HEALEY, JR.
BEYOND THE BEARD

LAWRENCE W. VERRIA

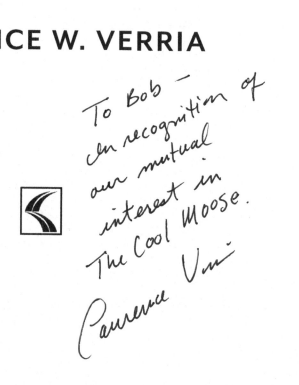

*To Bob —
in recognition of
our mutual
interest in
The Cool Moose.

Lawrence Ver...*

ISBN: 978-1-958217-87-0
Library of Congress Control Number 2022914296

1 2 3 4 5 6 7 8 9 10
Written by Lawrence W. Verria.
Cover and interior design by Matthew St. Jean.
Cover photo by Janet Muscarello.
Published by Stillwater River Publications, Pawtucket, RI, USA.

Names: Verria, Lawrence, author.
Title: The cool moose : Robert J. Healey, Jr. beyond the beard / Lawrence W. Verria.
Other titles: Robert J. Healey, Jr. beyond the beard
Description: First Stillwater River Publications edition. | Pawtucket, RI, USA :
          Stillwater River Publications, [2022] | Includes bibliographical references.
Identifiers: ISBN: 978-1-958217-87-0 | LCCN: 2022914296
Subjects: LCSH: Healey, Robert J. | Political candidates--Rhode Island--Biography.
          | Political campaigns--Rhode Island--History. | Rhode Island--Biography.
          | LCGFT: Biographies.
Classification: LCC F85 .V47 2022 | DDC: 974.5043092--dc23

To my father, Lawrence M. Verria—
the lifelong champion of the underdog.

"They're afraid of what I offer them...real change...not phony hope."
—Robert J. Healey, Jr.

TABLE OF CONTENTS

Foreword   *I*

Preface   *V*

1. Death of The Cool Moose   1
2. Growing up Bob Healey   11
3. Make School Cool   33
4. Healey's Short Honeymoon   41
5. Healey Did What?   67
6. The Year It All Hit the Fan   79
7. A Moose on the Loose   121
8. Not Business as Usual   133
9. What Healey Thought   157
10. The Cool Moose for Governor   175
11. The Best Lieutenant Governor You'll Never Have   221
12. So Close   241
13. The Final Campaign   263
14. The Will   287
15. What Was It All About?   297
16. Epilogue   309

Acknowledgements   *313*

Bibliography   *350*

About the Author   *366*

FOREWORD

BY MATT ALLEN, WPRO TALKSHOW HOST

I've always had a fascination with talk radio. Even as a kid I would tune in to see what was going on. Not because I understood what was being said, but more because I liked that people were communicating with one another. It gave me a strange sense of comfort. Little did I know that in a few short years I would work in the medium and make it a career. It would also be where I would meet Rhode Island's warrior poet, Robert "Cool Moose" Healey.

The first memory I have of Bob Healey probably stems from his second gubernatorial campaign in 1994. I can't pinpoint the year with complete accuracy, but I remember being a teenager at the time listening to Arlene Violet's afternoon talk show when she had Bob Healey in studio to discuss his running for office. There came one phone call from an older woman who spoke with the typical, thick, and annoying Rhode Island accent (only Rhode Islanders are allowed to call it annoying). She said something to Bob Healey that he had heard a million times before but I had only heard for the first time:

"I'd vote for you if you'd only cut your hair."

That moment I was appalled. How dare this lady judge a man's ability to lead or impact lives solely on the length of his hair!!?? The injustice! The short sightedness! What small-minded thinking!

Now mind you I couldn't tell you what Bob's platform was from that day, but I will tell you that that woman's statement and the reaction it invoked in me was the basis of my fascination and respect for Bob going forward through the rest of the time I knew him. He was a man that was misunderstood and principled! Unfairly maligned! He was someone who should have had power because he would know how to manage it properly! Believe me, I wanted him to win. I had him on my show so many times in 2014. When he garnered 21 percent of the vote that election, a campaign operative from the Fung camp called me on election night and swore at me. She said it was my fault that Allan lost because of my support for Bob Healey. I was a true Healey believer. Not so much because he had any radical ideas to make things all that better or different but because he wanted to earn the office based on merit. He wanted to earn someone's vote through his or her intellect and reason, not through flashy promises and expensive marketing. To Bob, the way you won was as important as what you did while in office. Perhaps it was more important. It wasn't like there weren't opportunities for him to raise a little money and put out some creative ads. I often wonder if Bob were still alive, would he have had the ability to adapt to the social media world and get all the free publicity needed to gain whatever office he wanted? We will never know.

Having some time to reflect on Bob Healey's impact, I've come to wonder whether or not it was best that he never won. Maybe he would have been a terrible leader and his best lesson and gift to the people who knew of him would have been clouded by the way he led in office. Maybe the best thing about Bob Healey was that he ran. Period. Maybe the really important thing was that he got 21 percent of the vote in the 2014 race for governor. He had substantial support in a race where he spent $37 and others spent a million. Before that, he got 40% in a race for Lt Governor while running to get rid of the office. All of that would have been sullied if he'd actually won. You know how people say, "It's the journey, not the destination"? With Bob it was the running and the campaigning that really mattered. It's only as I reflect on his life now that I can say that. It reminds me of a line from a Batman movie: "You either die a hero or live long enough to see yourself become the villain." We have enough villains. We definitely don't need anymore. To some, Bob died a bit of a hero. A local one. One that maybe not everyone would understand unless you knew and followed him.

You never really know how much time you have in life. One of the oddities of being human is that we know we are finite but act like tomorrow is guaranteed. Looking back, there are many questions I would love to be able to ask Bob Healey. What was it that created his golden rule regarding money and politics? What drove him to eschew offers of and/or ask for financial support of any kind? Many earnest people actually believed in the possibility that he could have won if only he shaved his beard, cut his hair, or spent a little cash, but he outright refused to do any of that. Why? One time in an in-studio interview, the man told me that he really never watched TV. Rather, he would sit in his living room at night and read or write. He had stacks of position papers on every subject you could imagine. When you wanted to know his take on a specific issue, he'd supply you with a yellowed, cigar smoke infused white paper he had printed out early in the 90's or 80's. His thoughts were his thoughts. They never seemed to change. I've been interviewing political types for over 20 years and I can tell you Robert Healey was the only person to ever do that. The man was unique in his simplicity.

I'd often sit there and talk to him and wonder, "What makes this guy tick?" What was it about Bob's childhood, or his education, or his family that created this enigmatic personality? He had business dealings in foreign countries, a wine label attached to wine made from the leftovers of other people's wines, a law practice, a cheese shop, and he was reportedly a wealthy man but drove a car that looked like it had been rescued from a junk yard. Those are just the idiosyncrasies I can name off the top of my head. There are probably many more that I just don't know. I was too young to remember his time on the Warren school committee. What drove his interest in education and government? Who were the people around him? Did he have a girlfriend? A boyfriend? Was his childhood happy? Sad? The day Bob died, the possibility of hearing his answers to those questions died with him.

I'm writing this forward before reading any of the text that follows. It was a purposeful act. I wanted to give you my perspective on Robert Healey before I learned more about him. I wanted to delve into the story of The Cool Moose with you, the reader. To go along on this adventure with you in spirit if not in reality. I'm wondering how my perspective on the man will change, if at all. What insight will it offer on the politics and people of the state I grew up in? I'm ecstatic at the chance to find out.

I'd still like to know the answers to my questions about Bob or at least have enough information and perspective to figure them out on my own. They are worth knowing. Robert Healey and the impact he had on a small corner of the world is worth knowing. It's the story of the impact that one principled, quirky, and kind individual can have on his home and the people in it. For me, it's the story of how one person, using no force other than his mind, his example, and his authenticity, can make you reflect on your own presuppositions about all kinds of things. He didn't just challenge the status quo. He challenged your status quo.

I'm happy that those of you who didn't know the Cool Moose will get a chance to do so, even just a little bit. I knew Bob Healey. I don't know how well. I'm about to find out.

PREFACE

One evening as I drove in heavy traffic through Warren, Rhode Island, I took notice of a tall figure about a hundred yards ahead to the right. He wore a white shirt and black tie, framed by an oversized, dark-colored suit jacket. As I drove closer, I noticed the man stood on a slim strip of grass that had grown almost two feet high. That sliver of lawn served as the only separation between a yellow ranch to the man's back and the busy main road to his front. As my vehicle drew nearer, I recognized the person on the side of the road as Robert J. Healey, Jr., the perennial third party candidate.

Bob, known widely as *the Cool Moose*, held a smoldering cigar between two fingers in his right hand, nestled a phone between his cheek and right shoulder, and cut the grass with a sickle clasped in his left hand. His multitasking included receptive body language to drivers who tooted their car horns as they passed his home, which also served as his law office. The whole impromptu arrangement provided the perfect backdrop for a vintage Cool Moose photo op. As his flowing hair blew in the wind, he enjoyed the smoke, listened to a caller's phone message, and tended to a primitive form of landscaping. He relished the state affairs, unconcerned about others' perceptions of him but intent on acknowledging them all the same with a grin or head nod.

As I drove past Bob, I smiled to myself. He often had that effect on me.

Bob and I crossed paths numerous times between 1983 and 2016. During those years, our talks became more meaningful, but never very personal. Still, a friendly comfort developed between the two of us. I do not know what he made of me, but I came to see him as a melody of normally incompatible descriptors: engaging, self-effacing, familiar, mysterious, brilliant, at times odd, and always fascinating.

Bob Healey appeared eternally young to me. He acted young, too. Ready to engage, eager to make a point, and ever present, he embraced life as a youthful spirit pursuing an unending adventure. As such, when I first thought to explore his political career, I didn't feel hurried to undertake my research. I thought I had lots of time. As it turned out, Bob Healey did not.

To some onlookers, Robert Healey presented as an alien, hairy political candidate in a familiar world of polished and preppy politicians. Looking like a hodgepodge of Grizzly Adams, Frank Zappa, John Lennon, and Jesus Christ, he stood out to a sizable number of prospective voters as either an active hippie or a 60s leftover. Neither characterization comes close to capturing the Cool Moose's essence. Others saw him as an individualistic showman, and the hair and beard factored into the act. That portrayal proves erroneous as well. Those who read his political position papers and platforms may have thought they understood Bob Healey. They probably did not. Bob Healey defies surface-focused descriptors. His substance does not communicate from a look or stance. To discover Bob Healey's core, one must delve deeper, and look wider.

Undeniably, Bob made an indelible mark on Rhode Island's political scene. By the early 2000s, it seemed almost every Rhode Islander knew of him. Though in many cases that familiarity extended only to appearance recognition, over a 30-year span, no political figure (with the possible exception of Providence Mayor Vincent "Buddy" Cianci) garnered more consistent attention throughout Rhode Island (and beyond) than Robert J. Healey, Jr. From 1982 to 2016, Healey's unconventional appearance, head-turning campaigns, and candid informative commentary enticed inquiring looks, occasionally incited spontaneous laughter, and ultimately caused political and personal reflection. He drew national media controversy and conveyed a base message that could resonate across the political spectrum. Robert Healey made people think, and challenged them to act. Even a Healey detractor would have to acknowledge that at the very least, Healey elicited consideration and fostered contemplation. Some politicians would spend handsomely for that acknowledgment. For Healey, the attention came free of charge, literally.

I first thought to write a biography about Robert Healey in 2013. I did not tell him of my intention. I had numerous questions for my welcoming, thick-bearded acquaintance. Did he truly want to win election to a statewide office? How might he have governed, had he won? What made him tick? Was he an overlooked third-party prophet, or did he amount to little more than an endearing cultish political figure? But all those questions aside, one overriding factor compelled me to learn more about his story: the man intrigued me. He still does.

Biographies typically tell the story of winners. Even though failure might enter into the plot, the main character's victories make them narrative worthy. Employing that qualifier, Healey falls far short of the biography prerequisite. For all his efforts over a 30-year period, encompassing eight campaigns (including seven runs for statewide office), he never served as Rhode Island's governor or lieutenant governor. In fact, as even the most ardent Cool Moose fan club member has to admit, he never came close to winning a statewide election. Regardless, Bob Healey's allure endured all the disappointing political defeats.

Bob presented to most as a political anomaly. Among other considerations, that made him interesting. But his distinctiveness and originality do not account for his significance. Clearly, Robert Healey mattered. But how so? And from what origin? And to what end?

This work pursues the answers to those questions.

CHAPTER 1

DEATH OF THE COOL MOOSE

In early March 2016, the phone rang several times at 75 Sowams Drive in Barrington, Rhode Island. When no one picked up, DeWolf Fulton left a message on the answering machine for Robert J. Healey, Jr. Known widely as "the Cool Moose," Healey had gained a major political following over the years, and enjoyed wide name recognition throughout Rhode Island and beyond. Fulton expected Healey to return his call shortly.

A former newspaper reporter and Providence school teacher, Fulton had organized a Bosworth Lecture[1] to discuss the upcoming presidential election. He wanted the audience to hear participating speakers' conflicting ideologies in a balanced and open environment.[2] That goal presented a tall challenge. For many, the charged Donald Trump-Hillary Clinton presidential race had taken a turn from predominantly political to primarily personal. Fulton worried that the seeping partisan bloodline from that contest would alter any semblance of equilibrium he wanted to maintain in his planned forum. To encourage a healthy give-and-take discourse, he needed a moderator of stature who could manage a range of ideas amongst passionate politicians with competing platforms. Robert Healey, a perennial candidate for governor and lieutenant governor, came to mind as a "disarming moderator."[3] Fulton thought Healey had established the presence and earned the respect to maintain an issues-focused discussion.

Fulton first met Bob Healey in the early 1980s. At the time, Fulton worked as an editor at the Bristol Phoenix. He had learned from colleagues at the Warren Times-Gazette that Healey, then the Chairman of the Warren School Committee, presided over meetings in his bare feet. That struck Fulton as "pretty remarkable."[4] And when he heard that Healey had run for election under the banner of "a strange man for a strange job," Fulton felt compelled to meet him.[5]

Finding Healey proved easier than Fulton had anticipated. The Warren School Committee Chairman made almost daily appearances on the town's Main Street sidewalks, often promoting one cause or another. Lanky, usually barefoot, and sporting shoulder-length hair and a beard that extended just north of his chest cavity, Robert Healey stood out in most crowds, especially in a small and predominantly mainstream town like Warren.

Though Fulton resembled an aging son from the 1950 television series, *The Adventures of Ozzie and Harriet*, he took an immediate liking to Bob, who could have blended seamlessly onto a 1969 Woodstock stage. While Bob's appearance gained a smiling recognition from Fulton, the Chairman's persona and purpose attracted Fulton more. In addition to Healey's amiable disposition, Fulton later commented about the young Chairman: "And of course as a journalist you want that watchdog attitude as you're looking at government…He [Healey] had that same watchdog attitude that the press has. So, we had that affinity."[6]

When Robert Healey did not return his first call in March 2016, Fulton tried two more times during the week to make contact. Again, an answering machine recorded Fulton's messages. Healey responded to neither communication. That struck Fulton as unusual. Healey almost always answered his calls personally, or returned the contact shortly afterward. Fulton wondered why he hadn't this time.

Unbeknown to Fulton, parties close to Healey had observed other changes in Bob's behavior, and health. Claire Boyes, his live-in companion, political cohort, and frequent confidant from 1991 to 2016, had taken particular notice of Bob's sagging spirit in 2015. He moved slower and smiled less. She did not know for sure if his sluggish pace stemmed from the off-season election lull, or something more serious accounted for his languorous deportment. She had reasons to determine the latter. Earlier, in 2014, she learned that Bob's blood pressure had spiked alarmingly high. Despite her pleas for him to seek medical attention, Bob refused. He reasoned that a doctor's recommendations for his potentially life-threatening condition did not amount to a cure. As such, he saw no point in pursuing medical services,[7] and therefore rarely did.

Around 2014, Bob's face intimated his progressively failing health.

According to many friends, by 2014 heart disease and political stress accelerated the aging of Robert Healey.

Surrounded by an increasingly gray mane, his brown eyes looked often glossy. His eyelids drooped at the corners, and sunk increasingly further into his skull. His face appeared drawn and gray tinted. His skin sagged, and seemed to have lost much of its luster. Some concluded that too many political battles accounted for his fatigued presentation.[8] And, in part, that may have proved true. But a doctor's examination might have revealed a graver prognosis.

Bob's cousin, Ruth Ellen Stone Seymour, knew of Bob's physical ailments by 2014 as well. She and Bob had grown up like brother and sister at their grandmother's Barrington home during the late 1950s and early 1960s. Both had learned of their family's history with cardiovascular disease. One family member had died of heart ailments at 51 years old.[9] While Ruth Ellen vexed over her cousin's failing health and potentially shortened life, Bob worried more about becoming old and existing in a deteriorated state. Neither Ruth or Claire understood just how far his condition had progressed by 2014.[10]

As 2015 approached and Bob's health issues advanced, he started to reflect more on his life. His old high school friends, Tom and Nancy Tracy, took notice.[11] Tom had graduated in 1975 from Warren High School with Bob; Nancy had graduated a year later. While they had lost touch with Bob in the years immediately following graduation, in more recent years they rekindled the friendship. During those later years, Bob would often drop by unannounced to smoke a cigar and drink bourbon in their backyard, situated not much further than a stone's throw from their old high school, now a regional middle school. Tom and Nancy enjoyed Bob's impromptu visits. Their ensuing talks often took place around a fire, and extended well into the night. As their get-togethers continued, Tom noticed that his old high school friend talked increasingly about his life, and theirs. Bob marveled out loud at their, and his, comfortable surroundings and economic security.[12] On several occasions he reiterated the good times they had enjoyed. As 2016 approached, he spoke more often in past tense.[13]

Joseph DePasquale, a Warren Town Council member from 2002

to 2010 and 2012 to present, came of age knowing Bob Healey, who played with Joe's older siblings. Joe, nine years younger than his brothers' friend, grew close to Bob in the middle 1980s. Joe looked up to Bob, referencing him as a mentor, and confidant.[14] In 2015, Joe started to notice changes in his older friend. At first it seemed to Joe that Bob had lost a step or two. Later, he grasped that Bob's slower movements demonstrated a more serious condition with increasingly concerning repercussions. The first incident that made that realization clearer to Joe occurred in late 2015. Bob had called Joe over to his Metacom Avenue law office in Warren. Bob needed help clearing a large area of littered tree limbs atop uneven ground. Bob helped Joe with the job. At some point Joe noticed that Bob had lied down amongst branches and brush. Joe figured Bob had tripped and elected to rest rather than resume work. That was not the case. Bob had experienced a dizzy spell, lost his balance, and had passed out. Before getting to his feet, Bob had to wait an extended period of time for his heart to stop racing and his head to clear.[15]

Another even more concerning incident occurred when Bob attended a Warren Town Council meeting in early 2016. Joe DePascuale served as the Council Chairman at that meeting. While waiting for his opportunity to address the Town Council, Bob worked on a crossword puzzle, as he often did to kill time. When his turn to speak arrived, Bob approached the podium in front, and soon had to lean on the lectern for support. Shortly into his speech his voice sounded increasingly marbly. Eventually he couldn't finish his sentences. His voice dropped off to a barely audible level. Saving his friend from further personal embarrassment, Joe DePasquale knew enough of what Bob spoke of to help him finish his statement and move the matter along. And he had done more than that. As Bob told his younger friend the next day, while at the podium he had temporarily lost the ability to function.[16]

Jade Gotauco, a close friend of Bob's during the last seven years of his life, noticed the same downturn in his overall vitality that others had. Jade first met Bob in 2009. She enjoyed his quirky sense of humor and fun disposition.[17] Their relationship developed quickly, unbeknownst to many other people in Bob's life, at least until years later.[18] Jade started to notice significant signs of Bob's declining health as early as 2014. Bob experienced increasing shaky spells and dizzy episodes.[19] Once, while representing a client in court, he fainted. While he did see a doctor for a short bit afterward, again Bob resisted any kind of prolonged treatment. Though he complained about his health, he refused to do anything significant to diagnose or counter the problem. This became a source of disagreements with Jade, and other people in his life, especially his closest friend, Brian Fortin.[20]

Fortin first met Bob when he was 13 years old and Bob was 11. They resided in the same neighborhood, and, years later, lived together, even after Brian married and had a son. From the 1980s onward, Brian ran several of Bob's campaigns, from school committee to governor. While growing up, the two friends talked about everything: girls, religion, aspirations, politics, and then later, around 2012, increasingly Bob's health. Bob complained about his worsening condition to Brian well before he had to others.[21] As time went on, Brian noticed more indicators of his best friend's declining fitness. These signs included a slower delivery and a more subdued manner.

As Bob's health deteriorated, he continued an unhealthy lifestyle. He exercised rarely, if ever, and smoked cigars often.[22] While a vegetarian, he ate fried foods almost every day, especially French fries, for which he had an appetite that bordered on an affinity. It seemed as if he had a life goal to find the "perfect French fry."[23] When he walked into Rod's Grill, a prototype 1950s-style diner in Warren, he didn't have to verbalize his order. The cook, Ray Rodriguez, knew to serve Bob his breakfast: black coffee and French fries.[24]

Many knew about Bob's love of the fried potato. Over 30 years earlier, Robert Craven, a fellow student at New England Law School, and later a long-standing Rhode Island state representative, remembered that Bob's eating habits wreaked havoc on arteries struggling to remain clear. Near the New England Law School in Boston, Bob and many of his peers frequented a cheap eats restaurant. Some of the law students limited themselves to a salad plate or an occasional sandwich. But not Bob Healey. He ordered sandwiches smothered with feta cheese and mayonnaise-based sauces. And then there were the French fries, which, as Craven recalled, Bob Healey couldn't consume fast enough.[25]

When his health further plunged in 2015, Bob agreed to see a friend's doctor, who prescribed medicine and supplements as initial treatment. For a short while Bob reported feeling better, but soon after determined the prescriptions had run their course and no longer offered benefit. Bob discontinued the treatment.[26] According to friends, as time passed, he seemed to increasingly choose resignation over medical intervention.[27]

Bryan Rodrigues, who had first met Bob when he interviewed him for a school history class project in 1986, also learned of Healey's poor health nearing 2015. Over the years Bryan looked up to Bob as a mentor and friend. Bryan knew of Bob's heart problem, but said Bob held on to a "Mr. Natural attitude" that called for "no extraordinary measures."[28] Even when Bob had encountered a slipped disc problem in his back, he chose to sleep on a wooden table and let his legs dangle rather than seek a doctor's care.[29]

Bob's high school girlfriend, Katherine Kittell, grew increasingly concerned with Bob's compromised health, too. In January 2016, she and her husband called Bob to see if he could help them move a piano, which Bob agreed to do. Shortly into the endeavor, both Kathy and her husband Bill noticed Bob's reddening face. Later, Kathy pleaded with Bob to do something about his health. He responded, "Yes, Katherine," a phrase Bob had used regularly to fend off Kathy's suggestions over the years.[30]

Bob's declining health affected his psychological well-being, too. According to Jade Gotauco, his feelings and judgments turned bleaker as his heart disease progressed. He researched philosophy more, grew pensive, and changed his perception of others. He lost faith that people really wanted change. Though the 2014 governor's race rejuvenated his spirit somewhat, two months later discouraging thoughts again possessed his thinking.[31]

Some close political confidants, who did not know of Bob's heart problems, nevertheless took notice of his diminishing drive and outward fatigue. Gloria Garvin, an active Cool Moose Party advocate and organizer, thought that growing pressures plagued Bob after the 2014 election. She felt those rising stressors accounted for Bob's increased anxiousness and failing spirit.[32] Grant Garvin, his campaign manager for the 2014 governor's race, arrived at a similar conclusion.[33]

On Super Bowl Sunday, 2016, Bob told Brian Fortin, "I'm dying."[34] At that point Bob had lost weight and felt increasingly tired. During the game Bob confided to Brian, "They [presumably doctors] can't do anything for me."[35] Brian encouraged Bob to seek other opinions, pursue alternative treatments, and get more help. Bob refused. Brian responded, "I'm going to bust your balls until you do right by yourself."[36] He called Bob almost every day from that point on, encouraging and later berating his friend to get help. Bob didn't do that, and eventually stopped answering his phone.[37]

As March 2016 approached, Bob's health continued to plunge. Regardless, his unhealthy behaviors persisted. During that time, he maintained a full social calendar. He continued to live life on his terms. During that month, Bob met up with his younger friend, Bryan Rodrigues, at a party. Bob drank wine, smoked cigars, and made no mention of his health conditions.[38]

Bob Healey's actions during the first half of March 2016 suggest he might have had a grasp on his fast-approaching termination. During that time frame he asked Kathy Kittell about friends whose future prospects concerned him.[39] Not understanding the specific context of his questions and unable to foresee his immediate future, Kathy responded that everyone would be fine. The talk between the former high school sweethearts took on a more personal quality than prior years. Kathy recalled later, as Bob left that day "he gave me a wonderful kiss and said thank you for everything. Almost like a goodbye."[40]

Jade Gotauco lived at Bob's Metacom Avenue ranch in March 2016. On Friday, March 18, Jade planned to work at the artist co-op business on Main St. in Warren. She and Bob had started the co-op as a business venture. That night Bob texted her a short message. It read, "Just wanted to say thank you."[41] His text did not specify anything more. Jade thought that was odd, but didn't think much more of it. She didn't see or hear from Bob on Saturday. That didn't concern her. Often, they would go a couple days without meeting or talking to one another.[42]

On Friday, March 18, Claire Boyes visited family in Denver. She talked with Bob by phone that night. Claire thought he sounded fine—upbeat, in fact. He said that Gregory Rufo, an old friend and fellow Scrabble player, had arrived back from Florida and that they might get together. Bob thought he would go to a local art gallery earlier in the evening. He told Claire that if they didn't talk beforehand, he would pick her up at the airport on Tuesday.[43]

On Friday, March 18, during the late afternoon, Bob went to the art gallery to view the work of Adam Tracy, the son of his friends, Tom and Nancy. Adam, a practicing artist and art teacher at Tiverton High School, spoke with Bob at the exposition. Bob told Adam that if he needed anything, please let him know.[44] As usual, Bob appeared interested in Adam's continued success as an artist.

After leaving the art gallery, Bob visited with his friend Scott DeSilveira. The two smoked a few cigars. A couple times during the visit Bob said he had to leave to meet someone in Providence, but ended up staying well into the night with his friend. Scott doubted Bob ever went to Providence. Scott later told his friend Joe Moniz, "Bob didn't look good that night."[45]

Sometime before 1:00 a.m. on Saturday, Bob arrived home. Later,

Healey talks with Adam Tracy, a local artist and Tiverton High School art teacher, on Friday, March 14, 2016, at approximately 4:00 P.M. at The Collaborative in Warren, Rhode Island. This is the last known photo of Bob Healey.

he wrote a brief note to Claire. He placed it on the side table by his bed. He dated and timed the note: Saturday, March 19, 1:00 a.m. When Claire later saw the note, she did not initially understand the message. She would later.

People who phoned Bob on Saturday, March 19, heard Bob's answering machine message. He didn't return any of those calls. Greg Rufo grew increasingly concerned. On Sunday, just before 10:00 p.m., Rufo entered Bob's bedroom in his Sowams Drive house in Barrington. Rufo found him "lying in his bed under blankets, as if sleeping."[46] Bob was unresponsive. The police ruled shortly afterward that he had died suddenly. Like so many actions Bob undertook in his 58-year life, his untimely expiration surprised, stunned, and shocked Rhode Islanders. [47]

CHAPTER 2

GROWING UP BOB HEALEY

On May 3, 1957, a seamstress and a plumber welcomed the birth of their son, Robert J. Healey Jr. Given Robert Healey's off-beat personal and political life, one might expect that he came into the world differently from most other newborns. However, by all accounts, it seems one could describe his arrival as quite conventional, even by the 1950s' conservative expectations. This ordinary debut would prove a stark departure from almost everything else in Robert Healey's life for the next half century.

Robert Healey's mother, Mary J. (Martinelli) Healey, sewed handkerchiefs for much of her 57-year career at I. Shalom, in Warren, Rhode Island.[1] From May 1957 onward, Mary's life would revolve around her son. Her husband, Robert J. Healey Sr., worked as a journeyman plumber at Dallaire Plumbing Company, also in Warren.[2] Though both parents came from relatively large families, they raised Robert J. Healey Jr. as their only child.

Most of the time Robert and Mary called their son Bob, presumably to avoid confusion when referencing the father or son. Bob grew up in a small, two-story, weathered, shingled home with a Gambrel roof. Built in the 1920s, the rented home stood close to the road,

Though the Healey family had little in the way of monetary wealth, by all accounts they shared generously with everyone who entered their rented humble abode. This photo from the 1970's includes from right to left, a young female visitor, Bob Healey, Jr., Mary Healey, and Robert Healey, Sr. (Photo courtesy of Brian Fortin.)

situated in the middle of a 600-yard dead-end lane on the west side of Warren's Main Street. A four-car garage that took up the lion's share of the backyard made the house stand out from the rest in the work-ing-class neighborhood. This fact bore no particular importance in 1957, but in addition to making the property unique, the structure served a practical and somewhat peculiar function years later.

Running perpendicular to Route 114 (Main Street), Bob Healey's home street and early stomping grounds connected the town's main drag directly to the Warren waterfront. If one stood on the small moon-sliver-shaped beach that separated Healey's home street from the Warren River, they could view Bristol to the left and Barrington to the right. During incoming high tides, Warren River's constant current drew strength from Narragansett Bay and snaked northward by Warren's Water Street toward Barrington, where the flow seemed to pause and rest along the Wampanoag Trail close to Seekonk, Massachusetts.

Bob looked across the Warren River numerous times during his early life. When he did, he could see Rumstick Neck (diagonally across the water), a very wealthy section in Barrington. Rumstick Point's lavish homes, large lawns, and long piers contrasted Warren's western shore of tightly packed modest houses and postage-stamp yards, which neighborhood children had worn down to packed dirt. On many occasions, an impressionable young Bob Healey stood at the end of his neighborhood street, looked across the bay, and took notice of the obvious disparities that separated him and his friends from the well-to-do. He processed those inequities continuously and profoundly during his childhood and young adult years.[3]

In some respects, Bob Healey's young station in life exemplified the town he inhabited. Two celebrated communities sandwiched Warren. Historic Bristol, standing stoically to the south, boasted a renowned Fourth of July parade and the longest continuous Independence Day commemoration in the nation. To the north, Barrington identified proudly as Rhode Island's second most affluent suburb, and arguably the state's most desirable sleepy town. Warren, the smallest town in the smallest county in the smallest state in America,[4] remained through the 1970s a predominately lower middle-class town of approximately 10,000 people, many of whom lived in tenement houses. Warren's renters could choose to attend one of several Roman Catholic churches in the area, and, if they could afford to do so, quench their thirst at one of its numerous small-town bars.

The Healey homestead stood five houses east of the Warren River and a few steps west from the East Bay Railroad tracks. Burrs Park, where Warren children met to play basketball and baseball and socialize with other neighborhood boys and girls, lay a short walk northward from Bob's home. By the early 1970s, the nearby tracks served more as a walking path to Burrs park than a busy line running from Providence to neighboring Bristol. Still, young Warren boys and girls who traveled along the line on foot or by bike had to be careful of the occasional approaching trains during the day.

If the river, tracks, and park outlined the outer reaches of Bob's early years, the Healey family home served as his childhood safe-hold—and, later, a neighborhood meeting place. And if his father was the king of the castle, by all accounts he ruled as a quiet monarch, who looked over his manor with striking blue eyes.[5] Though Bob's father had not pursued formal education beyond high school, he read the paper religiously and finished *The New York Times* crossword puzzle daily, never leaving a blank box.[6] The career plumber endeavored to instill an intellectual curiosity in his son, perhaps evidenced by purchasing a subscription to *Soviet Life* for Bob at a young age.[7] But above all, Father Healey taught his son to not let anyone define him.[8] The senior Healey, who died in 1990, didn't much like his own profession. He told his son, "I want you to be anything you want to be, except a plumber."[9] At age 62, Robert Healey Sr. retired, sold his tools, and self-relegated to a plumber of solely dire squirting, spraying, or streaming household emergencies.[10]

Robert Healey Sr. laughed loudly, which complemented his welcoming smile.[11] He had an "endearing quality of ease" and possessed the "patience of a saint."[12] But ease and patience did not qualify him for sainthood candidacy. In earlier years, Robert Healey Sr. carried on as a bar-drinking gambler and womanizer who developed a knack for showing up in the wrong place at the wrong time.[13] At least one of these predilections continued into fatherhood. Bob's father frequented the Raynham track on Friday nights to bet on dog races. While the senior Healey placed his bets, Bob and his mother did not leave the car, which remained parked in the dog track's lot. Bob would sometimes complete his homework assignments while sitting in the back seat. If the father had a good evening at the track, Bob would get a hot dog and other treats at the end of the night.[14]

While his father nurtured the quieter, intellectual side of his son, his mother taught Bob to debate, unceasingly. For that purpose, Mary

Healey coached by modeling. The mother-and-son debates would go on for days, or occasionally weeks.[15] To one childhood observer, disputes of one sort or another seemed a constant state of being between the mother and son.[16] Sometimes disagreements would start as a "nagging session," then metamorphosize into several days of spirited debate. Both mother and son exhibited stubborn streaks. Usually, the debates focused on a principle, and occasionally started up just for the purpose of spirited competition. On rare occasions, marathon debates brought about prolonged cooling off periods where neither spoke to the other.[17] But normally the disputes did not rise to the level of blood sport.[18] Eventually the debate fizzled out, with little or no lingering bad feelings. As Bob's adult experiences would suggest, his mother taught him well. Bob offered, in future decades: while my mother "was no intellectual match for my father…She taught me that every day was a new argument."[19] Debates aside, Mary Healey brimmed with pride over her son, often commenting on his humble disposition.[20]

So, while the Healey family offered its share of eyebrow-raising moments, the family remained close, welcoming to friends, generous to visitors, and well-received by most if not all who came to know them. Bob and his friends looked back fondly on their days at the Healey homestead.

Up to age five, Bob visited five days a week at his grandmother's home while his parents went to work. During that time, the Martinelli grandmother helped raise Bob and his cousin, Ruth Ellen. While he and his cousin got along well, Ruth Ellen described him years later as a "loner."[21]

Most mornings at their grandmother's Sowams Drive home in Barrington, Bob and Ruth Ellen watched Captain Kangaroo and enjoyed their grandmother's cooking throughout the day. Her specialty dishes included fried foods, especially fried red peppers, which Bob devoured.[22] He never lost his appetite for fried foods.

When Bob turned five, he attended kindergarten at Warren's Main Street Elementary School. With his short hair neatly cropped, he arrived every day to class wearing his ironed collared shirt and bow tie.[23] During most of Bob's elementary education, he remained a professed loner who stayed away from other congregating students, but took careful notice of their interactions. He recalled years later, "I spent most of my hours alone on the playground until I would hook up with other social misfits."[24]

In fourth grade, Bob's social status changed a bit. That transformation took place largely owing to the arrival of Mike Ferri, a new student from California. Mike had a way with Warren's elementary school girls, due in part to his blond hair, which apparently stood out as an irresistible rarity in Warren.[25] Mike's lure of female attention made him unwelcome competition amongst the other boys, who initially ostracized him. Isolated from most of the local male youths, Mike took to "finding" Bob.[26]

Mike and Bob developed a habit of leaning against a school wall during recesses. There, separated from others, they talked about many things, but most often Mike's *past* life. Mike's earlier involvements and the vocabulary he crafted to explain those occurrences differed radically from anything Bob had experienced or heard of in his insulated world. For example, Mike talked about his interactions with girls in explicit terms. While encounters of that sort interested Bob little in fourth grade, he noticed that knowledge of those exploits soon elevated his new friend's prominence and influence with the other boys.

Bob's takeaway of all this is interesting, more for its later reported effect than the initial questionable logic he employed to process his conclusion. A young Bob Healey had noticed that Mike's experience differed dramatically from most Warren boys. In some ways, Bob thought, Mike even came across as peculiar. And that served Mike well. This revelation impacted Bob Healey definitively. In his nine-year-old mind, Bob determined that maybe his own idiosyncrasies could lead to desirable developments, too. Being different, even eccentric, held hidden benefits.[27] Making that notion all the more spectacular, standing apart from others came about effortlessly and naturally to Bob.

While Mike and Bob's friendship lasted only a few months, the

According to a childhood friend, during his younger years Bob Healey's mother often dressed her son in a pressed shirt and bow tie. (Courtesy of Ruth Ellen Stone Seymour)

California transplant's effect on him proved transforming. Bob later reflected on Mike Ferri, "He was, in the limited world of nine-year-old boys, free…At that time of life, it allowed for me to fathom just what it was to be different and survive in a world of conformity."[28] According to Bob, his elementary school yard friendship opened for him a "world of rebellion… without a cause,"[29] even if only vicariously. Bob expounded further, "I was then, a rebel by default. I had yet to understand the need to have cause, the need to find the perimeters of the subject and exploit them by standing on the boundary line. I had no idea what intellect would play as a part in the ability to stand alone. But I knew that I was on to something big.… Mike had shaped a loner into an individualist in a few short months."[30]

In fifth grade, Bob attended Joyce Street Elementary. He despised his new school. To cope, the recently found individualist asserted his free thinking by bunking school repeatedly.[31] While it is not clear where he went while bunking school, the practice did not continue much after fifth grade.

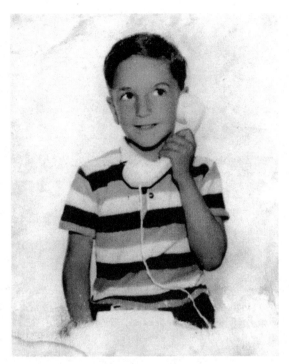

Bob Healey presented as the typical well-groomed boy of the early 1960's.
(Courtesy of Ruth Ellen Stone Seymour)

Sometime around Bob's 10th birthday, another change agent entered his life. Though very different from Mike Ferri, her roll proved just as significant. Barbara Value moved into Bob Healey's neighborhood in the mid 1960s. Recently divorced, she had three children. Initially, she stood out from her new neighbors in two ways. For one, she had earned advanced education degrees. Secondly, her family relations included former President John F. Kennedy, a first cousin on his mother's side. In Warren, a Catholic enclave, claiming John Kennedy as a relation elevated Barbara Value to royal stature. In the mid-1960s, most of Ms. Value's Warren neighbors probably had her cousin's image framed and hung in their front entrance halls, beside Pope Paul VI and Robert Kennedy (her other famous cousin).

Standing on their own, neither of the above two points impressed young Bob Healey very much. Though he took notice of what he perceived as Barbara Value's advanced intelligence, initially he just enjoyed going over to the Value family home to play with her son. When Bob visited his new neighbor's home, over time, he noticed newspapers and books strewn over the parlor coffee table. Soon, he took further notice of Ms. Value's well-read background, interest in art, and communicated grasp of many subjects. He liked that "she was sure of herself."[32] That Ms. Value remained grounded in a neighborhood of "regular folk" impressed him more than anything else. She apparently didn't need to flaunt her superior educational background. It appeared to Bob that she did not cling to the "the trappings she had been afforded."[33]

Bob took away three primary points from his experiences with Ms. Value. First, "You don't have to let your position in life transform your existence…She transcended the 'us versus them' class warfare, probably without a thought that she was such an envoy."[34] Second, Barbara Value's indifference to social standing endeared her to a neighborhood inhabited mostly by undereducated laborers. As such, Value's Warren neighbors responded well to her. Third, she taught those of modest backgrounds that they need not be intimidated by the more educated, the financially well-endowed, and the better connected. Of this third takeaway, Healey offered many years later, "As a child of the working poor from a small factory town, I could have easily been intimidated or even envious or antagonistic when I found myself in the company of the privileged."[35] Ms. Value taught him that feelings of inferiority and deflation need not result from encounters with the rich and well educated. In the coming years, Bob thought often of the lessons Barbara Value imparted by example, and which she embedded, probably unknowingly, in her attentive young admirer.

Bob went to Hugh Cole school for sixth grade, where he met Gary Lavey. Surprisingly, they became close friends "instantly."[36] While Bob remained yoked in his loner state, Gary, renowned around town for his dominant athleticism,[37] enjoyed celebrity status within several social circles. But for a number of reasons, Gary took an immediate liking to his new acquaintance. Gary appreciated that Bob came across as "his own person," a bit eccentric, and brilliant.[38] Bob engaged people to think different ideas. At 11 years old, Gary had never met anyone quite like Bob.[39]

And, other, shallower factors cemented the two sixth graders' friendship. Gary took notice of Bob's lunches. While other kids ate deviled ham or fluffernutter sandwiches, Bob brought lunches that stereotypically (and accurately) suggested he had an Italian mother. Mary Healey prepared all kinds of pasta dishes and other Italian foods for her son that seemed exotic to other pre-adolescent boys.

From age 12 onward, those Italian-influenced lunches contained no meat. In 1969, Bob had a hamburger that did not sit well. He decided not to eat meat anymore. Later, the reasoning for choosing a vegetarian diet broadened to, "I really believe in not abusing your body."[40] However, he also confided, "I smoke cigars, drink bourbon, and eat fried foods with lots of salt."[41]

Gary and Bob remained lifelong friends. Bob would later reflect that Gary influenced him more than almost anyone else in his life.[42] While he did not expound as to why that was so, it may have been that Gary, of the crowd Bob had earlier noticed from the outskirts of an elementary school yard, had ventured to befriend him before most others even noticed his existence. Gary accepted and liked Bob, never ignoring nor rejecting him for other, more popular friends.

Over the coming years Bob and Gary played at Burrs Park regularly. Unbeknownst to some, Bob possessed considerable athletic skill, blessed with great hands that served him well the many nights he, Gary, and other boys faced off in pickup basketball games. Gary remembered Bob as extremely competitive, referencing him as a "beast."[43]

While not one to fight, a young Bob Healey demonstrated unyielding perseverance. On one occasion Gary tried to use his superior strength to make Bob say "uncle." In the process of that attempt, Gary had Bob in a headlock and began rubbing a wire brush back and forth on Bob's forearm. Bob would not give in. Gary persisted. After a time, Gary noticed Bob's reddening and raw forearm. Still, Bob would not relent. He didn't cry. He didn't beg for mercy. And he would never say "uncle." Finally, Gary stopped what had turned into a torture game. After Gary ended the contest, he marveled at his friend's demonstrated resilience, and lamented how long he had permitted himself to inflict harm to a person he considered as close as a brother. Gary never again hurt his friend, but found it difficult to forgive himself for his own actions on that occasion. He would remember always his best friend's stalwartness.[44]

Over the coming years Bob and Gary grew inseparable. They loved to watch Hogan Heroes and the Beverly Hillbillies. They listened to The Beatles. Bob's questioning and sometimes negative disposition reminded Gary of John Lennon.[45] Both Bob and Gary served as altar boys at St. Mary's of the Bay, joked about certain priests, questioned Catholicism, and studied other religions. As they grew older, both became paper boys for the *Warren Times Gazette* (published once a week), worked at the Blount Seafood Company picking out full-size shells, and hung out in Bob's cellar, which the Healeys had furnished with old restaurant booths. Bob's house functioned as the hub for an expanding group of close-knit friends. During those years, Gary Lavey recalled, Bob "never stressed out. He was cool as a cucumber," and steadfast. Bob often said of those who disagreed with him, 'If they don't like it, too bad.'"[46] Even at a young age, Gary remembered Bob "never wanted to sell out. He would rather lose then sell out."[47]

In 1970, Bob Healey entered Mary V. Quirk Jr. High School. There, he gained the increased notice of his classmates. As would become Bob's signature, initially he resorted to odd extremes to draw their attention. By seventh grade he had developed the capability of raising his legs from a sitting position and, without the use of his arms, throwing his wiry body upward to come crashing down on his knees. Fellow students (and occasionally a teacher) encouraged him to do so.[48] Bob enjoyed the notoriety—and the looks he attracted from female students.[49]

Though Bob grew increasingly comfortable with himself as he

progressed to each subsequent grade, he did not come out of his shell completely during junior high school. According to Joe Marques, his eighth-grade math teacher, while Bob scored well on tests in his upper level math class, "He didn't seem to fit in, interacted little," and just "didn't bother" much. Mr. Marques remembered a presentation he did on Volkswagen cars, noting Bob had a lot of interests outside school.[50]

In eighth grade, Bob Healey attended the Mary V. Quirk Jr. High School spring dance. At what must have been quite the gala event, the boys stood on one side of the gym and the girls on the other. Bob and Gary goaded each other to ask a girl across the court to dance. Bob didn't. Gary finally did. Apparently feeling a sense of accomplishment, even if only by association for Bob, after the dance the two friends decided to celebrate Gary's coming of age breakthrough by walking down the middle of Main Street on the way to Bob's house. At some point they decided to lay down on the yellow dividing line. They considered the act funny. A police officer in an approaching squad car did not. When the officer attempted to apprehend the two delinquents, one fled while the other froze. Gary made his way eventually to the Healey household, sure that Bob would arrive shortly. When he learned otherwise, he asked Mr. and Mrs. Healey if he could go upstairs and wait for Bob to "catch up."[51] He didn't think it would take much longer. He miscalculated.

Bob had not moved when the police officers ordered him to stay put. The officers who apprehended Bob wanted to know where the other boy had gone. Bob claimed to have no knowledge of the other culprit. The police might have expected that drugs had contributed to the two boys' bizarre behavior. After all, what else would possess a young man to lie down in the middle of a main road at night? When the police searched Bob, they found only a breakfast bar and a piece of spearmint gum.[52] Apparently Bob had tucked them away just in case a reason developed at the dance that called for an energy boost, and fresh breath.

At some point around 10:00 p.m., Gary heard the telephone ring at the Healey residence. The ensuing phone conversation did not last long. After hanging up the phone, Mrs. Healey's voice rang out, "Gary!" Within seconds, Gary found himself in the back of the Healey family car as Mr. and Mrs. Healey made their way toward the Warren police headquarters to pick up their deviant son. After meeting with the police, Mrs. Healey ordered the two boys into the back of the Healey car. Both boys accomplished the task quickly and quietly. On the ride back to the Healey homestead, Mrs. Healey had some thoughts to share with her son. She made sure he heard them. For that matter, probably everyone within a block or two of Mr. Healey's moving vehicle could hear her. Bob knew better than to rebut his mother's points on this night. The two boys sat uncomfortably in the back seat and did not dare utter a sound.[53]

Though Bob spent much time with Gary during his Mary V. Quirk days, he also found time for one particular female friend. While Kathy Kittell had known Bob since kindergarten, at Mary V. Quirk they became better friends. A little later in life, she would influence him profoundly.

In high school, Kathy and Bob's friendship rose to another level. At Warren High School, Kathy and Bob took many classes together. One political science course taught by Michael DeLeo, a very popular social studies teacher at the school, stood out as their most memorable class. During that school year, Bob expressed often a counter viewpoint to that argued by Mr. DeLeo. Bob relished the challenge and Mr. DeLeo seemed to enjoy the banter. And the other students in the class encouraged the spirited debate between the two, partly because once the exchange started, the rest the class could sit back and take in the show. Mr. DeLeo's and Bob's discussions often involved higher level reasoning that some other students struggled to follow. Still, most willingly took on the role as entertained audience members.[54] These exchanges between the popular teacher and his capable student occurred frequently, and in good-natured fashion. Bob and Mr. DeLeo always smiled around one another and enjoyed a good rapport.[55]

During their senior year in high school, Bob and Kathy started to spend more time together, usually at the Healey homestead. Kathy became a mainstay at the Healeys', and particularly enjoyed Bob's father. Kathy recalled, "I would sit and watch *Soul Train*, *Hee Haw*, or *Monty Python* with Mr. Healey. We loved to laugh out loud. He was a gentle soul. He was wonderful."[56] When not laughing with Mr. Healey, Kathy spent time in the kitchen with Mrs. Healey. Mrs. Healey cooked constantly, much to the approval of Kathy and Bob's friends. She made many vegetable dishes to feed her vegetarian son. Her specialties included soups with mustard greens, escarole, and beans, as well as dandelion salad.[57]

Bob and Kathy's young relationship demonstrated an "earthy quality."[58] Kathy recalled, "We used to make dandelion wine, and cheese with cheese cloth in his cellar," which they would hang from the floor joists. Kathy shared, "We would buy old grapes they couldn't sell, and crush them with our bare feet. We made wreaths from princess pines...and his father would make pickles. At other times we went blue shell crabbing. I liked all this."[59]

When they didn't make or consume food, they played music, of sorts. Kathy played piano, while Bob played the washboard, and his longtime friend, Brian Fortin, banged the tubs. They were kind of a country jug band that played obscure folk music.[60] Bob rarely sang, as he couldn't carry a tune.[61] During gigs, the band members rarely wore shoes. For that matter, they didn't wear shoes outside much, either. Bob almost never wore them.[62]

Bob's friends, including Gary Lavey, could not figure out how Bob "got" Kathy, the high school prom queen who was widely recognized as the prettiest girl in school.[63] But Kathy had lots of reasons for dating Bob. She found him "kind, interesting, and adorable."[64] She offered, years later, of Bob, "He would write letters to me in the voice of another character. Sometimes the character was someone else's name spelled backwards or a homeless guy or an adventurer. I mean, what kind of high school boy does that? Most boys have raging hormones.

In comparison, other boys were dullards." [65] One could describe Bob in many ways, but certainly not as a dullard.

And Bob saw something different in Kathy that boys his age over-looked. While most coming-of-age male youths fixated on her "cute smile and well-proportioned body," her "free spirit," a rarity in a "small, stuffy town," attracted Bob more.[66] Bob found himself following her lead, even when he initially disagreed with her. Bob did not like to follow anyone, except Kathy. Though he never explained the reasons for such willingness, perhaps Bob permitted Kathy to lead because her persistence wore him down. Maybe he trusted her. Or possibly he just liked that she cared so much for him. Whatever the reason(s), his experiences with Kathy taught him that he could let someone else lead, sometimes,[67] dependent on identifying a reason to follow. Bob's future actions and decisions suggest he met few Kathy Kittells in the coming years.

Though his grandfather had worked as a local barber, shortly before he dated Kathy Kittell, Bob never again went to a barber shop. While he never explained to his girlfriend why he had let his hair grow out, according to his father, Bob never liked haircuts, at least after 1970. During that year his mother took him for a haircut at Mike's barbershop, situated on Main Street. After that infamous hair-cut, his father recalled; "Bob was mad as hell. When he came home, he found an old wig around the house and he put it on and went right

At some point in the early 1970's, Bob Healey arrived home furious over a "bad haircut." From that point onward he decided to grow his hair long and never to seek the services of a barber again. (Photo courtesy of Ruth Ellen Stone Seymour)

back to Mike's to show him. Oh, he was mad."[68] Years later Kathy offered to cut Bob's split ends so that his hair could grow stronger, but Bob insisted that his locks not be touched.[69]

During his senior year in high school, Bob decided to let his beard grow out as well. While it amounted to little more than peach fuzz by graduation, he never shaved from that point forward. Again, he offered no reason to Kathy for doing so, but years later told a friend who inquired about his abundant facial hair, "Well, let me put it to you this way ... You never saw what's under the beard. Even my mother wouldn't love me based on what's under there. So that's why I keep the beard." His law school friend added; "I think he thought he was an ugly guy."[70] While Bob may have perceived himself as ugly, pre-beard photos do not suggest such.

Throughout his high school years Bob came across as unique, different, and at times maybe even a little odd. His individualism and

Bob Healey's 1975 Warren High School senior photo sports his long hair, but predates his mustache and beard growth by about one year. (Photo courtesy of Gary Lavey)

eccentricity divulged themselves in comedic actions. One example involved his role on the Warren High School baseball team. Though he did not play on the team, he did serve as a student coach, of sorts. In carrying out his coaching duties, he would "prepare" baseballs from the dugout. This preparation mostly involved Bob writing on each ball before entering it into the practice field, "This ball has been prepared by Robert Healey."[71] Demonstrating another example of Bob's off-beat sense of humor, he submitted to the 1975 Warren High School Student Yearbook Committee that he had participated in the varsity weight lifting team. His inclusion made it to print. Not only would his streamlined physique suggest otherwise, but no such official club existed at Warren High School. For senior superlatives, his classmates voted him one of the class individuals. That stood to reason.

During their dating period, Kathy Kittell took notice of Bob's peculiar behaviors that came to mark, early on, his personal style. She noticed that he liked to get under people's skin. He enjoyed making people uncomfortable, mostly to see how they would react. This deportment surfaced most often when Bob debated informally with another party.[72]

Kathy also noticed that Bob never demonstrated a jealous vein. Kathy drew the attention of many boys. That never bothered Bob, as best as she could determine. In fact, he seemed unphased by such things. Once a girl slapped his rear end and Kathy questioned the action immediately. He said, "What? No big deal. Who cares?"[73] Kathy did. Bob didn't.

During the middle 1970s, Bob drove a 1967 turquoise Pontiac Bonneville, most often while wearing frayed edged bell bottoms and no shoes. He never talked to Kathy about buying a new car someday. He had no interest in such things. He was one of the most unmaterialistic people she ever met.[74]

Though many of Bob's former classmates remember him as a strong, even brilliant, student, Bob finished 70th of 135 graduates from the Warren High School Class of 1975, and scored just above average on his SAT scores.[75] In 1985, his father offered about his son's

Bob Healey and girlfriend Kathy Kittell enter the Warren High School gym during their 1975 graduation ceremony. Healey credits Kittell (and friend Gary Lavey and cousin James Healey) for eventually pursuing a college education. (Photo courtesy of Kathy Kittell)

unimpressive high school academic record, "In high school, I could see he had it if he wanted to push himself, but he didn't want to; he just wanted to be a normal student."[76]

After graduation from Warren High School, Bob determined "normal" meant pursuing a career as a house painter, just as his uncle had trained him. And this he did for a short while after high school, while Kathy Kittell went to Rhode Island College. Bob recalled years later, "I had decided that I wasn't [going to college] and instead would paint for the rest of my life. I wanted to live a simple life away from the maddening crowds."[77]

Though Bob and Kathy never underwent a distinct breakup experience, they drifted apart soon after graduation. In late summer 1975, Kathy saw Bob at a job site painting. She recalled, "He wore painter paints, with no shirt on. It was hot. He was wiry, and was up high on a ladder. I yelled up, 'Hey Bob, you gotta get to school [college].'" He replied, "Yes, Catherine," as he often did when he didn't want to bother with what Kathy had to say.[78] For her part, she started to think, "What a waste. With all his capabilities...I mean, he worked hard and made money...But I started to think, maybe I am wasting my time. I thought he had so much potential. I found it too aggravating." Kathy soon "started in" with an artsy group who were more dedicated to their studies.[79] Though she never stopped liking Bob, they lost touch for a considerable time.

While Kathy Kittell doesn't recall having a significant impact on Bob Healey, he remembers their first year out of high school differently. While he did not follow her, per se, his old girlfriend's advice influenced him. After his and Kathy's painting ladder exchange, Bob started to think that maybe life did hold something different in store for him, if he had an education. The following year, Bob entered college and would graduate in three years.[80] At Rhode Island College (RIC) Bob transformed into a student who valued learning for its own sake.[81]

In 1979, Bob graduated from RIC with a BA in English. In his senior year, Bob student-taught at Warren High School, under the direction of the English Department Chair, Mary V. Parks. In 1970, the Rhode Island Department of Education had recognized her as the state *Teacher of the Year*. The Parks/Healey pairing did not proceed smoothly.[82] Parks, approximately 60 years old, strict, conservatively dressed, and well read, had a penchant for rule-following. State educators respected her. Warren revered her. However, she and Bob did not match up particularly well. Ms. Parks practiced her craft in the old school style, tried and proven. Bob Healey thought to pursue other approaches. In the end, Bob passed student teaching, and later substitute taught at his old high school. Most students received him well.

Bob continued his education after graduating from RIC. In all, he attended 10 different colleges, universities, or professional schools.[83] He earned a Master's in education at Boston University and, in 1983, graduated from New England School of Law. Later, he earned another Master's degree in English at Northeastern University and pursued a doctoral degree in education at Columbia University.[84] For the rest of his life, he credited his high school girlfriend[85] for changing his life's path.[86]

In 1979, shortly after earning his BA, Bob went to Japan, partly owing to a woman he met at college. During his time in Japan, he proved an adept student of Japanese culture and language. While in Japan, he taught school, and he took courses at Santa Clara Law School at Tokyo University, where he studied international trade and Japanese law.[87]

In early 1980, Bob went to Oregon to meet up with friends Brian and Debbie Fortin. Brian and Debbie had moved out to Oregon in 1978. Brian made the move because in third grade, his geography teacher delivered a very persuasive presentation on the area. Brian had decided then and there to one day move out to Oregon.[88]

Bob stayed with his old friends in Oregon for several months. Brian and Debbie Fortin lived in a primitive mountainside cabin that had no running water. Bob left the cabin on Freak Mountain[89] five days a week to teach at the Trillium School in Jacksonville, Oregon.[90] The school had been founded a year earlier as a small rural learning center serving students from preschool through high school.[91] Somewhat like a commune school, students at Trillium directed their own learning more than they would at more traditional schools. They also helped build and maintain the facility. This approach had its benefits, and one might think it presented as a good fit for Bob Healey. And that proved true, for a while. Healey reported of his experience teaching at the free school in Oregon: "We were working with children and letting them learn at their own rate. And part of every day, the children and the teachers spent building a schoolhouse together."[92] Healey thought that the arrangement created a connection between the students and the school's physical structure and fostered a bond with the faculty. However, he hedged, the approach made sense "...if the kid is going to go out and build schools for the rest of his life. But I also knew those kids were not reading at their grade levels."[93]

The Oregon experience helped Bob work through changes that had affected his life since 1979. When Bob had decided to pursue

Shortly after graduating from Rhode Island College in 1979, Bob Healey ventured out to visit with friends Brian and Debbie Fortin in Oregon. During that time, he taught at a local high school, and sought his purpose in life. (Photo courtesy of Brian Fortin)

post high school studies, his increased drive and goal focus encouraged productivity—but also brought on stress, self-induced and otherwise. Brian Fortin recalled of Bob's time in Oregon, "About the only time he [Healey] really unwinds is when he takes a long drive or walk in the country. In Oregon, we lived in a very rural area, and Bob would take walks for miles in the mountains."[94]

While in Oregon, Bob Healey told Brian that he had made up his mind to return to Rhode Island and enter law school. He based his decision not on the stature or wealth a law degree might make possible, but rather so he could help the people of Warren who couldn't afford legal services.[95]

But for all his education, thinking, and decision making during the late 1970s and early 1980s, Bob Healey still sought a profound meaning to his life. He had thought earlier that destiny called him to a greater cause, but determined that everyone must entertain such thoughts about their being.[96] Even upon entering New England Law School in 1980, he had yet to recognize, but continued to wonder

Brian and Debbie Fortin stage a shotgun wedding in the hills of Oregon. Healey is holding the gun in jest.
(Photo courtesy of Brian Fortin)

about, a foreordained direction and purpose.[97] Little did he know it then, but by 1979, Bob's past experiences had already cast in iron the mold of the man he would come to fully embody. In 1982 he pursued a longshot prospect that would define his existence and guide his path from that time forward.

CHAPTER 3

MAKE SCHOOL COOL
THE FIRST CAMPAIGN

During a bus ride home from Boston's New England Law School in early fall 1982, Bob Healey leaned toward his law school peer and friend, Robert Craven, and asked, "You know a lot about politics, don't ya?"

Not exactly sure what to make of Bob's question, Rob replied, "Yeah, well, we talk about politics."

Bob clarified, "No, I mean, like getting elected in politics."

Rob offered, "Yeah, I know a little bit."

Apparently that response made Rob Craven enough of a credentialed source to seek his input on a campaign Bob Healey had begun to organize. Bob showed Rob a campaign brochure for a school committee position in Warren, Rhode Island. In the forefront of the printed page appeared Bob Healey, long haired and bearded, wearing a tuxedo as he strutted barefoot down Main Street. Because the photographer positioned and angled the camera to look up at Bob with his foot raised, one could not overlook that Bob wore no shoes. While one might have found the young candidate's decision to shed footwear bizarre, perhaps they could rationalize away the appearance as an oversight on the young candidate's part. But if such reasoning did enter Warren viewers' minds, the campaign countered such considerations by printing on the right side of the brochure, "Bob Healey for School Committee: A Strange Man for a Strange Job."

After Rob Craven finished looking at the image and reading the brochure, he gathered a long breath, stared forward at the back of the seat in front of him, and thought for a few seconds. He then turned toward Bob and asked, "You're running?"

Bob responded energetically and without hesitation, "Yeah, yeah!"

Rob inquired, "Do you think it's a good idea to characterize yourself as a strange man, and—maybe even more so—that the job I am assuming others are seeking is a 'strange job?'"

Healey offered, "I think people think that way."

Craven said, "Well, it will definitely be different. And I'm sure it will be the subject matter of some article in the local newspaper. I am sure of that."

Healey exclaimed, "That's what I want!" At age 25, he felt he needed the press's attention to make up for the fact that he had entered the race for the Warren School Committee as the youngest candidate by several years.

"Well, then you're going to get it."[1] Craven's prediction proved accurate, but an underestimation.

—·

Bob Healey stood as one of six non-partisan Warren School Committee candidates who vied for three positions that paid no money, promised public scrutiny, and would "subject them to lots of verbal abuse from belt-tightening taxpayers."[2] Bob's competition for the thankless job included: John J. Killion III, who issued seven statements outlining his stances pertaining to education in Warren[3] and who promised not to vote on any bills that presented a conflict of interest over his wife's roll as a Warren school teacher; Paul Edward

Brule, an outspoken local farmer and no stranger to the town's political scene; Leo R. Bouffard, who announced he would not raise nor spend a penny on his campaign; Spencer Hackley, who said in reference to the School Committee budget that if the people of Warren wanted surprises, they could buy Cracker Jacks;[4] and Anthony N. Nunes, a veteran School Committeeman who had served in that capacity 12 of the past 14 years.[5]

One has to wonder if the above five candidates worried much about the competition offered by Bob Healey's candidacy. The 25-year-old Healey didn't have a job. He had never run for office prior and didn't belong to a political party. He had never attended a School Committee meeting. And he didn't *look* like a candidate for the school committee, or for that matter, any other office. The odds stacked up against a successful first run for the youngest candidate on the Warren ballot.

Brian Fortin, Healey's campaign coordinator and friend, acknowledged the challenge before them, feeling that mainstream Warren voters would not be able to get past Healey's long hair and beard.[6] Even Healey himself thought he had little chance of winning. So, he decided to make the campaign fun. Healey explained, "Life is a goof, and this was the ultimate goof."[7] Still, Bob saw a path to a long shot victory. People in Warren knew him well. Like his father and grandfather, he had lived in Warren all his life. He still resided in his childhood home.[8] Expressing agreement with Healey, a long-time Warren Democratic town chairman offered a somewhat underhanded compliment: "He was a native, he went to the local schools, and let's face it: there is not a great deal of talent that runs for the School Committee."[9]

But Healey had talent, and smarts, but some people hadn't figured that out initially. His father offered, "With his beard and long hair and all, a lot of people think he is a stupid guy. But when they get to know him and talk to him, they realize he's pretty smart."[10] Brian Fortin added, "He's very bright and he knows what he is doing; he *always* has a plan."[11]

And the long-haired Healey *did* have a plan to secure a School Committee seat. Part of that plan included making comments that called attention to his credentials. Bob said that running for School Committee made sense because "...I had been a teacher; I knew the committee would have legal problems; I had the qualifications—there is always some logic behind what I do."[12] And while his actual education experience qualified him as little more than a novice teacher, he could boast about higher education credentials than his competitors. And he knew to sell those qualifications. Remembering his days at the Trillium School in Oregon, Healey stressed that he believed in some traditional educational wisdom. Healey explained, "I think the parents are the key. I think children grow up to be very much like their parents. If there is no encouragement at home, if the parents don't read to their children, if the child doesn't have a role model who cares [about learning], then forget it."[13] He described his ideal teacher as one who cares about young people and "doesn't talk down to students," but added he did not think any singular teaching method ranked superior to another. He believed teachers must adapt to their students. Referencing his educational credentials again, he added, "It was a real experience for me to teach in Boston, where there are a lot of minority students." Healey concluded, "The discipline problems, the whole thing was a lot different than in a basically homogenous town like Warren."[14]

While normally the Warren Town Council race drew more attention than the School Committee contest, in 1982 the opposite proved true. The town's Republican Party did not seriously contest the Council seats, seemingly accepting the dominance of the town's Democratic Party. And further, the School Committee race presented more plot and ploy. In May 1982, the School Committee had pleaded before the voters at the Financial Town Meeting that they required more money to help a School Department reportedly in a dire financial state. Instead of voting for the additional funds, the voters cut the education budget. Months later, the same School Committee announced a large budget surplus. The School Committee blamed Superintendent Wilfred R. Marchand and Business Manager Dennis Lima for poor management and communication. The taxpayers didn't know what to make of that charge, but did question the School Committee's credibility.

Part of the credibility gap between the Warren School Committee and the Warren voters also stemmed from the Committee's 1982 negotiation of a three-year teachers' contract. The ensuing agreement awarded Warren teachers annual raises of 7.5 percent, 8 percent, and 8 percent. Leo Mansini, the chair of the 1982 negotiating team, felt the committee had saved the town money on the 7.5 percent increase in salaries because they had budgeted for an eight percent increase for the 1982–83 school year.[15] While it should be noted that during the 1980s interest rates soared, the economy boomed, inflation ran high, and town school committees commonly bargained large raises for unionized teachers and other bargaining units, many citizens of Warren's large working class saw the 1982 three-year contract as an overly generous dispersal of their money. Healey did not publicly share his judgment of these raises during his campaign for the Warren School Committee. He would have much to say about them later.

During the 1982 campaign for School Committee, the 25-year-old Bob Healey commented on an array of other education issues. For instance, similar to competing candidates, he supported combining the Superintendent's job with that of the school's business manager, presumably with a new hire.

The cornerstone of Healey's campaign involved improving relations between teachers, administrators, students, and School Committee members. And how did he plan to do that? He would "make school cool." He offered, "I'm looking to bring everything together… We have to consolidate our plans and move as one…It sounds rather simplistic, but it's to make school cool, like I said in my handouts, and make it run better." He explained further what he meant by *cool*. "Cool comes from a feeling when everything's OK, when everything functions smoothly." He wanted to make school a "nice place to be; not

Taken in 1982 during his student days at New England Law School, this photograph captures Robert Healey on the cusp of his political (and legal) career. (Photo courtesy of Gary Lavey)

a job, but something they [teachers] want to do." He concluded, "But the only way to make school cool is through communication."[16]

To further his "cool" agenda, Bob Healey eyed the people's role in the governmental process. He explained this facet of his campaign message as follows: "I am not here to make decisions instead of you; I am here to make decisions with you... An elected official should never be anything more than a mouthpiece of the people; however, in these busy times people often forget this reason for government, and the people's voice has grown silent..." He continued, "Too often, politicians only hear from the people when something has gone wrong. Too often, people only hear from politicians when it is election time."

To make sure he did not sink to the latter, Bob promised to issue frequent press releases to the people. He trusted that informing the people would naturally lead to their involvement and empowerment. Bob declared, "education is not someone's job, it's everyone's job."[17]

In addition to his ideas and philosophies, Healey shared a bit about his faith, of sorts. He let it be known that, "I *believe* in letting body hair grow." He added, "I've given up jobs to keep my hair." Bob explained further that muggers passed him by because, "They think, 'He [Healey] can't have anything. He's a strange person,'"[18] And in line with such pronouncements, Healey acknowledged that in Warren's blue-collar traditional community, his appearance could hurt his election prospects.

Healey might well have had a point on the appearance front. And that argument extended beyond Warren. By 1982, people across the country had transitioned from the late sixties and seventies unkempt look to the eighties ultra-neat image. 1980s trend setters chose to wear straight-legged and flared pants instead of bell bottoms. Preppy pastel colors replaced earth tones. The young opted for the two-shirts, double-collar look over a single shirt with a wide lapel. Young women dressed in plaid skirts, not bright-colored short dresses. Many chose boat shoes over sandals (and certainly over bare feet.) Whale and fox insignias appeared on teal-colored shirts, as tie dyes faded into the past. And perhaps most notable, tightly cropped hair trumped men's long hair. Given such decade contrasts, in the eighties, Healey came across as a throwback. His long hair flowed everywhere. He wore unpressed, dark clothes in loose fitting fashion. And he opted for no shoes, unless frigid weather or the law required footwear— which Bob, the burgeoning lawyer, would no doubt challenge. In an era that clearly promoted a clean-cut, Tom Cruise, conservative look, Bob Healey sported a Frank Zappa do-as-I-please image. That model appeared rarely in the 1980s political scene, and for that matter, seldom made a presence in 1960s and 1970s political circles.

His apparent lack of electability aside, Healey seemed to relish his mane, and his unconventional appearance. He had developed a "brand" before people talked much about such strategizing concepts. So, instead of over worrying about the predictable chatter surrounding his exterior image, the long-haired candidate for the Warren School Committee embraced his look and focused on his inner message. School had to be cool.

On Tuesday, November 2, 1982, close to 70 percent of eligible voters in Warren turned out to select their School Committee and Town Council. Warrenites voted in large numbers for the long shot candidate, Robert J. Healey Jr., who garnered more tallies than any of his five competitors. That election night's result plowed aside the rule of conventional wisdom, at least for the time being. Apparently, a candidate's appearance factored little into a successful campaign. Many teachers reported that they voted for Healey as well. The Warren voters also selected John J. Killion III, and Paul E. Brule to serve on the School Committee. Anthony Mogayzel and George Gemp, whose terms were to expire in 1984, remained from the past committee.

A couple weeks later, the Warren School Committee selected their chair. They chose Robert Healey to lead them. Bob said his election as Chairman surprised him in the sense that he hadn't sought the post. Still, considering the election of new members to the committee, the choice did not shock Healey. Bob reflected, "We wanted to work for unity. Hopefully the new image of the committee will bring unity."[19]

And with that, the new School Committee Chairman took hold of Warren's education reins. Healey would work to unify the Warren School Committee, the teachers, the teachers' union, and the Warren Town Council toward common goals. Improved communication would be the cornerstone of such laudable intentions.

CHAPTER 4

HEALEY'S SHORT HONEYMOON

Robert Healey, the newly elected Chairman of the Warren School Committee, spent no time surfing the ways of his predecessors. In short order he made his own waves, and continued churning up turbulent seas throughout his tenure. With Healey at the helm, calm waters appeared nowhere in Warren's distant horizon.

In one of their first orders of business in late 1982, the Warren School Committee set out to hire one or more secretaries to handle clerical matters at the schools. Bob Healey did not agree with their proposal, and made his stance known immediately. He recommended, "There are other alternatives to hiring secretaries. One includes using students who no longer can participate in the former work-study program at the school." (An earlier school committee had eliminated that program due to budget cuts.)[1] While Healey's proposal may seem insignificant, he had just introduced publicly his approach toward all subjects coming before the Warren School Committee over the next four years, and by extension, how he would engage almost every challenge throughout his political life. The new Chairman would not support carte-blanche solutions that maintained the status-quo when other options could prove more beneficial, at least in his view. Under Healey's chairmanship, the business-as-usual model vanished.

As Healey had promised during his campaign, he made frequent use of the Warren Times-Gazette to report on School Committee decisions, and more notably, proclaim his own thoughts on developing circumstances. Occasionally reading like a President Franklin Roosevelt radio fireside chat from the 1930's, Healey used his weekly Warren Times-Gazette statements to inform Warren citizens about education and related town business.

In one early published weekly statement, Healey penned a message that could have included segments from one of his past Warren High School history teacher's lectures. In a somewhat elongated communication, Healey shared;

> *"When Massachusetts Colony passed the 'Old Deluder Satan Act' in an effort to educate the people to keep the devil from controlling the society, public schools were born in America. These schools were to be funded by the public because the public as a whole benefitted from an educated population. Since 1641... the funding source has remained the same. The taxpayer funds education.... As you might know, in recent years the Town Council and the School Committee in Warren have been at odds over the school budget. While the people of the town are not against education, they are against wasting money. It should be remembered that the School Committee is also interested in providing a good education at the lowest possible cost. It is time the two groups work together because both are seeking the same end."*[2]

A week after Healey's above *fireside chat*, he made the first use of his weekly column to cast disparaging commentaries about the previous school committee. With little apparent regard for the two senior Committee members' feelings, the new Chairman offered the following public remark about legal matters facing the current School Committee; "... I am aware of the lack of credibility the people of Warren

Healey meets with the Warren School Committee in 1982. Soon his relationship with some committee members turned combative.

have had in past committees. I want you to know that this committee is trying to do the job you put us here to do." [3] As would become increasingly clear, Healey's mention of the "present Committee" referenced the body's three new members.

Though Bob Healey made several other comments during his short 1982 School Committee Chair tenure, none created much stir. The same could not be suggested of 1983, or for that matter, the rest of his chairmanship through 1986. Often, his statements shocked or delighted readers of the Warren Times-Gazette. Many of those comments and subsequent actions drew state-wide and even national attention.

In January 1983 Healey attracted major front-page coverage in the Warren Times Gazette and The Providence Journal. (See Chapter 5, *Healey Did What?*) On that same date a smaller less noticeable headline, "More money needed for schools – Healey," ran at the bottom of page three in the Warren Times.[4] That article explained the School Committee had begun developing its budget request for the 1983-84 school year. A cursory reading of that piece suggested the school committee had undertaken to build a typical school year budget. They did not. In early 1983 the School Committee put forward a $5.3 million budget for the coming school year, which included an increase over the past year's budget. That budget did not include the $25,000 necessary to fund the sports program or a $100,000 settlement involving a school nurse from a couple of years earlier. Healey explained proudly that the taxpayers could decide separately from the regular budget whether or not they wanted to fund the sports program.[5] However, he warned, "If it's cut, it's cut. We don't have the money for it." [6] He hoped they realized the committee had no funds to reinstate the program should the resolution be rejected at the upcoming financial town meeting. Healey later explained his rationale for separating the sports budget from the general budget; "As a committee, we did not want to force a vote [on the overall budget] by threatening sports."[7]

In addition to referencing the separate sports budget, Healey further stressed, "The schools can be run on as much money as you give us, but the quality of the schools will diminish if our requests go to deaf ears."[8] In one of his weekly statements he added, "If the vote is to cut the budget, there is no choice but to cut programs. I am not trying to scare you. I am trying to tell you that only so many oranges can be taken away from the bottom of the pyramid before it topples. I leave it up to you."[9]

At several junctures during the work on his first school budget, Healey continued referencing negatively the prior school committee's impact on his current decisions. Apparently aware of his repetitive refrain, Healey said that he realized people must get tired of hearing him say "it's not this committee's fault." He assured them that he too was tired of saying it. Regardless, he continued the refrain over the coming months and years.

Some argued that Robert Healey had "shirked" his responsibilities by passing along the decision making to the same people who had elected him to assume such duties.[10] Healey responded to the criticisms in such a way as to introduce an aspect of his political philosophy then, and later. "I cannot give the people the choice of hiring teachers, providing insurance for schools or cutting programs guided by the state. These are my concerns – the ones I was elected to oversee." Regarding the alleged avoidance of his obligations concerning the school department's sports budget, he pointed out, "I find it hard when people complain when you give them power. Any decision that can be made by the people should be made by the people."[11] In his weekly statement, Healey expounded on his thinking further: "I will not usurp power. I voted for this because this was an issue [the sports budget] the people themselves could decide just as easily as the committee... To give powers to any government without good reason is encouraging dictatorial rule."[12] Healey went on to explain that he did not know whether the committee would reinstate a sports appropriation in the operating budget if the state education department said the two cannot be separated.[13]

Robert J. Healey Jr.'s early performance as School Committee Chairman impressed his former high school social studies teacher, Michael DeLeo. Shortly after Healey presented on the budget, the two crossed paths by the entrance to the second floor Warren High School teachers' lounge. DeLeo complimented Healey, pointing out that he had made it clear that the people would get what they paid for, adding that he had just given the people the facts with no theatrics. Healey appeared somewhat humbled by his former teacher's flattering review. Leaning forward and bobbing his head appreciatively, Healey looked to his former teacher with wide opened eyes and a serious and somewhat dubious expression, which could almost pass for a frown. He appeared a bit apprehensive in front of his former teacher. DeLeo nodded with an approving smile, and assured the Warren High School graduate that he had done a good job. The two parted amicably.

As the School Committee grappled with the 1983-84 school budget, concerns over keeping the Warren School Department operational into the future picked up momentum. With Warren's school age population declining, soon future graduating classes would dip below one hundred students. Many questioned whether Warren citizens could afford to offer a comprehensive education for a declining populace. A study prepared by *The Warren Study Committee* recommended that the town's taxpayers choose to send Warren students to another community. Healey referenced their recommendation as "extreme," but continued that the School Committee would need to consider the possibility should the taxpayers no longer wish to fund the schools adequately.[14]

As Healey and the rest of the Warren School Committee tried to garner public support for their school department budget, they entered into contract talks with school clerks and custodians. The committee asked the clerks and custodians to take a zero pay increase. Their negotiation team agreed to consider the offer, with one important condition; other town employees would need to take a freeze as well. Most likely the clerks and custodians' negotiating team knew no other unionized group would support such a notion. As such, their ploy would affectively suffice to end talks of zero percent raises. But Healey didn't flinch. He liked the idea. In fact, he loved it. Healey decided to run with the notion. He exclaimed, "I think this [the clerks and custodian's suggestion] presents a golden opportunity to hold the line in both the town and the schools. After all, what is good for the goose is even better for the gander..." He then continued, as if to deliver a pep talk in support of the union bargaining teams' proposition; "Some may say that it would be difficult to achieve. They will argue that the contracts with the town employees are already negotiated. I say reopen them. We, as a committee, asked our teacher union to re-open. It is apparently harder to achieve than first expected, but if the national steelworkers can re-open their contracts and take a cut, I think the town can re-open their contracts and negotiate a freeze on wages." Healey then counseled, "Face it, if you were going to take a pay freeze to save the town's schools, wouldn't it make you feel better to know others in your position are making a similar effort? Sure it would..."[15] As soon as the teacher's union agreed to *discuss* the idea, the Warren Times Gazette chimed in, "Sharing between the committee and union is commended ... This attitude and the willingness of the union to rediscuss its contract only confirms what Warren residents have known all along: that we have a first-rate teaching staff dedicated to our students."[16]

At the same time Healey tried to gain support from Warren town employees to open their contracts and take wage freezes, the School Committee Chairman continued his efforts to win public support for the town's current proposed school budget. In his March 20, 1983 weekly newspaper statement, Healey enrolled the help of a children's tale he authored to further entice the public's backing for the School Committee's 1983-84 school year budget.

"Once upon a time in the kingdom of Nerraw there was a school committee. This body was given the task of making sure the schools ran smoothly. Each year the people who held seats on the committee would dress up and go to the coliseum to fight against the representative of the local ruler. During this clash both parties would shout demands and the one group that was the loudest won. They did this craziness because people would not give money to run the schools. The reason why the people did not freely give money for education was not that they wanted to remain poorly educated. In fact, the reason was that they had been asked for money from their then well ladened purses. The years passed. The same cries continued. "Money. We need money or else we cannot offer art." It became so common that people paid no attention to the cries. Then one day, not so very long ago, when looking at budget figures, the school committee seriously found itself in need of money to keep the schools operating at present quality levels. Without money the course could not be offered and soon the schools would close. The committee decided to ask the people for money, but they knew that the people were not really listening. They had heard the cries of "wolf" one time too many. The picture looked rather bleak. But the story had a happy ending. Somehow the people of Nerraw were not backwards after all. The teachers pitched in, the janitors and secretaries did their part, and through some miracle, the taxpayers gave the money to the schools to operate. And although it did not solve the problem forever, it did not hurt. I know another Grimm tale that is rather similar."[17]

Whether or not Healey's story telling talents would sway Warren voters remained to be determined. Certainly, it would take more than a good story to sway Warren teachers to erase a bargained eight percent wage increase in the coming year. But some good karma seemed to transfer over to the negotiations between the School Committee and the union representing custodians, secretaries, and maintenance personnel. During early April the two sides reached a one-year contract deal. The agreement included a 5.3 percent pay increase for maintenance employees at the top of the pay scale, but a 6.2 percent for those at the bottom.[18]

Both the School Committee Chairman Robert J. Healey Jr. and the union expressed satisfaction with the agreement. The union leadership offered about the new contract; "It's not bad considering we started with zero. The package sounds decent to me."[19] While the union leadership tried to sell their negotiated contract as "not bad," given the times and other town workers' recent contracts, the custodians, secretaries, and teacher aides would be hard pressed to describe the settlement's terms as particularly *good*. A comparison to other awarded town contracts negotiated over the past few years suggest that Healey secured the agreement more to his liking than the union's. And he knew it. Healey reflected, "We came out with a pretty good deal. Even with benefits it figures out to be less than the 45 cents an hour the Town Council allowed for other town employees." He added, "We wanted to get off the percentage raise" because "...It builds up too rapidly. You're compounding percentages on percentages."[20] He further pointed out that the forgoing of one across-the-board increase helped out the lower-paid members and saved the tax payers from funding top-scale workers the same increase.[21] While the Healey led School Committee hadn't won a convincing victory, they had moved one bargaining unit a couple of steps toward their side of the ledger. Not only had the union not secured a raise along the lines they had hoped, their one-year deal fell short of the three years pact they expected. Given the times at hand, the accomplishment ranked more impressive than Warren voters might have realized.

Perhaps the *win* over one union caused Healey to reflect differently upon another group he continued to bargain with in good faith, at least for the moment. On April 27, 1983 Healey offered the following in his weekly press release: "One major gripe many people have with this budget [school budget] is the large amount of money going to the teachers in the form of pay raises and benefits. Some see the teachers as bandits making off with all the town's resources. First, let me say that teachers are easy targets… Warren has many fine teachers who are more than willing to help a student learn. I rank Warren's education among the best… as for the amount of money being paid out in raises and benefits, these are under a contractual obligation… People will argue that these tax increases are killing the people. Taxes are a way of life." Perhaps wishing to counter his overly generous spirit, he followed by sharing; "My personal hope is that the school committee's budget version is passed, and then, have the teachers, as a show of good faith, renegotiate their contract. This would be the best of both worlds."[22]

In May 1983 four-hundred Warren taxpayers passed the town's $9.1 million school budget. The assembled crowd exceeded the previous year by fifty-three people. According to the Warren Times-Gazette, many of the voters were "employees of the school system who were told by the administration to show up to support the budget." [23] Nevertheless, Healey interpreted the outcome as proof that the taxpayers supported the schools and had confidence in the School Committee's "good-faith effort" to reduce its original operating request.[24] Healey felt empowered. In receipt of the people's good faith, he pivoted toward the Warren teachers' contract and delivered a new proposal.

"Teachers, if they concede a 1 percent reduction, would provide enough money to do the roof repairs, and they would show the community that they are interested in preserving the school system rather than taking money while they can….. Warren is trying to keep its schools open. Teachers need to realize this fact. Sure, teachers are getting the same throughout the state,

but realize that while other communities' packages are tied to horses, Warren's package is strapped to a pony. It is a small town with a small amount of children… In any case, the ball is now in the court of the teachers. I hope that they will seriously consider the situation. The voters of Warren at the meeting showed that they will support education. As educators let us not let the people down."[25]

The Warren Times-Gazette agreed with Healey's suggestion.[26] The teachers did not.

While the teachers knew their current contract had exceeded even their own expectations at that time of negotiation, they feared that future contracts might be far less generous. For teachers, the notion of giving up a gain from a hard fought and successful past settlement flied in the face of rational thinking, and fair play. Further, the people of Warren had just passed the budget, the one proposed by the School Committee and endorsed by the Warren Times-Gazette. The teachers agreed with all three parties. As such, they saw no need to open their contract. Healey disagreed with the teachers, once again publicly and demonstratively. He warned, "If the teachers refuse to renegotiate, next year the taxpayers will take it out on the schools… And I don't blame them."[27]

The same month Healey made his position on an updated teachers' contract known, he announced he had no problem with increasing administrators' salaries. He reasoned that administrators worked eleven months a year, not nine, as did the teachers. Without higher pay, he questioned the incentive to be an administrator.[28] Teachers had responses ready to his rhetorical question. But nobody asked for their opinion. Some teachers remarked sarcastically to each other, "Did you hug your administrator today?"

As the hot days of summer took hold in 1983, the heated indirect exchanges between the Warren School Committee Chair and the towns' teachers chilled for the season. The cooling off didn't mean that

Healey forgot about the matters that he and the teachers disagreed over, nor that he had a change of heart. Rather, his attention had turned elsewhere, specifically drinking water and bare feet, at least for a time. (See Chapter 5—*Healey Did What?*)

In September 1983, Robert Healey's School Committee dealings soon took over the headlines again. Healey's biggest concern as he entered the 1983-84 school year remained communication, an issue he promised to address and improve when he ran for School Committee in 1982. But the spirit and definition of that communication underwent a transformation from his earlier campaign days. In the fall of 1983 Healey referenced the union as "intractable," and stated that improving communication required a "two-way street."[29]

In a "final attempt"[30] to improve two-way communication, Healey introduced a monthly letter to employees of the Warren School Department. If he truly meant for the effort to build a better working relationship between the School Committee and the teachers, he should have introduced the initiative in a more positive tone than the version he ultimately chose. Healey explained, "These letters, if read, will serve as a source of information. Many teachers have told me that they were in the dark as to many of the issues discussed between the union and the Committee. The union has even stated publicly that its members `do not read the papers.' I hope this monthly letter to the staff directly will not go unread."[31] Healey titled his monthly letter to the Warren schools' faculty, *What is about to Hit the Fan.*

In addition to the teachers and their union, Bob Healey had combative exchanges with other parties. For instance, Healey criticized the work that Atwood Construction completed in one of the Warren Schools. His complaints referenced drooping and missing panels. As it turned out, state Representative Michael Urban's (D-Dist 89) brother owned Atwood Construction. In response to Healey's charge, Representative Urban expressed in curt fashion his thoughts about Healey's statements. Healey offered soon after, "Perhaps the knife cut too close to a political nerve, and for that I am sorry. Politics is not my

While Robert Healey played the front man, grabbing most of the attention and headlines during his School Committee Chairmanship, behind the scenes Paul Brule had great influence on Healey as an immovable force against the teachers' union.

business. My job is to oversee the operation of a school system." However, not to strike too conciliatory of a tone, he added; "Rest assured, I will not succumb to political pressure."[32] Over time Healey strengthened his resolute disposition and associated commentary.

In addition to local school topics, Chairman Healey took every opportunity to comment on larger education issues that emanated from lands beyond Warren. Most of the time these commentaries laid down his political philosophy—a viewpoint that over the years would continue to develop, but rarely waiver from its original philosophical foundation. In November 1983, he commented on the Basic Education Plan (BEP), which the state could use to assert greater state oversight of local school curriculums. The BEP laid down fundamental curriculum requirements that every Rhode Island school district had to meet. Healey contended, "A statewide curriculum will effectively usurp the power of the local school committee. This power will go to state bureaucrats in the RI Department of Education, known affectionately as RIDE... Powerless, local communities will be able to do little more than roll over and play dead.... Personally, I favor adopting this curriculum as a guide for state unification, but certainly I cannot accept it as being mandated from Providence without any concern as to the needs of the local level."[33] Broadening his point, Healey added, "'Local control is the key to the success of the American schools... Having frequent discussions with members of foreign ministries of education, I am constantly reminded that their countries are still underdeveloped because they lack a reputable local body to implement federal plans."[34]

At other times Healey did not shy from chastising indirectly the electorate. In one such instance, after requesting citizens to write their legislatures about tenured administrators, he questioned the citizens' lack of carry through; "In a discussion with Rep Michael Urban (D-Dist 89) I was told he had received only one letter. He said it was mine. Needless to say, the legislature adopted the bills and now we have tenured administrators in the school."[35]

As time went on, Healey focused his attention and ire on the Warren teachers, and more pointedly, their union and contract. And as his chagrin and related actions increased, so too did the teachers' resentment of their young School Committee Chairman. The examples of the deteriorating relationship numbered high. An early instance of this ilk involved Healey's treatment of a Rhode Island General Assembly bill that would allow teachers to defer taxes on their pension contributions, if their town of employment permitted them to do so. At that time teachers paid taxes on their pension contributions upfront, and then did not pay taxes on their initial retirement check up to the amount they had contributed. Under the new option, teachers would not pay taxes on their pension contributions, but would pay taxes on their pension upon receiving their first retirement check. Most communities had rubber stamped the change. Warren had not. Healey saw the potential benefit as valuable trading bait. The Chairman wondered, if the teachers preferred the change in benefit, what would they give up at the bargaining table to realize that alteration? Because the change would come at no cost to the town of Warren, teachers could not fathom why the School Committee, and specifically Robert Healey, would prevent them from opting for the alternative arrangement. But Healey felt, "To simply give this away without getting anything for it is ill advised." To illustrate his point, he added, "Why even Jack got a magic bean for the family cow. Are we not as impoverished as Jack and his mother? Can the town's taxpayers afford a give away?[36]

The standoff over the pension tax structure circulated bad blood between the teachers and Healey, and amongst the members of an increasingly fractured Warren School Committee. After weeks of contentious talks and debate, on March 26 the School Committee voted by a three to two margin to allow teachers to defer taxes on the income they contributed to the state's teacher retirement fund. The vote tally mirrored that of many decisive issues moving forward: George E. Gempp Jr., John J. Killioin III and Anthony Mogayzel supported the pension vote, while Paul E. Brule and Roberty J. Healey Jr. opposed the measure.

Making the pension vote particularly contentious, Committeeman John J. Killion III's wife worked as a Warren teacher.[37] During his campaign for office, Killion promised not to vote on any matters that could benefit his wife monetarily. In this case Killion made the exception because the teachers "deserved" the benefit. Further, Killion claimed that as best as could remember he did not say he would not vote on all issues affecting teachers. Healey recalled Killion's comments differently. Healey researched 1982 back issues of the Warren Times-Gazette to determine whose memory better served the truth. Upon reviewing the newspaper's back issues, he announced to Warren voters that Killion had said; "I will abstain from anything concerning her (his wife's) salary." Healey expounded, "... I cannot let the public be misled by inaccurate or incomplete press statements." Healey labeled Killion's explanation for doing other than what he had promised as "limp."[38] Healey added, "This coming May we [the School Committee] must ask you for your hard-earned bucks to pay an outrageous pay hike for teacher contracts, and yet less than two weeks ago the committee was seen throwing benefits around without concern. The taxpayer in me shudders just thinking about this."[39] Healey said he ranked teachers last on his priority list, behind students and taxpayers.[40] Healey explained his thinking further, "I am not here to play

Santa Claus year-round. Since taking office, nothing has personally upset me more than this [pension] issue."[41]

Soon other matters irritated the Warren School Committee Chairman even more. Once again, he found teachers entangled in the crosshairs, and took aim. On one such occasion he spoke about Warren teachers' higher than normal absentee rates. He thought to publish records that he felt proved his assertion. The teachers expressed their outrage over Healey's threatened use of the local newspaper. Healey disagreed with the premise of their outrage and, again, shared his views in the Warren Times Gazette; "There are many within the schools that feel I should not speak to the people through the newspapers. I feel these people are wrong. I feel that you, the people, have put me here to keep you informed... While I can agree that the newspapers sensationalize stories, it does not detract from their value as the watchdog of the public... My position then, and my position now, is one in the same. I will not hide or color facts. I will comply with any and all reasonable requests for factual material, and I will bring the schools to the people by way of the press."[42] For the immediate time being, teacher absentee rates did not appear in the Warren Times-Gazette.

Healey also used the press to lash out at other government leaders he felt did not do enough, if anything, to help the Warren School Department or education in general. In one press release to The Providence Journal he charged that special interest groups firmly positioned in the General Assembly slaughtered school committees throughout the state. In that same article, to further his point Healey wrote of a meeting between the Warren School Committee, the Warren Town Council, and the town's General Assembly delegation (Senators Gardner F. Seveney, Richard M. Alegria and Michael B. Forte, and Representative Michael J. Urban Jr.) and most of the Warren School Committee. At that meeting Healey wanted the town representatives to oppose mandatory arbitration of teacher contract disputes and the Basic Education Plan, and to better support school systems trying to fire incompetent teachers. After the meeting Healey commented to the press that he found the delegation's response to the committee's concerns and requests "unacceptable" and characterized the group as "next to impotent."[43] He added, " I know that it is hard to introduce legislation that will be unpopular. It risks losing friends, but damn it, the legislature is not a clubhouse."[44]

The next day a "shocked" Representative Urban characterized Healey's comments as "unfair and unfounded." Urban added that Healey had "expressed no displeasure" at the meeting and "just sat there." Urban finished, "He should have said something there and not have run to the newspapers with his remarks."[45] Town Council members also expressed dismay at Healey's comments. Councilman Walter S. Felag Jr. referenced Healey's public remarks as a "backstabbing," while Councilman Paul J. Harvey offered, "They [Warren's state delegation] took the time out to come down here and meet with us and have to put up with this stuff. Lately, it seems, Mr. Healey just has to put articles in the paper."[46] Healey responded to Harvey's charge, "My use of the newspapers to let people know what should not be kept quiet is done because many people should know what happens at public meetings." Healey added, "It's another David versus Goliath situation. This time Goliath is the local Democratic Party and I'm still David."[47] Healey concluded, "I think writing [letters] and letting people know is better than talking behind closed doors in Town Hall."[48]

Before the exchange between Healey and other Warren government officials had much time to cool, Healey turned his attention to an issue that would consume him, just about everyone else in Warren, and several Rhode Island state officials for the foreseeable future. As if to shoot off the first warning silo of a future burgeoning long war, Healey stated, "This is the last year of the teachers' contract. After that all eyes will focus on the committee to see if it will live up to its talk. But for now, this committee is still tied [by the earlier negotiated contract]. Watch us in the next year when we will be able to do something more than complain. If we do not keep our promises, then you should do something more than complain. You should get rid of us."[49]

While the School Committee Chairman and the Warren teacher's union tolerated a tense affiliation up to December 1983, from early 1984 onward that relationship turned toxic. Exchanges between the two sides grew increasingly combative. Soon neither side could cover up their disdain for the other. Over the next two years any salvageable aspect of their working relationship degenerated further. The decline played out publicly, in accordance with Healey's plan.

In February 1984, Healey attacked the union in his newsletter to the teachers, *What is about to Hit the Fan*. Healey alleged that the teachers' union had performed an "about face" on opening their contract after Warren's citizens had agreed to do their part in supporting the budget. Healey shared, "Needless to say, this has caused me to lose respect for the union."

Andy Duperron, a Warren High School math teacher and President of the Warren teachers's union, wrote in reply that the union had never agreed to re-open the current contract and charged that Healey had carried-out the about face.[50] Duperron, bald, spectacled, and usually conservatively dressed in a tie and sports jacket, looked the part of a college professor (a position which he later assumed.) The contrast in hairstyles and attire between Duperron and Healey accentuated their separate takes on matters before them. The bald-headed President and long-haired Chair battled out their conflicting interpretation of who said what when in the Warren Times-Gazette. Over the coming months the debate widened and spread throughout the streets of Warren. Couples, co-workers, classmates, children's parents, and casual acquaintances began to make accusations, take sides, and point fingers. With fired up bases on both sides of impending related school issues, contentious parties readied for a town family feud, the likes of which Warren had never experienced.

The Warren Times-Gazette soon started receiving upticks of letters to the editor on issues related to the approaching school contract negotiation. Early on many of those letters came from parties representing the teachers. In one of those letters Andy Duperron called attention to what he identified as a discrepancy between Healey's earlier statements and his more current actions. Healey fired back to Duperron's public criticism aggressively; "...let me say that I am tired of the union and its featherbedding. When I said that we should be working for the same goals, I meant the education of children and the relief of the taxpayers. I guess Mr. Duperron thought I meant saving teaching jobs. Clearly, what we have here is a failure to communicate."[51] At this point no one, not even Paul Newman[52], could argue that any semblance of good faith bargaining existed between the Committee Chair and the teachers' union.

Moving forward, it seemed the Warren teachers interpreted everything Healey said or did as controversial and open to interrogation. A case in point occurred in Spring 1984. On that late March day, no certified English substitutes had come forward to fill a Warren High School English teacher absence. Robert Healey, conducting research at the central administration building, learned of the vacancy. Healey, a certified English teacher, volunteered for the assignment for no compensation. Of the teaching experience that day, Healey commented, "It's nice to see how things are going in the trenches. You forget what it's like to look at it as a teacher."[53] What Healey also forgot, maybe, was what constituted proper attire for a teacher at Warren High School. Healey wore jeans when he substituted that day. That clothing choice violated Warren High School's *understood* teacher dress code. Someone brought the infraction to Principal Herman Grabert's attention. Grabert, who even on the hottest days wore a tie, and most often a suit jacket, called Healey into the front office to discuss the dressing code violation. While technically no official written dress code for teachers existed, Grabert had established a clear expectation of teachers' professional attire. Acceptable clothing included collared shirts, shoes, and slacks, not jeans. Grabert explained his policy to Healey and the issue dissipated quickly. No further discussion on the matter ensued.

Healey's attire infraction concerned Warren High School teachers little. The fact that School Committee Chairman Healey filled the substitute position himself did disturb them. Andrew Duperon questioned whether other substitutes could have filled the vacancy, and more importantly, whether the Chair filled the high school teaching position so that he could evaluate teachers.[54] Healey responded to Duperron publicly and in scolding fashion. "When he [Duperron] says that perhaps he [Healey] was there to see if teachers were doing their jobs, he is in fact saying that I am doing what I was elected to do. Furthermore, I had no reason to think that something might be going on without my knowledge, but his comments make me think there is something being hidden."[55]

The continuous back and forth public banter between Healey and the teachers appeared at times petty, and arguably more focused on personal issues than professional matters. In 1983, Healey had expressed concerns over teachers' high absentee rates. In February 1984, he decided to publish each teacher's monthly absentee numbers in the Warren Times. According to Healey, "individual teachers" had confided to him that *other* instructors had abused sick leave. Healey admitted that determining systematic abuse proved difficult because the teachers collectively duck for cover behind their union. Healey wrote in his monthly newsletter to the teachers, "As a former student and teacher in the Warren system, I am well aware of the joy some teachers get out of having the union put one over on the committee."[56] Healey later added, "It's hard to say students should be here every day, too. We have to run a school system on the idea of 'not as I say, but as I do.'"[57] Duperron responded that despite Healey's charges to the contrary, school authorities had brought forth no official charges of teacher sick leave abuse for the union to react to one way or the other. Duperron added that instead of Healey making frequent use of the town paper to air his accusations, "He should pass along those remarks at School Committee meetings, so that I and anyone else can comment."[58]

In March 1984, the Warren teachers' average daily number absentee rate dropped from 6.86 to 2.85. This encouraging absentee decline did not impress Healey. In fact, he expressed skepticism over what the recent drop in teachers' absences truly meant, and, once again, shared his thought process in the town's newspaper. Healey shared, "It is interesting to note that the Times article showing the teachers and the sick leave records came out in the middle of February '84. This may explain the drastic drop in absentee rates per day in March '84.'" Not only did he callout what he saw as teachers' attempts to draw attention away from their past abusive absentee behaviors, he also took aim at those who seemed more sympathetic to the teachers' circumstance, including members of the School Committee he chaired. Healey reasoned, "In any case, this method of having the public scrutinize the records seems far less expensive than the methods proposed by the teacher coalition of this School Committee. Public lectures make far more impact than the tongue lashing in the principal's office as proposed by Mr. Gempp and Mr. Mogayzel."[59]

Healey's public denouncements of public officials, who he felt ignored the will of the people, increased during the Spring 1984. So did those officials' responses. And Healey almost always rejoined, seeming to relish the attention and opportunity the back and forth provided him, sometimes at a cost to his opponent's personal and political reputation. In one such turn of events Healey took aim at Rep. Michael J. Urban Jr. on the grounds that the representative had not supported bills that would benefit the Warren School Department. In response to a letter Representative Urban had published in the paper, Healey countered by alleging that in an earlier verbal exchange Urban had called him a "dope pusher," threatened to strike him, and that "he [Urban] should give me a backhand instead of a bill."[60] Healey further offered, "It's unfortunate my physical appearance causes people to unjustly challenge me."[61]

Some of the most spirited debates over school issues occurred among School Committee members, all involving Healey front and center. In one ongoing public debate, School Committeeman John J. Killion III pressed, "In the future I do not want Mr. Healey speaking for me in his articles to the press. I will also ask the entire committee to formally vote on this issue at a future meeting. [George E. Gempp Jr. and Anthony Mogayzel joined on via a School Committee vote.] I personally feel that a leadership crisis has developed within the committee, and that steps should be immediately taken to correct the situation before it continues to affect the schools and the staff in a negative manner." Killion widened his criticism of the Chair. "When Mr. Healey assumed his position as chairman of the School Committee he made it abundantly clear that school and staff morale were essential to the educational process. In fact, in one of his statements he commented that morale within the school department had risen since the new committee had taken over the operations of the schools. Well, Mr. Healey, I have news for you. Staff morale is probably at an all-time low, and most of it is directly attributable to your newspaper articles and your negative letters to staff." Killion finished, for now, "None of us need to be intimidated in our voting with the threat of bad publicity."[62] School Committeeman George Gempp added that Healey's weekly letters had made the Committee the "laughing stock" of Warren.[63]

Healey blasted back to his oppositional Committeemen. "I am sorry Jack, George and Tony. I am not here to change the Warren School Committee into the Warren Teacher Protection Agency… Low morale in the teaching ranks, is far more acceptable to me than low morale in the taxpaying ranks."[64] The internal strife between Healey and his three fellow School Committee members continued and intensified over the coming months.

As the tension between School Committee members tightened, some Warren residents wrote letters to the editor critical of the Committee in general, and Healey more specifically. One disgruntled and politically engaged citizen wrote in a letter to the editor, "If the School Committee, the Town Council and the teachers union continue to exchange political crossfire, we may find ourselves with a below-average school system, taught by disgruntled teachers and unhappy pupils."[65] In a stronger specific reference to Healey, another citizen directed, "If credibility is a problem, perhaps narcissism and dema-goguery should also be considered as possible causes."[66]

Despite inter-squabbling, the School Committee did settle on a 1984-85 school budget to present to the Warren Town Council for funding. However, the Council decided the budget should be cut by $100,000. And though the town charter empowered the Council to make such a cut, and left what to cut to the School Committee's deter-mination, Healey criticized the council for the "round figure" decrease because "It shows they haven't studied the budget."[67]

And Healey had more to say about the Council's $100,000 cut. "... I would rather have the council stay out of the committee budget mat-ters entirely. I say, 'render unto Caesar that which is Caesar's and render on to the Committee that which is the schools.' The Council should not meddle in the committee's budget simply to meddle."[68] Healey went on to call attention to the differing treatment of municipal requests to that of school requests. "The council rejected the school's request for money to maintain the high school's boilers, but on the town's side, approved boiler repairs at fire stations. Do not the school's boilers need the same type of attention? Apparently not... I cry hypocrisy."[69]

"But why stop there?" questioned Healey. And he didn't. "Let's look elsewhere. What about Paul Harvey's protest on Feb. 27 that we should not award raises to our administrators, who as I shamefully note are vying for the title of lowest paid in the state. Well, it seems that the town budget approved by the council raises its administrators at a rate of about 7 percent in many cases. Why should the town get such handsome wages while the schools suffer?"[70]

Though the School Committee did make the needed adjustments to the school department budget necessitated by the Town Council cut, agreeing on the cover letter for the upcoming Financial Town Meeting proved more challenging. The point of contention centered on Healey's written acknowledgement. "... I would be lying to you if I said that this committee used everything in its power to get the best deal for the taxpayers of Warren (I refer to the pick-up plan.)" When

School Committeeman George E. Gempp Jr. asked Healey why he referenced the "pickup plan" (allowing teachers to make tax deferred contributions to their pension) in the report, Healey responded, "I asked for approval, not editing."[71] Healey, *compromised* later, "We'll have blank pages this year," instead of a cover letter. Gemp countered that the budget would have a cover letter, "and there won't be any catty remarks about a pickup plan." Gemp later remarked of the young Warren School Committee Chairman; "I've got a 12-year-old who behaves better."[72] In the end the Committee Budget contained two cover letters. One written by Healey which included Paul E. Brule's name. Mogayzel, Killion, and Gempp wrote the other letter.[73]

In addition to his fallout with three School Committee members, Healey fired more public charges toward the Warren Town Council. He asserted that the Council had critiqued the School Committee budget as a "smokescreen" to deflect attention from the town's budget which outpaced the growth of the school's budget significantly.[74] Healey further stated in the Warren Times-Gazette, "... there is much information around that can make this committee look bad. The reason it is around is because this committee has no secrets. Political safety is best achieved by keeping things secret... There has always been an attempt to keep you, the taxpayer, informed as to what is happening on the committee. I have brought you the good and the bad. You know it all, unlike other bodies [mainly the Town Council] that keep their stuff under wraps."[75]

The School Committee agreed to have Healey speak for the group at the Town Financial Meeting, although recently that same group had told him he could not be their spokesman. Healey rationalized that they had changed their minds "because none of them want to get up before the crowd."[76] Healey added that other School Committee members had "lectured" him before the meeting not to antagonize the council[77] and that, "I have a feeling they [the Committee] might dump me after the Financial Town Meeting."[78]

As it turned out, the taxpayers approved a 9.3 million 1984-1985 school budget at the town's financial meeting, and the School Committee did not dump their Chairman. Soon after the back and forth attacks between the Warren Town Council and the Warren School Committee subsided. The same development did not occur within the School Committee.

Instead, as the 1984-85 school year took hold, publicized arguments within the School Committee turned even more nasty, as exemplified in one particularly negative exchange between newly elected Anthony N. Nunes and Chairman Robert Healey. At a November School Committee meeting, tensions between Healey and Nunes built up. Nunes poked at the inflated tension balloon in the room, puncturing the thin wall that maintained any semblance of decorum at the meeting. He "exploded" over the Chairman's "sarcasm." Healey later criticized Nunes in the press over the incident. "Does this guy know what he's doing?... It is unfortunate that Mr. Nunes does not wish to be part of a team, but I will admit that it would be far worse if he had his own team."[79] Nunes had pointed out that Healey did not approach him over a decision the Committee had made before the meeting. Healey retorted in his weekly press letter, "I ask him [Nunes], for what reason would I give the decision to him almost a week before the meeting? In case he ran out of toilet paper? Hardly. It was to get his opinion."[80] Despite such troubling exchanges, the School Committee did not appear too upset with Healey when in November they reelected him as their chairman by a 4-to-0 vote. Nunes abstained.[81]

As 1984 wound down, Healey shared, "..some people have noted that my comments are harsh, often biting, and at times sarcastic." He acknowledged, "Perhaps they are..." Rather than continuing with the softened tone, Healey finished with, "...if you can't take the heat, get out of the kitchen."

Rumbles of thunder associated with the approaching budget year could be heard throughout Warren, and to a lesser degree (for now) the rest of Rhode Island. And in case Warren teachers somehow did not hear the cracklings, the Chairman turned up the decibels in his last monthly newsletter to the teachers. Bob Healey wrote that despite circulating rumors, the teachers should not "celebrate" yet over his removal as School Committee Chair, and that he might assume a seat on the upcoming negotiating team for the teacher contract set to expire in 1985. He chided, "Now is the time to send that card to St. Jude." While Healey might have inserted the line for humorous tension relief, his later forthcoming comments in the same letter negated any realized good feeling. In a blatantly sarcastic tone, Healey injected, "For all those teachers who complain about this 'dismal' newsletter [*What is About to Hit the Fan*], let me personally thank you for not contributing a single word in response to my call for ideas … Good job." He closed out what would be his last direct letter to the Warren School Department's teaching faculty, "I'll be blasting you." [82] His last line proved prophetic. It was all about to hit the fan.

CHAPTER 5

HEALEY DID WHAT?

Most considered Robert J. Healey Jr. an intelligent, industrious, and impassioned advocate for his many causes. Many of those same people perceived him as unconventional, controversial, and comical. The former traits established Bob Healey as memorable. The latter traits made him unforgettable.

In 1983 the Providence Journal published its parting thoughts of 1982. The states' premier newspaper took the opportunity to reflect on the newsworthy passing year and awarded certain parties for making it so. Even though Healey had served as the Warren School Committee Chairman for less than two months in 1982, The Journal presented Bob Healey the *Last Laugh Award*. In explaining their choice, the newspaper announced, "They laughed when long-haired Robert J. Healey Jr. announced he was a candidate for the School Committee in Warren. Healey laughed too... He won the race. Not only that, he got more votes than anybody else. Now he's the chairman of the School Committee."[1]

Only a few days after the Providence Journal reported the above recognitions, Healey grabbed the attention of the same newspaper (among other news outlets) again. In January 1983, the Warren

Police instituted random drug checks on local school buses. They had received complaints from parents about students smoking in one of those vehicles. Warren Police Chief Emilio D. Squillante Jr. did not inform the town's superintendent, high school principal, or School Committee Chair about the ordered school bus checks he instituted.[2] Over a two-day period in January, the police went on board three buses looking for evidence of students smoking marijuana. Though they detected the smell of Cannabis, they could not determine if the students possessed the drugs.[3]

When Bob Healey first learned why the police had conducted the bus checks he said, "'I'm telling the students not to smoke pot on school time," adding, "School shouldn't be that cool."[4] He stressed, "It [smoking marijuana] shouldn't be going on." Referencing the policemen's part in the operation, he cautioned, "They have their jobs to do as long as they do not abuse students' constitutional rights."[5] All of these commentaries fell within the realm of how one would expect a small-town School Committee Chairman to react to the circumstance before them.

But Healey had more to say. And that proved problematic. Healey offered, "If students want to smoke pot, they should do it on their own time. I don't think the schools should force any opinions down the throats of students. Making people believe what the government wants people to believe is something done in less free nations."[6] Whether the long haired and bearded School Committee Chairman knew it or not, he had stepped into a pile of stereotype manure, too often used to smear people of his appearance. And on cue, the public responded hastily, casting disparaging judgements on the Chairman. Healey addressed those comments forthrightly, calling attention to the bearded elephant in the room.

> *"People say because he has long hair he must be saying it's OK to smoke pot at home, but I thought people had realized that having long hair does not mean that a person shoots up every night, deals drugs to little kids, steals purses from old ladies and*

all the other elements of the stereotype... the reaction to this whole event... could have been expected... Still, I was shocked that people immediately read into my statement the way they did. I meant that smoking pot, if done, would not be done on school time. I did not give a license to smoke pot at home— quite frankly, that is not my problem."[7]

Speaking in wider terms, Healey concluded, "Finally, maybe you do not agree with my views. Maybe you wanted a stronger statement such as 'Smoking pot causes insanity' or something to that effect. Well, I guess I could tell you what you wanted to hear, but I thought you deserved the truth. I remain firm in my commitment not to tell students how to live their lives off school time." [8]

The Warren Times Gazette leapt to Healey's defense, as they often would over the coming years. The local paper made their position clear.

"Most residents like to think that days of basing opinions on a person because of his race, religion, or his appearance are long gone. Whether or not this is so in Warren, however, is uncertain after Robert J. Healey Jr., chairman of the School Committee, said some residents have decided he is an advocate of drug use because of his full-length beard and below-shoulder-length hair..... Healey makes a good point when he says it's not his place to tell students whether or not to smoke pot—it's the parents' responsibility. Those same parents should realize that long hair worn by Healey or anyone else doesn't constitute a drug user. We tend to think that if Healey's remarks had been made by any of the other members of the School Committee, the connotation would have been different..."[9]

The Warren Times Gazette got it right. At about the same time Healey shared his views on Warren High School students allegedly smoking pot, fellow Committeeman John J. Killion III said to a Providence Journal reporter, "If they're going to do it, they shouldn't do it with anything that is connected with the school. Let them do it at home."[10] While arguably Killion made a more controversial statement than had Healey, no one expressed public outrage over Killion's assertion. Of course, Killion did not sport a beard, a mustache, or long hair. Apparently his more mainstream appearance caused people to hear his commentary at face value. They *heard* his statement differently than they did a similar utterance from the School Committee Chairman.

While Healey's hair and beard typically gained peoples' attention and drew their commentary, further south another feature of his appearance, specifically his feet, also could incite interest and reaction. Healey had a long-standing practice of walking barefoot in public. That habit didn't cause much of a stir until he continued the behavior elsewhere, most notably at the Warren School Committee meetings. There, people interpreted the behavior as lacking proper decorum. Many people expressed concern, but not everyone. Some Warren students found the shoeless look *cool* enough to mimic when they returned to Warren High School in September 1984. That style choice drew more attention to Healey's attire, or in this case, lack thereof.

While pressure built for Healey to put his shoes on at School Committee meetings, the Chairman checked with the state Education and Health Departments and discovered no law prohibiting bare feet in a public building.[11] However, a school department policy required that students wear shoes while at school.[12] And with that, Healey agreed to wear shoes, once the school year began, figuring, "...you can't walk barefoot in the winter."[13] But of course, Bob Healey had more to say about the matter. "...I have been said to have turned the committee into a laughing stock of the world. I have been told that I am an elected official and that this means that I must wear shoes. Well, to that I must take exception. America is still a free country, and

I am not violating any rule or law. On bare feet I will take a firm stand. I was not elected to wear shoes. I was elected to oversee the operation of the Warren school system. While I would be very concerned if my decisions made the committee the laughing stock of the world, I am not concerned about my appearance. To mandate appearance would be taking away part of the freedom America is so famous for. And besides, what would be next, mandatory shaves, haircuts? Now, I am sorry to waste such precious space over senseless matters."[14]

Healey chaired the next School Committee meeting wearing footwear, specifically wooden sandals. He also wore socks, one blue and the other brown, blue jeans, and a red and white striped summer blazer, with a multi-colored shirt.[15] With his point made, Healey moved onto other issues.

About a year before Healey's shoeless lifestyle gained statewide notice, his stand on another more important issue garnered attention as well. In the summer of 1983 Robert Healey prepared for his Bar Exam, but not on the day before the assessment. On that day Robert Healey took on another cause: drinking water. While other law students most likely reviewed material associated with the next day's pivotal test, or rested, Healey walked Warren sidewalks draped by a sandwich board, carrying a bottle of tap water, and urging Eastbay residents to sign a petition for better drinking water. He intended to deliver hundreds of signatures demanding water quality improvement to the Bristol County Water Company. To entice pedestrians to sign his petition, Healey filled a bottle with his home tap water. That liquid resembled "sun tea."[16] Later that same summer Healey handed out information entitled, "Everything You Always Wanted To Know about H2O but Were Afraid to Ask," a clear reference to Woody Allen's 1972 comedy film, "Everything You Always Wanted to Know About Sex but Were Afraid to Ask."[17] To offset Healey's impact, Robert L Amman Jr., vice president and manager of the Bristol County Water Company, explained that the discoloration of Healey's bottled home tap water resulted from a street cleaner that had run too close to a fire hydrant by Healey's home system. Nevertheless, Healey continued his campaign for cleaner water.[18] Healey formed a group unofficially known as "Friends of Good Water," with the slogan, "The Stink in Your Sink is Not Fit to Drink."[19] In an October 1983 letter to the editor, Healey vowed, "...I believe the people of Warren want pure Scituate water, not a concoction of Bristol water and Scituate water... Because I feel that the water of Bristol is bad, I am demanding pure Scituate water. ... I will continue to bring my findings to the public."[20] And he did much more than that.

One month later Robert Healey got out of bed at 4:00 A.M. determined to set out on an eight-hour trek to Scituate. He had three motives. First, he wanted to support a first ballot question that would establish a state water board to which municipalities could apply for funds to upgrade their systems. Second, he wanted an affirmative vote on a Bristol County ballot to form a local water authority. And third, he wanted to have a glass of "good" water.[21] On that November 1983 morning, Healey left the Bristol Water Company in Bristol and continued walking down the Wampanoag Trail, through the East Side of Providence, and up Route 6 into Scituate. One television station filmed part of his journey, which they shared on that night's news with James Taylor's song, *Walking Man*, playing in the background. Fatigue aside, Healey said the journey pained him little, minus walking for a while with a pebble in his shoe, and dodging a stone thrown at him by a youngster in Providence. When he arrived at his destination, Healey had a cup of Scituate water. Minutes later friends picked Healey up and drove him home to Warren.[22]

While Healey had made the news walking, on another occasion he grabbed headlines by standing. One morning he positioned himself by a crosswalk in front of Mary V. Quirk Jr. High School. He had good reason for doing so. Quirk faced Warren's busy Main Street (Route 114). At that location drivers often passed by at speeds far exceeding limits legislated for school zones. Though the circumstance proved very concerning, to be fair, one can understand why drivers might have had a tendency to speed by Mary V. Quirk. First, the school overlooked a straightway with no lights north or south for a considerable distance. Second, when a driver cleared the congested Warren business district on route to Bristol, they often attempted to gain speed as they approached the gradual upward plain that would turn into Bristol's Hope Street. At that location the speed limit jumped to thirty-five miles per hour. Conversely, drivers from Bristol felt a temptation and had a tendency to maintain their speed from driving down the hill toward Warren, especially when running late for work in Providence during the morning rush. A crosswalk painted in front of Mary V. Quirk Jr. High School did not result in slowing approaching cars because drivers could not see the white lines clearly until they practically drove over them. The school's cross walk appeared at the top of a slight hill.

Making the traffic situation in front of the school all the more hazardous, in addition to morning and afternoon arrivals and departures, physical education classes used the crosswalk to make their way to Burr's Hill Park where students played on the basketball court, baseball diamond, or open field areas. Further adding to the treachery, school buses could not park in front of Quirk and therefore arrived and left by a side street. Had the buses dropped off students in front of the school, their blinking red lights would have forced approaching traffic to stop. Healey stressed that only a small sign, attached too high on an electric pole for a passing car to see, warned approaching drivers that they should be on the outlook for excitable adolescents crossing the street. The mix of accelerating cars, limited warning, and impulsive children who had to cross the street at least twice a day, created a concoction for disaster. Chairman Healey worried aloud about the disastrous possibilities that awaited a child in front of the school he once attended. Healey explained, "You don't know a school is there until it's too late. I don't want to wait until a kid gets killed to do something."[23]

While other town and state officials had pursued the legislative process to deal with the concerns over children's safety in front of Mary V. Quirk Jr. High School, Healey grew impatient. Within weeks of sounding the alarm, he undertook more drastic means to secure a blinking light by the school's crosswalk. To that end, during a Thursday morning rush hour Healey positioned himself in front of Mary V. Quirk wearing a sandwich board that read, "25 is Cool." He was only getting started.

Warren School Committeeman George E. Gempp Jr. reached out to Healey after the sandwich Board campaign and told him to pursue "proper channels" to secure the blinking light. Healey responded, "I told George he could go through channels. I'm going to the public."[24] Earlier, Healey had offered of George Gempp, "I only wish to say that George Gempp has been very involved in this matter in that he spoke with various officials to attempt to solve the problem. I'm just the jerk with the sign who believes actions speak louder than words. [25]

Other government officials joined the campaign for a blinking light in front of Mary V. Quirk Jr. High School, notably State Representative Michael J. Urban Jr., often Healey's adversary. On the Friday after Healey took to the street in front of Warren's only Jr. High School, the state Traffic Commission notified Representative Urban that the state had denied Warren's request for a warning signal in front of the school. The Commission based its decision on a study it had conducted on June 13, 1984 from 2:15 P.M. to 2:30 P.M. Engineers said "gaps of up to 20 seconds per minute..." provided sufficient time to cross a forty-eight-foot span of roadway. The engineers recommended that the Warren police should enforce a posted parking ban in front of the school. This would improve passing drivers' visibility. (Teachers parked in front of the school to avoid a long walk to the school's front door.)

Urban complained about the commission's determination, "I think it's a poor decision. If any place needs it [a traffic light], it's Mary V. Quirk." Urban said he would get together with Healey to see what the School Committee wants to do next, including possibly appealing to the Traffic Commission or to put forth another solution such as placing a stop sign by the crosswalk. Urban apparently shared Healey's determination saying he would continue to pursue the issue, including, if necessary, filing a bill in the next session of the General Assembly to appropriate funds for the traffic light.

In the meantime, Healey continued to take to the streets by the Jr. High School. Sometimes he parked his car in front with several signs about the need to reduce car speeds attached. At other times he wore his sandwich board with various slogans, including "Slow is Cool." In addition, Healey spoke before the Town Council to gain their support for the blinking light. In response, Town Council President Paul J. Harvey assured Healey that "The work order has already been issued for warning signs and speed limit signs."

Harvey's assurance did not placate Healey who continued his on-street campaign because, Healey explained, the state "... can say they are doing a lot of things, but seeing is believing."[26] Regarding the installment of signs instead of a blinking traffic light, Healey stated, "If I'm satisfied the kids are safe, I'll stop. If not, I'll be down there."[27] About a month later the state Department of Transportation (DOT) installed two signs to reduce the speed limit. The move saved the state thousands of dollars over the money required to install a traffic light.

Within a month of the signs' installation, Healey decided the DOT's offering fell short of securing the children's safety in front of Quirk. So, he upped his anti. In mid-October, he created a "traffic stopper." This contraption amounted to a plastic container, yellow wrapping paper, and some lights Healey rigged up to a battery which could fit in his back pocket.[28] The entire getup cost him $3.50. On an October 1984 morning, Healey put his traffic stopper gadget to work for the first time. For that purpose, he stationed himself to the north on Main St., a little over a block away from Mary V. Quirk Jr. High. At that location he lit up a cigar, and placed the homemade contraption on his head and turned on the blinking lights. He intended to draw attention. He succeeded. Motorists passing by responded to the

School Committee Chair's blinking light protest by honking horns and waving enthusiastically. On that morning, Warren School Superintendent Wilfred Marchand joined the demonstration. Marchand observed of the drivers, "They're not going 20. You can tell some of them left late; they're drinking coffee." He added, "I tell you one thing. If I was chief of police, I'd have a field day here. I'd have the cars lined up to Bristol. If they left late, they would be a lot later." Paul Canario, a Quirk Jr. High School English teacher, who walked along Main Street to school daily, shared his thoughts of the traffic situation that same morning. He said while the signs helped at first, "... they're [motorists] back to their old form." Marchand worried, "Yesterday, after school, a kid almost was hit while crossing the street." He said he would be in front of the school once a month until "we get what we want."[29]

Shortly after Healey's traffic stopper debut, Warren acting Police Chief Robert Pare ordered patrolmen to Mary V. Quirk in the morning and afternoon to run radar. The action resulted in ten motorists ticketed for speeding, and another ten given warnings. The police handed out tickets to drivers exceeding thirty-five miles per hour. One driver passed Mary V. Quirk driving forty-five miles per hour as school was letting out. Pare referenced the situation as a significant problem.

Superintendent Marchand offered of Bob Healey's efforts; "The guy has got a message to get out and he's getting it out. You can write editorials and articles, but they will never get the results he gets." Though State Representative Michael J. Urban Jr. did not stand out in front of Quirk with a "traffic stopper" on his head, he planned to talk to the state's General House Speaker, Matthew J. Smith, about the ongoing concern. Referencing two separate lights installed by the state at other locations in Warren, he complained, "It's outrageous. They can put two lights doing the same job and not add a blinking light at the Mary V. Quirk." He added that if his talk with Smith did not prove fruitful, he would again put a bill in next year's state budget for the light.[30]

October turned into December. The sun rose later and set earlier.

To call attention to the need for a traffic light in front of Mary V. Quirk Middle School in Warren, Rhode Island, School Committee Chairman Healey stood beside a speed limit sign, wore a blinking yellow light "traffic stopper" that he rigged up himself, and smoked a cigar as students entered the school.

As a result, increasingly motorist struggled to see students in front of the Main Street school building. And still, no blinking light existed in front of Mary V. Quirk Jr. High School. Healey's frustration rose. So did his determination to affect change. As the holidays approached, Healey showed up on Main Street, this time south of Quirk, draped in a sandwich board in the shape of a Christmas tree with a blinking north star on his head. He printed on the board a politically correct statement; "All Faiths… Go Ye 20."[31] Of the spectacle, Healey commented, "It's not every day you see a walking Christmas tree."[32] Healey added, "When people saw me there, most automatically slowed down. There were only four or five people who acted like jerks and sped by."[33]

Referencing Police Chief Emilio D. Squillante Jr.'s alleged minimal concern over the lack of a blinking light at Mary V. Quirk, Healey offered, "When we had radar down there it worked quite well. But they [police] haven't been back there since." Calling attention to Acting Police Chief Pare, who had run the radar trap during Police Chief's Squillante's absence, Healey suggested in the form of a question, "Maybe the chief should go on another vacation?"[34]

Paul Harvey, the Warren Town Council President, did not fully support Healey's efforts to secure the light at Quirk. Healey reported of that reality, "... I wish to inform you that at the last council meeting, a request for legislation to put a light in front of Quirk was tabled. Paul Harvey apparently convinced the council that they should wait for a report of this traffic commission before supporting a bill for the light. Take the bull by the horns, will ya? There is little doubt that a light is needed there."[35] Eventually, the state agreed, or at least succumbed, and installed more traffic control measures in front of Mary V. Quirk.

While some might not have agreed with his train of thought or approved of his high-profile antics, undeniably Robert Healey provided extraordinary head-turning performances. Whether referencing students smoking pot "on their own time," trekking miles for a drink of reservoir water, or standing in front of a school with a blinking light on his head to slow drivers, people of all political persuasions took notice. How could they not? As the Warren Times-Gazette reported in September 1984, Healey produced the best show in town, and beyond.

And the local paper gave Healey high marks on his other related undertakings. Of Healey's strategies and activities, the paper referenced the "Marco Polo Healey Show" as a "a mini series in which a newly elected School Committee Chairman explores new worlds by trying to keep government business in the open. He meets opposition from all sides and nearly gives up hope, but he is given courage by voters who tell him to stick to his guns." [36] And for the remainder of his term of office as Warren's School Committee Chairman, he continued to do just that.

CHAPTER 6

THE YEAR IT ALL HIT THE FAN
1985—1986

Representatives of the Warren School Committee and the Rhode Island National Education Association (NEA) Warren[1] met in January 1985 to begin contract talks. The current contract expired on September 1 of that year. Based on past negotiations in Warren, conventional wisdom suggested nine months provided ample time to work out a mutually agreeable contract between the town's School Committee and the Warren Teachers Association.

At their first negotiation meeting, the two sides exchanged lists of proposed ground rules for the upcoming negotiation sessions. After three hours of arguing over how to proceed, the parties came to agreement on only two matters. First, they would meet again in two weeks, and every Wednesday after that date until mid-February. If needed, they would schedule more sessions. Second, both negotiating teams decided they would share their proposals at the next meeting. Neither side could submit anything new later. Each party found that understanding reasonable enough.

At the next negotiation meeting NEA-Warren presented ten pages of proposed changes to the existing contract, including benefit and pay increases that would boost their teachers' compensation slightly above the state average. Their submission resembled what the School Committee probably expected based on the teachers' initial offerings during past negotiations. The School Committee's representatives, Robert Healey and Paul Brule, put forward a proposal that bore no resemblance to anything proffered by past Warren School Committee negotiating teams. Their list amounted to thirty-five pages of changes to the current contract.[2] Their offering took the NEA's team aback. In essence, the two-man committee had just opened up every line in the old contract for negotiation. While the teachers had suggested a revisit of several items, Healey and Brule had called for a wide-reaching overhaul of the current contract. If accepted, the resulting agreement would differ dramatically from any Rhode Island teachers' contract negotiated in modern times. Just the suggestion of the proposed changes favored the School Committee. The earlier agreed upon ground rules empowered Healey and Brule to reference anything in the contract for change, while the teachers' union could not.[3] The two men representing the School Committee had flat footed the teacher union's five-member delegation. That circumstance did not result by chance. Healey later explained of their proposal, "NO ONE had copies, not even other committee members or the superintendent of schools." Healey explained of their strategy, "We wanted to hold our cards close."[4]

The hand they held conveyed that business as usual had no place at *their* bargaining table. Healey and Brule's proposed revamp of the contract challenged long-standing practices and understandings. Across the state school committees and the teachers' unions typically negotiated three-year contracts. Brule and Healey proposed a nine-month contract that would adjust drastically the teachers' working schedule, benefits, and compensation. Under the Committee's plan, teachers would work 200 days (up from 182 days), eight hours on site (up from six hours and forty-five minutes), and do so for a pay cut of approximately ten percent. While under the Brule/Healey proposed contract teachers on lower steps would receive a raise, most Warren teachers were on the top step (ten years of service or more.) Healey and Brule proposed that top step teachers undertake a salary reduction in excess of $2,000. Other proposed changes from the Committee included increasing class sizes up to thirty students, and less paid sick days for teachers, annually and cumulatively.

In an apparent attempt to calm the waters he and Brule had stirred up, Healey said, "It's important to understand that things could change drastically. It's like buying a used car. You talk to the person and work out a deal."[5] But before he would deal, Healey further strengthened his bargaining position. When Healey found out that the school department's business manager, Dennis Lima, had budgeted eight percent for teacher raises during the 1985-1986 fiscal year, the School Committee chairman demanded that the school department eliminate those figures from the budget. Healey explained, "If we budget 8 percent, anybody who understands the budgeting process could look and see that a certain amount of money was in there and they would fight for that amount." By erasing that line item, Healey insisted, "... the committee can really bargain and negotiate in the true sense of the word."[6] Looking further down the road, Healey added that if the two negotiating teams could not reach an agreement by the annual Financial Town Meeting in May, he would ask taxpayers not to set aside any funds for teacher raises. Instead, Healey explained, if the teachers inevitably negotiated raises, Warren citizens could decide at a special Financial Town Meeting whether or not to support the proposed funding.[7] To do otherwise, Healey thought, set the committee up to get "jerked around like a monkey on a string."[8]

If the Warren Education Association thought that things would run more smoothly after their first negotiation meeting with Healey and Brule, they learned quickly that both School Committeemen had prepared for a long battle. Early on Healey decided to record the negotiation meetings. Jeanette Wooley[9] (National Education Association Rhode Island (NEARI) negotiator,) didn't like that idea. After approximately one minute into Healey's first taped session, Wooley objected to the practice and called her five-member team into caucus. Despite the protest, the tape recorder remained.[10] The negotiations proceeded, on Healey's terms.

In January 1985, the two bargaining parties achieved little success toward reaching an agreement. In February, negotiations worsened. After a February 6 negotiating meeting, according to Healey, Wooley said, "If you're smart, you'll settle this contract next time." [11] Wooley probably made her remark in reference to a state law that empowered teachers to pursue arbitration after thirty days of unsuccessful negotiation. She figured the teachers would fare far better with a neutral party than continuing talks with an obstinate force in the form of Healey and Brule. *Next time*, February 13, 1985, Robert Healey brought a party hat to the negotiations, as if in preparation for a contract settlement celebration. If Healey truly expected a festive occurrence, he left disappointed.[12]

While exactly how well the teachers would fare with an arbitrator remained an unknown, clearly the relationship between the union and School Committee continued to deteriorate. At one late February meeting, Jeanette Woolley requested that the School Committee raise travel compensation for teachers from fifteen cents a mile to twenty cents a mile. The committee suggested eighteen cents. When Wooley refused the offer, Superintendent Marchand asked her why she would not accept eighteen cents. Wooley replied, "Read my lips—we don't want eighteen cents." When Healey questioned Wooley regarding her refusal to accept the three-cent a mile increase, Wooley replied, "It's an insult." Healey retorted, "Everything insults you."[13]

When not *negotiating* with the teachers' union, Healey continued to attract attention and make news as he called out individuals in government offices. In one instance the School Committee Chairman demanded the Rhode Island General Assembly's local delegation support bills he had identified as educationally sound. At another point he turned his attention to the Warren Town Council, criticizing the body for selecting Patricia Read to replace Paula Cruz's seat on the School Committee in March 1985. (Cruz had been elected in the November 1984 election and died tragically.) Healey charged of Read, "She holds great loyalties to the teachers because of her work with them as a volunteer and the fact that she was once a teacher in the Warren Schools."[14] At other times he clashed with veteran School Committee members. In one instance he referenced the past contract that current School Committeeman Nunes had helped negotiate as "...a three-year, 25 percent monster."[15] Occasionally Healey even eyed the electorate. In one such occurrence, he implored Warren residents to attend the school department negotiation meetings, pointing out that almost no one had attended the last contract negotiations despite that "teacher contracts are probably the single most expensive item in the town..."[16]

In mid-March, Healey sought Town Council support for the School Committee's budget, which continued to present teacher salary cuts of approximately $2,000 per teacher. When one councilwoman inquired what would happen if teachers succeeded in negotiating raises, Healey lashed back, "You're approaching this with a defeatist attitude. We might as well throw in the towel if we assume they will get a raise..."[17] The Council eventually backed the School Committee's budget with no allowance for a teacher raise.

While Healey continued to grab more attention than his negotiating partner, one should not overlook Paul Brule's critical part in the team's assertive dealings with the town's teachers and the NEA. From the beginning, Brule pushed Healey to up the heat on the teacher's union.[18] One might rightfully wonder if Healey would have been so dogmatic during negotiations had Brule not encouraged him so insistently behind the scenes. Jeanette Wooley picked up on Paul Brule's role early on, recalling years later that Brule wanted first and foremost to keep taxes from increasing and as such had it in for the teachers.[19]

Though both Brule and Healey agreed that the Chairman served their collective endeavor best as the front man, each man also understood that Brule knew the town's people well, and that he presented as fearless and brutish.[20] Accordingly, the two committeemen assumed their respective role and teamed seamlessly. Healey pushed the argument at the frontline while Brule held their position squarely intact along the backlines. Healey did most of the talking, and Brule played the part of a less loquacious immovable enforcer. If the teachers' negotiating team underestimated the two Committeemen, and they may have at first, that miscalculation would come at a great cost.

At future contract talks Healey continued with intent to aggravate the opposing negotiating team, especially Jeanette Wooley. He slouched in his seat, clipped his toenails,[21] and in the eyes of Wooley and others, demonstrated little proper decorum. Wooley once commented about Healey, "And his publicity stunts—I think that's how he gets his kicks."[22] Beyond commenting on his semantics and style, Wooley questioned the degree to which the Chairman bargained in good faith. She contended, "From the beginning, he has not wanted to negotiate. He wants to negotiate with the public and wants to embarrass the teachers... He doesn't care about education... I find him very arrogant. He is just trying to undermine the union and take his case to the public instead of bargaining with NEA-Warren." One night Wooley took notice of Healey slumping behind a table during a negotiation session. Wooley asked him, "Do you think you could possibly sit up? It's so annoying." Healey did not change his posture.[23] Shortly afterward negotiations between the two parties broke down and the process headed for mediation.

Healey didn't only aggravate Wooley, he annoyed the teachers, again, presumably by intent. In late March the Chairman asked Superintendent Marchand for copies of teachers' lesson plans. Lillian Ridgewell, the Warren High School Business Department chair, pointed out that Marchand had not complied when administration had made the same request of him when he taught.[24] Marchand assured Healey that teachers wrote up lesson plans. The Superintendent did not force teachers to turn in their teaching plans.

Also in late March, Healey asked the citizens of Warren if the teachers "need" a raise.[25] To help them make up *their* minds, he instructed, "I do not think that people realize that in addition to their average salary of about $29,000, the teachers are getting an additional $6,000 to $7,000 more in before-tax benefits."[26] To further guide citizens to arrive at their opinion, Healey wrote, "The teachers union is asking too much…."[27] And in case people still couldn't arrive at a personal judgment, Healey sought to tutor them on the sidewalks of Main Street, distributing mimeographed copies of teachers' salaries and benefits. Healey's handouts read, "It is time to stop the senseless slaughter of Warren taxpayers."[28] The printed sheets informed pedestrians that teachers worked 180 six and ¾ hour days, twenty of which qualified for sick leave and two additional days for personal leave. He made no reference to obvious rebuttal points. Further, Healey charged, the teachers enjoyed "top shelf" benefits which included two pension plans.[29] (The two pensions Healey referenced included the state pension system and social security, both to which the teachers contributed via bi-weekly pay deductions. Bob Healey chose not to include that information in his address to Warren residents).

The Warren teachers' union President, Andrew L. Duperron, challenged the legality of Robert J. Healey Jr.'s sidewalk tactics on the grounds that the Chairman violated state laws. Duperron charged, "The issues he's bringing up have never been brought up at the bargaining table. Yet he chooses to paste [them] on a board and go up town."[30] Duperron further supposed, "I guess he's looking for public outcry to tell him what to do instead of sitting down with us and doing what he was elected to do."[31] Not surprisingly, Healey disagreed with Duperron, and inquired, "Is handing out public records a violation of the law? Has the First Amendment right to free speech been repealed?" After his referencing of the Constitution, Healey drew attention to NEA-Warren's tactics during negotiations. "They [the teachers' union] have taken to personal attacks on me in the form of name-calling. To which I say, if you can't talk to the facts, try to make fun of the speaker."[32] Further, Healey declared, "I will continue to distribute the truth until there is a court order telling me to stop. The people have a right to know and I have the right to free speech."[33] Of the people's response to his questions, Healey shared, "I have found that with the exception of teachers and their relatives, many people are supporting the committee on these negotiations,"[34] and those people "...want to know how to help even more." He advised Warren taxpayers, "The best thing to do is to call or write to the School Committee and tell them 'Enough is enough' and that you support Paul Brule and me in the negotiations. Without the support of Anthony Nunes, John Killion and Patricia Read, the negotiating team will not be successful."[35]

In late April, the School Committee voted to publish the names, salaries and benefits of all Warren School Department employees in the Warren-Times Gazette, and to pass out the information at the May 20 Financial Town Meeting."[36] The vote to do so did not attain unanimous consent. Committeeman Anthony N. Nunes thought Healey wanted to publish teachers' salaries for his (Healey's) "own publicity purposes." Nunes added, "I don't think it's our jobs to embarrass our own employees...," and "lower morale."[37]

In one of Healey's weekly May press releases, he appeared to back away from comparing Warren teacher's salaries with other communities' teachers. The omission did not signal a retreat or a peace offering, but rather a maneuver to attack from another vantage point. Healey explained; "...Warren is Warren. It is not Providence, Westerly or Newport. The issue is what Warren teachers should earn. Each side could easily cloud the issue with higher and lower paid teachers." Pivoting, Healey then angled for his next shot; "... people should remember that teacher wages are not subject to a free market economy. Teachers' jobs are protected. Comparisons are for shoppers who, when discovering they can get something for less, buy it. Since teachers do not exist in a supply and demand economy, the use of comparisons is less than informative and almost foolish."[38] So, if Warren teachers' proposed salary raises put them on par with other communities, Healey had

Bob Healey talks with Warren resident about teacher salaries and benefits in front of the Warren Town Hall.

in essences negated that point and widened his argument to question the legitimacy of teacher salaries in general.

As the spring progressed, people voiced increasingly their opinions on the school contract talks. Most, not all, expressed concerns over the effects of Healey's take no prisoner approach to negotiations. Many of these critics had an established connection of one sort or another to the teachers. Healey responded to almost all letters that took a negative view of his position or tactics. In one instance, Healey corrected (in his view) and chided a writer about their letter to the editor; "Had you attended my most recent matinee performance... it [his contract proposal] does not, as you claim, ask for a $3,000 pay cut... the average Warren teacher was asked to take a cut of $1,701." In responding to Ginger DeSocio, the wife of a teacher who referenced Healey's general approach to negotiations as a "circus performance," Healey scolded, "The fact that I chose to use my spare time to inform the public should not concern you. I do not tell you what to do with your time. In concluding, let me make it clear. The show must go on."[39] And it did.

Anthony Annarummo, a Warren political enthusiast for twenty-five years, might have offered one of the more insightful opinions up to this point. He said, "Bob doesn't like it when I tell him this, but he is a better politician than most politicians I have seen. He knows how to use the media. He is a great publicist. He's a lawyer, and like any good lawyer he knows how to put the best light on his arguments."[40] If one did not take into account Annarummo's assessment of Healey and dared to argue a position contrary to the full-time Chairman, part-time lawyer, they could expect a most directed and often cutting personal retort.

As summer 1985 approached, the teachers' frustrations with their School Committee Chairman grew. Healey communicated no notion of compromising, and conducted his affairs as if he would stop at nothing to make his case before the Warren voters. As such, the teachers' Association looked more and more to the arbitration process for results. That procedure called for a neutral arbitrator to hear-out both sides and then render a binding decision on non-money issues only. Many school systems adopted the arbitrator's award (including non-binding monetary recommendations) in order to avoid teacher strikes, or to just end the misery of dead-end talks. With both thought processes in mind, in May Jeanette Wooley asked that seventeen unresolved issues between the Warren School Committee's negotiating team and the teachers' union be submitted to arbitration. Healey referenced Woolley's request as "tactical" and for the purpose of delaying negotiations. He charged that when teachers' unions go "...before an arbitrator, they have much to gain and nothing to lose."[41] Healey attacked the arbitration procedure, asserting, "Arbitrators are generally liberal spenders, especially when they know their awards are non-binding. The union knows this. They want a piece of paper to try to make the people think they really deserve it, after all. They will tell you that an arbitrator said they should get this. They will not tell you about the process."[42] Since arbitrators live and work from outside the town to which they render their decision, Healey reasoned, most spend the neighboring taxpayers' money liberally.[43]

Though Healey drew the lion's share of the press's attention during the negotiations, in time other less colorful parties of interest got their opinions in print as well. Union President Andrew Duperron, one such less showy party, entered into the published discourse fairly often. On one occasion Duperron challenged Healey and Brule's arguments: "I can't see where you can say they're bargaining in good faith when they say they have no money for us in the budget. Next year's committee budget has an increase of $400,000 over this year's.[44]

While the townspeople's opinions on the contract negotiations did not suffer from short supply, the late May annual financial meeting drew fewer than 400 of Warren's 5,000 plus registered voters. While reasons for the relatively low turnout ranged from inclement weather to other plans, more than likely the fact that neither the School Committee nor the Town Council had requested a tax increase bred limited public interest,[45] for the time being.

As the 1984-85 school year came to a close, the two sides continued to battle on. Remarks perceived as cutting by one party inflamed passions and built stubborn resolve on the other side of the table. Most of these digs, at least of the published sort, came from Healey, directed squarely at the teachers and / or their union. When Healey's comment barrages portrayed teachers in a negative light, he irked the rank-and-file educators. Most often Jeanette Wooley would push back on behalf of the exasperated teachers. For instance, when Healey suggested teachers did not work very hard, she remarked, "This I find ironic coming from someone who has dedicated his entire life to remaining unemployed."[46] Healey, rarely at a loss for words, attested shortly afterward: "I could never see spending the best years of my life in a 9-to-5 job. I always thought the best way to do it is to put retirement at the early part of life and enjoy it until I'm old enough to join the workforce. What do I need money for, a tank of gas?"[47]

The transition to summer did not inspire hope for a contract settlement by September. Just the opposite seemed truer. Healey widened the scope of his attacks, taking on any group that he thought created an undue financial burden on the taxpayer. For instance, he offered of the school departments' clerks and custodians, among the town's lowest paid employees, "The union [for clerks and custodians] is opposing the Committee's going out to see how much a cleaning service would cost. Perhaps they are worried that it is less expensive to have someone come in. If they are hard working for low pay, as they claim, then why do they fear some competition?"[48]

When not taking on the secretaries and janitors, at the end of the 1984-85 school year Healey targeted the only two teachers in the system who had received lay-off notices, and who otherwise would have made up the minority of the teachers slated to earn raises under the School Committee's proposed contract. Since a laid-off teachers' final payment occurred at the end of June, they could apply for unemployment benefits as of that date. Healey opposed that practice on the grounds that even though a teacher does not earn a salary during the summer months, technically a teacher's contract runs to September 1. As such, he argued, a teacher should not qualify for unemployment benefits during July and August. On those grounds, Healey asked the Committee to authorize the business manager to make no payments to the Department of Employment Security to laid off secondary level English teacher, Lawrence Verria (and later laid-off science teacher Laura Lawrence), and further to seek the opinion of the Department of Employment Security regarding making future such payments to other laid-off teachers.[49] While Healey moved quickly to stop such payments, all the commotion proved for naught as neither Verria or Lawrence had sought unemployment benefits.

Though from 1984 to 1986 Healey rarely offered Warren's teachers a compliment, exceptions did make it to print. Perhaps owing to a moment of sentimental remembrance, Healey made a point on one occasion late in the 1984-85 school year to praise Mike DeLeo, his former history teacher and occasional good-natured debating opponent. The twenty-eight-year-old Healey offered of his former teacher; "I was especially impressed with the genuine concern of the Coordinator of Student Activities, Michael DeLeo. His dedication and hard work in the matter did not go unnoticed."[50] Not much time would pass before the former student and his past teacher drew each other's attention again.

When the 1984-85 school year came to an end, Chairman Healey made sure to notify the public, and no doubt the teachers, about the school department's financial state. He shared, "In the past the cost of paying teacher wage increases meant that some areas of the budget went with little or no funding. Textbooks got old. Buildings wore down. Libraries were unfunded… We are spending almost $500,000 more on the students this year than last. The only difference is that the money is in programs for student supplies and such rather than for wages."[51]

Though the public may not have followed the school contract negotiations over the summer, nonetheless developments continued to unfold. For one, the arbitration hearings, scheduled in late July and late August, took place in Warwick. Healey thought the hearings should be heard in Warren. He offered of those meetings, "…but do not fear. I am hoping to have them broadcast on cable television."[52] He then informed the public of his whereabouts in July and August, "Finally, my street theater is into summer stock. Pick up the latest handout."[53]

One particularly important summer development involved School Committeeman Killion's decision not to vote on the Warren School Department's teacher contract. He had no choice. The state's Conflict of Interest Commission determined that as the husband of a Warren teacher, self-interest would likely dictate Killion's judgments involving his wife's salary. The news of *his* decision crippled the teacher's bargaining position. In all likelihood Killion would not have supported Healey's hardline position during the continuing teacher contract talks. In an indirect reference to Killion's compromised role, Healey surmised, "they [teachers' union] might take us a little more seriously now."[54]

Even though by then the teachers certainly took Healey and Brule's formidable (and in their view, ruthless) negotiating skills seriously, that realization did not bring about a breakthrough in the contract talks. Just the opposite seems truer. At a July morning negotiation meeting, the Warren Teachers Association bargaining team did not allow a reporter to cover the session, as Healey had arranged. The School Committee then walked out on the session because Healey did not want to risk a fine for violating open meeting rules.[55]

Later in July, the teachers' union asked the School Committee to agree to binding arbitration as a means of moving the intractable negotiations to a conclusion. Healey responded in animated fashion, as usual, and publicly, as always; "Can you believe this one? … The union suddenly decided on July 26 to ask the negotiating team of the school committee to agree to final and binding arbitration on all issues. Under RI labor law, teacher arbitration is only binding on non-money matters…. We might not be the slick professional negotiators that they are, but surely we are not bumbling idiots." Healey went on, "Remember this, it was the union, not the committee, that sought arbitration. The committee is in arbitration to uphold its steadfast commitment to bargaining in good faith. But good faith bargaining does not mean that we must be fools. The union is asking the negotiating committee for permission to take a sucker shot at us."[56]

When parents expressed concerns over the potential effects of a looming teachers' strike on the sport's program, Healey responded with the authority of law, specifically, RI General Laws 28-9.3-1. That law stated Rhode Island teachers couldn't strike. Though Healey made it clear, "That's the law,"[57] he did comment on matters of the undetermined future; "But should teachers consider themselves above the law and strike, the sports teams will not be affected."[58] Since the teachers' contract did not cover coaches' salaries, their existed no obligation for sport teams' personnel to strike with the teachers. And Healey assured parents that coaches would not disobey the law.[59] Healey went on to blame the teachers for the community's anxiousness over a potential coaches' strike. Teachers' "little talks" with the community, Healey pointed out, cause parents to "worry" so "…they no longer think logically."[60]

As the summer approached its unofficial end on Labor Day, angst over the possibility of no settlement between the Committee and the teachers' union grew. Tensions spiked within the School Committee as well. School Committeeman Anthony Nunes undermined his chairman's bargaining position with the teachers' union by saying, "The time for posturing is over and I think we should sit down and start talking like adults. This is ridiculous because we've got $400,000 extra in state aid, we've got a tax cut and we're asking the teachers to take $2,000 pay cuts."[61]

Though Warren teachers had not elected to strike since 1975,[62] on a muggy late August 1985 night, fears of the far-reaching effects of another walkout drew an overflow crowd to a Warren School Committee meeting. School Committee members, teachers, union officials, tax payers and press members gathered in close proximity to one another at the Warren Town Hall. Late arrivals who could not find standing room became part of the overflow in the adjoined hallway and outside. And regardless of where the attendees sat or stood, they all waited, listened, and sweat for two hours as the School Committee discussed other school department matters. Finally, the School Committee got to the last agenda item. Expectations rose. One community member described what happened next; "We expected some serious and concerned talk, some questions and answers, some explanations, some assurances…. But they quarreled. They argued among themselves over a technicality. Then, in a matter of five seconds, they moved to adjourn, voted, got up, and began to leave. It was so fast! All of us in the room just sat there for a minute trying to take it in. The meeting was over. The committee obviously did not choose to recognize the concerns, answer the questions, or consider the advice of its constituency."[63] Healey responded to the woman's concerns in his weekly September 4 press statement, saying that she had blamed "… the Committee for obeying the Open Meeting Law… and not straying from the posted agenda."[64]

With community anxieties peaking, in an August 28 letter to the editor Healey sought to inform and perhaps comfort the citizenry with nine numbered points of information. In point nine the Chairman responded indirectly to the teachers who had charged that the School Committee had circumvented its responsibility to meet and negotiate with the union. Healey argued that while the Committee's and the union's contract proposals were in arbitration, "We [the School Committee] are in no way obligated to be jerked around by the union. Returning to the negotiation table before the end of arbitration is rather ridiculous."[65]

On the night prior to the students' scheduled return to school, 107 of the 114 NEA/Warren teachers attended a called union meeting at St. Casimir's Church. At that meeting, Jeanette Wooley reminded teachers that they had never gone back to school without a contract.[66] Still, Warren teachers voted 106 to 1 to return to school. Healey responded to news of the vote, "I'm really glad to see the teachers are setting a good example by obeying the laws of the state of Rhode Island and going to work."[67] The Warren Times-Gazette editorial adopted a more reaffirming tone. Under the headline, "Teachers deserve credit for going back to school with [out] contract," the editor wrote, "Keeping a reasonable attitude in difficult times is to be commended and we offer kudos to the teachers."[68]

Good tidings aside, the same body that voted to return to school without a contract also empowered their union leadership to call a strike if the School Committee did not accept the anticipated arbitrator's contract award. Joseph Marques, a 17-year veteran teacher and math department chair at Mary V. Quirk Junior High School, captured best the essence of his union's reasoning; "We've never had this before—non-negotiations."[69] Regarding the teachers' vote to strike later if the School Committee did not meet their conditions, Healey commented, "What they're saying to us is take binding arbitration or else. We'll cross that bridge when we come to it. But I'm not threatened by the union pointing a loaded gun at my head."[70] The Warren Times-Gazette elected to make no comment about the union's position on binding arbitration in their editorial.

As Healey's relationship with the teachers soured, so too did his collegiality, what was left of it, with School Committeeman Anthony Nunes. Nunes' support of the teachers bothered Healey. And the outspoken leader of the School Committee shared his concerns forthrightly. Healey charged, "Mr. Nunes, the person who negotiated the last contract of about 25% for raises in three years, has sided firmly with the teachers' union. He seems to forget that the senior citizens who voted for him are living on fixed incomes. His approach of throwing around taxpayers' money is appalling and most definitely a betrayal of his constituents."[71] As bad as the relationship had become between the two committeemen, in the coming weeks their rapport worsened.

While NEA/Warren waited for the arbitrator's decision, they also brought unfair labor charges to the Labor Relations Board against the School Committee, most pointedly their Chair. At that meeting on September 30, the teachers' union charged that:

1. *"The School Committee is bypassing the process and guilty of bad faith bargaining. While unavailable to bargain with the union, the chairman of the School Committee is on the street corner in Warren advertising individual teacher salaries."*[72]
2. *"The Warren School Committee is engaged in bad faith bargaining in its action of bypassing and undermining the union and attempting to enlist the support of its bargaining proposals by going directly to the public at the Town Financial Meeting."*[73]

Bob Healey called the charges "absurd." "In short," he added, "the union is saying that I have done something wrong by telling you [the people] what is going on."[74] Healey assured, "The School Committee sees no problems in defending this matter."[75] The Chairman, moved to speak in biblical terms, lectured; "...last week the teachers union itself distributed green and blue handouts on Main Street, advertised in the local paper for support, and had coffee hours to bring matters to the public rather than discuss them at the bargaining table. LET HE

AMONG YOU WHO HAS YET NOT SINNED CAST THE FIRST STONE. Is this not the same conduct they are charging me with? I imagine I could also file an unfair labor claim, but I feel the public should know and the teachers' union has the right to speak out as long as it does so responsibly."[76]

It wasn't long into September that the Warren teacher contract negotiations, or lack thereof, gained increased attention throughout Rhode Island. Ronald DiOrio, President of NEA Rhode Island, and soon to be Governor Edward DiPrete's policy coordinator, offered about the School Committee's two chief negotiators, "... Healey and Brule have been erecting obstacles throughout the negotiations process. They have engaged numerous antics ..."[77] DiOrio expanded his criticism to the Warren Superintendent as well. "Wilfred Marchand has been strangely agreeable while Healey has assumed an unprecedented role in manipulating the Warren school district according to his own convoluted objectives."[78] In response to DiOrio's criticisms, Healey said he did not care what DiOrio thought about the committee's negotiating strategy. He stressed, "We are acting in the best interests of the people who elected us, not in the interest of the teachers' union." Of DiOrio personally, Healey commented frankly; "There is one person whom I don't take seriously. Like a rat leaving a sinking ship, DiOrio goes to the governor's office."[79]

During September, Healey used his weekly press piece to speak to the current contract in more macro terms. Addressing the state as a whole, Healey proposed ending teacher contracts on June 30. In so doing, he argued, the new termination date would match up with the end of most communities' fiscal calendars, and as such "... teachers could strike illegally all summer long. The only sure loser would be the teachers' travel agents... Ending the contract June 30 is a viable alternative to the fall ritual [teacher strikes], and it would be in the best interest of education. No longer could children be used as pawns to a job action." Knowing his proposal had little chance of adoption, he concluded, "So far, NEA-Warren has flatly rejected our proposal to end the contract in June. Much like the swallows that return to Capistrano, the teachers' unions are doing their best to ensure that the ritual continues."[80] Widening his point further still, Healey added, "It is interesting to note that even without binding arbitration and the right to strike to help the teachers' unions, Rhode Island teachers are the fifth highest paid of the 50 states and the District of Columbia. Obviously, a General Assembly infested with teachers and teachers' union sympathizers has seen to it that teachers are well protected in this state."[81]

Apart from his arguments against teachers' unions in general, the new school year did not bow well for Healey. From September 1985 through March 1986, almost every decision, development, and published opinion rang counter to Healey's mission; to settle the teacher's contract in accordance with the terms he and Brule had outlined. The barrage of critical reviews and contrary developments tested the fortitude of the "unflappable" School Committee Chairman.[82]

Upon entering back to school, Warren students became increasingly concerned about the effects a possible teacher strike could have on their school year. Understandably, potential graduates of Warren High School's class of 1986 worried more than their underclassmen. Denise MacDougall, senior class president, and Rosalie Walsh, student council president, wrote letters expressing their worries to Superintendent Wilfred Marchand, NEA Warren President Andrew Duperron, and each member of the Warren School Committee. Both students saw themselves as neutral and intended to remain so.[83]

The union responded to "Ms. MacDougall" and "Ms. Walsh" in two days, expressing gratitude for the students' interest, and updated both class leaders about the negotiations. The Warren Teachers Association concluded in their response to the students, "It is crucial that your viewpoint as students continue to be presented before the School Committee. We respect your efforts and concerns during these difficult times."[84] The tone and tenor of the letter impressed the students.

The same day the students received the teachers' reply, an article ran in the Providence Journal which quoted Bob Healey's verbal response to the students' letter. The article reported that Healey said the students' letter represented "a nice gesture on their part" but that "...they are a little naive in terms of the contract."[85] The students felt Healey's comments smacked of a condescending tone and took offense to his characterization of them.

Soon after learning of Healey's comments, in October MacDougall and Walsh wrote a letter to the Warrant Times-Gazette editor describing to the public how the School Committee's handling of their earlier inquiry differed from the teacher's reply. The students said that they now knew how the teachers felt, what they might accept as a settlement, and that they would accept any possible losses in the arbitration system. In that same letter to the editor the students asked, "but how does the School Committee feel?" They then explained the reason for their question; "Their spokesman has yet to inform us, the student body, as to their position on the negotiation issue, but has seen it fit to demeans us by stating we are 'naive.'" And the students didn't let it go at that. They continued, "Although we may not be of voting age, we feel that as people who are most affected by this issue, we should be informed of our educational future. If the school committee spokesman would like to inform the students of Warren High School as to the school committee's position, we are easily accessible at the number [telephone number omitted here]... Afterwards we hope we will not be called 'naive.'"[86]

Following the students' public rebuke of Healey's published comments, in mid-October, Commissioner of Education Troy Earhart recommended that binding arbitration (whereby before reviewing the proposed settlement each side agrees to accept the neutral arbitrator's award) be adopted by both the Warren Teachers Association and the Warren School Committee. Healey lashed out, "I'll be spearheading the campaign against arbitration... Binding arbitration is nothing but a veiled benefit for teachers' unions in the state... It is costly to the people of the state."[87]

Before the ink could dry on Commissioner Earhart's recommendation, the Rhode Island attorney general's office weighed-in, sort of, regarding NEA/Warren's desire to close arbitration sessions to the public. Assistant Attorney General Sheila T. Swan said she would not offer an opinion as to whether school committees and teacher unions' arbitration meetings are subject to the state Open Meetings Law. Swan termed the issue moot since for the time being both sides had agreed to meet in open session.[88] Swan's rendered opinion upset Healey who said, "The attorney general's office is definitely ducking a decision," and that "The attorney general [Arlene Violet] is pro-teacher and pro-union."[89]

As if to pile on Earhart and Swan's judgements, in November Governor DiPrete let it be known that he wanted to see "last best offer" utilized in the Warren teacher pact impasse.[90] Again, Healey responded briskly and emphatically. In a Providence Journal letter to the editor, Healey remarked, "After months of watching Governor DiPrete play ball with the state's teachers' unions, your article... came as no surprise. His selling out of local school committees is beyond belief. ... This 'bold move' by the governor is little more than political posturing. Reelection in Rhode Island is tough when unions oppose you. Still, I am further amazed that his move for the last best offer comes only weeks after the governor appointed long-time teacher union president Ron DiOrio to a policy-making position."[91]

In mid-December, strikes at Healey's position relative to the Warren contract negotiation continued to land. The state Conflict of Interest Commission decided to allow School Committeeman John Killion III (whose wife was a Warren school teacher at the time) to vote on whether to accept binding arbitration as a means to settling the continuing impasse between the Warren School Committee and the teachers union.[92] Rae Condon, executive director of the conflict panel, explained the Commission's reasoning; "...voting to send the dispute to a disinterested party (arbitrator) ... is a separate issue [from voting directly on a spouse's salary] and the commission doesn't see any conflict on sending that issue out to disinterested people, even if it includes teachers' salaries."[93] While Killion nor Patricia Reed expressed initially whether they would vote on the binding arbitration award, Healey did not wait for his two colleagues on the School Committee to weigh in. Healey charged; "I think binding arbitration is wrong. It allows some outsider, in this case some dude from Vermont, to order a teachers' salary increase and set the tax rate for the town of Warren. It amounts to taxation without representation."[94]

The Rhode Island Labor Relations Board had no *dude from Vermont* within their group when, days before Christmas 1985, they (in response to an April 1985 charge filed by the Warren teachers' union) ordered the School Committee, and more specifically Bob Healey, to cease publishing the names, salaries, and benefits of the town's teachers. Though the board acknowledged in its five-page statement that Healey had shared public records information, they explained; "It is clear to us that for the chairman of the Warren School Committee to act in the way that has been outlined . . . meant to circumvent the collective bargaining process… The committee is ordered to cease and desist from further actions of this kind."[95] The sticking issue did not concern the physical handing out of public information but rather the position and role of the person distributing the information. The board's opinion stipulated, "Ordinarily, we would have no quarrel with this information being disseminated, if someone other than the chairman of the School Committee had seen fit to remonstrate in this way. But for the chairman of the School Committee whose obligation . . . is to sit down with the duly certified collective bargaining representative for the purposes of collective bargaining at the bargaining table, certainly merits our concern."[96]

Healey responded to the Labor Relations Board in no uncertain terms. "I may sit down, but I'll never shut up… Just because I am chairman of a school committee, I will not be made a second-class citizen… The labor board is attempting to silence elected officials who wish to have an informed public." Healey questioned. "Is this democracy?" He had an answer to his rhetorical question. "Hardly."[97] Healey went on to point out that the labor board had considered fellow School Committeewoman Patricia Reads' opinion that he (Healey) had "evil motives" in distributing the public information.[98] Healey stressed, "Such is unbelievable. The information was made available to people so that they could be informed. Informed citizens create a democracy. Using public records is simply not evil."[99] Healey further questioned his alleged use of public information for purposes of teacher humiliation; "...please tell me what is embarrassing about saying a Warren teacher earns $29,000, before counting benefits."[100] Healey concluded that the board's ruling "...closes open government," and emphasized, "It has no place in the land of the free."[101] Despite the State Labor Board's cease and desist order, Healey continued to distribute flyers and pamphlets with teacher wage comparisons from across the country.

As both sides continued to await the arbitrator's award that would not be forthcoming until late March 1986, official negotiations came to a halt for months. Serving as partly pressure release valve and alternatively as pressure pump, communications in the newspapers became a substitute vehicle for dialogue, or a nasty semblance thereof. Helpful or destructive to the process, newspaper letters to the editor served as one of the only means available for continuing the interchange over the teachers' contract between competing parties. During that period letters to the editor increased in volume, and to a significant degree, function. Most challenged or criticized the School Committee Chairman.

While Healey responded to almost all of the letters in his weekly press release, to some he did not offer a reply. Peter Gray, a veteran Warren High School faculty member, penned one such letter. Gray wrote, "Robert Healey has successfully degraded, humiliated and demoralized a fine group of 'public servants' and has triumphed in returning endless columns of negative publicity to a school department that has worked hard over the past 20 years to improve its academic standing and image."[102] Given that Healey did not reply to the letter, one has to wonder if Gray's published correspondence gave Healey, known widely to be unaffected emotionally by criticisms, at least a moment of pause.

In another letter to the editor in the Warren Times-Gazette not responded to by Healey, Robert Evans, the Mary V. Quirk Jr. High School English Department Chair, addressed the Warren School Committee Chairman in direct terms. Evans rationalized, "As far as is known, the delays [in contract negotiation] have been legal. You've covered yourselves in that respect. No, you've not violated the law as written. You have done something far worse. You have violated the spirit of the law." Evans then charged that during the negotiations "No real or actual give and take has happened," and that Healey's "tactics" raised concerns. In his teacher's voice Evans finished the letter with a question; "Robert, why are you stalling?"[103]

The commentaries that seemed to bother Healey most emanated from within the School Committee. Perhaps the best example of this ilk came from School Committeewoman Patricia Read. She had much to say about Robert Healey in a Warren Times article published in January 1986. She offered, "...I was an old-time member of the town and teacher. Bob Healey said that I would be pro-teacher and I expected that he would say that. I didn't think he would be foolish enough to print it. I've been teaching longer than he's been alive, but that doesn't mean I'm going to be pro-teacher. It means I'm going to be favorable to good teachers."[104] Read allowed, "I was very impressed with Mr. Healey's professional grasp of basic issues. He was selfless in his work, tireless in his research, he got opinions from everywhere."[105] However, Read made it clear that, "... I have been puzzled, frustrated at times, and sometimes embarrassed because even at social functions I have been tinged with the same cookie brush as our illustrious leader."[106]

Shortly after the publication of the full-page article that focused almost solely on Read's review of Healey, the School Committee refused to back their chairman in appealing the recent state Labor Relations Board decision. In a response letter to three of the four other committee members Healey wrote, "I am truly disgusted by the back stab dealt me by this committee. I take it as a personal affront. Perhaps it may be better to have a new chair. I cannot, in all honesty, represent people that I find so unsure of my legal judgment in committee matters."[107] Healey threatened to resign from his chairmanship of the committee unless he secured a vote of confidence. Little moved by Healey's aversion to recent developments, Patricia Read made the following demeaning judgments about the Chairman; "He is sulking. He always sees his side of things and thinks only in terms of his own ego." She also said that Healey's tactics polarized the committee and spurred "testy" contract negotiations with the union.[108] While Paul Brule indicated he would back Healey "100 percent," Anthony Nunes made it just as clear that he would not; "He has never had my confidence… I guess now he's not so cool…" Continuing, Nunes said, "When you play ball, sometimes you win the game and sometimes you lose. Bob has been winning so far, but now that he loses one he can't handle it."[109]

But Healey didn't lose. In late January, School Committee members voted 2 to 1 in support of Chairman Bob Healey. Based on that vote, he decided to remain as the committee's leader. With his own vote added in, Healey believed he had secured the 3 to 2 working majority[110] to push forward his hardline stances involving the contentious teacher contract negotiations. Healey thanked his supporters on the Committee and said, "It appears right now that Mr. Nunes and Mr. Killion are the only two people willing to oppose me or the positions I support."[111]

At a January Warren School Committee meeting five high school teachers appeared before the committee. The group included Mary Parks, Healey's cooperating teacher during his student teaching experience, and Mike DeLeo, Bob Healey's former favorite teacher. DeLeo read a statement signed by the attending five teachers. While the upfront issue centered on submitting mileage vouchers of fourteen cents each to compensate for driving one mile to attend a curriculum meeting,[112]DeLeo characterized the vouchers as "symbolic." (As apparently agreed upon earlier, the teachers withdrew the voucher request later that night.) The statement focused on Healey's leadership of the committee during the contract dispute. DeLeo said, "I guess we all know that 14 cents is pretty petty. Then why would five teachers with over 100 years of teaching experience put a voucher in for 14 cents? Certainly we knew the chairman would make a big deal out of those 'greedy' teachers. Then why? We are trying to call attention once again to the blunders that are made."[113] DeLeo continued, "I am tired of being laughed at everywhere by fellow educators and people throughout the state because of the chairman's antics... The chairman has the right to disagree with teachers, but it can be done without media attention, ridicule and the demeaning nature he has used.... It is criminal what has happened to this school system in the past year all because of a lousy contract."[114] DeLeo stressed further, "I am not out to rape the taxpayers of their hard-earned money, but neither am I going to be raped by taking away 10 percent of my hard-earned money and along the way listen to the garbage being spread about my profession."[115]

Healey replied at first with light resignation. "I have to take it with a grain of salt. It was all done for a platform to make his [DeLeo's] statement. Hey, I understand p.r. Some people go uptown and hand out teachers' salaries, some people hand in 14-cent vouchers,"[116] Later, after more thought, Healey's assessment of and tone toward his old teacher hardened. "Using his self-created public forum, he [DeLeo] chastised me for publicizing issues unfavorable to his union. In response, I say, I'll take Main Street and you take 14-cent vouchers.... If the grudge is against me, then why are the students being used as the whipping boy? I simply cannot believe that our teaching staff would do such a thing."[117]

At the next School Committee meeting in February, the Committee made it clear in a 3-to-1 vote[118] that when Bob Healey submitted statements to the media spoke for himself, not the whole Committee. Committeeman Anthony Nunes explained, "The motion made was that nothing should be disseminated to the media by a member, on behalf of the committee, without the prior approval of the committee."[119] Healey's reaction to what he saw as censorship came across like a Patrick Henry oration; "I will not be silenced... PAST COMMITTEES disastrously kept the public in the dark. I will continue to expose what these three wish to be kept hidden. I reiterate, I may sit down, but I will not shut up."[120] Committeeman Nunes responded, "We're not gagging anybody, particularly Mr. Healey, who walks up and down in a sandwich board. We just don't want people to think he's speaking for all of us."[121]

Healey used his February 12, 1986 weekly press release to lambast his fellow School Committee members. "These three [Patricia Read, Anthony Nunes, John Killion] would prefer an uninformed public so they can avoid public outcry when they burn taxpayers they supposedly represent." Healey continued, "Mrs. Read's understanding of free speech is disturbing. She has no right to decide what I can say. Sorry Pat. Instead of playing censor, spend 39 cents on your very own pen. Public debate is much more democratic than censorship... If my words are wrong, I expect rebuttals: Censorship simply demonstrates the words are on target. Maybe these three members want to discredit me. If people do not listen to me, these three members escape public eyeing of their actions. They can then appease their friends and interest groups at taxpayer expenses. ... I will continue to expose what these three wish to be kept hidden."[122] Healey charged that the Committee members' comments indicated a step toward accepting the upcoming arbitrator's award.[123]

With the charges heated to a boiling point between Healey and several parties, the Warren Times-Gazette apparently thought it prudent to cool the rhetoric, or at least try to do so. On March 19, 1986, the local paper worried that "It would be unfortunate if both

Refusing to be silenced in his efforts to confront the local teacher's union over "generous" contract provisions, Healey took his case to the streets of Warren, again.

sides in this long dispute have painted themselves into a corner with flamed rhetoric."[124] The Warren Times-Gazette published an editorial entitled, *Time for a school settlement is now.* Their written statement came across as clear as the article's title; "The school year grows old. The time to negotiate is now. The time to settle is now."[125] While the School Committee and the teachers' probably read the article, The Warren Times' plea affected them little. The two parties remained entrenched, far apart, and primed for continued hostilities.

By March 1986, Healey had endured a six month barrage of personal attacks, disappointing outcomes, and decisions that conflicted with his positions and practices. Opponents' unending bombardment of disparaging remarks had attacked the chairman's self-image and pride. Still, he persevered. The onslaught may have forced Healey's knees to buckle on one or two occasions, but he never collapsed to the canvas. He kept his bearings, re-engaged, and continued swinging. As

Spring 1986 took hold, cowering before no one, the bruised and bat-tered Chairman again readied to take the fight to his opponents. Ed DiPrete stood near the top of that list. With more rumors circulating that the Governor would use last best offer binding arbitration to settle the ongoing dispute, Healey wrote to DiPrete *clarifying* that the Warren School Committee answers to the General Assembly, not him.[126]

In late March the arbitrator's award arrived. Both the award and everyone's reaction proved predictable. Rather than fueling the dispute, the offering affected all parties in anticlimactic fashion. With three annual 6% raises, the award gave the teachers less than what they had asked, but much more than the School Committee had offered initially. While the Warren teachers accepted the award, the Warren School Committee did not. The School Committee offered to renew negotia-tions, and put the award to the people for a machine vote. Healey reiter-ated that the arbitrator's award would not restrict him, but promised to bind his vote to the referendum's outcome. The Warren Times-Gazette continued to plead for compromise, warning, "The state (and probably the nation) is looking toward this particular contract as an example either for or against the need for binding arbitration or last best offer legislation. Let's not give Warren and its school notoriety."[127]

Healey paid little attention to the Warren Times' pleas, probably because he saw a populist themed pathway toward his campaign's ultimate success. Playing to that anthem, Healey declared, "Let the people rule."[128] Peppering the Warren teachers and their leadership, Healey chided, "Perhaps the union fears the people's will... The union doesn't want the people to decide. The people support the Committee. If the union has the popular support it claims, then why not put the issue to a vote of the people. The union would have an opportunity to get the award and avoid a strike."[129]

Of course, Healey knew that the teachers would not let their contract be determined by a popular vote of the very people who would have to pay the resulting salary and benefits. After three more days of painful and unproductive negotiations between the School

Committee and the teachers' union, the talks broke down. At an Association meeting in St. Casimir's Church, with 104 of the town's 114 teachers present, the rank and file voted unanimously, no contract, no work.[130] After a year of exhausting talks and fruitless bargains, the vote to strike emboldened the teachers. Healey saw the teachers' actions differently. As Healey saw it, the teachers' vote to strike positioned the bargaining unit exactly where Healey wanted them; out of their classrooms, apart from their students, and in plain view of working parents who had to arrange for child-care on a day-to-day basis.

News of the teachers' vote spread quickly throughout the town. Warren voters heard that the teachers had *chosen* not to work. Information explaining the teachers' position did not make it to the townspeople. No matter. At this juncture, such news wouldn't have resonated with the public anyhow. As Healey already knew, and the teachers soon learned, their support throughout Warren had dwindled to fellow educators, a declining number of students, a few townspeople, and nobody else. And Healey commanded a public relations strategy that threatened to destroy the last vestiges of their backing.

Some parties, once sympathetic to the working teachers' plight, jumped ship and took positions contrary to the striking teachers. Even the School Committee came out increasingly in favor of their chairman's thinking and actions. By mid-April, the workingmen and women of the town lined up against their children's teachers, and had less apprehension about saying so and demonstrating such. To make matters worse, those students and parents who remained on the side of the teachers, offered at best, lackluster support. Only 100 of the 1,400 Warren public school students' parents managed to attend a "well publicized meeting" where the School Committee would decide whether or not to accept the arbitrator's award.[131] The relatively small turnout disappointed the teachers. In an act of frustration, Warren teacher and Senior Class Co-Advisor Claire Frye wrote in the Warren Times, "They [Warren students' parents] have contributed to it [the current circumstance] out of sheer indifference."[132]

Ms. Frye's assessment of the parents' cool support proved painfully accurate but did not account for the teacher's main woe. Another dynamic, well positioned, wide spread, and in plain view assumed that mantle. Warren ranked among the state's poorer communities. Most people in town earned less money than the teachers. Healey understood intimately that condition. Whipping up this economic phenomenon, Healey framed the developing encounter as a clash between the town's haves and have-nots. That depiction picked up momentum as Spring 1986 heated up. Increasingly, the townspeople saw the ensuing developments as a revolutionary movement with their unemployed School Committee Chairman, born of and raised within the community's working-class base, as their savior and champion. And at the point they needed him most, he had returned home from law school to lead their crusade against the town's *privileged and greedy* educators. By April, all the pieces were in place for a Warren working men and women's rebellion.

In support of the revolt, in late April the Warren Times-Gazette, who had earlier praised Warren educator's restraint and later called for the School Committee and NEA to compromise, now opposed openly the town's teachers. In a newspaper editorial the publication appealed to the town's socio-economic vein when they editorialized:

> *"It [Warren] is an ordinary community made up of extraordinary people who work hard, enjoy a few beers, love their sports, and want the best for their children. Part of what's best for their children is a good education. How providing ... good education got tied to underwriting the cost of medical and dental coverage for the children of teachers up to the age of twenty-five is beyond us. The idea is ridiculous in a community where the head of a family feels fortunate indeed if able to provide a Blue Cross plan with any kind of Delta Dental rider. The lesson our children are learning is that if you don't like a rule, break it, then ask for more time and money to do it again. We call that bad education."* [133]

And by bad education, the Times may have inferred not so covertly, and unfairly so, bad teachers.

As the 1986 spring's temperatures continued to rise, the Warren Times-Gazette printed more editorial letters than usual. (According to Warren teachers, the paper did not print many of the letters in explanation of their position.[134]) All the published letters stressed the need for the strike to end. Most of the letters supported the teachers returning to the classroom, but did not back the teachers specifically.

While the teachers remained united, they understood increasingly the ever-growing challenge before them. And though their solidarity remained impressive, surface cracks appeared on their outer shell. One high school teacher, Charles VA January, found the strike "immoral, unprofessional, unethical, and... illegal."[135] Though he agreed with his colleagues' cause, and expressed no support for Bob Healey, he removed himself from his union's strategy.[136] Soon after, Warren High School principal, Herman Grabert, who had earlier assured his faculty he would come out in support of them at the appropriate time, wrote a letter to the editor that fell short of his prior promise. Far from a ringing endorsement of his teachers, Grabert offered, "I have made the statement that we must do everything possible to get the teachers back to school even to the point of getting an injunction, and if they violate the injunction, take the necessary steps to enforce the injunction. I certainly do not want any teacher sent to jail or fired, but we got to get our students back into the classroom."[137]

Healey garnered the support of the masses, the press, and the administration. Even a teacher who remained in full support of the union's cause, admitted of Bob Healey's tactics, "He has played the town masterfully."[138] And that he had, as became increasingly apparent by the end of April. A photo taken by Warren Times-Gazette writer Don Stevens illustrated the town's leanings in a most telling fashion. In that printed picture five young men, most clad in flannel shirts, stood in front of the school administration building holding a handcrafted sign that spelled out in large letters, "JAIL THE

Warren citizens, young and older, share their views on the beleaguered teachers.

TEACHERS—THEY ARE NOT ABOVE THE LAW"[139] The soldiers in Healey's growing army of fed-up Warren citizens had tired of the teachers' proposals and looked forward to putting them in their place.

Warren's good old boy faction may have made up the bulk of Warren's most boisterous citizens, but they did not raise their voices in solitude. People from every town demographic criticized the teachers openly in public. At times they delivered their taunts from moving cars that passed by picketing teachers.[140] The townspeople's actions demoralized the teachers, many who lived in Warren or neighboring communities.

In an effort to increase pressure on the School Committee, on April 29, 1986, teachers decided to stop advising and coaching extracurricular activities if they could not reach a settlement on the contract by that coming Friday. The move further alienated the teachers' eroding base of support. In growing numbers students began to speak out against their teachers. Some did so in a particularly demeaning fashion. Tammy Arruda, a senior at Warren High School complained, "We're left out in the cold to do our own senior prom by ourselves, to plan our senior week by ourselves, to plan our graduation by ourselves. The teachers said they didn't want to hurt the students but now they're hurting the students." Arruda finished, "This was totally uncalled for.

While most Warren High School students supported their teachers, over time their allegiance waned. (© The Warren Times Gazette / All rights reserved)

It's a slap in the face."[141] Even the Senior Class President's weigh-in fell far short of supporting teachers' latest decision; "I don't like it. I can see why they did it, I can understand why they did it, but I don't like it."[142]

One day prior to the date teachers had drawn a line in the sand over discontinuing their advisorship of extracurricular services, the School Committee had scheduled the public non-binding referendum vote on the arbitrator's award. Bob Healey explained, "It will say, 'Should the Warren School Committee accept in total the arbitration award—yes or no?'" Committeeman Nunes referenced the referendum's wording as "… no longer germane to what's really on the table."[143] As the teachers had already stated, they agreed to a lesser offer than that offered in the referendum. But fair or not, Warren voters prepared to vote their preference on the referendum as originally stated.

Before the vote, Chairman Healey had *instructions* for voters and the reasoning behind the guidance he offered. In a letter to the editor Healey directed:

> "*Warren has a town financial meeting system of government. Historically, voters controlled their fate at these meetings. But, two years ago, the Exeter-West Greenwich case changed that. The people were stripped of their voice. That case, decided by the RI Supreme Court, held that any bill legally voted by the*

majority of the School Committee must be paid regardless of what the people say at a financial meeting. That's the law. Now, the Warren committee is asking your opinion before entering into the bill. In doing so, your voice in local government is being restored. I personally urge people to vote "NO." A strong rejection will tell the union to be reasonable at the negotiating table.... Think how disastrous approval would be."[144]

As the clock ticked toward a Thursday, May 1, 1986 referendum vote, the School Committee and NEA/Warren continued to negotiate, as the Town Council had ordered. At Saturday's session Chairman Healey arrived with a sleeping bag in toe. On that Saturday night the School Committee offered Warren teachers a three-year contract with pay increases of two percent in the first year and four percent in the second and third years. The teachers' union referenced the offer as "nothing new." Though more negotiations took place, the teachers wanted an offer that at least resembled the arbiter's award. The School Committee made no such offer. Their thinking aligned with comments made by Town Council President William A. Estrella Jr. who voiced that teachers "ought to resign themselves to the fact they're not going to get six percent—they're not going to get more than the people of Warren are getting."[145] Healey saw the referendum in wider terms; "The real issue is, who says what teachers are going to earn—the state, the people of Warren, or the teachers' union?" Healey added, "What happens in Warren is going to impact what happens in the rest of the state."[146] The referendum would mark the first time that Rhode Island voters would be asked their opinion of an arbitrator's award.[147]

On the night before the referendum vote, Warren teachers held a rally. They had decided to boycott the next day's referendum, which in effect conceded the predicted outcome of that vote. The teachers prepared sandwich boards, picket signs, shirts, posters, and the like, making their feelings of Bob Healey ever clear. The Chairman's likeness appeared everywhere. One artistic creation depicted Healey as "an angel of death mowing down teachers with a scythe."[148] Healey trashing abounded. History teacher Mike DeLeo announced, "If you like Laurel & Hardy, you will love Healey and Brule. But the joke is on Warren."[149] Harvey Press, the newly elected president of the state National Education Association, spoke of "not knowing where that gentleman that looks like Tiny Tim[150] is coming from next."[151] The gathered crowd of teachers and teacher supporters applauded his commentary enthusiastically.[152] Some students joined the gathering and distributed Healey-buster lapel badges.[153]

While the demonstration may have raised the teachers' spirits temporarily, Healey flipped the teacher demonstration on its head. Healey explained, "When people don't want to face the issues, they start dealing with the personality. It's the first sign of a weak argument." Healey then reminisced, "When they came into the first bargaining session, they expected to deal with a real flake. They played out their cards as though I was a bimbo. And they got trapped in their own game."[154] When teachers and some community members blamed Healey for the strike, Healey shook off the charge. "I personally forced 114 people into doing something they don't want to do? They had no other choice but to break the law? "I don't buy it. It's a PR move."[155]

On May 1, forty-three percent of the voters turned out for the referendum, considerably shy of the sixty-nine percent who voted in the 1982 general election.[156] However, considering the polls stayed open for a shorter period of time than normal, and that Warren teachers boycotted the vote, the turnout registers more impressive than first reactions suggested. Turnout aside, the final tally left no doubt, Warren voters' blaring judgment proved deafening, and could not be misinterpreted. The final result registered 2,092 to 218 against the arbitrator's proposal. Duperron tried to minimize the vote's impact declaring, "It's my opinion that that was a vote against a $3 tax increase and not a vote against the teachers."[157] Even affording Duperron the benefit of considerable doubt, by a ten to one spread, Healey had produced a landslide result by tapping into the working-class veins of his fellow Warrenites. And as far as the town's people now saw it, the teachers had bargained away their souls. The teachers stood alone before an empowered electorate and their warrior School Committee Chair who had the stature and gumption to say loud and clear what a growing portion of the local population felt.

The strike and negotiations between the supported School Committee and the demoralized teachers continued. The day after the referendum the School Committee offered the following pay scale to the teachers: 2 1/4 percent increase in wages for the first twenty pay periods of the 1985-86 school year, 1 percent for the remaining six pay periods of that school year, a six percent raise the second year, and a five and a half pay hike in the third year.[158] School Committee lawyer Vincent J. Piccirilli stressed, "This is the final offer. This is it."[159] Duperron found the final offer "insulting." Responding to School Committeewoman Patricia Read's charge that the NEA-Warren had not properly informed rank and file teachers of the Committee's offers, Duperron stood in front of the Town Hall after hearing the last offer and announced, "We're inviting Mrs. Read to present the final offer to the membership so there will be no doubt it will be presented accurately." Read responded, "I'd love to be there, but I'm going into the hospital for tests."[160]

The teachers held an "emotional" meeting to consider the latest contract offer. After one hour Warren teachers rejected the contract offer in a 93-16 secret ballot vote. They readied to go to jail, if necessary, to secure what they viewed as a fair contract. The teachers sustained a loud cheer when Duperron read the final vote tally and presented him with an ACI inscribed hat and a T-shirt printed, "property of the ACI." Duperron said, "I've said all along that we would do what's necessary to get a fair contract."[161]

As the teachers voted to reject the latest contract offer, the courts initiated the injunction process. At the injunction proceedings in Superior Court, with Judge Paul P. Pederzani Jr. presiding, NEA lawyer Natale L. Urso pleaded that the court consider the unfair labor charges levied earlier against Chairman Robert Healey. Pushing aside the union's concerns, Warren School Committee lawyer Vincent J. Piccirilli stressed that irreparable harm had been done to the students. That argument swayed Judge Pederzani more. Piccirilli stood on firm ground in making his case. As Healey had pointed out prior to the court proceedings, State Education Commissioner J. Troy Earhart had written a letter to the Warren School Committee where he expressed his belief that irreparable harm to students had occurred.[162] Healey added, "I think we've got a good case, just from the sheer passage of time, and the fact that we'll be going into July to end the school year."[163]

Judge Pederzani thought the issue "isn't whether the adults can agree or not, but whether the children are being harmed."[164] Pederzani willingly listened to the particulars of the bargaining in bad faith argument against Chairman Robert Healey, but that consideration had no effect on his decision. Warren School Superintendent Wilfred R. Marchand testified to the effects of the school closure on handicapped special-education students, and poor children.[165] In the end, Superior Court Judge Paul P. Pederzani Jr. ordered the Warren teachers back to work.[166] The two- and half-week strike ended.

The next day teachers entered their respective schools defeated and discouraged. In the process of making their case for a just contract (as they saw it) they had more or less lost a most loyal support base: their students. Cindy Simal, a thirteen-year-old seventh-grader made that clear when she said, "It's not fair. They [teachers] shouldn't get more money—they make enough already. What they taught us before (the strike began April 21), we forgot all about it." Tara Kee, an eighth-grader, explained angrily, "We lost respect for the teachers. I think they deserve to be fired." Becky Tavares, a seventh grader implored, "If they cared more for us, they wouldn't have struck until the summer."[167] Other returning students noticed an uneasy air to the school.[168]

On the Wednesday evening the teachers returned to school, the

School Committee denied the union's request to hold a negotiation session. This refusal pinched the teachers' raw nerves. At a union meeting the next morning, in short order the teachers decided not to return to the classrooms until they reached agreement on a negotiated contract. On Thursday morning, May 9, the students arrived at school to find their teachers picketing, again. Unlike the night before, on Thursday evening the School Committee found a way to meet. In the emergency night session, the Committee decided to seek a contempt of court order against the teachers, advertise for new instructors, and ask the Commissioner of Education to revoke the striking teachers' certifications.

Before the School Committee's decision could proceed, Superior Court Justice Paul P. Pederzani Jr. ordered the School Committee and the union to meet with him. At that meeting Justice Pederzani asked Chairman Healey how many days long would a strike be in place before doing irreparable harm to students? Healey responded with a question; "How many angels can dance on the head of a pin?" The judge did not receive the Chairman's quip warmly.[169] Moving beyond Healey's remark, with the consent of the Committee's and the union's lawyers, and at Governor DiPrete's request, Justice Pederzani appointed Rhode Island Education Commissioner J. Troy Earhart as "special master" to impel the Warren School Committee and NEA/ Warren to negotiate. Union lawyer Natale L. Urso agreed with the move saying, "As long as Healey and the committee have complete control over this situation—with the threat of sending teachers to jail—there will be no meaningful negotiations."[170]

On Saturday, May 10, Thomas Soares (Special Mediator from the Department of Labor) and Commissioner Earhart "shuttled" between the Committee and the union for about six hours. Probably more out of fatigue than good will, the two sides reached an *agreement*. The teachers received a two and half percent raise for the first year, retroactive to the beginning of the school year, and five and a quarter percent the next year.

On Sunday, May 11, the union held a two-hour meeting at St. Casimir's Church. The teachers accepted the contract, not unanimously, and with no celebration. A fruit basket went untouched, a box of candy remained unopened, and a bottle of champagne went uncorked.[171] The teachers agreed to return to school on Monday. The school year would stretch to July 9.

As best he could, Warren Union President Andrew L. Duperron tried to sell the notion of a teacher victory. In addition to nearly a six percent raise the upcoming year, Duperron said, the contract offered a lump sum upon retirement of $150 for each year taught.[172] He added, "We hope to go back to a School Committee that will be more favorable to education."[173] Sylvia Blanda, vice president of the state NEA, thought that the Warren strike had strengthened the argument for collective bargaining statewide. She said, "I think they [union] proved a point: You have to bargain collectively. Healey didn't want to do it all along, but in the end he got it shoved down his throat."[174]

But not everyone on the Warren teachers' side of the ledger saw the conclusion of the contract negotiation so positively. In a parting shot approximately a week later, Jeanette Wooley, Warren NEA's chief negotiator, responded to an earlier published letter to the editor; "As for the referendum, the School Committee submitted a question to the voters (should the School Committee accept the Award in total) which, if approved, would have cost the taxpayer more than the teachers had at that time agreed to accept. Indeed, hats off to the hippie and the farmer [Bob Healey and Paul Brule] for a brilliant performance."[175] While Wooley never came to a peaceful resting place with the memory of the most contentious contract negotiation of her career, she later reflected that Healey got away with his "shoot from the hip" style because of his intellect and bold manner. In the end, Wooley admitted of the 1986 late term negotiations, "We had to settle,"[176] and hope to make-up for the loss in the next negotiation two years later.[177]

The *hippie and the farmer* had a much easier time making a case for their take on the recently settled contract than did the teachers' union. Healey rightly pointed out, "I think they're [the union] trying to put a good face on a package that's distasteful to them."[178] He added, "It's a very, very nice contract for the people of Warren. For the most part I'm very happy with it."[179]

The frenzied school year ended in mundane fashion. Warren High School's class of 1986 graduation took place later than usual. Though students asked teachers to attend, fewer teachers than normal took part in end of year festivities. Student absentee rates ran high in late June and early July. Finally, on July 9 the school year came to a quiet close.

In the immediate post negotiations era, Healey and the union continued to fire parting shots at one another, though with much less frequency than before. In one such instance, referencing a recently settled negotiation with the clerks and custodians, Bob Healey proverbially kicked the teachers and their union while they were down. Of the negotiations with the clerks and custodians, Healey lectured, "The give and take was exactly what the bargaining process is all about. There were no hard feelings and no bitterness. Maybe other unions should take note."[180] (Healey did not mention that the School Committee had offered the clerks and custodians far more generous terms than they had the teachers.) Glenice Sousa, Communications Chair for NEA/Warren, for her part continued to pepper Bob Healey and the School Committee about the monetary cost of their doing business against the teachers over the past two years.[181] She emphasized that Healey did not refute her reporting of the $500,000 cost encumbered by the town of Warren for taking on the teacher's union. Sousa argued the figures she quoted remained indisputable, and "most conservative." She went on, "Too much money has been spent giving one person a practicum of work experience in law, when these dollars were allocated by the taxpayers of Warren and the State of Rhode Island for the purpose of improving and supporting education."[182]

That summer a reporter asked Healey whether or not he would repeat his actions of the past two years. With no hesitation, he answered, "Yes, I would do it all again. It is the seniors and working poor who need our sympathy and support instead of affluent teachers with a penchant for greed."[183] He further reflected; "As each day passes, I grow more pleased thinking that my service as chairman of the Warren School Committee resulted in Warren's seniors and working poor having a small bit more to spend while still allowing Warren's teachers to earn a generous wage."[184] Paul Brule reflected years later on the same ordeal and the tactics thereof, "It had to be done."[185] And for better or worse, it had been so.

With his conscience clear, in the fall of 1986 Bob Healey could look back with a great deal of self-satisfaction at his Warren School Committee chairmanship. Less than four years earlier, he had yet to graduate from law school and had little stated ambition to pursue a full-time law practice, or for that matter, any other line of work. Against great odds, he ran for the Warren School Committee, garnered more votes than any other candidate, and earned the confidence of his fellow Committee members who elected him to the School Committee Chairman post. Now statewide people recognized him as the heralded Chair who took on the powerful teachers' union, and won. His popularity in Warren soared. His battles and victories had made headlines throughout Rhode Island, and in national publications. He could run confidently for School Committee again. Many talked of him seeking a seat on the Town Council. Other's thought he should pursue higher public office. At every turn he reinforced his disinterest in such pursuits. Still, despite such declarations, in late 1986 many continued to wonder about the young sensation's future political fortunes. And as would soon be evidenced, so too, did Bob Healey.

CHAPTER 7

A MOOSE ON THE LOOSE
THE 1986 RUN FOR GOVERNOR

I n September 1985, a moose meandered into Rhode Island and
quickly assumed celebrity status. With the help of citizen leads,
an infatuated press reported the massive animal's daily movements. Eyewitnesses described the traveling moose as fully antlered
and weighing about 1,000 pounds. The moose lumbered through the
state's West Bay area, including at least one saunter by the Warwick
Sewage Treatment Plant off Route 95.[1]

The large Ocean State visitor's minute by minute location soon
consumed Rhode Islanders' curiosity and concern. "Where is the
moose?" became a popular question among local residents. Some went
in search of the alien creature. Even Rhode Island Governor Edward
DiPrete ventured to secure a look at the stealthy roving tourist.[2]

While a topic of welcoming fascination, the moose clearly didn't
belong in the smallest state in the union. The ungainly stray animal,
lost in a tiny state known more for its oceanfront than its forests, must
have found the accommodations uncomfortable. The moose's normal
habitat included secluded ponds, thickly treed woodlands, and
sparsely populated and spread-out human dwellings. That landscape

contrasted drastically Rhode Island's congested traffic lanes, clustered tenement houses, and crowded towns. Nonetheless, the awkward and alluring moose made the best of the situation, at times seemingly unphased by his foreign surroundings. If he took notice of the increasingly inquisitive onlookers or a mainstream press that played the part of Moose paparazzi, he did not let on. According to Frank J. Williams, a Department of Environmental Management conservation officer, the moose just "loped" along "nonchalantly."[3] One might have observed rightly that he appeared to be a *cool* moose. Bob Healey, the Warren School Committee Chairman took something more from the animal's approach. He offered, "The Moose is representation of the average citizen. A moose just plods along. This is sort of the Rhode Island mentality."[4]

After much fanfare over several days, dozens of police, conservation officers, and private citizens captured the moose and tranquilized him in preparation for transfer to the animal's natural habitat in New Hampshire. Unfortunately, despite efforts to keep the moose alive, the animal expired on route to the *live free or die* state. Before his demise, the moose had won over Rhode Islanders' hearts and stirred their imaginations, including that of the cool School Committee Chairman from Warren.[5]

—

In late spring 1986, Robert Healey Jr. announced his intentions to gather a slate of like-minded candidates to run for several government offices, including the Warren Town Council, treasurer, tax assessor and state representative. These pioneering recruits would make up the first class of Healey's brainchild political organization, the Cool Moose Party.[6] Healey claimed to model his political creation after the former Bull Moose Party,[7] which Theodore Roosevelt created in 1912. Roosevelt broke away from the Republican party when they chose his former friend and the current United States President,

William Howard Taft, to serve again as their presidential candidate in the upcoming election.[8] Having recently fallen out with Taft, Roosevelt bolted the Republican convention and took his cause directly to the people. While Robert Healey didn't bolt a convention, he did try to burst onto the Rhode Island political scene and in that sense saw himself as Teddy Roosevelt like. Albeit, the Cool Moose Party candidate's political philosophy and platform differed distinctly from that espoused by the early 1900's Bull Moose Party candidate.

The Cool Moose Party took liberal views on civil liberties and espoused conservative fiscal policies.[9] Healey offered, "The main point of the Cool Moose Party is to give people an alternative to the same old faces. There are major divisions within the two parties in town. Since that's the case, maybe the best alternative is to start a new party."[10]

The *best alternative* got off to a slow start. Early on, Bob approached five individuals to run as Cool Moose Party candidates. They turned him down. Others agreed to take on the cause.[11] Undeterred by the marginal support, Healey continued to spread his vision for the new political party, and remained upbeat. The School Committee Chairman proposed that if the Cool Moose Party really drew support, he might just run for governor. He explained kiddingly, "It depends if public opinion polls show me way in front of Ed DiPrete."[12] Since initially Bob had vowed no interest in higher office,[13] people probably presumed Healey offered up his state office aspirations for comical relief purposes. And that may have been the case. However, after successfully defying the odds during his four-year term as the Warren School Committee Chairman, Healey's bolstered confidence might have set in motion grander aspirations then he let on, even, perhaps, to himself.

While it might not have been his original intention, at some point in 1986, Robert Healey decided that for the good of Rhode Island, the Cool Moose Party needed to put forward a candidate for governor. At age twenty-nine, he thought he could fill that void. He knew the odds of winning the race amounted to highly unlikely, at best.

Still, he figured that even a modest showing would offer measurable benefits. Healey thought if he could entice just five percent of Rhode Islanders to vote for him in 1986, in the 1988 election he would earn placement on the ballot under the Cool Moose Party designation.[14] If successful, his party's placement could attract more attention, and potentially votes, as opposed to other third parties that garnered less than five percent of the vote and got lumped together, apart from the dominant Democratic and Republican Party candidate.

Even with Healey's compromised aspirations, winning over five percent of the electorate presented real challenges. For one, approaching the November election day, his party treasury had less than $7,000.[15] Republican Governor Edward DiPrete and Democrat business mogul Bruce Sundlun had accumulated well-funded war chests that dwarfed Healey's resources. Unlike the two frontrunners, Healey could not afford full spread newspaper advertisements, attention grabbing television commercials, catchy radio spots, or for that matter a large inventory of pens, pins and other campaign paraphernalia.

In addition to monetary concerns, Healey did not stand out as the only alternative to the two-party system. Tony Affigne, of the Citizens Party, also threw his hat in the ring. A veteran Providence social activist speaking on behalf of the state's poorest neighborhoods, Affigne espoused peace, a cleaner environment, human rights, and social justice. He garnered support from the poor, rank-and-file organized labor, and Hispanic and African-American citizens.[16] And he had a progressive style battle cry. Affigne charged, "Elections run by millionaires and the consultants that millions can buy are getting further and further away from the people."[17] He claimed his constituents did not support Governor DiPrete or Democrat Bruce G. Sundlun. Affigne did not *look* like the Cool Moose Party governor candidate, but his pronouncements resonated similarly. As a result, Healey could not gain consideration as the sole rebel candidate.

Healey tried in vain to separate the Cool Moose Party's message from the Citizen's Party. Like the Citizen's Party, the Cool Moose

Party aspired to be the ordinary person's voice and a movement Healey's parents and childhood neighbors would likely support. Healey explained, "The Cool Moose Party is attempting to get people involved in the political system…" Accordingly, he organized fundraising efforts that the average working family could afford. "People participation is our goal,"[18] Healey assured. True to the point, the Cool Moose Party charged $15 per person and $25 per couple for a fundraising brunch that included baked ham, seafood Newburg, and eggs Benedict.[19] The effort proved purposeful in that the brunch raised money for the campaign. However, the undertaking did little to separate Healey apart from the other third-party candidates in the race.

And arguably, most of Healey's ideas came across less maverick than Affigne's calls for change. Healey advocated for an increase in the state income tax and a reduction in the property tax. Voters had heard these ideas in one form or another before. When he did put forward more sweeping changes, such as the elimination of the sales tax, (Healey explained that because the sales tax is collected at an equal rate from all citizens, it harms the poor and elderly disproportionately compared to other sectors in society,[20]) Affigne agreed. Healey struggled to communicate an exclusive novel campaign message.

Similar to the plight of other third parties, initially the public did not give serious consideration to the Cool Moose Party, at least certainly not to the point that they might actually consider voting for the party's governor candidate. The media helped solidify that low contemplation status for Healey, and Affigne. Even public media outlets overlooked third party candidacies. While in 1986 four candidates met the qualification to run for governor of Rhode Island, the League of Women Voters of Rhode Island, which produced the Channel 12 and Channel 36 (WSBE, Rhode Island's public television station) debates, announced that only candidates who had garnered fifteen percent in public opinion polls qualified to participate in their political forum. Governor DiPrete and candidate Sundlun met their requirement. Affigne and Healey did not. Debate organizers believed the two

independents had little chance of winning.[21] Ray Fass, WSBE's director of programming, explained that the station served the people of
Rhode Island best by allowing only "the candidates that have a chance
to win the office" to participate in their debate. Anticipating inquiries
as to how they arrived at that determination, Fass emphasized, "...
and yes, we make that judgment."[22] Healey had some judgments of
his own to share on the matter. He argued that his (and Affigne's)
exclusions from the debate underestimated the lure of their message
and weakened their campaigns.[23] In essence, Healey argued, the pro-
ducers' rulings fulfilled their professed prophecies.

Healey and Affigne refused to drop the debate participation issue.
They argued that the law favored their inclusion in the 1986 Governor's debates, especially the event on Channel 36.[24] Both independent party candidates had a point. Federal laws generally required
equal treatment of candidates.[25] On the other hand, established rules
favored the right of television and radio stations to limit the participants in a political debate.[26] Competing interpretations aside, in the
end neither Healey or Affigne participated in either the Channel 12
or Channel 36 debates.

Undeterred, in October 1986, Anthony D. Affigne challenged
Governor DiPrete (and the other two governor candidates) to a
debate on Channel 10, WJAR-TV. Interestingly, Affigne called for
the debate without first approaching Channel 10 to see if they would
agree to host the program.[27] David B. Baer, Channel Ten's news director, referenced Affigne's invitation to the candidates before consulting
the *involved* news station as "unusual and unorthodox."[28] Baer went
on, "Our position would be we are still interested in a gubernatorial
debate between Bruce Sundlun and Governor DiPrete."[29] Regarding
the inclusion of Affigne and Healey in those televised debates, Baer
submitted, "We would have to consider the campaign situation at that
time, and make a determination then."[30]

As the debate about the debates continued, the Rhode Island affiliate
of the American Civil Liberties Union (ACLU) approached Channel

36 to reconsider their decision to exclude Affigne (and by extension, Bob Healey) from their gubernatorial debate on the grounds that a public-TV station should sponsor broad election coverage. While acknowledging that the law might support the station's decision, the ACLU contended that a "fundamental policy question" existed when a publicly funded station excludes certain candidates while including others.[31] In an apparent attempt to placate Healey, Affigne, and probably more so the ACLU, Channel 36 offered both third party candidates the opportunity to appear separately or together as part of a special half-hour program. Healey declined the offer because doing otherwise served as an admission of a "second class" candidacy.[32] Instead, he threatened to pursue a complaint with the FCC.[33] Affigne's campaign also rejected the separate show offer because accepting the invitation would relegate Affigne "to an exotic corner of Channel 36."[34]

When not challenging WSBE's position on political debate participation, Affigne took on the League of Women Voters methods for determining the fifteen percent debate qualification rule. Affigne said that a recent pollster had called his house and only inquired about supporting DiPrete and Sundlun. When his wife let it be known her intention to vote for her husband, the pollster hung up.[35] In essence, the alleged polling practice assured that a third-party candidate could never attain evidence of surpassing the fifteen percent voter support threshold needed to participate in future political debates. As such, the two-party system remained securely in place via a practice that in effect barred Affigne, Healey, and other independent candidates' purposeful political participation.

Other media sources also gave the lion's share of coverage to the two highest polling candidates for governor. The Cool Moose Party treasurer called attention to this fact in a published Providence Journal letter to the editor. Deborah Fortin wrote:

"In almost every one of your recent articles, only two candidates running for governor are mentioned when actually there

are four. I have seen very little coverage on the two independent candidates… If you are really out to convey the news fairly to the public, the public should be made aware the opinions of all the candidates, not just those of the two major parties. Your near monopoly of the Providence news market also gives you a responsibility to be fair, something that you clearly are not. Only informed voters can then make the right decision about which gubernatorial candidate to vote for."[36]

In an attempt to attract increased media coverage, as he had during his campaign for Warren School Committee in 1982, Healey's 1986 bid for governor utilized off the beaten path campaign strategies. He handed out campaign combs instead of buttons.[37] He passed out leaflets and posters created by Gary Cavey, childhood friend, which were often run-off on copy machines.[38] One of those handouts showed Bob Healey holding a mask of his own likeness with the caption, "What you see is what you get." A Cool Moose Party leaflet read, "Put *The Independent Man* in the state house, not on it." To further that point, Cavey pasted Healey's face on to the body of The Independent Man. Healey's strategy meant to draw voters; attention first and inform them second.[39] And this he did, maybe at times with too much of the former. Healey explained, "You have to be different to experiment with third party politics... the gimmick is to get people interested in you. Then they read the pamphlets, and when they read them, they're hooked. Because what I'm saying is not so radical."[40]

During the 1986 campaign for governor, Healey referenced lessons he had learned from prior candidates and government officials. For example, Healey recalled when Providence's mayor painted "Mayor Joseph R. Paolino Jr. & the People of Providence" on city trucks. The public criticized Paolino for that decision as an improper use of public property to promote his own candidacy. Healey promised, "I'm going to put my name on the side of my car and say it's not the property of the people of Warren."[41] And maybe that cautionary approach made

Bob Healey strikes a somewhat stoical pose, perhaps in the hope that voters would give his 1986 candidacy for Governor serious consideration. (Photo courtesy of Gary Lavey)

sense enough. But of course, regardless of how Healey adorned his vehicle, no one would have likely noticed or cared. Healey owned a 1973 yellow Volkswagen "spotted with beige and silver rust-repair patches."[42]

To inform people about the Cool Moose Party, Healey pounced on invites that more established candidates avoided by citing supposed scheduling conflicts. High school audiences populated by few eligible voters often met with such *schedule conflicts*, and for good reasons. From the mouth of babes could come some harrowing questions. A front-runner candidate had little to gain and much to risk by participating in such forums. While a local news source would not likely report much on a successful campaign outing, a candidate's *wrong* response to a minor's inquiry could make for a damaging headline. As such, in the fall of 1986 only one candidate for governor attended a

Portsmouth High School library forum. At that venue students asked Healey some pointed questions that older voters might not have ventured to ask, at least not is such blunt terms and direct delivery. In one such case a Portsmouth High School student questioned Healey, "Do people take you seriously?" Rarely bothered by insulting inquiries, intentional or otherwise, Healey responded to all questions head on. In this instance, Healey used the student's question to deliver a predetermined speaking point; "Once they hear me, they do; before that, they think it's a joke." Healey then shifted to deliver his wider point; "We're out to transcend party lines.[43]

Another Portsmouth student asked Healey whether or not a candidate should take a drug test. This question might have harkened back to the Warren School Committee Chairman's 1983 publicized comments regarding students' alleged use of drugs on a school bus. That episode had garnered state and national attention. (See Chapter 5, *The Chairman Did What?*) His handling of that matter might not have boded well for a governor candidate. But Healey didn't flinch. He humored, "My big drug is aspirin, so I thought I'd offer myself up for testing. That would have gotten me a lot of media coverage. But I don't believe in drug testing unless it's for something super sensitive. I think it generally violates (a person's) privacy. I can't support it."[44]

In another rather pointed question, a Portsmouth student asked, "If you're elected, what's to stop your party from becoming like the others?" Healey admitted, "That's a danger. If you're there [in office] for any length of time, you become the jerk you replaced. Hopefully there would be other parties that would follow us, that would replace us."[45] After the session at Portsmouth High School, students continued to talk to Healey up close "...as if they were trying to figure him out,"[46] a tall order for any voter. Clearly, at the very least The Cool Moose candidate piqued their curiosity.

Not all high school visits in 1986 ended up as successful as the one to Portsmouth. At North Kingstown High School's Candidates Day, Healey took the stage in the school auditorium to address approximately three hundred students. As he did so, another waiting government official leaned toward one of the school's social studies teachers and shared with a gestured reference to Healey, "That's why Warren is so fucked up." Regardless of whether the assessment of Healey's performance in Warren rang true or not, few would have disagreed that Bob Healey's 1986 North Kingstown High School speech came across as unremarkable. That judgement would not characterize his future political orations at the same school.

As the November election day approached, Healey's chances of securing five percent of the electorate's support seemed to decrease further. He had failed to gain the traction needed to challenge either of the two front runners. And the continuing lack of election news coverage did not help his cause. Within a week of election day, the Providence Journal shared the governor candidates' views on the arts. In a piece that ran almost 2000 words, the Journal *saved* Healey's views on the subject for the article's last 86 words. The newspaper even afforded Affigne additional commentary and a more advantageous article placement.[47]

A week prior to election day, Healey's chances of a strong showing in the election experienced yet another setback. Charles Bakst, a widely read Providence Journal political columnist, reported on the Rhode Island Women's Political Caucus's ratings of nine Rhode Island major office aspirants, including Bob Healey. (During the fall of 1986, women's issues had gained increased attention from the public.) The caucus had questioned the candidates on a wide range of women's rights topics, including support of comparable economic equity legislation, the state's Equal Rights Amendment, and abortion related issues. (Question 14 on that November's ballot concerned an anti-abortion state constitutional amendment.) The women's 130-member caucus rated candidates who answered their questionnaire on a 100-point scale. When a reporter at a State House news conference asked Marlene Roberti, the caucus chair, whether a ten-point difference between two candidates for the same office mattered much, she replied; "There's a big difference between the 100 percent and the 90 percent. If they got a 90 percent, that meant that they filled in the questionnaire wrong on one of our very important issues."[48] John Holmes, Republican candidate for the House of Representatives, scored a 100, as did Republican Arlene Violet and Democrat James O'Neil, both candidates for attorney general. Governor candidates Bruce G. Sundlun and Anthony D. Affigne scored 100. Governor DiPrete scored an 80. The Providence Journal reported that Robert Healey scored a 50.[49]

On the eve of the state election, a Coventry Junior High School mock vote proved an impressively accurate indicator as to who would win the state governor's race. The Coventry school's results read as follows: Edward D. DiPrete (R) 446, Bruce G. Sundlun (D) 196, Anthony D. Affigne 33, Robert J. Healey Jr. 12.[50] On the actual election day, Edward DiPrete retained his governorship easily. Healey captured 1.85% of the state vote.

Healey often said, "If it doesn't hurt, then you're not trying hard enough."[51] If Healey felt any significant pain during the 1986 election, he let on little. And even though Governor DiPrete had trounced the Cool Moose Party candidate in his first run for governor, the former Warren School Committee Chairman demonstrated no outward humiliation or smarting. Instead of admitting to the political pasting he had endured or acknowledging that perhaps he had set his sights too high at this early juncture in his political career, Healey rationalized away the embarrassing election results. At times he even expressed a degree of pride over his numbers in the 1986 race. While his evident high self-esteem might encourage another run for governor, if Healey wanted the voters to take him more seriously in future political contests, he would have to follow his own mantra more intently and try harder.

CHAPTER 8

NOT BUSINESS AS USUAL
HEALEY OUT OF POLITICS

Many knew Bob Healey, the candidate. But from 1982 to 2016, Bob spent a substantial part of his life as a success-ful lawyer, a sometimes-prosperous businessman, and a professional and voluntary educator. To understand the Cool Moose Party founder more fully, one must explore Bob Healey the attorney, the entrepreneur, and the teacher. In Healey's pursuits of these profes-sional domains, stories and examples highlight his personality, mind-set, and disposition, thereby providing a more revealing look at Bob Healey's personal and political entity.

LAWYER BOB HEALEY

In August 1980, Robert Craven entered New England Law School in Boston with Bob Healey. When he first met Bob, Craven thought "he had a Jesus Christ SuperStar look."[1] According to Craven, Bob's long hair and beard presented as an alien look with fellow law stu-dents. Craven took lesser notice of Bob's facial appearance than other budding law students. However, Bob's feet drew his attention more. Craven explained years later, "What I noticed most was that he had no shoes on in the middle of Boston. When it came to the middle of November, he still didn't have shoes on. I asked him, 'Gee, Bob, when do you put shoes on? In the snow? And by the way, doesn't it hurt? Don't you step on nails, glass? This is Boston.'" Healey responded, "Well, I don't like the restriction of shoes." Craven thought that was "unusual," but accepted the answer. A few days later Healey showed up wearing sandals. He came up to Craven and said: "You don't have to worry anymore." Both laughed out loud.

Craven soon learned that Healey's shoeless preference—and more notably, his reasoning for the penchant—proved analogous to so many other facets of his school peer's life. Not only did Healey dislike the restriction of shoes, he rejected most forms of conformity. This aversion helped explain in part his look, deportment, and eventually his practice of law.

Most of the law students at New England Law School secured apartments in or around Boston, living with one or two other students. Considerations of budget and socializing dictated such decisions. Living together built camaraderie, as future lawyer colleagues learned about each other's families, sense of humor (or lack thereof), and aptitude for law study. Bob Healey didn't seem so concerned with camaraderie. He lived in a small third-floor room-and-a-half apartment in Boston's North End. For much of his law school years, he had no fellow law student roommate.[2] Though Bob sometimes maintained his distance, fellow law students liked him. They found Bob friendly, easygoing, and approachable.[3]

During their law school years, Rob Craven and Bob Healey became friends. That friendship grew throughout the rest of Bob's life, though in sporadic spurts. Over a 36-year span, the two crossed paths often, checked in with one another occasionally, and enjoyed each other's company at every presented opportunity.

But Bob and Rob's first names, legal backgrounds, and

long-standing amicable relationship did not amount to a likeness in appearance or practice, legal and otherwise. Rob Craven followed the *rules*. He thought those rules read clearly. "You go to church. You dress a certain way. You part your hair a certain way. You get married to Emma Lu and you have 2.3 kids and you have a house with a white picket fence. Those were the rules."[4] According to Rob, "Bob didn't follow any of them."[5] While a lack of rule following might not sink one in politics, the culture of law exhibited less patience for deviations from the well-established norms. But even in the less tolerant land of statutes, precedents, and legal judgements, Healey would come to push the constraints many other lawyers adhered to steadfastly.

Rob and Bob pursued initially different paths upon graduation from law school. Rob Craven's path fell in line with what one might expect of a successful graduating law student. Craven became an Assistant Attorney General for the State of Rhode Island from 1983–1992, served as their lead trial lawyer, and became Chief of the Public Corruptions Office. Craven dealt with the infamous Joe Mollicone case, corruption charges against Governor Edward DiPrete and Judge Antonio Almeida, and other very public prosecution cases. Bob Healey entered politics right out of law school, and from 1987 to 1994 (and beyond), enjoyed success in business. Healey's law practice would not become well established until a few years out of law school.

Healey's career as a lawyer defied standard description. He practiced law as he approached many things in his life, in accordance with his unconventional personal style. For one, when Bob went before a judge he rarely if ever possessed a piece of paper with his notes on the case. Everything associated with his delivery had an "off the cuff" semblance.[6] This approach stood out as highly unusual, and for good reason. A lawyer can't always anticipate the questions a judge might ask, or if the opposing lawyer is going to bring up an unforeseen line of reasoning. In such circumstances, a lawyer can look down at their notes, flow chart, or other information to guide their comments. Bob "had none of that."[7]

While Bob might not have had any of *that*, he did have "a lot of balls"[8] when in court. Sometimes a judge will say something that a lawyer thinks has no bearance on the matter before the court, but for a whole host of reasons, most lawyers decide not to introduce that notion to the presiding judge. Bob thought otherwise. On one occasion Bob presented a case before a Rhode Island Supreme Court. At that hearing, a judge asked Healey a question. Bob didn't think the inquiry had particular relevance to the case. And so, Healey looked up calmly and said to the presiding judge, "You're off the mark on that question. It's got nothing to do with this case. Anything else you want to ask me?"[9]

Though initially Healey did not intend to practice law in Rhode Island (he had trained to be a Japanese trade attorney or a Japanese educator),[10] the New England School of Law graduate nevertheless put his lessons in law to work within days of graduating. As Chairman of the Warren School Committee, Healey reviewed a ruling by the Rhode Island Conflict of Interest Commission. That Commission had determined that fellow Committeeman John Killion's vote on a budget item that affected his wife, a Warren School Department teacher, should not enter into effect "...because she was part of a group that benefited as a whole."[11] (This circumstance is raised in Chapter 6, *The Year it All Hit the Fan*, but does not include most of the background information discussed here.) Bob Healey disagreed, emphatically. In making his counterargument, Healey cited a case in Newport similar to the one in question in Warren. In the Newport case, that town's councilman, William Nagel, also a teacher in that town, had married a Newport school nurse. Councilman Nagel had sought counsel from the state's Conflict of Interest Commission regarding potential circumstances that might call into question his actions. The commission advised in opinion #84-22 (June 19, 1984), "...that a potential violation of RI Gen Laws S 36-14-49a0, (d), and 9e0 (1) would arise for Mr. Nagel if he participates in the discussion of or votes on the school department's budget while his wife is an employee of the department. However, no violation will arise under these circumstances if he votes on the city's budget as a whole even though the school department is contained within it."[12]

Healey offered of the commission's advisory opinion, "This seems to say that there would be a conflict if there was a vote or discussion of a line item in the school budget by a councilman." Turning attention to the case in Warren, Healey implored, "Just think, we have a committeeman voting for such, and the commission has apparently let this matter go unchecked. Maybe the only real conflict is with the people who are on the conflict commission."[13]

In another legal-based development during his tenure on the Warren School Committee, Bob Healey issued a complaint to the State Attorney General's office that the Warren School Committee violated the Open Meetings Law when it elected to go into a closed session on June 11, 1984. (Chapter 6 also raises this issue, but not to the extent discussed here.) According to Healey's rendering of the occurrence in question, Committeeman George E. Gempp Jr. requested the closed session for the purpose of discussing personnel matters, which is considered an appropriate use of a such a session. However, Healey reported that Gempp used the session to attack the Chairman for a letter he had published in the local paper. Healey had published many such letters over the past year.

Healey charged, "Under the Open Meetings Law, such a discussion is not an exemption to meeting in public."[14] Healey added in his letter to the attorney general, "The (closed) session privilege should not be so abused. The matters discussed in closed session could have been completely addressed in open session. Further, I found the practice of stating the session was for a personnel matter when no personnel matter was discussed was a bit deceptive."[15] After waiting a month for the attorney general's reply, Healey complained, "The attorney general's office has two speeds, slow and dead."[16] (The attorney general saw the case as of a lower priority since the Committee had spent no money in the subject session.) In August, the attorney general's office determined that the Warren School Committee had violated the Open Meetings Law that past June. Assistant Attorney General Thomas Caroulo added, "If Mr. Gempp gets engaged in another shouting match with Mr. Healey, it will have to be on stage."[17]

Years later, when Bob Healey represented clients, sometimes he and his old law school classmate, Robert Craven, presented opposing arguments before the court. One of those cases involved a Central Falls City Council candidate, Edna Poulin. She had decided to run for the Central Falls City Council. The next day, Poulin learned no one had opposed Charles D. Moreau for mayor. She thought to run against him and sought the 200 signatures to qualify for that race. By the time she secured 44 signatures, Poulin learned that another candidate entered the race against Moreau. With that news, she decided to run for the City Council District 2 seat, and secured the 50 signatures necessary to qualify. And that's when things got contentious. Councilman Richard G. Aubin Jr., her opponent for the District 2 seat, contested Poulin's candidacy for that office on the grounds of a 2005 state law that said a candidate cannot file to run for an office "if that person has declared to be a candidate for another elected public office."[18] Poulin disagreed with Aubin's reasoning. Both brought the matter before the Board of Canvassers. Craven represented him. Healey represented her.

Craven argued that Poulin couldn't run for City Council or Mayor because her final choice of candidacy (mayor) overruled her City Council filing. And since she didn't secure the required signatures to run for mayor, she did not qualify to run for that office as well. Healey argued that while Poulin couldn't run for both offices, nothing in the subject law stipulated that the board had to disregard her first declaration. The Board of Canvassers decided in favor of Craven's client. Afterwards, as Craven gathered up his materials, Healey approached him and said, "Well, … I don't think I will be successful in front of the board of elections because you will still be their lawyer, but the Supreme Court should be fun…I can't beat you in places where you have to be normal…"[19]

The Board of Canvassers arrived at their decision due in part to board solicitor Christopher Petrarca's analysis, offered in a session prior to the public meeting. Healey felt uncomfortable with that *prior* session. He argued, "It was clearly a closed meeting," and added, "I think they had reached their decision before I walked in the door."[20]

Shortly after walking out that door, Healey determined to bring the case before the Board of Elections on behalf of his client. At that Board of Elections meeting, Healey argued that the Board of Canvassers had earlier misinterpreted the law. Healey clarified, "The first sentence of 17-14-2(b) is explicitly clear. No person shall be 'eligible to file.' The argument should end there. Any second filing made after the original declaration is deemed to be by a person who lacks the eligibility to file such a declaration."[21] As such, Healey maintained, Poulin's first declaration, that which she declared to run for the Central Falls City Council, supersedes her second declaration to run for mayor. Healey also cited two other previous cases that favored his interpretation in this matter.[22] The Board of Elections reversed the Board of Canvassers decisions in a 6 to 0 vote.

Of course, Bob Healey did not win all his cases before boards and courts. Still, even in losing endeavors, the long-haired prosecutor penetrated the heart of matters and raised thought-provoking arguments. In July 2010, while running for Lieutenant Governor, Bob Healey sought to abolish straight-party voting. He served as one of 11 plaintiffs in a lawsuit filed in the United States District Court. The claim named as defendants Rhode Island Governor Don Carcieri, Rhode Island Secretary of State A. Ralph Mollis, members of the state's Board of Elections, and the heads of the state's Republican, Democratic, and Moderate parties.

The lawsuit alleged, "The use of the party lever in conjunction with optic scanning technology has created several discernable and distorted voting patterns. Using the optic scan ballot, no marks are visible as to the vote cast in each race. As a result, communities that hold non-partisan elections demonstrate a marked decline in civic participation, showing that voters often fail to cast votes in non-partisan municipal contests, mistakenly believing that the party lever has triggered votes in all races."[23] Furthermore, "Plaintiffs alleged that the existing Rhode Island ballot format [for straight ticket voting] causes great ballot confusion to the extent that it denies voters the right to vote guaranteed under the United States Constitution."[24] The suit's primary point stipulated that "...established political parties are the sole beneficiaries of the straight party ticket voting" and "are favored over Independent candidates."[25] Healey offered that the Secretary of State and the Board of Elections acknowledged that straight party voting is "a source of confusion" and therefore should be repealed.

Bob Healey testified first in court on behalf of the plaintiffs. He stressed that straight-party voting levers lessen the votes cast in local races as non-partisan elections are not registered under straight-party voting.[26] Healey explained that voters who utilize the straight-party voting levers are not likely to vote in non-partisan office races (or for an office that no one from their party has run for) because they may overlook doing so. As such, straight-party voting levers harm independent candidates, and indirectly disenfranchises voters. US District Court Judge William E. Smith saw the matter differently. In his decision, Smith explained that much of the plaintiffs' case relied on speculation as to how and why people voted. Smith advised that the matter go before the General Assembly instead of reintroduction into the courts. (In 2014, under legislation HB 8072, Rhode Island banned straight-party voting by lever.)

Robert Healey's most notable legal triumph probably involved a case heard in the United States District Court, The Cool Moose Party v. State of RI, 6 F. Supp. 2d 116 (D.R.I. 1998). Future related court decisions around the country referenced the case in deciding political challenges of various forms. With Judge Ernest C. Torres presiding, in the subject case, Healey and The Cool Moose Party questioned "...whether statutory provisions that prohibit members of one political party from voting in another party's primary prevent "write-in" voting at primary elections and require voters to identify the primary in which they wish to vote impermissibly infringe on rights to freedom of association and/or privacy that are protected by the First and Fourteenth Amendments and whether such provisions violate the "Qualifications Clause" contained in Article I, Section 2, Clause 1 of the United States Constitution and the Seventeenth Amendment."[27] Specific arguments brought forth in the case included:

Whether R.I. Gen. Laws § 17-15-6, which requires political parties to select their nominees by means of primary elections, violates CMP members' right to freedom of association by preventing them from selecting candidates at a caucus open only to CMP members.

Whether R.I. Gen. Laws § 17-15-24, which prohibits members of one political party from voting in another party's primary, violates the plaintiffs' right to freedom of association because it prevents the CMP from allowing members of other parties to participate in the selection of CMP candidates.

Whether R.I. Gen. Laws § 17-15-24 also violates the "Qualifications Clause's" requirement that electors for federal office have the same qualifications as those of electors for state offices, because the CMP does not nominate candidates for federal office.

Whether some unspecified Rhode Island statute (presumably R.I. Gen. Laws § 17-19-31) that prohibits write-in voting at primary elections also violates the "Qualifications Clause."

Whether some unspecified Rhode Island statute requiring voters to "publicly" identify the party primary in which they wish to vote violates the plaintiffs' First and Fourteenth Amendment right to privacy.[28]

Healey's arguments convinced the court to declare R.I. Gen. Laws § 17-15-24 unconstitutional "…to the extent that it prohibits any otherwise eligible voter from voting in a party primary when the bylaws of that party would permit them to do so."[29] Other findings in the Court's conclusion did not bode well for the remainder of Healey's challenges. Judge Torres stated in his opinion that "All of the plaintiffs' remaining claims are denied and dismissed"[30]

So, like almost every attorney, Bob Healey won and lost cases. But how did Bob Healey size up as a lawyer? Several sources ranked Healey among the state's best. Arlene Violet, the former Rhode Island Attorney General who, at least on one occasion, Healey had referenced as biased, wrote of Healey, "So many times I ran into Bob Healey in court…Always professional, Bob's word could be trusted. He was an attorney extraordinaire."[31] Representative Robert Craven said of Bob, "There are 10,000+ lawyers roughly…less than 1,000 that frequent the court. There are about 300 that frequent a courtroom regularly. And there are less than 100 who are proficient in trying cases. He was in that less-than-100 group." Craven further expounded of his former colleague, "He thought outside the box because he lived outside the box…[which is] very helpful in arguing a case where you were asking the court, whether it be the Supreme Court or whether it be the District Court or anything in the middle, or even federal court, to change the law. Bobby looked like a change agent…He knew that was his fastball…He could argue for change because…he had the talent and he was seen that way by those that perceived him and listened to him."[32]

Shortly after Bob Healey died, Rob Craven argued an East Providence gun case. Following the rendered decision, a spectator approached Craven. He asked Craven how he had composed himself during the hearing, unfazed by the other lawyer's confrontational manner. Craven responded to the inquiry in two words: "Bob Healey."[33]

The highest praise for the lawyer Bob Healey came from those he represented in court skillfully, successfully, and often without compensation for his legal services. Those free services contributed to his personal goal to donate one million dollars before he passed. One recipient of his legal assistance, Vickie White, a Warren resident, had contended with a legal matter that she worried would cost her greatly. Stretched financially, she did not know where to turn for help. Friends suggested that she have Bob Healey look at the case. She later said of Healey's legal counsel, "He found some obscure law that made our case. He could just do that. He was unbelievable."[34]

Shortly after Healey's passing, Probate Judge Steven Minicucci reminded those in attendance in court that day that Healey had argued many pro bono cases throughout his career. Minicucci held a moment of silence in his courtroom in Healey's memory.

BUSINESSMAN BOB HEALEY

Right out of high school, Bob Healey wanted to be a house painter. He had learned the craft from an uncle, and liked the lifestyle associated with the vocation. In that profession, he reasoned, people would let him be. For a couple reasons, mainly the advice of a girlfriend, a cousin, and longtime buddy, he changed his mind. When he decided to go to college, he gave considerable thought to being an English teacher. However, he never pursued that path in earnest.

By the late 1980s, Robert J. Healey Jr. found himself at a crossroads. Just shy of 30 years old, he had yet to establish a clear career path (though he was credentialed in two vocations) and had accrued no significant wealth. In addition to his brief teaching experiences, he had held a post as Chairman of the Warren School Committee for no pay, and mustered a long-shot campaign for Rhode Island Governor that had won over less than two percent of Rhode Island voters. Around 1990, he decided he needed to exit his current circumstance. While his law practice sustained him financially, the prospect of a small-town lawyer did not excite him, for the moment.[35] He needed a change.[36]

At the invitation and convincing of his friends, Bobo and Helen

Fischer, Bob (and his girlfriend, Claire Boyes) went to Uruguay. Bob had considered vacationing in Mongolia, but the Fischers offered to put Bob and Claire up in their time share in Uruguay. Soon after arriving in the South American country, Bob fell in love with the area, its culture, and the people. He found the nation unspoiled. "People trusted each other there more. They didn't lock their doors."[37] Bob decided to extend his stay in Uruguay.

Even though most Uruguayans he met could not speak English, they welcomed Americans. Since Bob spoke some Spanish, he conversed in simple terms with his new neighbors. His rudimentary command of Spanish sufficed to meet his limited needs, usually.

But some occasions gave over to the unusual. During one such occurrence Bob and visiting friends from the United States decided to go out and get chicken wings to barbecue.[38] Bob's Uruguayan residence, like most others in the area, had an outdoor grill attached to the house, situated behind an indoor oven. Before venturing out for wings, some of his friends from the States expressed concerns about communicating with the locals. Bob assured them that he spoke enough Spanish to communicate their order at the nearby grocery store. When they arrived at the store, the largest in the area—approximately the size of a typical CVS store in the United States—Bob placed his order for chicken wings. The meat department clerk looked confused by his request, seemingly unable to understand why the Americans before him wouldn't want the whole chicken. But, intent on pleasing his American customers, the butcher said that they would process the order as instructed by Bob. In a half hour, the Americans returned to pick up the order. The butchers had cut the tips of the wings, as Bob had requested in Spanish. His friends chided him for the rest of their visit, "Yeah, you speak Spanish really well, Bob."[39]

During Bob and Claire's extended stay in Uruguay, Bob befriended Omar Rodriguez. The two combined their funds to purchase a large lot of land. They later sold off individual tracts as financial determinations dictated. Healey did well by those dealings.[40]

In the early 1990s, Bob returned to the United States and, shortly afterward, decided to try his hand in the business arena. He wanted to make money. While that explanation would not make for a revelation in the business world of budding entrepreneurs, Bob's values and tendencies do not support the same snap assumption. Not wanting to venture out on his own, he chose to pursue a business partnership, approaching his high school friend, Joe Moniz. Moniz had graduated from Warren High School in 1976, a year after Bob. Though friendly in high school, the Warren High School graduates' relationship developed significantly in the early 1980s.

Joe Moniz, a self-assessed average student in the Warren school system, embodied a work ethic and aptitude that served him well in his post-secondary education business pursuits. Soon after graduation from high school, Joe worked at a couple union jobs but found the experience limiting. The top pay step did not satisfy him, and he determined that the union just protected some lazy workers. Those two factors prompted Joe to pursue other business options. In the mid 1980s he started his first significant successful business. He created New England Tool Company, a machine shop. Joe had contacted Bob Healey to do the legal set up for the company. The experience reinforced what he expected of his former schoolmate. Joe determined that his old friend knew his craft well, carried out his work earnestly and honestly, and cared about serving his clients' best interests. From that point on, any time Joe had a legal question, Bob got a call.

Joe Moniz did not ruminate long over Bob's business proposition. Two considerations guided him to a swift decision. For one, Joe valued Bob's legal mind. Secondly, he trusted his old friend. Soon after, the two past high school friends started a wine and liquor distribution company, Global Horizons. They generated two million dollars in their first year. Their intake jumped substantially higher in the coming years. Bob had never generated that kind of money before.

The business partnership between Joe and Bob worked well, but not perfectly. If the duo parodied as the business world's Abbott and

Costello, Bob took on the role of Costello. Bob came across funny, informal, and loose. Joe, more the straight man, normally handled the commercial part of their joint endeavors. Bob took care of the legal issues, and sometimes public relations.

On occasion, Bob would meet up with clients. Sometimes those sessions developed in humorous fashion. One such memorable instance involved a potential high-powered client who expressed interest in a line of Pinot Grigio that Joe and Bob hoped to popularize throughout the country. While new to the United States market, Joe thought the foreign wine product could develop into a mega-market favorite. To advance that intention, Joe agreed to meet up with a prospective buyer who he believed could be the connection to a lucrative deal. He imparted this thinking to his business partner in direct terms: "Now don't embarrass us. Don't blow cigar smoke in his face." Bob agreed not to do either, and promised more than that. He would break out his best car to escort their valued client around Rhode Island. Despite Bob's assurance to drive his finest automobile, Joe worried, and understandably so. Bob had an affinity for old cars, and usually spent around $200 or so for each addition to his fleet. Under this restricted budget, he grew his inventory to approximately six very used cars. He had done so with purpose. Bob had reasoned that if a car couldn't run one day, he would just swap in another for free.[41] For this prized client, Bob picked his top-of-the-line automobile, a Volvo, early 1980s vintage.

When the prospective buyer arrived to confer with Joe and Bob, he looked the part. He dressed professionally, conducted himself in reserved fashion, and spoke in measured terms. Shortly after his arrival, Bob drove the potential client from Warren to Wakefield, in South Kingstown. At the end of that day when the client returned to Warren, he had a tale to tell to Bob's business partner. The disheveled New York buyer made an insistent request of Joe Moniz: "Don't ever send me out with him [Bob Healey] again."

Joe, concerned, inquired, "What do you mean?"

The client explained to Joe in an emphatic tone, "We were driving along and it started to rain. And the sunroof was open. I started getting wet, so, I asked him, 'I'm getting wet. Aren't you going to close the roof?' Bob said matter-of-factly, 'Oh, the roof doesn't close.' He [Bob] then reached back while he was driving and brought forward a newspaper and handed it to me. I asked, 'What am I supposed to do with this?' He instructed me to, 'Put it on my head.'" The frazzled prospective client went on, "So we're driving down the highway and I'm feeling like an asshole with a paper on my head. And while this is going on, people are beeping their horn at him [Bob]. And he just waved at all of them. It was like he knew everyone in the state."

While revisiting the day with Joe, the client demonstrated his anger in no uncertain terms. But about halfway through the telling, he and Joe broke out laughing, almost uncontrollably. Joe assured the client jokingly, "And you got the good car!"

"Oh, good," the client roared, "but I don't want to get trapped in that car again!"[42]

In another *Abbott and Costello business episode*, Bob and Joe wanted to attract high-end wine buyers from California. To do so, they decided to rent an upper echelon venue so they might impress and entertain potential clients. Robert Mondavi, of wine fame, owned the property in California they chose to rent. One morning at the Mondavi estate, a conservatively comported and attired female client visited around 8:00 a.m. That morning, the sun rose brightly upon the early day Sonoma Valley landscape. Joe decided to take advantage of nature's offering and talk business outside. Sitting on the patio, the client had her back toward the Mondavi house. Joe sat facing the house. Their talk flowed easily for a short while as they discussed niceties and general business interests. At some point in their conversation, Bob came out of the house to join them. As soon as he did, Joe flashed an intense look toward his business partner. As Bob approached, Joe couldn't keep from widening his eyes at the sight before him. Even for Bob, his attire had a shock value.

He wore orange shorts, black socks, black oxford shoes, an

untucked and wrinkled long-sleeved white shirt, and a straw hat. He smoked a cigar held in his left hand, and balanced a glass of bourbon in his right. Joe did his best to signal Bob back to the house without drawing their prospective client's attention to the matter at hand. He did not succeed with either endeavor.

When Bob arrived at the woman's side, puffing and sipping, he said in a jovial fashion, "How ya doing?"

Joe said in a monotone voice to their prospective client, "This is my business partner."[43] The woman appeared horrified.

After the meeting, Bob asked Joe, "So, how did we do?"

Joe replied matter-of-factly, "Not good, Bob."

Bob inquired, "Why?"

"Because of you,"[44] Joe answered frankly.

Joe and Bob did not secure a deal with their business visitor that morning.

Bob smoked cigars often. According to several sources, most days he puffed through five to eight stogies. While Joe rolled with many of Bob's relaxed behaviors, including his affinity for cigars, on at least one occasion, he got particularly upset with his business partner's comportment. During that instance, Joe told Bob that too often, his clothes reeked of old cigar smell. He expounded in demonstrative fashion, "People like you, so they don't tell you, but they don't want to get stuck in a room with you. The smell is that bad."[45] Apparently Joe's tirade hit a nerve with his friend and business partner, but to little purposeful effect. A couple days later, Bob showed up freshly showered. But since he didn't blow dry his long hair, the wetness transferred to his shirt, which appeared soaked. To make matters worse, on his way to see Joe, he smoked a cigar in his tiny, beat-up Fiat. When Bob arrived, he strolled in with his hair and shirt reeking like an old, dampened, burned-up cigar. The scent presented stronger than any Joe had smelled before. When Joe commented about the odor, Bob didn't understand his concerns.

"You told me I smelled like an old cigar. So, I showered and put on a clean shirt before coming here."

Joe retorted, "But then you smoke a cigar with everything wet, causing an even worse smell."

Though Bob thought about how his relaxed habits might affect business, he stressed to his old friend on more than one occasion, "This is who I am."[46] He would repeat that statement many more times, in varied applications, over his life.

One Christmas Eve, Joe and Bob decided to rent a limo and go out to liquor stores with which they did business to pour the owners and managers a glass of $400 wine. Even though the liquor store owners had these same bottles in stock and for sale, rarely, if ever, had they enjoyed a glass of their finest wine. After a day of sampling the wine with their business associates, they decided to go to a Japanese restaurant in Cranston. At the restaurant, Bob addressed the waiter as if he were Japanese himself. Once again, Bob's behavior concerned Joe. He thought Bob pretended to speak Japanese in an insulting, mimicking way. As Joe soon learned, Bob could speak Japanese. The waiter and Bob conversed about vegetarian cooking.[47] Years earlier, Bob explained to Joe, he had learned the language when attending school in Japan. He continued to practice Japanese over the coming years.[48]

In 2002, Joe shopped their liquor distribution business to see what it would bring on the market. A prospective buyer offered a seven-digit figure that would net out to over one million dollars for both Joe and Bob. Joe asked his partner what he thought. Bob responded nonchalantly that he could go either way.[49] They sold the business. Bob became a millionaire.

Bob went on to pursue other business interests, none reaching the success of the venture with his Warren High School peer. Some of his future enterprises proved failures. While Bob's law background and warm persona served as assets for his business undertakings, he had relied heavily on his former partner's business acumen to reach his prior success. To his dying day, Bob continued to approach Joe Moniz about his ideas for other business enterprises.[50] Sometimes he followed his old friend's advice, and other times he did not.

Like his political office campaigns, Healey promoted his business enterprises creatively and boldly. (© The Providence Journal—USA TODAY NETWORK / All rights reserved)

Shortly after selling the profitable liquor distribution business, Bob took his share of the profit to South America where he invested in more land and other business ideas. He started a liquor company in Uruguay to import California wines to the resort area of Punta Del Este. Later, he opened a wine and cheese restaurant in Warren, Rhode Island, and a yacht provisioning service, both which terminated after marginal success.

Bob conceived of many business ideas via out-of-the-box thinking, and more than a little optimism. While by almost all accounts Bob was a brilliant man, at times his commerce decisions exemplified flawed business acumen. For one, he lacked interest in "wooing" people with marketing strategies. According to his close friend Jade Gotauco, Bob "had ideas, a lot of them great and some of them only great in his mind, but [he] never felt the need to convince anyone. That mindset surely hindered his success in business ventures. Essentially, he got a kick out of himself and his ideas, but didn't mind when others didn't see the same."[51] And while this "kick out of himself" mantra remained true to Bob's "This is who I am" persona, as Jade Gotauco suggested, most of the time neither served his economic bottom line particularly well.

However, in one commercial venture, Healey's unique business approach proved advantageous. In this business start-up he introduced an ice cream line made at Warwick Ice Cream. Healey offered four Cool Moose Ice Cream flavors.[52] Uncharacteristic of the company's founder, Bob elected to go with the mainstream flavors: vanilla, chocolate, coffee, and strawberry. His advertising campaign reverted back to his off-the-beaten-path approach. To help sell his ice cream, he introduced six T-shirt styles and 40 trading cards that celebrated the company's founder, Robert J. Healey Jr. The cards, the product of friend Bryan Rodrigues and Izwuz (a Rhode Island-based graphics workshop), reproduced famous works of art. On those reproductions, Rodrigues superimposed Healey's hairy likeness. The advertising team accompanied each visual with a humorous caption. In one such example, they superimposed Healey's facade onto Napoleon's uniformed body with the caption, "Let them eat ice cream."[53] The savvy advertising campaign proved genius.

Other tendencies plagued Healey's efforts to jumpstart business enterprises. Some of these inclinations proved otherwise flattering of the corporate owner. For instance, he exhibited an ever-generous spirit. Even before a new enterprise gained steady footing, his charitable nature took priority over savvy business decisions. Again, one can turn to his ice cream business to make the point. In 2011, Rudy Cheeks, originally of radio fame, ran a nonprofit radio reading service for blind and visually impaired Rhode Islanders. Cheeks wanted to thank the volunteer readers with an ice cream social event. He called Bob Healey to see if he could provide the ice cream for about 75 people at a discount. Bob said, "No." Instead, he showed up to the Warwick location and donated all the ice cream and partook in the event so he could celebrate the volunteers' efforts.[54]

Sometimes the fates did not work out well for Bob Healey, the entrepreneur. Though not purely a business endeavor, during the 1990s Robert Healey wrote a children's book entitled, *The King Needs Sleep*. He wrote the book about a benign ruler who looked more than a little like an older version of the author. The story centers on a king who becomes upset one day when the sun does not set. The book ran about 100 pages, perhaps a bit long for a children's book, as reviewers had expressed to the book's author. Such advisory opinions didn't matter to Bob. He liked it. That mattered more. But to publish the work successfully he needed to secure the services of an artist to illustrate the book. This he did. However, before that work could commence, the illustrator died unexpectedly.[55] Later, Jade Gotauco, a talented artist, created the images for his children's manuscript. Her work served his literary offering well, but Bob did not get to publish the book before his untimely passing.[56]

Similar to his legal and political undertakings, Bob ran his businesses in accordance with his personal instincts, core principles, generous spirit, and unending concern for his fellow human being. And while that mindset did not always serve his bottom-line well, he rarely (if ever) deviated from that approach. He knew what he thought, and had little interest in pursuing matters against that grain. When he died, he left behind several ideas for undeveloped business endeavors, including a religion hall of fame.

TEACHER MAN[57]

Robert Healey's undergraduate and graduate studies prepared him to pursue a career as an English teacher. He continued to study the profession and associated subjects throughout much of his life. However, though he often referenced his educational experience in political campaigns, he taught only briefly. Counting Healey's four-month student-teaching training, a short stint teaching in Boston's schools, a few months instructing at a school in Oregon, some substituting at Warren High School, and a brief college position in Japan, his entire professional teaching career amounted to approximately two years of intermittent appointments. And by age 25, that teaching career had ended. While the numbers do not add up to much experience, there are indications that he served as an effective teacher.

First-hand accounts suggest that Healey appeared vested in his teaching, committed to student improvement, and quite capable. While those attributes usually identify an effective teacher in the making, a teaching career might not have ever been in the offering for Healey. The teaching profession and Bob Healey did not match up well. First, as evidenced in his political career, Bob often thought in radical terms. When Healey identified profound failings, drastic change had to follow. Despite rhetoric to the contrary, most school settings have a low tolerance for immediate, sweeping change, and when an aptitude for change exists in a school community, arriving at what that change looks like most often proves debatable. The career teacher Bob Healey in pursuit of change would have had to bite his tongue often and hold his breath for extended periods of time. One might doubt his willingness to do either.

Second, while schools do not operate within a strict military style chain of command, they do adhere to regulations, rules, and restraints. Further, curriculum mandates, administrative dictates, and union-bargained contract language govern schools. That trio would have restricted, tied up, and tortured Bob Healey.

Third, while many teachers dream big and give chase, they must also operate within a very scheduled and orderly paradigm. Healey could have done that in the short term, but not over a 30 to 40-year career. The Cool Moose liked to roam freely, unimpeded by restraints. School schedules and calendars would have caged Healey.

And fourth, day-to-day teaching requires, among other qualities, a large reservoir of patience. Every September required the educator to restart from the beginning that which they finished the previous June. Healey had patience, but of the volume that would fill a small pond, not a vast ocean.

While Healey may not present as the ideal teacher prospect, initially he did train for a career in education.[58] And Healey did teach, though via a method more in line with his strengths. He mentored. And within this mode of operation, he taught effectively.

For the most part, his mentees sought him out. Usually, his political background, not his education preparation, drew his students to him. Joseph DePascuale might have presented as his first such pupil. DePasquale first learned of Bob Healey through his sister, who befriended Bob in high school. Joe, several years younger than his six siblings, liked and looked up to Bob. Over time, Joe grew friendly with Bob, and often asked his advice on matters of all sorts. As time went on, Joe gained an interest in politics. Bob took him under his wing.

In 1998 and 2000, Joe DePasquale ran for the Warren Town Council. He lost both times. In 2002 he ran again. During this run, Bob counseled Joe that if he wanted to get elected, "You need to know the answer. Not how to get the answer."[59] More importantly, Bob instructed, Joe needed to draw attention to his campaign. People needed to *see* him, and *remember* him. Joe took the lesson to heart.

Approaching the 2002 election, several residents complained about the Warren Department of Works not doing enough to clean the town's streets. This claim gained credence when a woman slipped and fell in front of St. Alexander Church on Main Street. Acting on the advice of Bob Healey, Joe DePascuale took to the streets with a broom in hand and started sweeping. The Warren-Times Gazette picked up the story and printed pictures. Warren's readers learned of his efforts and *saw* the evidence. On election day, Warren voters *remembered*. They elected DePascuale to the Warren Town Council that year. He went on to serve several terms on the Council, and eventually became President of the Council.

Another of Healey's mentees, Bryan Rodrigues, first learned of Bob in 1986 when he ran for Rhode Governor. During that autumn, Bryan decided to focus his 10th-grade social studies project on the Cool Moose.[60] From that point onward, Rodrigues maintained contact with Bob Healey. In addition to a developing a friendly relationship, over the years Bryan contributed to Healey's campaigns by drawing and Xeroxing Cool Moose Party content. In later years, Bryan aided the Cool Moose campaigns in several forms, including painting the Cool Moose

Mobile, setting up the candidate's Facebook and webpage, and creating the black-and-white facial caricature of Bob Healey which came to serve as the party's de facto trademark emblem. In 2007 to 2008, Bryan and Bob wrote a satirical newsletter on Rhode Island politics entitled, "Rhode Island Diogenes."[61] (Bob identified with Diogenes.[62])

Over the years, Bryan learned from Bob in part by observing his mentor's conversations with many people. Bryan noticed that Bob used these verbal exchanges to "test his ideas."[63] These ideas interested Bryan. Over the years, Bryan and Bob discussed topics of societal importance regularly. Bryan said of these talks that "Bob's ideas were fixed" and that he "...couldn't beat Bob in debate. Bob always had a retort."[64] On further reflection, Bryan added, "I suppose he would relent if you persuaded him that your idea was better..." When on the ropes in a debate with Bob, Bryan would say, "Well, we will have to tell all the rugged individualists in Calcutta."[65] At such points, Bob "... appreciated the remark and let it stand. That was as close to winning an argument with Bob as one could get."[66]

While Bryan did not consider himself on the same page as Bob Healey with all things political, he recognized Bob as a trusted friend and respected mentor, and continued to seek his advice over the years. In 1996, Bryan Rodrigues ran for state representative of District 96. In Bob Healey style, Rodrigues spent 12 dollars on the campaign, and lost, to Mary Parella. Bryan credited Healey with helping him to think in deeper, more meaningful ways about issues he otherwise might not have.

Another protégé, Grant Garvin—a son of a political activist family—took to Bob at age 14. Bob impacted Grant's thinking profoundly. Later in life, Grant grew out his hair and beard to resemble his mentor.[67] In his 20s, he helped Bob Healey with graphic designs for the Cool Moose Party. Bob adopted enthusiastically his role as Grant's mentor, and wanted to transfer all of what he thought, and knew, to his apprentice. Grant was a sponge. Later, he became an integral part of Cool Moose political campaigns. In 2014, Grant ran Bob

Healey's last campaign. (See Chapter 12, *The Last Campaign.*) Many considered that campaign Bob's most successful political endeavor.

—

Robert J. Healey could have spent his entire professional life as a lawyer, an entrepreneur, or an educator. He had the capabilities to practice each well, and this he did, as the opportunities presented and his inclination motivated. But another vocation beckoned him, repeatedly. And he answered that call, every time.

CHAPTER 9

WHAT HEALEY THOUGHT

Throughout his political career, Bob Healey's outspoken manner and unfiltered delivery generated a long trail of attention grabbing, and sometimes provocative, written articles, letters to the editor, web page announcements, radio spots, and televised news clips. Typically, those publicized utterances reverberated candidly and humorously, as Healey had intended. This work chronicles many of his quotes, in part because they provide significant insight to his thought process. But there are other prepared sources that delve deeper into his political mindset and stance on specific issues. Healey's 41-page 2006 political platform might provide the most insightful exploration into Bob Healey's viewpoints and reasoning.

Of his 2006 platform, Healey declared years later, "If you read nothing else, read this document."[1] Healey alternatively entitled his 2006 creation, "If I Were the King of the Forest." He produced the detailed platform while running for the lieutenant governor's office. Ironically, he ran for that office so he could abolish the position (See Chapter 11, *The Best Lieutenant Governor You'll Never Have*, and Chapter 12, *So Close*). Nevertheless, he developed the 2006 platform document to inform and assure potential voters that he stood willing and ready to assume the governor's responsibilities should circumstances necessitate.[2] Since Healey's core philosophy did not change over the years, the exploration of his 2006 platform provides an insightful look at the ideas that informed his runs for governor and lieutenant governor from 1986 through 2014.

Healey's political positions sprang from rooted core governing philosophies. In explanation of those principles Healey said, "Our founders... called for self-governance, subject only to the powers ceded to the State, and even then, such powers were only on loan. The power resides in the citizens. We have bastardized their vision, much to our detriment."[3] Healey sought to rectify what he saw as a disturbing development.

Healey, a professed capitalist, argued that campaign promises from one political party or the other (exclusively Democrats and Republicans) determined what the victor party would do "with someone else's money."[4] He identified the "someone" as primarily the middle class. And considering only two parties in Rhode Island take turns at assuming "king of the mountain" status, he reasoned that those parties perpetuate the political cycle because doing so serves their collective interest. And to keep a dutiful middle class compliant with the party rotation, Healey pointed out that the government made up "wars" on everything from drugs to poverty to instill fear in the electorate. They did this so the elected politicians might offer protection as a route to establishing more government control during their party's governing cycle. In the case of the war on poverty, which Healey characterized as "unwinnable," the controlling party could allocate middle class resources to fund programs to supposedly end the plight of the poor.[5]

Healey promised he would work "to restore a middle class."[6] Toward that end, his 2006 platform addressed a litany of issues. Identifying himself as a liberal on social issues (he favored the right to an abortion and believed in privacy), he wrote most extensively on education, economic development, the law, and the legislature.

EDUCATION

Given his raucous tenure as the Warren School Committee Chairman, teachers across the state might have expressed grave concern over the prospect of a Governor Healey administration. Perhaps with that in mind, Healey offered, "While I have had my battles within education, I have never lost respect for teachers. I have bruised their egos and have waged battles with their unions, but I do feel they are doing a great social service. It is my vision to make this [Rhode Island's education system] all work more efficiently and effectively. I truly wish to empower teachers to allow them to perform to the best of their abilities, unhindered by contractual matters."[7]

In another apparent attempt to contextualize more positively his actions as Warren School Committee Chairman, he offered,

> *"When I was the Chairman of the Warren School Committee in the early 1980s, I was often at odds with the educational establishment. Because contractual obligations were funded by local property taxation, I was forced by my elected duty to take a hard bargaining approach to teacher contracts in order to protect those who chose me to be their government representative in matters of education as well as its funding. Now, two full decades after a teacher strike in Warren, I still see the same inadequacies in the system. I can say first and foremost, I honestly never thought that the teachers in Warren were bad teachers. To the contrary, having worked in the school system as well as having studied under them, I found Warren's teachers to be, with limited exceptions, highly qualified professionals. While at times they considered themselves prima donnas in the workplace and cringed at corrective criticism, they were highly effective given the social demographic community they served. The problem was with the system, namely the local negotiation of the union contract and the eventual method of paying the obligation incurred."[8]*

In 2006 (and later), Healey spoke almost glowingly of teachers and at least acceptingly of unions. He added to the above statement, "I truly believe that teachers deserve to be well paid. They are highly educated professionals. They shape the minds of the future."[9] He also understood that unions existed in education to "protect the teachers and education from unwarranted political intrusion, nepotism, and workplace abuses."[10]

The real "flaw" with Rhode Island's education, Healey argued, involved ill-equipped school committees. While well meaning, he felt the school committees could not negotiate with "buzz saws" (state level union negotiators.) The mismatch of bargaining skills resulted in inflated contracts that, in turn, elevated local property taxes. Those signed agreements inevitably led to face-offs between townspeople and teachers. To improve the relationship between the two parties, Healey suggested the state's legislatures negotiate and fund a state-wide contract. Local school boards could then focus on education issues. In Healey's ideal scenario, the state legislature would offer two-year teacher contracts that expired prior to the elections in November to allow for at least indirect public oversight.[11]

Healey did not see state regionalization of education as the "panacea" that others envisioned. He thought any resulting advantages did not outweigh the "fact that communities with different socioeconomic and cultural differences do not merge well." He argued the point further, "…education is better when it is locally based, especially in elementary grades."[12] He also felt that published reports inflated the financial benefits of regionalization.

Regarding school choice and voucher systems, Healey did not see either as a solution to Rhode Island's public education woes. He argued private school vouchering was "indisputably an asset to those being vouchered," but that the action "would cripple the public school system." Instead, Healey suggested "having public schools arranged based on achievement and subject matter" as "more reasonable…[and protective] of the public's reliance on publicly financed education."

He explained his reasoning further: "Public education must be maintained to allow for the social classes to transcend socioeconomic levels. While it is ludicrous to think that no child will be left behind, it is completely inane to think that public policy should stand as an obstacle to equal opportunity for social advancement."[13]

Concerning higher education, Healey thought Rhode Island needed to "dovetail" education programs with anticipated state business and social needs. For instance, he recommended, "If Rhode Island is going to be dependent on tourism, then teach our middle class to operate in that environment." In doing so, Rhode Island's higher education institutions should provide employable training, thereby preventing a "brain drain" exodus. Otherwise, he further rationalized, a class of young middle-class workers in the best position to support a quality education system would go missing.[14]

ECONOMIC DEVELOPMENT

Economic development stood as a cornerstone of Healey's platform. His reported unflatteringly of past state efforts to improve the Rhode Island economy. Healey charged in somewhat crude fashion, "Rhode Island has long maintained its commitment to drive-by economic policy making. This whimsical whoring ourselves out to whatever economic engine comes along is counterproductive and will not sustain growth."[15] According to Healey, this economic "whoring" rose to a state of being. The dealing started when a business let it be known that they might consider relocating to Rhode Island—dependent, of course, on the particular terms floated by the state. That process ended, according to Healey, with the state giving away the house to gain the interested business's favor. Healey explained that this approach amounted to a "method of spending one's way out of debt." He warned of this mode of operation that the "...ill-conceived idea works, but not indefinitely, and never achieves the stated goal of getting out of debt."[16] To keep this downward spiraling game going on longer, Healey explained, the Rhode Island General Assembly acted like "a drowning person [who] will grasp at the smallest piece of wood while surrounded by ravenous sharks."[17] In addition to serving up sweetheart deals for lucky businesses, the state used "magic money,"[18] such as tobacco settlement funds or gaming revenue, to prolong the flawed spending formulas.

Healey's economic prognosis spelled out a bleak future. He predicted, "There are no quick fixes, and it may well be too late to save the patient..."[19] Healey told of two possible depressing economic outcomes:

> "In a capitalist society there is production of wealth. In a totalitarian society all wealth belongs to the state for its disbursement. The more the state operates in a totalitarian manner, the less the incentive for the individual to produce wealth. In a capitalist society, wealth production provides growth that can then be taxed. This is not an exhortation that the rich are the means of success in capitalism. Far from it. It is an observation that it is the working middle class of people that are responsible for the well being of any true capitalist state. Therefore, if the state is to survive, it must increase the value and commitment to its working class. To promote policies that are an anathema to the working middle class is merely a path to totalitarian rule or revolution. While the first is the more likely outcome, the second is not so far-fetched."[20]

"So what is a state to do?" asked Healey. Initially, he outlined what *not* to do. Do not, he stressed, pursue solely industry-based solutions that are really "government spending campaigns in disguise."[21] Healey then added, *do* reign in public sector employment. The lure to do otherwise is innocent and sinister, he claimed, and under either condition, bad for the economy. In the innocent storyline, the state employment programs hire people that pay taxes and stay off unemployment rolls. However, "recycling state money" produces no goods. Therefore, "Eventually, slippage will occur and the money is gradually removed from the flow. Its long-term prognosis as an economic development policy is nil."[22] In the more sinister model, Healey explained that offering state employment did and does secure voter loyalty. This amounts to the spending of someone else's money by state politicians to secure their power base.[23] While Healey acknowledged that the government needed to maintain public sector employment, his disagreement centered on the extent to which officials increased such public spending.

Healey suggested private sector solutions as an alternative to public managed projects, but worried, "Private sector economics, left unguarded, gets fashioned by greed and contempt." Healey thought "the solution lies in a middle ground that is about a 75/25 split with a reliance on private over public…The state should provide the proper climate conditions…The growth is left to the private sector." But again, Healey warned of the private sector, "Businesspeople are whores, perhaps on a level of a politician. They are not interested in much more than the dynamics of a good deal."[24] The relationship between the businessman and the politician in an environment of "unbridled capitalism" presents dangers to the public good. In simplest terms, the business gets a great deal in public tax breaks or other incentives, and the politician gets their campaign funded generously by the private sector. Both outcomes contribute to the economic detriment of the middle-class citizen.

To illustrate the above point, Healey referenced Rhode Island's tourism industry. "If the industry is as strong as economic data would indicate," Healey questioned, "then why is there a need to subsidize hotel building and conversion?" Healey suggested, "either the data is being massaged, or the people are being had in the name of economic development."[25]

So, Healey warned that private incentives need to be watched just as closely as public spending. The formula for a good private investment, according to Healey, would first involve taking inventory of

what the state has to offer. In Rhode Island, Healey identified gerontology (the study of old age and the outgrowths thereof) as one possible example. (While a purposeful identification, Healey's reference
to gerontology hardly stood out as a groundbreaking idea. Others
had identified the issue and its potential positive ramifications for the
Rhode Island economy over two decades earlier.) Since census figures
made it clear that Rhode Island had more than its fair share of elderly,
Healey suggested using "...our resources to attend to the elderly of
Rhode Island while making it a laboratory for gerontology."[26]

Healey thought that the crowning consideration for Rhode Island's
economic future prosperity lay in thinking outside of the box. That
amounted, he thought, not to catching the wave that had already crested
and ebbed toward a crash landing on the shore, but rather to anticipate
rising waves on the horizon and position the Ocean State to take advantage of that next developing upsurge. Healey discussed one example he
identified eight years earlier. This involved capitalizing on the import/
export service market to Brazil and the rest of South America.

Healy explained, "that market was showing signs of growth. We
have a population that is fluent in Portuguese and Spanish. We were
a natural. Instead of locking ourselves into a business that would be
hard to relocate, we worked on the financial institutions, a sector of the
business world that is capable of operating anywhere a telephone exists."

Healey explained of his economic approach's wider rationale:
"Businesspeople are shoppers. They will go where the best deal exists.
If we use taxpayer dollars to subsidize their private sector operations,
they have succeeded. It is that simple. Businesspeople, while shoppers,
are also keenly attuned to the idea of looking at the bigger picture.
Given a good business climate, a responsive government, a reasonable
level of taxation, and an educated populace, a business will forego the
quick fix and will more likely stay put..."[27]

Making this point all the more salient, Healey referenced industries
that had moved their operations to Mexico to capitalize on wage concessions only to realize that necessary employee training and equipment

mishandling ended up costing the company more than had they stayed in their previous location.[28] As such, Rhode Island, and other states, had much to offer. Rhode Island needed to play its hand accordingly.

In the end, Healey acknowledged, no one prescription could cure what ailed the Rhode Island economy. However, Healey argued, tenets consistent with the examples he provided could make the state more commercial friendly and help improve the state's financial standing. Healey's most salient business point stressed that whatever the process, the resulting economic arrangement should not be "rich person friendly,"[29] and must be carried out always with the intent of benefitting the middle and lower-middle class.

THE LAW AND LEGISLATURE

Healey applauded several Rhode Island developments in the legal and legislative realms that empowered the people. These improvements included the following:

1. Even though too many politicians continued to seek only their own best interest, several had been exposed and prosecuted.
2. Government body meetings had become increasingly open to the public.
3. Public records, thanks to computerization and the will of public servants, had been made more available to public scrutiny.
4. Internet access to government workings in The Secretary of State's office and in the General Assembly—and, to a lesser degree, the Courts--had increased citizen oversight.
5. The Ethics Commission had increased its role "as a fourth branch of government."[30]

Healey wanted to improve upon the positive changes brought forth in recent years. An amended voter initiative process ranked chief amongst these ideas. Companion changes included increased regulation of special interest influence in elections and altering the legislation process.

While Healey had several suggestions for judiciary reform, by his own admission a majority of his ideas came up against systematically entrenched practices. He asserted that exerting time and resources to opposing the status quo amounted to "spitting in the wind."[31] Still, it is interesting to read his recommendations, as they demonstrate his thinking in an area he is well suited to offer a qualified opinion.

Regarding criminal enforcement, Healey worried about the over-criminalization of society, especially with drug offenses. While understanding the need for law and order, he felt incarceration to the degree employed against the poorest citizens demonstrated a "societal admission of defeat." Further, Healey thought poorly planned undertakings to correct such problems had led to a litany of other negative outgrowths. For instance, Healey explained, "due to the deinstitutionalization movement that began in the 60s, governments released thousands of patients on the premise that they were not dangerous to self or others. Many of these lacked the coping skills required to simply exist, and soon found themselves re-institutionalized, only this time in a prison setting."[32]

While "on the whole" Healey found the judges serving in Rhode Island courts to be a "respectable lot," he did favor reforms that impacted justices. For example, Healey said, "I am in favor of a judge's review by election every ten years, excepting the Supreme Court."[33] He also favored a constitutional amendment to "allow individuals to seek judicial redress for rights granted them under the Constitution."[34]

Perhaps surprising to most, especially given his support of a judge's review every ten years, Healey did not believe in term limits for legislators, because the Rhode Island government would lose the benefit of historical perspective in the legislative process. In a related matter, he argued, "It may be prudent on the surface to limit the leadership positions by term limitation, but that would only be a ruse. The powerful coalitions that make a speaker powerful would not be diluted. Thus, it is an exercise in futility that appears to be in the name of good government."[35] Of the legislature, he believed that the body should remain part-time, using off election years to pass a budget only, thereby reducing "the current flood of inane legislation…"[36]

Perhaps more than any other single issue, Healey passionately supported a host of reforms he thought would create more voter empowerment, and by extension, perhaps more voter participation. Campaign financing changes topped his reform list. Crediting the thinking of Rhode Island Supreme Court Justice Robert Flanders, Healey supported a fully state-funded system for all state candidates qualified to be on the ballot. Further, should a candidate choose not to participate in the state funding program, their political party would lose state funding as well, thereby causing the party to think more about their endorsements. In limiting the use of outside money in support of certain candidates, Healey reasoned, elections would "not be susceptible to being bought and sold by special interests."[37]

Healey wanted the Rhode Island General Assembly and Senate to reconsider the conditions by which the state granted (or did not grant) political party status. At the time, only a party that ran a candidate for governor could earn official party status. Healey thought that a party that ran any statewide candidate and garnered 20 percent of the vote should earn the official party status. However, Healey qualified, "Having once enjoyed political party status, I would have to say it isn't worth fighting over."[38] This is an interesting admission, considering that he steadfastly sought the Cool Moose Party's official recognition.

Healey strongly supported runoff voting. Under this system, rather than a voter selecting one candidate after the field had been narrowed by earlier primaries, the voter could choose from a wider field in the general election. Under Healey's preferred system, the voter would select their first, second, third, and fourth choice. Each placement vote earned the candidate an assigned point value. This system would allow people to vote for their candidate of choice without skewing the election results. Healey referenced this point as the "Nader factor." He explained, "While many people may have considered or even supported him [Nadar] for President, the fear of voting for a predetermined loser diminished, if not preempted any chance of him winning. Their vote for Nader, a Democrat alternative, would result in a decisive victory for the Republicans."[39] Further, Healey suggested, people vote in low numbers because "by voting they merely vindicate the mistaken perception that they are in favor of a candidate with which they find little merit."[40]

Also, Healey expounded, the runoff system would eliminate the expense of primaries at the state level. He clarified, "Political parties could still endorse candidates, but all candidates would reach the ballot." Though Healey wrote extensively on this subject, and felt strongly it should be utilized, he conceded the chances of such a system's adoption in a "party entrenched General Assembly" amounted to "zero."[41]

Healey also supported a hodgepodge of other initiatives affecting the legislative process. He articulated his reasoning for such proposals more succinctly than prior topics. These entries included the following:[42]

1. A line item budget veto to allow for the governor to adequately convey which parts of the budget are at issue.
2. A Constitution amendment that disallows the governor from making lame duck appointments (not requiring senate confirmation) that extend beyond their term of office.
3. A two-year election cycle for statewide office to better keep "elected officials on task."
4. A state budget that is clear enough to be read by an "eighth grader" so that "people know how their money is spent..."

5.   The maintenance of a relatively small rainy-day fund with a "pay as you go" budget.

6.   "Funding for pension obligations and other such expenditures need to be current. Underfunding of such obligations is merely transferring the problem to a future generation."

7.   The hope to broaden the peoples' power of recall.

8.   "At least 50 to 100 more items."[43]

PUBLIC SAFETY AND WELFARE

At his core, Healey cared deeply about the good of the whole and the equal sharing of burdens. While he thought much of this concern fell to the legislature, he thought the governor could employ the bully pulpit to affect the legislative process. He emphasized, "The Legislature imposes and the Governor disposes."[44]

Healey saw Rhode Island as a "tax mecca." To illustrate his stance, he referenced a long list of tax burdens: property taxes, cigarette taxes, income taxes, gasoline taxes, sales taxes, restaurant taxes, corporate taxes, and the fees for services. He added, "...and, if one considers gambling a tax on the poor, then that too."[45] Despite the flourishing stream of revenue, Healey pointed out, the state grappled with budget deficits. Rhode Island spends too much, he exclaimed.

While many politicians call for tax reform, Healey pointed out that too few have called for the necessary spending reductions. Healey equated the circumstance to "pushing on one side of a balloon only to have the other side expand." Healey thought the state's tax prognosis bordered on hopeless. "I honestly see no easy answer to the problem I describe here. I wish it were different, but it ain't." [46]

Still, Healey had a plan: a "triage budget."[47] This amounted to budget cuts (Healey identified few specific reductions), a higher emphasis on economic development (including public necessity projects "where appropriate"), and consideration to a one-time elimination of certain exemptions. Healey would also up efforts to collect taxes from "deadbeats." Despite these measures, Healey acknowledged, "All of this, however, cannot substitute for actual and real growth in the economy..." Otherwise, he warned, "We are a bunch of Okies just trying to keep everything together so that we can make it to California and redemption."[48]

Healey supported universal healthcare, but worried about special interests capitalizing on the reform effort. These parties included doctors ("who would be social workers if they weren't in it for the cash"), insurance companies, and politicians. Healey argued that "doctors often line up with Republican interests" and "malpractice lawyers with the Democrats." He added, "The interesting point here is that the middle class is the most likely to lack healthcare coverage and yet it is the overtaxed middle class that is making healthcare available to the poor and subsidizing the healthcare of the rich."[49]

Healey thought Rhode Island could attain universal healthcare by building on what the state already had in place. Healey explained, "If we look at the healthcare offered to employees of the state and municipal governments, along with their spouses and children, the people on RITE care, the numbers that are on other support services out of the Department of Human Services, along with all the other programs that include healthcare, it seems that universal coverage is nearly here... The secret here is to use the existing fabric to extend the security blanket."[50] Healey advised that middle class healthcare coverage could be accomplished by the state looking to its worker compensation system, utilizing managed accounts, expanding state funded medical services, capping malpractice awards, and establishing a state-owned insurance pool, among other possibilities. Despite what seemed like a surge of possibilities from Healey, as in other areas of need, Healey doubted that the government had the will to solve the healthcare challenges facing them.[51]

Healey also addressed transportation in his platform, including roads, bridges, the Registry of Motor Vehicles, the Rhode Island Public

Transportation Agency (RIPTA), sea-lanes, and other related topics. Healey suggested that the problems facing Rhode Island resulted from past deals and arrangements that, from the outset, appeared too good to be true. And such was the case, he argued. Healey explained that Rhode Island (and other states) had accepted federal transportation dollars, thereby empowering the federal government to impose its will (then and later) on certain aspects of Rhode Island's transportation system.[52] Federal government upfront short-term funding of projects too often led to long-term state financial burdens. He stressed that the state needed to stop that practice.

Healey argued that Rhode Island's size and urbanization made the state the perfect location for expanding the public transit system. However, despite the associated benefits of a limited landscape, he identified obstacles blocking real progress in this area. Candidly, and potentially politically costly, he identified Rhode Islanders themselves as the main obstacle. Healey explained that Rhode Islanders liked their vanity plates and the convenience of car ownership and use. Also, people's time did not come cheap, and using public transit eats up time. Healey observed frankly, while public transit is a "worthy objective," problems of greater concern relegated addressing this issue to back burner status.[53]

Without an expanded public transit, Healey stressed the need to maintain proper road surfaces and bridge structures, even during the worst economic times. He explained, "It is always good policy to maintain what has already been bought and paid for."[54]

Clearly, Healey did not have solutions for every governing problem facing Rhode Island. And with some problems, he threw his hands up right out of the gate. For instance, though he wanted to improve the Registry of Motor Vehicles, he observed this problem plagues many areas, even outside the United States. He confided, "I am not sure that this is a problem that can be solved given the scope of the operation and the fact that just about everyone over the age of 16 has some contact with the agency..." To no discernable end, he concluded, "...this is another area that needs attention."[55]

In a similar vein, Healey addressed the state's land resources. He felt, "Rhode Island has an obligation to protect open spaces and water resources." His solution, though worthy of consideration, required further development. His recommendation offered no plan to accomplish what one might conclude served as an obvious goal. Healey offered that any adopted "policy must address the need to provide for more affordable housing without exploitation of our lands."[56]

Healey, like almost all Rhode Island political campaigners for everything from school committee to governor, emphasized water as a critical lifeline to the Oceans State's survival and prosperity. He understood the need to protect the state reservoirs for healthy drinking water and realized that the bay stood as the backbone to the state's tourist industry. But outside a strong statement favoring protective vigilance of both water sources, he offered no specific plan to accomplish the said worthy goal.

Healey's ideas for emergency management amounted to heightened concern, but again, no specific plan of action. He recommended, "Fear mongering should be limited. The watchword is preparedness." However, outside a laundry list of rather obvious proposals (e.g., adequate signage, maintenance of emergency supplies), he offered no instructions for realizing the end game. Healey's last words on this issue realized only a heightened sense of concern and an admission of defeatism: "The bottom line is that in a crisis, most will survive, but we could have always done better."[57]

The last specific platform item Healey addressed in his 2006 platform directed the need for the governor's line-item veto capability. He felt this leverage would better permit the governor to "...ensure that the money is being adequately, appropriately, and reasonably well spent."[58] Healey remained skeptical of the Rhode Island General Assembly to move forward with this long-pending suggestion.

At the end of the day, Healey saw himself as a government minimalist.[59] But he clarified, "I am not fully libertarian in that I believe there are some very legitimate functions for government..."[60] As he would continue to make clear in the coming years, a Healey administration would work to serve the public welfare based on core conservative principles and with a sympathetic eye to those most in need.

CHAPTER 10

THE COOL MOOSE FOR GOVERNOR
THE 1994 AND 1998 RACES

S hortly after Robert Healey's disappointing 1986 bid for Rhode Island governor, he disappeared from politics, more or less. In 1987, he hinted that he might run again, one day. That same year, he let Rhode Islanders know in a published *Providence Journal* letter to the editor that his leftover "campaign war chest" from the 1986 governor's race amounted to $151.28. He quipped, "While it may not be enough for a trip to Las Vegas, a rental car, or even a week of law school, it is enough to put toward a future political campaign. Almost unthinkable, isn't it?"[1]

Bob Healey's activities between late 1986 through 1993 suggest that he thought a political rebound of any sort remained unlikely, if not inconceivable. But Healey's mid-1980s performances had piqued an enduring curiosity from others. Though Healey didn't enter the political news stream until late 1982 and went without any significant mention in the media from 1987 through 1989, in 1990, *The Providence Journal* thought Bob Healey had made a big enough splash in the 1980s to reference him in their "The Decade in Review" article. In that piece, *The Providence Journal* pointed out that while Healey no longer presented as an active candidate, he still took aim at political targets with adept skill. To support their claim *The Journal* article quoted Healey's satirical reflections about his public role and the current state of politics: "It's fun to light fires and watch politicians run like rats from a sinking ship."[2] Of his future plans, Healey shared, "I'd really seriously consider doing a talk show." He clarified, "Old politicians don't die, they just do radio."[3]

As best can be determined, Healey made no move to participate in any state or local political races during 1988, 1990, or 1992. He confined his infrequent political utterances to local Warren politics. Those statements rose to a barely audible decibel. In 1988, he questioned the Warren School Committee's appointment of his sometimes ally, often times nemesis, Rhode Island Representative Michael J. Urban Jr. to an eighth-grade social studies teaching position at Mary V. Quirk Jr. High School.[4] Healey objected to the selection out of concern over "…having yet another teacher in the General Assembly."[5] Urban, the then-vice chairman of the House Committee on Health Education and Welfare, estimated that teachers accounted for only 15 percent of the legislators in the General Assembly.[6] In the end, the School Committee stood by their choice.

In a similar vein, Healey also criticized Warren School Committee member Richard Blouin, who voted for his brother, Romeo Blouin, to assume the principalship of Hugh Cole School. However, Healey's objection did not gain traction because before Blouin voted, the other Committee members had supported the appointment unanimously.[7]

Bob Healey's diminished political appetite may have had something to do with the arrival of Claire Boyes in his life. In 1978, Claire had moved from England to Barrington, Rhode Island. Her new dwelling stood within a short walking distance to a house owned by Bob Healey's grandmother. When the grandmother passed away a couple years later, her Will transferred ownership of the Sowams' property to Bob's mother. She, in turn, rented the home to Bob's close friends, Brian and Deborah Fortin. When Bob graduated from law

Healey dresses as Elvis Presley at one of his and Claire Boyes' annual "Halloween Christmas" parties. (Photo courtesy of Brian Fortin)

school, he moved in with the Fortins. Soon after, he met Claire Boyes. A friendly relationship developed between them. Claire found him to be a "character."[8] She saw Bob as the lawyer next door who made her laugh. His "antics" included tying a rope to the back of his old car (did he ever own any other kind of car?) and then having someone drive the vehicle while he held onto the rope. Claire recalled of Bob during those days, "He was a prankster."[9]

In 1992, Claire and Bob's friendship developed into something more substantial than a friendly dating arrangement, but "serious" never came to aptly describe their relationship—or at least, not their time together. The new couple laughed more than they contemplated grave societal issues. Accordingly, during the early 1990s they sought pleasurable pursuits over politics. For instance, they organized Christmas parties that borrowed traditions from Halloween. At these parties, everyone dressed up in costume and participated in a gift exchange. During one of those gatherings, Healey outfitted himself as a longhaired Elvis Presley.[10] The party soon became a well-attended tradition among their widening circle of friends.

Over the years, Claire Boyes became much more to Bob Healey than the pretty and amusing girl next door. In addition to her part in the longest romantic relationship of Bob's life, Claire later proved to be a dedicated campaign consultant, worker, and ally. Her devotion to his cause would last to his dying day.

With a burgeoning relationship in his life and a voice relegated to that of an occasional concerned citizen, by 1993, one could conclude confidently that Robert Healey's political career had amounted to a mid-1980s flash in the pan. Few early 1990s political observers would have challenged that notion.

THE 1994 RACE FOR GOVERNOR

On a cold February 1994 morning at the Warren Town Hall, Robert J. Healey Jr. announced that he would run for governor. Bob had not publicized his announcement. Had his mother not crossed the street from her workplace (the I. Shalom Handkerchief factory), only five people would have heard him declare his candidacy for the state's highest office.

At his announcement to run for governor, any one of the six observers would have noticed that Healey's appearance had changed little since his last run in 1986. He still sported long hair with a matching roaming beard and dressed in an oversized dark suit and black tie. However, by 1994, he often wore socks and shoes.

From atop the stairs of the Town Hall building, Healey avowed, "It is time for a real change in Rhode Island. I offer that real change."[11] He continued, "As I look about Rhode Island, I see high levels of unemployment, slow economic development, an educational system in need of repair, and governmental waste and corruption. It is time we Rhode Islanders say, 'I've stood all I can stand and I can't stand anymore.'"[12] Healey assured those gathered that he would run a "...a no-frills, all-thrills campaign." Further, he assured, "I have no political ties. A vote for Healey is asking to allow yourself to determine your destiny."[13]

Although Healey held onto some anger over the media slights from his 1986 run for governor, he expressed pride over securing almost 6,000 votes in his first statewide candidacy.[14] In 1994, once again he felt ready to challenge the system. Directing what some ascertained as his disappointing prior run for governor, the 32-year-old former School Committee Chair explained, "We had limited campaign funds and had no concept of running a campaign. This time around, we're a little more experienced."[15]

Also, this time around, Healey had rallied up a larger team of working campaigners. He, Claire, and a network of friends and followers put in 10-hour days addressing, stuffing, and licking envelopes, running off campaign materials, and expanding contacts.[16] Sometimes people they thought would come forward to support the campaign did not carry through.[17] But other individuals that Bob did not expect to help, did offer assistance. Some of the new volunteers had met Bob through his law practice or remembered him from his earlier campaigns. From either origination, Healey had impressed them so profoundly that they decided to support his run for office in 1994.[18] In all, Healey's second governor campaign attracted a more expansive staff than his first run for the same position.[19]

In addition to benefiting from past campaign experience and a larger political network, in 1994 Healey hoped to catch the tailwinds of Ross Perot's 1992 impressive third-party presidential run against George Bush and Bill Clinton.[20] Perot's challenge had gained significant national attention. Had he not removed himself from the race only to rejoin shortly afterwards,[21] and not chosen former Navy Vice-Admiral James Stockdale as his vice president running mate,[22] Perot could have taken his challenge to the two-party system to even greater heights. Perhaps to remind Rhode Islanders of such possibilities, Healey proclaimed, "A strong third party is good for Rhode Island. The Cool Moose Party is just that party…"[23]

In a four-page campaign flier mailed to 57,100 voters, Healey explained his position on several key issues. In the coming weeks, he took every opportunity to augment those stances. Regarding the ongoing debate over abortion, Healey offered, "We believe that people, not government, should make personal decisions." Regarding crime, he held that, "Building jails only to fill them with small-time offenders is not the solution to the current crime explosion." Healey specified that only "egregious offenders" should be incarcerated. While not offering a personal stance on gambling, the Cool Moose Party supported "allowing people to control their own lives." And on education, once again Healey argued that the General Assembly should oversee the bigger ticket aspects of a town's education, including the negotiations for two-year statewide teacher contracts.[24]

The most important issue of Healey's campaign remained the people's empowerment. To that end, he promoted voter initiative as the cornerstone of his political movement. He emphasized, "We believe that there must be an amendment to the Rhode Island Constitution to allow the voters of this state the opportunity to create laws."[25] And he wasted no time lashing out at politicians who opposed him on this front. Healey charged that such candidates wanted to "override" the people's right to make decisions for themselves.[26]

Healey described the Cool Moose Party as a bastion of libertarian ideas.[27] And this rang true, but not to the extent his comments suggested. He differed with pure libertarians on some issues and agreed to certain extents on others. Healey saw more of a role for government to play in rectifying society than did libertarians.[28]

Acknowledging that his political bid for governor remained a long shot, Healey said that he hoped to get enough votes to secure the Cool Moose Party major party status. That way, he reasoned, the party could gain better funding and a more prominent placing on the election ballot the next time he or another party candidate took on the established Democratic and Republican Parties' candidates.[29] To attain major party status, the Cool Moose Party would need to secure at least five percent of the Rhode Island votes cast for governor.

In March 1994, the governor's race heated up ahead of schedule, thanks to spirited challenges in both major parties. The contenders read like a list of who's who in Rhode Island. In the Democratic Party primary, Rhode Island State Senator Myrth York challenged Governor Bruce Sundlun. If York won the general election, she would become Rhode Island's first female governor. On the Republican side, Lincoln Almond, a former United States attorney, ran against Congressman Ron Machtley.

With the early political season matchups forged, Providence College, the Journal Bulletin, and the Greater Providence Chamber of Commerce invited all the candidates for governor to a Business Expo forum moderated by the Journal's financial editor, Peter Phipps. Well, all, that is, accept for Robert Healey. The debate organizers had not invited Healey to participate in the high-profile debate because he did not belong to a major party with a primary. Nevertheless, the Cool Moose candidate vowed to make an appearance.

During the debate, the two Democratic candidates and the two Republican candidates sparred in energetic fashion over Congressman Machtley's promise to not raise state taxes if elected governor. Candidate Robert J. Healey Jr. stood in the rear of the forum distributing Cool Moose Party literature. Of the exclusion this time around, Healey quipped, "I hate having to feel like a skunk at a lawn party, but if that is what I must do to get the opportunity to get my positions out to the people of Rhode Island, that is what I must do."[30]

Soon after the Business Expo Debate, Healey did participate in a candidate's forum organized by environmentalists. Governor Sundlun's firing of the Department of Environmental Management's (DEM) director, Louise Durfee, had upset the forum's organizers. At the forum, Sundlun offered no apologies and accused Myrth York, Congressman Ron Machtley, Lincoln Almond, and Robert Healey Jr.

of not taking a clear stand on legislation that, if passed, would weaken regulations that safeguarded wetlands.[31] The ensuing back-and-forth finger-pointing focused mainly on DEM's budgeting and fees. When the discussion turned to possible beach and park closings, Healey asserted, "I think the beaches and parks should be open, and that issue should not even be a question for the people of the state of Rhode Island."[32]

Healey's comments at the environment forum did not capture major headlines. Frankly, his commentary gained little notice of any kind. Still the Cool Moose Party did find reason to celebrate. The DEM invite marked the first time that he secured a seat at the power brokers' table. There, he could separate himself out from the rank-and-file candidates and expound on key issues that mattered most to Rhode Islander voters. The increased exposure, minimal though it remained, resulted in a notable improvement over Healey's earlier anemic bid for governor. Even during the early going, 1994 already looked better than 1986 for the Cool Moose Party founder.

Two April 1994 decisions, both emanating from an outside source, potentially increased Healey's exposure further—one in the short run, the other potentially in the foreseeable future. Barbara M. Leonard, Rhode Island's Secretary of State, announced two procedural changes for candidate placement on the voting ballot. A *first* lottery would decide the candidates' location on the ballot, rather than their last names. Of this change, Leonard explained, "An accident of birth won't place you on the ballot . . .We decided a lottery is fairer to all."[33] Though Healey supported the lottery approach, in the short term this change impacted him little. The new rule only applied to those parties that had garnered at least five percent of the vote in the last election. As such, immediately the change only affected the Democrats and Republicans. This change heightened the need for Healey to capture five percent of the vote in 1994.

For now, a second lottery announcement mattered far more to Healey. That lottery would determine the placement of all other parties on the ballot.[34] In addition, the name of each candidate's political party would appear on the ballot. Prior practice listed third-party candidates as "Independent." As a result, third-party candidates did not stand out from one another. Further, the rule inferred a lower standing to the candidates of the specified Democratic and Republican Parties. Now Robert J. Healey Jr. would appear on the ballot as The Cool Moose Party candidate.

Though the Cool Moose Party welcomed the ballot reforms for the potential increased exposure they provided third parties, organizations continued to exclude independent gubernatorial candidates from debates. One particular exclusion disturbed Healey more deeply than other debate snubs. In May 1994, the Rhode Island Association of School Committees and the Rhode Island Association of School Administrators did not invite Healey to participate in their forum. As a past member of the Association of School Committees when he served as the Warren School Committee Chair for four years, Healey found the slight most troubling. He commented about the circumstance, "I can only assume that they are afraid to listen to my ideas concerning education. I can think of nothing more repulsive in education than its leaders practicing censorship."[35] Both associations explained that they didn't invite Healey to their Newport Marriott debate because he did not face a primary challenger.[36] Tim Duffy, executive director of the Rhode Island Association of School Committees, said he expected the association would have another debate after the primary elections to which "all qualified candidates" would be invited.[37] "Qualified" went undefined. Duffy did not guarantee Healey's participation in the potential fall debate.

While Healey did not garner any new debate invites, he continued to deliver statements that sounded as if they had been launched during the throes of a debate. Addressing campaign funding, The Cool Moose Party candidate for governor charged, "If we are ever to get government free from outside influences, we must drastically alter the way we finance political campaigns."[38] Similar to his pronouncements made when he served as the Warren School Committee Chair, Healey cajoled potential voters, "People can cry for reform, but unless they take actions designed to make reform a reality, there will be little reform. It is that simple." Healey added, "We all talk about reform, but we also allow politicians to get elected by being the kept servants of special interests that provide campaign funds."[39] The truth of the matter, Healey stressed, is that "to spend a million plus on a gubernatorial campaign requires exhaustive fundraising. Therein lies the evil inherent to the system. If candidates were to voluntarily limit their spending, and that limitation was enforced by voters who rejected candidates who overspend, then there would be real reform in that the candidates would not be forced to prostitute themselves to the special interests."[40] On this front, Healey tried to lead by example. He pledged to limit his campaign spending to $139,800, half the salary he would receive over four years as governor, if elected.

Healey did not limit his criticism of big money campaigns to other politicians. He also lashed out against the media for what he saw as their self-serving part in maintaining a desperately flawed election process. Healey felt that the status-quo excluded rank and file Rhode Islanders from pursuing state and national offices. Of the media's part in advancing well-financed political campaigns, Healey charged, "Television, radio, and newspapers all benefit from campaign advertising revenues and, therefore, are quite willing to turn a deaf ear and a blind eye to the situation." Healey continued, "These vested media interests keep real reform efforts on the sidelines by giving the issue, and the candidates discussing this issue of true campaign financing reform, short shrift. In short, reforming campaign spending does not benefit the bottom line of the Fourth Estate [media outlets]."[41]

Healey charged further that the Fourth Estate protects its "stake in the political game…killing the messengers of reform through lack of coverage."[42] As such, Healey argued that the media "cheapens itself in the same way politicians do in accepting campaign financing from dubious sources in the name of good government."[43]

While one might question why a third-party candidate intent on getting their word out would take on the very institution that could help spread their message, the Cool Moose candidate fired off his accusations anyway. Healey might have figured he had nothing to lose. And he didn't. The media's treatment of his past and present campaigns included no debate invites, almost no television coverage, and buried references in long articles that focused overwhelmingly on Democratic and Republican candidates. If Healey wanted Rhode Islanders to learn about his message, then he would need to promote his cause and make his own headlines.

Most of the time the press only referenced Bob Healey's comments when he responded to another candidate's actions. Such was the case in June 1994 when Governor Sundlun's remarks drew critical attention. In an interview with *The Providence Journal*, Sundlun offered no opinion about Sara M. Quinn (executive director of the state Ethics Commission) stepping down from her position to run for attorney general. However, Sundlun did share some explicit thoughts about her physical appearance. He described Quinn as a "small woman with a relatively good figure."[44] The Governor later explained, "I gave a description of her that I might give if I was in a witness stand in court as to what she looked like." When initially questioned about his remark of Quinn, the governor did not apologize for the comment because, he said, "...there was no reason to apologize..."[45] And after all, he had commented on her appearance in somewhat flattering terms. Regardless, just about everyone else disagreed. While Quinn said the governor need not apologize to her, she did clarify, "I've already told the governor that I think it would have been better if he had focused on my achievements professionally as a woman instead of focusing on my physical appearance."[46] Others expressed a more alarming reception to the governor's statement. State Senator Myrth York charged, "Instead of commenting on the substance of Quinn's tenure at the Ethics Commission, the governor chose to talk about what she looked like. This is demeaning to women, inappropriate, and offensive."[47] Lincoln C. Almond referenced Quinn's comments as "sexist" and as demonstrating a "tremendous disregard for women."[48] Per usual, the *Journal* reported Bob Healey's take on Sundlun's comments in the last lines of the article. But Healey made the most of the placement. Healey stated, "The comment reeks of sexual inequality."[49] And then the Cool Moose candidate for governor added some color, off or otherwise, to his statement: "Does the governor, when asked about [Attorney General] Jeff Pine, say 'nice buns'?" Healey questioned further, "Does he realize that [Quinn] is running for attorney general and not Miss Rhode Island?"[50]

While Bob Healey continually tried to steer *The Providence Journal's* attention toward his campaign, press clips continued to quote Healey just as a means of covering another candidate. For instance, in one June 14, 1994 article, the *Journal* ran the headline, *Cool Moose Party candidate supports Mayer and reform.* Though that article referenced Healey throughout the piece, the main focus remained Mayer's performance, not Healey's. In the article, the Cool Moose candidate spoke in glowing terms of the Republican candidate for general treasurer; "Good government is open government. No one party or person has a monopoly on good government. That being said, I find that I must once again speak out in support of General Treasurer (Nancy) Mayer's efforts to bring to the public the operation of the pension system."[51] In response to the notion that the Republican treasurer's comments amounted to political grandstanding, Healey responded, "Politically, she doesn't need to do that. She could, were she so inclined, rest on her laurels. She chooses not to, and as a Rhode Islander and taxpayer, I applaud her."[52] Healey did manage to expand his commentary beyond support for Mayer's candidacy. He explained that "Bringing government into the light of day is often very threatening, especially for those seeking to keep matters tightly wrapped."[53] Of those matters, Healey offered, "There is politics being played in the matter of the Retirement Board. Unfortunately, it is the traditional defense political strategy of keeping the matter from the public's inspection. Reform is overdue."[54]

Healey's increased references in newspapers during the summer of 1994 did not attract coveted invitations to debate the other candidates before Rhode Islander voters. The Rhode Island Association of Realtors did invite five other candidates for governor to a debate at the Johnson & Wales Airport Hotel. Those five candidates (Brue Sundlun, Myrth York, Louise Durfee, Lincoln C. Almond, and Ron Machtley) made their pitches and answered questions from Jim Taricani (Channel 10), who moderated the debate. *The Providence Journal* reported of that debate, "Noticeably absent was Robert J. Healey Jr., a perennial political gadfly who is making his second run for governor as the Cool Moose candidate." The *Journal* explained that Tom Mulhearn, executive vice president of the association, had not invited Healey because he did not face a primary.[55] Healey did not accept Mulhearn's explanation and lashed out, "Once again I have been silenced." Healey added later in a statement, "While I can understand that having too many rings on stage would make too many Realtors' lips sore by the end of the day, I must object to this failure on their part to invite all candidates contending for the office."[56]

The Providence Journal referenced the Rhode Island Association of Realtors debate as "low-key."[57] Rarely would a source describe a debate with Bob Healey participating in such terms. Apparently, the only debate line to produce an animated response came from Sundlun acknowledging Machtley's "great speech" that, according to the governor, failed to answer the original question. When Machtley tried to continue, Sundlun told Machtley "to shut up for a minute" so that he could offer a response. Machtley fired back, "Watch out or we'll start talking about animal rights."[58] The audience responded in loud laughter, apparently recalling the prior year when Sundlun shot three raccoons from his deck to protect fox kits set up on his Newport residence.[59]

From August through October of 1994, *The Providence Journal* covered Healey's positions on key issues in a series called, "Campaign Briefs." While these short pieces rarely featured Healey in the main headline, the *Journal* referenced his views in the articles often. In an August

Healey campaigns with Claire Boyes for votes during the 1994 governor's race. (Photo courtesy of Brian Fortin)

1994 brief, Healey called out the Republican candidate, Representative Ronald Machtley, for "deliberately attempting to confuse the electorate by making it appear that he's proposing widespread tax relief [related to Social Security taxation] while in reality the policy Machtley is promoting is little more than relief for the upper middle class and above."[60] Healey referenced Machtley's distortion as "deliberate and disgusting" because it would not help pensioners who received less than $25,000 a year. Healey claimed, "Machtley understands this so-called tax break of his will not help the subsistence Social Security pensioner."[61]

In August, Healey struck at Machtley again. This time he took aim at Machtley's support of a crime bill, calling it "a costly approach to fighting crime."[62] In that same *Providence Journal* campaign brief, Healey reiterated his view on Political Action Committee (PAC) money, stating, "I have not taken any PAC money, nor do I intend to do so."[63] In another related article, Healey denounced the rules governing the state's matching-fund program. Before securing the offered money, the candidate had to raise $150,000 on their own.[64] Healey said that the practice favored already well-financed campaigns, while independent candidates in need of funds received no extra money. Healey lamented, "I would have to raise more than I have pledged to spend so that I could get more money to spend."[65]

In another *Journal* Campaign Brief, Healey let it be known that he opposed the November 8 ballot question that proposed a constitutional amendment to reduce the size of the legislature and increase legislative pay from $300 to an initial $10,000 annually, with built in cost-of-living increases. Healey called the idea a "threat to Democracy." Healey added, "smaller legislatures are far more dangerous in that they can be easily ruled by lobbying groups," and claimed the pay increase would amount to "little more than a contribution to keep incumbents in office."[66]

In early September 1994, Healey spoke out on a proposed gambling site bill, stating that if casino gambling came to Rhode Island, he favored placement of such a facility in a high tourist area, such as Newport. This placement capitalized more on out-of-state gamblers.[67] Of a proposed West Greenwich casino site, Healey said that "I may be wrong but it seems to me there is really about as much interest in the placement of a casino in West Greenwich as there is for the building of a toxic waste facility in Barrington."[68] He added, "...private interests would open a Providence casino after gaining voter support for a gambling facility".[69]

Bob Healey called for less government involvement in economic development, preferring instead a climate in which business can flourish. Healey explained about his position, "While there is a useful aspect to some government participation, the less involvement the better. We do not need to make business financing a new cabinet-level government department. If we create a thriving business climate, business will locate and prosper."[70]

Though Healey's views were disseminated by *Providence Journal's* Campaign Briefs, that exposure did not cause an uptick in his poll numbers. Those polls reported that Lincoln Almond, who had defeated Ron Machtley in the Republican primaries, found himself tied with Myrth York, who had defeated Bruce Sundlun and Louise Durfee in the Democratic primary. A Brown University poll had the two frontrunners at 38 and 37 percent respectively. According to the same poll, Bob Healey had captured 4 percent of the electorate's support. Twenty-one percent remained undecided.[71]

The recent poll results encouraged the media's continued focus on Almond and York. In one of those news stories, Almond accused York of "trying to run away from her (legislative) record...to posture herself as a moderate."[72] In late September, York had acknowledged in an interview that an earlier welfare bill she had co-sponsored proved unaffordable. In the interview, she communicated her intention to jumpstart dialogue on the subject issue. Almond quickly pounced on his opponent's alleged about face: "This sudden turnaround in position must come as a shock to the people that York has prided herself on trying to help. Could it be that she is simply now trying to appear more centrist in her views in order to get elected?" Almond went on, "Myrth needs to tell the people of Rhode Island where she honestly stands on these issues and where the money to pay for her proposals would come from."[73] Healey piled on, questioning York aggressively: "Which one is it? Old York or new York?...Is the change truly motivated by a newfound belief in fiscal responsibility or in the newfound realization that pie-in-the-sky welfare programs make good campaign strategy as a candidate for the legislature but not the office of governor?" Healey added, "My concern is that, after the campaign, will the position again evolve?"[74]

Unfortunately for Healey, he could only attack York in the papers, not in the upcoming televised debates. Adding insult to injury, Channel 10 had disinvited Healey to their scheduled October debate. The Cool Moose candidate had already accepted an April 6 invite to the debate from Channel 10's executive producer, Matt Ellis, but according to News Director Ted Conova, that invitation had been sent to "cover all the bases."[75] Since Healey failed to garner 5 percent support in the latest poll, Channel 10 referenced its standing policy to exclude candidates with poll numbers under that threshold from participating in their debates. Healey protested the rescinded invitation, arguing that his 4 percent constituency remained relevant given that only a point or two separated York and Almond. However, Channel 12 did not budge. To make matters worse, Channel 6 also prohibited Healey from participating in their upcoming debate.

In mid-October, Bob Healey did participate in a debate on WHJJ radio, moderated by the former-attorney-general-turned-talk-show-host, Arlene Violet.[76] Healey liked the radio station's rough-and-tumble debate format. On Violet's show, candidates could ask questions of one another. Healey thought a gloves-off debate approach allowed candidates to get to the core of issues far more than the common televised packaged format, whereby polished candidates responded with prepared statements to predictable questions.[77] Interestingly, when *The Providence Journal* reported on the radio debate in their October 13, 1994 edition, they reported only Almond and York in their article's title, referenced only exchanges between Almond and York, and made just one insignificant mention of Healey. For the benefit of those who hadn't listened to the radio debate, the *Journal's* report clarified that the debate had indeed "...included Cool Moose Party candidate Robert J. Healey Jr."[78] The paper did not include a single utterance of the Cool Moose Party nominee. Had Bob remained uncharacteristically silent during the entire debate?

Bob Healey took measures to assure others heard him during the campaign. Pledging to attend at least one council meeting in each community,[79] he intended his message to rattle the cages of complacency. He communicated that voting wasn't enough. People needed to take back their government. And he pulled no punches in explaining his reasoning. "Look at Myrth York. She has surrounded herself with union people. Look at Lincoln Almond. He's surrounded with Old Boy Republicans. That's change?"[80] Healey stressed further, "... if people are desirous of change, the only way to have that change materialize is to vote for someone that has not relied on the same old system to get elected...a capable person acting without the political baggage."[81] Healey warned against passive approaches: "If you want change, you've got to get change."[82] And in case he wasn't clear enough, he added, "The other candidates rely on their party machines. I'll rely on the people to pressure their legislators. That is the only way I could govern."[83]

In addition to speaking out against what he saw as party machine candidates, Healey drew attention to out-of-the-box solutions to persistent problems. For instance, Healey proposed a "one-stop shopping" system for citizens to access government services. Healey explained that the state could set up satellite offices using the "employees, computers, and telephones" already at work for the state. He offered, "The satellite concept can be used to make government operate more effectively for the people it must serve. It is time that we move into the technological future."[84] In addition to these space-age themed government service systems, Healey called for increased voter initiative and a more vigorous mindset to recall government officials.

Regarding business issues, Healey did not favor over-regulation. In addition, he supported developing Quonset Point as an international trade port and funding of education and training grants for job creation to keep young people in Rhode Island. However, he opposed the use of large amounts of taxpayer money for Providence Place. Sounding a bit like President Calvin Coolidge in 1924,[85] Healey coined the phrase, "Business should do business, not government."[86]

But Healey was no Coolidge. Calvin Coolidge campaigned little, took daily long naps, promoted the status quo,[87] and earned the nickname, Silent Cal. Bob Healey showed up where invited and not invited, raced tirelessly around the state, and offered colorful commentaries that highlighted his change agent message. Different from his 1986 run for governor, Healey issued daily news releases, wrote substantial reports on major issues, and made himself visible to Rhode Islanders. As in the past, he preferred to deliver his message from old vehicles. In this election, he drove around in a nine-year-old Chevrolet. At other times, he toured the state in the "Cool Moose Transit," a refurbished white minibus with his namesake painted boldly on the side.[88] The "Moose Mobile" came equipped with two helium tanks on board for blowing up campaign balloons at short notice.[89]

Whether calling out from the driver's seat of the Cool Moose Transit, the front seat of a 1982 Chevrolet, or pontificating while campaigning on foot, Healey continued to hammer away at his opponents. And in at least one instance, his two leading opponents made doing so easy. In October, Myrth York called out Lincoln Almond for accepting campaign contributions from Department of Transportation state contractors, and then admitted she had sought and collected funds from the same organizations for her campaign. The reporting presented as red meat to the Cool Moose candidate, who did not hesitate to take advantage of the offering. Healey decried against the actions of both and the hypocrisy of one. Healey bemoaned, "If campaign contributions came without strings on the part of those connected with business of the state, and Almond should return it, then why should York keep it? Better yet, why should the public tolerate it? If there is no influence from such contributions, then what's the fuss about? If there is reason to fuss, then why should any candidate accept such contributions?" Healey clarified, "The point is, campaign contributions from those with state business contact(s) are strands of invisible filament that serve to influence...If these strings were visible, the people would realize the puppet status of these candidates."[90]

Unfortunately for Healey, and perhaps for all Rhode Islanders, he couldn't further his above point at the next governors' debate at the Providence Holiday Inn, sponsored by Common Cause, a citizen's advocacy group. They didn't invite him. Not only did the group snub Healey, they slighted him as well. Common Cause's director, Philip West, explained, "We had a very brief amount of time available, and he [Healey] in our view is not a serious contender." Healey fired back at the affront: "While it may be in Mr. West's interests to kiss up to the powers that be, and while it may be his philosophy to sell short to the political power brokers, I find the reasoning to be questionable. I have gotten involved and I am a legitimate candidate for the office." Further, Healey questioned, "Who is West to make the determinations for the people of Rhode Island?"[91]

Perhaps Bob Healey would have preferred that students at North Kingstown High School make all such determinations moving forward. Healey accepted an invitation to the North Kingstown High School's tenth bi-annual Candidates Day. He had appeared at the school's 1986 forum, but that setup allowed for little interaction between candidates seeking the same office. In 1990, the school's Candidates Day coordinator started to invite aspirants for the same office to appear together on the stage before the students. Under the guidance of student moderators, sponsoring students offered short introductory comments of each candidate. After their introduction, candidates offered prepared one-minute opening remarks. After each attendee finished their initial speeches, audience members could approach the stage to ask questions of the candidates. During the question-and-answer segment, each candidate had up to one minute to respond. Each session ran approximately 45 minutes.

Lincoln Almond and Myrth York declined North Kingstown High School's invitation to the October 26,1994 Candidates Day. Both candidates offered to send representatives. While normally not permitted, the coordinator acquiesced in the belief that allowing the two representatives to substitute for the actual nominee offered more benefit for the students than hearing from just one third-party governor candidate.

At the October 26, 1994 governor's session, each sponsoring student offered a 30-second introduction of their assigned candidate (or substitute). The student representatives stressed how much *their* candidate "cared" about the students at North Kingstown High School, and throughout Rhode Island. The respective candidates then made their opening comments, which affirmed the student's prior introduction. Four hundred students listened politely.

With open remarks concluded, the student moderator invited questions from the audience. A pregnant pause of about 20 seconds ensued. Finally, a male student, positioned in the back row of the auditorium, several seats off the stage left aisle, stood and began to make his way to the microphone. He approached the stage walking in a demonstrative fashion, his upper torso motioning quickly from right to left. The student audience emitted a humming sound that became more audible as the young man made his way down the aisle. The students seemed surprised by their peer's courage to come forward. Their daring schoolmate's facial expression seemed to communicate anger, or serious pursuit of a mission. He pressed his lips tightly together, bent his eyebrows inward toward his nose, and clenched his fists. He moved briskly to the front of the auditorium, perhaps to avoid thoughts of doubt or apprehension from entering his mind. When the student arrived at the microphone, which stood upright about six feet from the stage's center, he wasted no time in making his point.

Speaking loudly, the student inquired, "Yeah. Not for nothing, but if you guys cared—" He made a head gesture toward the two female representatives sitting to Healey's left. "—then how come they [Almond and York] ain't here?!" As soon as the young man finished delivering his question, he turned abruptly around from the stage and made his way to the back row. As he did, the student audience cheered and applauded.

During the boy's question, each well-dressed female governor candidate representative on stage sat upright, clasping their respective kneecaps, which they pressed together tightly. Both sported pageboy style hairdos and positioned their calves to the right of their knees. They had listened attentively to the boy before he had spun around and returned to his seat. When the student moderator asked for the candidates to respond, both representatives shared a nervous grin. Bob Healey, who had smiled during the delivery of the student's question, slouched in his seat.

One of the female representatives responded to the student's question first. It mattered little which representative spoke first or second, because their mannerisms and message looked and sounded very similar. Both representatives stepped gingerly, in an upward and downward motion, as they approached the microphone on stage. When they spoke, each apologized profusely for their candidate's absence, and assured the students that both Lincoln Almond and Myrth York had children of their own, loved children, wished they could have been here, and said they were "sorry, really sorry...Sorry."

Throughout both representatives' painfully awkward explanation and apology, Robert Healey grinned, continued to slouch, and pulled at his beard, at one point doing so while looking up to the auditorium ceiling. After the second representative finished her apology, Healey stalled, looked out to the mostly silent audience, stood up, pulled up his sagging pants, and then made his way slowly to the microphone in the middle of the stage. When he arrived at the microphone, he glanced back at his opponents' two representatives, looked out to the students, took a deep breath, grinned, and declared, "Well, it looks like I'm the only one who doesn't have to apologize. Because I'm here," Healey gestured backward, half-heartedly, and exclaimed "and they're not!"

The students erupted into thunderous applause and loud laughter, followed by hooting and hollering. After approximately 10 seconds, Healey continued, "But they should be here. Because if something really matters to you, you show up. That's why I'm here. You matter!"

Again, the students offered a roaring applause, this time standing up to do so. Soon after, the same students who moments earlier seemed glued to their seats, began approaching the microphone to ask questions. The students directed almost every question toward Bob Healey specifically, the politician turned rock star, for the time being. For the next 20-plus minutes he owned his audience. Every Healey response to a student's question, issue-oriented or otherwise, aroused applause from adoring students. He owned the day.

When the North Kingstown High School students voted in a mock school-wide election soon after the forum, the results drew the attention of *The Providence Journal*. The state's paper reported, "If the high school's 20th annual [tenth bi-annual] mock election is a harbinger of what will happen at the polls statewide next month,

Rhode Island has a few surprises in store. Cool Moose Party candidate Robert J. Healey Jr. would become governor and the Moose mobile he motors around in would become as recognizable as former Gov. Edward DiPrete's mobile home."[92] Robert Healey secured over twice the number of votes casted for Myrth York, and almost four times higher than those tallied for Lincoln Almond.

Perhaps needless to say, North Kingstown High School's numbers did not match up well with a Channel 12 poll reported shortly after the student vote. In that poll, Healey attracted only three percent of the poll takers, down two percentage points from another recent poll. Almond showed a commanding lead within a week of Election Day.[93]

Healey, undeterred by his candidacy's poor prognosis, continued the fight, focused on the November election. And late October did bring some good news for his campaign. *Get Out The Vote of Rhode Island*, an organization intent on encouraging the minority vote, invited the three governor candidates to a forum at the Community College of Rhode Island campus on Hilton Street. However, the biggest news to come out of the event focused on Lincoln Almond, a debate no-show. Joseph Fowlkes, President of the Providence branch of the NAACP, did not mince words about Almond's non-participation. "We're trying to get the candidates to understand that there are important issues to this community...It's sad and greatly disappointing that Lincoln Almond didn't see fit to come."[94] Ed Morabito, Almond's campaign manager, said that their campaign now tried to limit the frontrunner's appearances because he had partaken in so many events already and they had consumed a tremendous amount of his time. Also, Morabito said that the Almond campaign had notified Fowlkes of their decision weeks earlier, a claim refuted by Fowlkes who called Almond's decision "hugely irresponsible" and "arrogant."[95]

At the *Get Out The Vote of Rhode Island* forum, York emphasized that many people are cut out of the political process and the related economic opportunities. She spoke to her three-part welfare overhaul proposal that addressed many issues she thought important to the assembled crowd of approximately 50 people. Healey focused his comments on the need to create enough well-paying jobs before offering meaningful welfare system reform. Healey wanted to make sure that the government would not cut off the co-pay system for housing and other needs prematurely when a welfare recipient first started to make more money.[96] All in all, the forum attracted limited attention.

Soon afterward, Channel 10's instant poll in November concluded two surprises. First, the poll reported that Myrth York now held onto a one-point lead over Lincoln Almond. Second, Robert Healey's numbers had jumped to 9 percent. If these two findings held, Myrth York would be the state's first female governor and Robert Healey's Cool Moose Party would become a recognized official political party in Rhode Island. As such, an upcoming Channel 10 debate took on added importance. The station invited Bob Healey to participate.

The final televised debate featured candidates entering the last round of what had seemed like an all-out 15-round slugfest. While Almond and York fired most the jabs and haymakers, Healey mixed it up as well. At one point, when the two frontrunners tried to determine who qualified as the greatest political insider, Healey contended, "I find this so interesting that we talk about insiders and outsiders, and we have inside outsiders here. We're looking at people who are coming from a political party system...(that) produces the people that are involved in these types of administrations over and over again, whether it's an old-boy network or the special interest groups."[97]

Bob's comments seemingly stung Almond, who retorted toward his Cool Moose Party rival, "You know, Bob, it's easy to say these things. But you know you've been in public life only for a couple of years on a school committee. Senator York's got less than four years. I've been around for 30-on years. Tell me a crony I've ever appointed...a scandal that has ever been a part of my life?"[98] Not only had Healey landed a shot against one of the frontrunners, but the fact that Almond mentioned Healey by name suggested that the Cool Moose candidate had taken on stature. Finally, Healey mattered, at least a little.

News panelist Dyana Koelsch asked the candidates what they would do if the police told them beforehand that a planned drug raid might involve their children, and that drug raid could turn ugly. Almond said, "They shouldn't tell the governor if he's got a personal involvement...That would be my instructions to them...I would immediately recuse myself from all decision-making, confer with the attorney general...tell him to handle it, and nothing else would happen."[99] York offered to the same question, "As a parent, I would be hard pressed to believe I wouldn't want to do what I thought was immediately best for my son and, my inclination is, I would tell him and try to encourage him to turn himself in."[100] Healey, the only candidate for governor with no children, and unmarried, responded, "Justice is blind, and we have to just apply that justice as we see fit, and go completely straight forward without getting involved in the process whatsoever."[101]

After the last debate, the press resumed their Almond-York focus. But with the last hours of the 1994 campaign season dwindling down, the candidates aired nothing of a breaking news classification. Finally, with the all the debates, campaign spending, and polling ended, the people could now cast their vote. And when they did, the electorate chose Lincoln Almond as governor. Gaining 47 percent of the vote to Myrth York's 44 percent, the contest proved close, but not a nail-biter. Robert J. Healey Jr. took 9 percent of the vote,[102] and won in his hometown. 32,822 Rhode Islanders had casted a vote for Warren's favorite son.[103] And though they had finished third, the Cool Moose Party could claim significant gains. Healey's third party took on prominence and official status. The lawyer from Warren eyed his political future optimistically.

THE GOVERNOR'S RACE, 1998

The 1998 governor's race began in early 1995, at least for Robert Healey. He had to feel good. A marked improvement over his 1986 drubbing, Healey had drawn significant support during the 1994 race for governor. Not only had over 32,000 voters selected him to be Rhode Island's next governor, but his beloved Cool Moose Party took on legitimacy, gaining 9 percent of the vote, 4 percent more than was needed to gain official party status. Due to changes made to the ballot's organization during the last election, the Cool Moose Party qualified to end up in the coveted left-hand column of the ballot. Legitimacy and visibility summed up to rising optimism for the Cool Moose and his followers.

In preparation for the anticipated and welcomed political battles, The Cool Moose Party held its first convention in February, 1995. Seventy-five people gathered at the Community College of Rhode Island to plan the party's future. They elected Bob Healey as their first chairman. No one voted against him.[104] A Providence Journal reporter asked the new party chairman, "Where were the 32,000 voters who wanted Healey to be governor this year instead of Democrat Myrth York or Republican Lincoln Almond?"[105] Healey offered something short of an assuring response: "It's a Saturday, and it's a nice day, and there's no money to be made here. That's the long and short of it…But the people who I see here are dedicated to the task of reforming government."[106]

Though not able to boast teeming numbers, like other political conventions, the Cool Moose Party convention included fiery speeches and impassioned pleas. Interestingly, most of those speeches originated with other parties' members and leaders, not Cool Moosers. These other parties lacked the official status that the Cool Moose Party now held. However, they may have eclipsed them in spirit. Joseph Devine, the Reform 92 candidate for governor, proclaimed, "If you're going to get freedom, if you're going to get what our forefathers wanted us to have, you must stand up at times and fight for it."[107] Anthony Affigne, co-founder of the Green Party, delivered the most emotional speech of the day. Affigne offered, "Bob [Healey] and I do go back a long way. We share the experience of not being taken seriously by the political elites in Rhode Island, having some difficulties with the media, having some difficulties with election laws and the election system, but I think it would be fair to say that both the Cool Moose Party and the Green Party have come a long way since 1986." Affigne charged that Democrats had put themselves up "for sale" and that Republicans had committed to an agenda of the rich. Drawing parallels between the Cool Moose Party and the Green Party, Affigne recalled how certain parties had minimized his fellow Green Party members when they called attention to the overfishing of Georges Bank. "[We said] if we don't change the way we fish, the day will come when you will not be able to fish on Georges Bank. And the naysayers and the Democrats and the Republicans and the scientists and the think tanks said, 'Those people don't know what they're talking about. Those people are trying to scare you.'"[108] Affigne finished, "We have tremendous problems in Rhode Island that are not being addressed by the Democrats or the Republicans, and that's why we need independent political movements like yours and like ours."[109]

At their first convention, The Cool Moosers, while in low numbers, presented themselves as strong willed and independent thinkers. That day, they put forward the lofty goal of coming to a consensus on a proposed 19-page platform. However, hours in, they had advanced through only seven pages. At the end of the day, they adopted a draft document, leaving the approval of a final version for the 1996 convention.[110]

While remaining a work in progress, the Cool Moose Party platform favored:

- Universal healthcare
- Work—not welfare—for the able-bodied
- Government neutrality on abortion
- Federally regulated "Indian" gambling
- Gay rights
- Affirmative action (with clear goals and an expiration date)
- Election of judges every 10 years (except Supreme Court justices)

- Shifting police attention from victimless crimes to the pursuit of violent criminals
- Abolishment of the parole system and adopting truth in sentencing.
- State legislature were to meet at night (so more working people could bear witness or run for office)
- Phasing out of taxpayer funding for the arts and historical preservation
- Support for the right to die[111]

Immediately following the convention, the Cool Moose chairman opted not to declare himself a candidate for governor in 1998, but clearly ventured to keep himself in the public's eye. In March 1995, Robert J. Healey Jr. marched near the front of the St. Patrick's Day parade. He reflected of that experience, "The recognition factor is pretty high from a political standpoint." Besides, he added, "St. Patrick's Day is always fun, and I'm a good Irishman."[112]

The good Irishman doubled as a fighting Irishman. In April 1995, Healey ridiculed *The Providence Journal's* Francis Mancini for an apparent oversight in one of his articles. In his letter to the editor, the 1994 Cool Moose Party candidate for Rhode Island Governor wrote, "I was somewhat taken aback to find that Francis Mancini had only two choices for Rhode Island governor in the last election. Did I miss something? Was this but a Freudian slip, wishful thinking, revisionary history, or just typical *Journal* editorial writer treatment of third-party candidates?"[113]

Though increasingly capable of making his own headlines, in May 1995, Healey again found himself in the paper, partially via the efforts of others. For example, the Rhode Island General Assembly voted 47 to 28 against legislation designed to include Cool Moose Party representation on local canvassing boards.[114] Representative Charles T. Knowles, a Democrat from Narragansett, argued that since the completion of the 1994 governor's race, the Cool Moose Party deserved to be represented on canvassing boards. However, other representatives pointed out that doing so would be a challenge for the local canvassers who would need to locate registered Cool Moose voters willing to serve on the boards.[115] The General Assembly vote incensed an East Providence resident and Cool Moose enthusiast so much that she wrote to *The Providence Journal*:

> *"The General Assembly has rejected, 47 to 28, legislation that would have allowed the Cool Moose Party on local canvassing boards. In doing so, the Assembly denies the wishes of more than 9 percent of voters in the last gubernatorial election, who struck a blow against politics as usual in Rhode Island by making the Cool Moose Party a legitimate third party.*
>
> *Not surprisingly, Democrats and Republicans are doing what they can to avoid sharing power. Such dirty pool is exactly what we voted against last November, and I find it very interesting that the Journal did not consider this newsworthy.*
>
> *Cool Moose Party Chairman Robert J. Healey Jr. has vowed to challenge this disgrace in court. It is, likewise, time for each one of those who supported the Cool Moose Party last November to contact their legislator and demand to know why it has been denied the chance for reform we earned in that election."*[116]

In May 1995, North Kingstown High School seniors invited Bob Healey to speak at their graduation. Healey gladly accepted. After his performance at the school's 1994 Candidates Day, Bob Healey had taken on a celebrity standing among the graduating seniors, almost all of whom would be able to vote in the next election.

Upon his return to the high school, the Cool Moose Party candidate received a "hero's welcome."[117] Healey's message resonated well with the over 1,400 celebrants present, which included 278 North Kingstown High School graduates. Healey encouraged the graduates to "Be yourself," the first of his 10 lessons for living. "If you're not your-self," he stressed, "you're only acting in front of others."[118] He added, "weird alternatives are okay, too."[119] In the end, he encouraged all in attendance to live, "That's it. Just live."[120]

In addition to the students at the high school graduation, Bob Healey impressed two prominent North Kingstown adult citizens, Bee Given (owner of the Wickford village Green Ink store) and her husband, Curtis Given (chair of the North Kingstown Republican party). After the graduation, Curtis Given asked Robert Craven, a Democrat on the town council and an old law school friend of Bob Healey, "You know Bob, don't you?"

Craven replied, "Yeah. We went to law school together."

Given then requested of Craven, "Could you come over the house with Bob Healey to have a little drink of wine or something?"

Craven responded, "Sure."

When Rob mentioned the invite to Bob, Healey replied, "Yeah, okay. If you want me to go, I'll go."

Craven thought Healey accepted the invitation as a way of secur-ing an audience who might listen to his political vision.[121]

Bee and Curtis Given, widely regarded as very "nice people,"[122] espoused a conservative political slant. Their attire and mannerisms came across to most as conservative, too. When Healey entered the Curtis residence, it seemed as if he had stepped back in time. The house, meticulously appointed, free of dust, and handsomely furnished, looked like a standard setting for a 1950s television show. Shortly after arriving at the Curtises' residence, Craven got the sense that his friends had invited Healey to entertain other guests as a "circus act."[123]

A few minutes later, when the Curtises went into their kitchen, Bob Healey said to Craven, "I feel like this is *Leave it to Beaver* and they're Ward and June..."

Craven mused, "Well, I'm Eddie Haskell. Who are you?"

Healey replied, "I'm not in the show yet."[124]

Shortly afterward, Bob Healey initiated a polite exit.

In November 1995, Healey grabbed headlines by pressing Claire L. Boyes to become the first Cool Moose candidate to win a seat on the Barrington Board of Canvassers.[125] However, because Healey had not registered the Cool Moose Party as a major party in Barrington, some felt Boyes could not take up a seat on the Board of Canvassers. Healey disagreed. He clarified that because state law supersedes local law, the Cool Moose Party candidates could be considered for the vacancy.[126] Healey widened his argument, pointing out, "I believe there should be an equal opportunity, and now they can't say I didn't know about the openings…The main thing here is the opportunity to appoint the first Cool Moose person to a state or local board." State Representative Mark Heffner remarked in agreement, "I think Barrington should send a message to the rest of the state that the Cool Moose Party, which plays by the rules and got itself recognized as a legitimate party, should be embraced by the political structure."[127] Claire Boyes went on to become the Cool Moose Party's first officer on the Board of Canvassers.

With an ambitious eye to the 1996 election, in November, 1995, Robert Healey announced, "The Cool Moose Party has set its sights on challenging every seat in the Assembly in 1996. It is our position that no seat go unopposed and that people deserve choice."[128] Others took up the Cool Moose mantra as well. Dark horse candidate Timothy Rossanno, who took 1 percent of the vote in his 1994 bid to become mayor of Warwick, eyed again the prize in 1996, this time under the Cool Moose Party. And why wouldn't he? Rossanno had proven himself even thriftier than Bob Healey. In 1994, Rossanno spent a dime on his campaign and secured 1 percent of the vote.[129] Despite the expanded expense account this time around (Rossanno suggested he might spend $1,000), Republican Mayor Lincoln D. Chafee showed no signs of worry. Concerned or not, Chaffee's Cool Moose opponent went on the attack. "I'm running to inform the people of better ways of doing business in the city." Rossanno clarified, "There's no deadlines on contracts. It takes a year and a half to do 32 yards of road…We're getting raped for lousy roads."[130] Of his reasons for embracing the Cool Moose Party, Rossanno offered, "We need to let go of manufacturing and embrace the market trend in service companies and in the tourism industry. That's the only way I can see to have the city and state pull itself out of this economic chaos."[131] His remarks aligned well with the Cool Moose Party chair.

The Cool Moose Party welcomed willing candidates and the brotherhood of other parties, which amounted exclusively and expectedly to the fledging and unofficial variety. At one point in 1996, the Green and Reform Parties (tied to former presidential candidate Ross Perot) joined forces with the Cool Moose Party to promote voter initiative, campaign finance reform, and election reform. As the Green Party's Tim McKee said of the trio, "We've been kind of cooperating for a while, but this is a little more public demonstration of it."[132] While all three parties intended to have candidates in the upcoming election, the Cool Moose Party qualified as the only "major party." However, the Cool Moose Party's high hopes did not generate the wave of candidates they had earlier predicted. Instead of sponsoring a candidate in every one of the 150 legislative districts, Healey later downplayed, "I think we'll have enough to be at least respectable for a new party."[133]

The Cool Moose Party's second convention in late August, 1996, presented as the political version of multi-mixed marriage. Parties of every variety mingled about, including the Sharecroppers' Revolt Party, the Junk Yard Dog Party, and the Don't Vote Paolino Party.[134] In addition, the Republicans and the Democrats joined in on the scene, suddenly interested in other parties' views. Most of this newfound interest probably stemmed from the realization that third parties had arrived, at least for the time being. Darrell West, professor of political science at Brown University, said that Rhode Island "is actually number one in the country for independent voters." West explained, "People are disenchanted with the Republicans and the Democrats. There is a lot of ferment in national politics which has allowed third parties to flourish, in the sense that we have a lot of them and they're a little more plausible" than in past elections.[135]

The most bizarre story that kept the Cool Moose Party in the news in 1996 involved the party's first primary season. Two candidates from Healey's party ran for the District 88 state representative spot. That seemed normal enough. It wasn't. Robert Healey submitted his name for the nomination, and then did the same for Brian J. Fortin, even serving as a witness for his so-called opponent.[136] (Democrat Mark D. Heffner, the incumbent, and Republican Maria T. Ferri of the Barrington Town Council, ran for the same seat.) When asked about the Cool Moose Party's bizarre arrangement in their first primary, the Cool Moose Party Chairman came across initially as coy: "The public has to decide who the best man is."[137] Later, in a more forthcoming fashion, Healey said that he designed the arrangement to set up a court battle over state-funded primaries.

The bizarre seemingly turned bogus. Healey explained, of the primary for the District 88 legislative seat, "I believe that my opponent is going to win. I know that I'm going to have to vote for him."[138] While the arrangement appeared foolish, the developing ordeal unfolded as planned. In order for the plan to work, Fortin had to win the primary. Healey wanted to lose the primary and gain his convention's endorsement. That scenario would put Healey in a better position to challenge the state primary system in court. In losing, Healey would appeal that the convention winner, not the primary winner, belongs on the November ballot. Hence, one could then argue that the primary did not really matter, so why do we use taxpayer funds to run primaries? Healey explained further, "Sometimes, the only way to attack those (primary) rules is from the inside."[139]

Healey challenged the current primary system in court by asking, "Why should we taxpayers pay for a beauty contest and horse race that benefits only the political parties, which are really private political organizations? These political parties are not part of the government." As such, Healey suggested, there existed "...no compelling state interest in holding these primaries."[140] Bolstering this point even further,

Healey said that, compared to other states, a very high percentage of Rhode Island voters register as independents. In his second point, he reasoned, since a registered Democrat cannot vote in a Republican or Cool Moose primary, Rhode Island should mandate open primaries or end taxpayer support for the closed primaries.[141] Otherwise, Healey explained, since the Cool Moose Party had no candidates for the House of Representatives or the United States Senate, the current system denied him the opportunity to write in a candidate. As such, according to Healey, the law disenfranchised Cool Moose Party members in the Congressional primary, which amounted to a violation of the United States Constitution's 14th amendment.[142]

On the morning of the September 10 primary, Bob Healey appeared at his Barrington Hampden Meadows School polling station. As a registered Cool Moose party member, the poll workers did not allow Healey to vote in the Democratic and Republican primaries when he made the request to do so. The poll workers also denied Healey's request to write in a Congressional candidate for either party. Healey then voted as a Cool Moose party member, presumably for Brian Fortin.[143]

And so much for the best laid plans of "mice, men, and moose."[144] While earlier Healey had joked, "our exit polling indicates that I'm going to lose,"[145] as is so often proven of real polls, Healey's *exit poll* misled. On September 10, 1996, Healey defeated Brian J. Fortin 7-6 in the Cool Moose primary for the State Representative District 88 seat. When asked what he would do about that primary result, Healey submitted, "Demand a recount, I guess."[146] And this he did. Healey's letter to the election board based his appeal on "questions raised as to the operation of the machine in light of the tally of fourteen having attempted to vote, but only thirteen votes being registered." He further argued, "Additionally, other concerns have been raised as to the actual count."[147]

Healey might not have been the first election winner to seek a recount, but past such cases most probably stemmed from a winner wanting to protect their slim margin from a paper ballot count.[148] Regardless, Healey won the recount, which, given the plan he had in place, resulted in a loss of sorts for the Cool Moose Party Chair. At this point, a *Providence Journal* reporter referenced Healey's campaign as one with a "Alice-in-Wonderland flavor."[149] And, still, Healey's plan took yet another weird turn. On September 13, Healey withdrew his candidacy, and with authorization from his party's executive committee, appointed Fortin as the Cool Moose nominee to represent District 88 in the state legislature.[150] (The ordeal set up the makings for the case of, *Cool Moose Party v. State of RI*, 6 F. Supp. 2d 116 (D.R.I. 1998). See Chapter 8, *Not Business as Usual; Healey Out of Politics*)

Within hours of being appointed a state legislative candidate, Brain Fortin's exposure jumped. Due to a lottery conducted by Secretary of State James Langevin's office, The Cool Moose candidate won a second column placement on the November ballot. The Democratic candidate would be placed to his right and the Republican candidate moved to his left, prompting a *Providence Journal* reporter to quip, "Move over, elephant, and make way for the moose."[151] Third-party candidates welcomed this development because, as Healey explained, "Statistical studies have shown a correlation between the first column and an increased percentage of votes, and has long been a source of controversy in election ballot court challenges."[152] Healey praised Secretary of State Langevin, a Democrat, for his even-handed stewardship of this long-sought ballot change.

And of those newly positioned second-column Cool Moose Party candidates, Healey guaranteed voters that every one of them running for the General Assembly supported Referendum No. 8 for voter initiative. He based his claim on a survey to which every Cool Moose Candidate responded. Healey stressed, "If the people want voter initiative, they can be assured that if they vote the Cool Moose candidate, they will have a vote for initiative in the legislature,"[153] Currently, Healey explained, "Rhode Island prohibits its citizens from proposing laws in that all laws must originate in the General Assembly."[154]

Electing officials in support of the initiative, Healey noted, deserved attention because the legislature must draw up the constitutional amendment that would appear on the 1998 ballot.[155] Healey warned, "This issue is of prime importance in this election. This is about the future of Rhode Island as to whether the people control at the ballot box or the lobbyists control Smith Hill."[156]

Though Healey did not run in the election of 1996, he chastised verbally Channel 10 for only featuring major party candidates, specifically Democrats and Republicans, on their televised debates. He charged, "These people are supposed to bring us the news, not censor it."[157]

In an ironic twist, Democratic Representative Patrick J. Kennedy refused to participate in any debate forums that did not include all four candidates for the 1st Congressional District seat. Bob Healey spoke positively of Kennedy's newfound political chivalry, saying, "... we credit him for standing up to Channel 10 in saying all candidates must participate." However, Healey hedged, "While we may question his sincerity, we must approve of his position."[158] Many thought Kennedy adopted his 1996 stated position for all inclusion debates to limit his Republican candidate, Giovanni Cicione, from gaining further exposure.[159]

From November 1996 to November 1997, the media covered Bob Healey little. In November of 1997, he wrote a letter to the editor that indicated his stance on campaign funding, and by inference, his intention to run for Governor again. Healey announced, "I wish to indicate that I have pledged—as I had in 1994—that I will not spend more than $139,600 in the race for governor."[160] He went on, "While many talk about campaign finance reform, I am willing to act. If a candidate truly believes in campaign finance reform, the candidate must practice what he or she preaches. To advocate campaign finance reform while raising and spending large sums of money is hypocritical, deceitful, and just plain wrong."[161]

Bob promised to run a low-budget campaign, unfunded by political action committee money. His campaign would rely almost completely on face-to-face discussions with the people. The conversations would center on the issues that mattered to Rhode Islanders. Healey declared, "By old-fashioned campaigning, I hope to win election."[162]

In preparation for the 1998 campaign season, the Cool Moose Party made organizational changes. At the party's convention in December 1997, they elected Rui Reis chairman of the Cool Moose Party for a one-year term. They re-elected Claire Boyes treasurer, and selected Victoria White and Norman Brunelle as the party's secretaries. With the party nearing 1,000 members, Healey anticipated a successful 1998 elections season, pointing to a growing number of young people registered and "the fact that people around Rhode Island are seeing the Cool Moose Party as a reasonable alternative."[163]

Healey made his official entrance into the 1998 governor's race on April 9, 1998. Addressing an assembled group outside the Warren Town Hall, he referenced himself as "the Cinderella candidate."[164] In what had become his signature self-deprecating humor, Healey explained, "It is said that one definition of insanity is exactly repeating the same process expecting a different result. While some may assert that this definition precisely describes my persistent gubernatorial aspirations, I assert that it equally applies to Rhode Island's traditional embracing of a two-party system. By continuing to go into the voting booth and electing political players from the two-party system, no one can expect anything less than the same outcome election after election."[165]

Much of Healey's 1998 platform hadn't changed from his earlier runs for Governor. In fact, at his 1998 announcement to enter in the governor's race, Healey read an excerpt from his announcement speech in 1986, addressing local property-tax relief, state financing of education, environmental protections, and limited government.[166] Healey stressed, "We still need to revamp our system of taxation, promoting progressive, graduated taxes instead of regressive ones." He added, "We still need to have the state assume its full, rightful, and constitutional role in funding education."[167]

Early in the campaign a reporter suggested a haircut might afford him some votes. Healey had heard this before. This time he responded, "I am myself. If I package myself for the people of the state of Rhode Island simply to get their vote, they'll think that I'm betraying them and betraying myself as well."[168] His moose curls remained flowing.

As he had in the past, Healey fired off jabs against his political opponents right out of the campaign season gate. Speaking to Governor Almond's energy and vision, Healey assessed, "I think the governor, for the most part, is probably deficient in both areas."[169] Of Democrat Myrth York, he offered, "I don't see her plans and policies as changing very much from the last election."[170] Of his chances of winning this time around, Healey stuck to a Cinderella theme: "This, if any year, has to be the year. It's a long shot…I may be able to get to the ball and, who knows, maybe the slipper will be mine."[171]

The Cinderella candidate garnered very little attention in the press from April to August. Bill Clinton wished he could have said the same of himself. With the Monica S. Lewinsky affair threatening to end his presidency, in August he admitted to the American people that he did indeed have "relations" with his intern. Most Rhode Island politicians responded in measured terms. Providence Mayor Vincent A. Cianci Jr., rated the confession a "B." Cianci clarified of his evaluation of Clinton's performance, "He went halfway…Last night was not the right time to do it. He looked tired. He looked burned out. His speech was too short, and rather general."[172] Myrth York, of the same political party as President Clinton, offered, she was "glad he accepted responsibility" but was "disappointed he hadn't done it sooner."[173]

Democrat Paul S. Kelly, majority leader of the Rhode Island Senate, for the most part stood by Clinton: "He admitted wrongdoing, apologized to the country and to his family…It's very difficult to go before the world and say, 'I made a mistake…' It took a lot of courage."[174]

Bob Healey had nothing positive to say about Clinton's courage, or just about anything else associated with the beleaguered president. "I think the guy's a liar and people should have realized all along he's a liar." Healey then stated that Clinton's actions did not rise to the level on an impeachable offense.[175]

While Healey usually had much to say, that didn't hold true all the time. At the Common Cause of Rhode Island candidate forum in October, Healey decided to offer no comment when his turn to speak arrived. He explained, "I've always been a firm believer that if you have nothing to say, don't say it." His comments drew laughter from the 350 Common Cause members at the Newport Viking Hotel.[176]

While he might have missed an opportunity or two to offer comment, his sense of humor remained opportune. His bumper stickers quipped, "Vote Cool Moose. Elect Healey Governor. Why Not? You've Done Worse."[177] When pounding the pavement, the longhaired candidate who drew comparisons to the likes of John Lennon and Jesus Christ, handed out red pocket combs with the question printed, "Can Healey shaving mugs and razors be far behind?"[178]

As election drew closer, Almond and York called in the big names to prop up their chances of winning. Governor Lincoln Almond invited New York Mayor Rudolph Giuliani to say a few words on his behalf. Myrth York's campaign secured Hillary Clinton to speak on the former Rhode Island senator's behalf. How does a third-party candidate compete with that kind of celebrity star power draw? Well, if you're the Cool Moose Party candidate you invite the world's beloved big purple dinosaur, Barney, and bill him as "one of the world's preeminent educators and advocates of peace."[179] As it turned out, Barney could not make it to Rhode Island, reportedly too busy "...doing the people's work in maintaining a safe, peaceful environment...certainly more important than a political appearance." Healey assured about the schedule conflict, "We have no hard feelings."[180]

As the election reached a fever pitch pace for the Almond and York campaigns, complete with gala events, high exposure advertisements, and perpetual smiles for camera cameos, Healey continued offering his legal services and stumping for votes on foot. In the dog days of the campaign, he secured no television spots or choreographed photo ops, and, probably, increasingly realized he had no chance of victory. He seemed to accept his lot, and jabbered less than he had in past years. He came across more contemplative,[181] too, perhaps owing to the fact he had entered his forties. He offered, "I don't see the value in being the candidate who keeps the others on the issues,"[182] at least not as his sole schtick.[183] Healey shared that 1998 would be his last run for governor, "unless I come in second or better, or come within 2 to 3 percentage points of winning."[184]

Though even Healey's most ardent supporters might admit that both of the above conditions remained beyond his reach, even his most vocal detractors had to wonder why the Cool Moose candidate did not build on the considerable momentum established in the 1994 campaign for governor. Perhaps, like last year's hairstyles and over-told jokes, four years later, third parties resembled a timeworn fad that no longer sold so well. Ross Perot might as well have been ancient history in 1998, a fate maybe applicable to Bob Healey, as well. One *Providence Journal* reporter wrote of Healey, "This time around, reporters sometimes forget he's out there."[185] When the *Journal* ran a story on class size as an educational high-profile issue, the paper sought the opinions of Almond and York, neither who are educators, and did not approach Healey, who completed the course work for a doctorate in education at Columbia University, taught in both public and private schools, and served four years as the Warren School Committee Chair. Further, he issued a 22-page position paper covering an array of educational initiatives including statewide teacher contracts, shifting power back to local school committees, and the formation of long-term plans rather than year-to-year short-sighted target statements. Healey responded to the *Journal's* slight with frustration, remarking of his grasp of educational issue, "I mean, I really know this stuff."[186]

In truth, while the *Journal's* coverage of Healey's campaign amounted to nominal, substantial opportunities did present themselves to the Cool Moose Party candidate. Owing in large part to his party's new official status, three media outlets invited the Cool Moose candidate to participate in key televised debates in October, one such contest within a week of election day. At the first debate on October 5, in addition to Lincoln Almond, Myrth York, and Bob Healey, businessman John P. Devine of the Reform Party participated. Interviewers included WPRO radio show host Steve Cass, *Providence Journal* political columnist Charles Bakst, and Rhode Island AARP President Ann Gardella. At that debate, Healey had numerous opportunities to make his case to Rhode Island voters. He performed unremarkably.

At times during the debate, questioners addressed only one or two candidates rather than the four assembled. (Charles Bakst never asked a question of Healey or Devine.) Sometimes, a candidate would gesture to speak to an issue asked of a different nominee. Despite the moderator's willingness to extend such opportunities, Robert Healey only spoke when addressed directly. In one instance, the moderator afforded Healey the chance to treat a question from Ann Gardella, but Healey said he had addressed that inquiry earlier (which he had,) and appeared aggravated by the repeat offering. He slouched in his seat, held his head up with his right hand, and protruded his forefinger along his bearded cheek. One might wonder if he still stewed over Bakst's earlier slights. Regardless, he came across detached and unresponsive, and passed on the opportunity to expound upon his thinking. At one point in the debate when candidates discussed government pay raises over the past year, the moderator said to Healey, "Mr. Healey, you have been very quiet in this segment. Would you like to tackle pay raises?" Healey smiled and offered, "Yeah, I didn't get between them [Almond and York] I guess. [laughter] I think that obviously we have to look at the pay situation on an individual basis..."[187] While his voice lacked a strong sense of expression, and his point did not resonate clearly, his comment nevertheless drew applause.

At times when Healey spoke, he rambled and provided responses that failed to inspire. He delivered his statements in a monotone voice that seemed to trail off at times. His answers read like a list of obvious talking points with no explanation of how to accomplish the stated goals. In short, his performance proved forgettable, maybe even deflating.

In the next debate in late October (again with all four candidates present,) Healey improved on his delivery, but still spoke quickly and to the point, sometimes abruptly so. When interviewers asked the candidates whether or not Rhode Island should use public subsidies to lure the New England Patriots to Rhode Island, Almond expressed his willingness to assist in financing, while York said it all depended on the actual proposal. Healey and Devine responded more succinctly. Healey answered, "No." Devine accentuated on Healey's response, "Not a dime."[188]

When asked, "Should we change the way we finance education in the state?" Almond said he would increase the state's contribution to local towns. York agreed but was not "sold on a specific way of changing the funding." Healey offered to "eliminate the property tax for education purposes, placing the onus on the income tax." Devine quipped, "If corporations want trained workers, let them help pay for them."[189] In other words, use inventory and corporate taxes to fund education. No candidate supported school cash incentives to improve test scores. Healey explained of his opposition on that subject, "If you give cash to places that are improving, you're just rewarding towns like Barrington and East Greenwich, where it is easy to improve the test scores. You have to spend the money where the problems are."[190]

All in all, the second debate lacked the personality and gumption one might anticipate with Healey's participation. Healey made few if any quick-witted responses or colorful contributions. Maybe Healey had tried to act more gubernatorial. Maybe the questions didn't provide the setups he needed to offer his snappy replies. Regardless of the reasons for Healey's substandard performance, an upcoming October 30 debate offered a final opportunity to improve his political lot—less than one week before Election Day.

Healey looked forward to the next matchup with Almond and York. This would mark the first time he had *qualified* for a third debate. He felt ready for the high stakes forum. He only had to get there. That proved more difficult than he had anticipated.

Healey's affinity for well-used cars suited him, and his candidacy. His vehicle choices connected him to the middle class and lower middle-class citizens he promised to represent. A working-class voter might rationalize accurately that Healey hadn't forgotten where he came from. His automobile choice served brazenly as an extension of his candidacy. His cars cost little, communicated an egalitarian spirit, and ran consistent with his espoused ideals. Those same cars broke down often.

On the evening of October 30, 1998, as Bob Healey and Claire Boyes made their way to the third governor debate, one of the wheels on their 1970s vehicle disembarked on Interstate 95. The car required immediate repair. It looked as if they wouldn't be able to make the debate on time, if at all. That likelihood stressed Healey. Suddenly, the notoriously unflappable candidate unraveled. He blurted out frantically, "What if they lock me out of the debate? What am I going to do?"[191] Claire Boyes had never seen him act like this. "He was crazed and out of control,"[192] she later recalled. Exasperated, Healey exclaimed, "I got to make a call!" Without further explanation, he sprang from the broken-down vehicle, darted across the highway, and leapt over a fence. A few minutes later he cleared the same fence and dashed back across the highway. Shortly afterward, help arrived and fixed the tire. He and Claire then sped to the debate, arriving fifteen minutes late.

By the time they arrived at the forum, Bob Healey had composed himself completely, as if he had entered into a zone, like a relief pitcher might as he got the call in the bullpen to enter the game in the final inning. As Healey made his way onto the debate floor, interestingly, Lincoln Almond and Myrth York appeared rattled and disheveled by the Cool Moose candidate's late arrival.[193] They scuffed their shoes, looked repeatedly downward, and managed nervous smiles. Their focus seemed broken. The two frontrunner candidates had locked into one another's fastball. They knew Healey could throw knuckle balls. Maybe they feared their timing would be off. The candidate *of the electorate* had

Arriving late to an October 31, 1998 debate, Healey made a somewhat theatric entrance, causing Governor Lincoln Almond and former state representative Myrth York visible angst. (© The Providence Journal – USA TODAY NETWORK / All rights reserved.)

entered the game after all. Was this part of some bizarre Cool Moose Party late game strategy? What was he going to throw their way?

Almond in particular appeared to sweat out Healey's arrival, literally. The Governor had battled a cold during the week, and now struggled with a scratchy throat and a mild case of laryngitis. As the younger and healthier Cool Moose Party candidate took his position, one has to wonder if it occurred to Healey in the short order that, for the first time in this campaign (or any other prior campaign for that matter), he enjoyed the upper hand.

If Healey's tardiness secured any advantage, its lifespan proved short. Myrth York composed herself quickly, incorporating Bob Healey's late entrance into one of her responses to a panelist's question. She offered, "The roads are a problem, they're a big problem. You only have to ask Bob Healey about that and he'll tell you. He's probably wondering why we're spending $8 million for signs that are telling him he's in a traffic jam."[194] While Healey's late arrival had nothing to do with a traffic jam, York had gained back her stride.

Bob Healey might have offered the most humorous comment of the night when he drew a parallel between himself and a daytime soap-opera star, Susan Lucci. Lucci had earned many nominations for an Emmy award, but never took the prize home. "Please," Healey beseeched voters, "don't make me the Susan Lucci of Rhode Island politics."[195]

But as in the past, Healey's comic relief did little to advance his candidacy. In fact, when *The Providence Journal* reported on the last debate of the 1998 governor's race, they mentioned only that Healey had arrived late, York's mentioning of him, and Healey's Susan Lucci line. Later articles marking the final countdown to the election followed the same pattern. One of the only mentions of Healey in *The Providence Journal* during the last three days before election day reported that he continued to poll in single digits.[196]

Election Day proved predictable, and anti-climactic. 1998's election story proved a retelling of the 1994 election, only with a worse finish for Healey. Almond won. York came in second. Healey finished a distant third, with a little over 6 percent of the vote, about three percentage points less than four years earlier.[197] (John Devine captured less than 1 percent of the tallies.[198]) Even worse for Healey, Warren, his hometown, abandoned their favorite son and voted for Governor Lincoln Almond.[199] The Cool Moose failed to win over a single Rhode Island town.

Not only did Healey lose, but in a way, so did the election of 1998. Just 306,000 Rhode Islanders cast votes statewide in the 1998 election, down from about 361,000 in 1994, a 10 percent drop in voter participation.[200] Like Healey, 1998 had failed to ignite the voters' passion.

In keeping with remarks he had made earlier in his campaign, the disappointing performance prompted Healey to announce that he did not expect to run for governor again. After three losing gubernatorial campaigns from 1986 to 1998, many probably predicted he would never run for anything again. His campaign strategies, while once of a head-turning and eye-popping variety, by 1998 came across as familiar and standard fare. At this point, the voters might have wondered if the Cool Moose had anything left to offer that communicated as fresh and relevant.

CHAPTER 11

THE BEST LIEUTENANT GOVERNOR YOU'LL NEVER HAVE
2002 AND 2006 LT. GOVERNOR'S RACES

THE 2002 CAMPAIGN

In March 2002, Charles Fogarty announced officially his bid for re-election to the lt. governor post. From the outset, the former Glocester Town Council member (1985-91) and state senator (1990–98) took his place as the odds-on favorite to reclaim his position. The popular incumbent already enjoyed a long list of endorsements, including that of former Rhode Island Governor J. Joseph Garrahy and United States Senator Jack Reed. Soon he would secure the backing of the state's most powerful party. Further improving his odds of re-election, Fogarty faced no substantial competition. The Republican Party put forth Larry Shetler, who worked in the Providence planning and economic development office. Rhode Island voters had little knowledge of nor interest in Shetler. The Cool Moose Party later nominated Robert J. Healey Jr. for lt. governor. Rhode Islanders *knew* Healey as a perennial third-place finisher in three bids for governor. In each of those bids, Healey never attracted more than single digit percentage support. By all accounts, Fogarty had a lock on a November 2002 victory.

Fogarty spoke of the office he once again sought in glowing terms: "That's what I see as the real power of the office…to be a catalyst to make things happen."[1] When he announced his candidacy for a second term as the state's lt. governor, Fogarty made sure to list the accomplishments from his first term. This list included efforts to use a portion of the state's tobacco lawsuit settlement for anti-smoking education, improving the state's mental health parity law, and lowering the cost of nurses' student loans. In addition, as lt. governor he had used his powers to improve antiterrorism planning and helped advance the RIPAE prescription drug-benefit program so low-income elderly residents could have increased access to the benefit.[2]

In addition to reviewing his past accomplishments, Fogarty announced his plans for the upcoming term, a portion of which he had already begun to implement. These goals included a new child-literacy program that would provide parents with free kits to assist their children improve reading skills. In the upcoming term, the lt. governor expected to have more time to help institute such programs. Next year, the lt. governor would no longer preside over the state Senate. But William V. Irons, a political ally and Senate Majority Leader, pointed out that while Fogarty would no longer have the same administrative role in the state senate, "We'll still look to him for a lot of advice."[3]

The same day Charlie Fogarty announced his re-election bid, Attorney General Sheldon Whitehouse endorsed the current lt. governor's candidacy. Fogarty had earlier endorsed Whitehouse as the Democratic Party candidate for Rhode Island governor. The back and forth between the two well-known Democrats expressed the makings of a political lovefest. Fogarty said that if Rhode Islanders elected Whitehouse and him in 2002, "I think there's going to be opportunities for me to take a more executive role, in addition to the roles I've carved out at this point in time."[4] Whitehouse's campaign manager, Bill Fischer, concurred, adding that a Whitehouse/Fogarty win would result "in a spirit of cooperation like no other governor or lieutenant governor before them."[5] Fogarty's and Fischer's commentaries called attention to the poor working relationship between past Rhode Island governors and lt. governors that resulted in part because both ran independently of one another.

On August 2, 2002, *The Providence Journal* published an article entitled, "Fogarty enjoys fundraising edge." The title proved misleading. His fundraising *far* exceeded that of his competitors. By June 30, 2002, Charles Fogarty had amassed a war chest of $168,142,[6] and with plans for television ads and numerous campaign functions, the Fogarty campaign team continued to raise more money. Further improving Fogarty's lot, Larry Shetler, the Republican's original endorsed candidate, dropped out of the race due to fraud charges in Massachusetts. On June 26, John A. Pagliarini Jr. replaced Shetler on the Republican slate. By August, Pagliarini had raised about $7,000.[7] The Green Party lieutenant governor candidate, Gregg R. Stevens, had amassed almost no money. When a reporter questioned Bob Healey about how much he had raised for his anticipated run against Fogarty, he responded, "squat."[8] Bob Healey had vowed not to accept contributions.[9]

While Fogarty stressed his first term record with Rhode Island voters, other candidates shared their thoughts for change. Pagliarini wanted to run the governor and lieutenant governor on the same ticket. The Green Party candidate ran for the office, in part, to warn of melting polar ice caps. Neither of these ideas gained much traction. Against Charlie Fogarty, the well-financed, widely endorsed, and popular incumbent candidate, one had to wonder what chance did any *competitor* have in dethroning the affable lieutenant governor. Even the most eternally optimistic Cool Moose supporters had to admit that an upset of this order called for the likes of divine intervention.

But Healey had a plan. The candidate who many 1998 voters wrote off as dry of fresh ideas surprised his doubters, once again. His maverick thinking made for a potentially show stopper campaign. He announced that he intended to destroy the office he sought. Though the idea sounded better suited for a kamikaze mission than an election campaign bid, Healey could not complete the undertaking alone. He needed the voters' help. And that, he pursued vigorously. To entice curiosity in his campaign this time around, Healey promoted the slogans, "The best Lt. Governor you'll never have,"[10] and "If nothing is what you want, Healey for Lt. Gov."[11] While the catchphrases were new, the idea was not. Healey and the Cool Moose Party had long supported eliminating the Lt. Governor position. And just like all of his amusing political promotions of the past, this time around a well-crafted thought process governed his campaign. Rhode Islanders, Healey rationalized, could save close to one million dollars annually by ridding themselves of the state's second highest office. Healey stressed that starting next year, the lt. governor's constitutional duties amounted to filling in for a governor, and only if needed. (In addition to replacing, potentially, a governor, the lt. governor would sit on several committees.) A transfer of power to the lt. governor would most likely require the death of a sitting governor. That had never happened in Rhode Island's history. Bob Healey, who ran part of his campaign while visiting in Uruguay, said of the post he sought, "It isn't very hard to wait for the death, incapacity, impeachment, or resignation of the governor. I can do that in my sleep."[12]

Former Attorney General Arlene Violet agreed with Healey. She offered later of the lieutenant governor's office, "There is just no need for the grooming salon that office represents. Jobs for that office-holder are made up through legislation and the official's personal 'causes.' Typically, however, the governor keeps a close eye on the #2 person lest they usurp the throne, so each plays 'nicey nice' as long as #2 knows that he/she is to acquiesce to the governor's agenda."[13] And arguably, Violet's reference to a "grooming saloon" spoke in too generous terms. Over the past 50 years only one lieutenant governor had gone on to become Rhode Island's governor.

Healey's hara-kiri attacks on the lieutenant governor position gave cause for the Democratic incumbent to defend his post. Referring to the funding of his office as money "well spent,"[14] and clarifying that the office earmarked only 1/100th of 1 percent of the state budget, Fogarty claimed he saved the state "millions" by arguing successfully in favor of lower-cost prescription drugs.[15] Further, according to Fogarty, while it may have seemed that little is asked of the lt. governor, recently state laws had added responsibilities to the position. Now the lieutenant governor oversaw public advocacy groups. Fogargty added, "Elected officials lead, set policy, and make things happen. That's the role of the lieutenant governor."[16] Providing proof of those assertions, a spokesman for the lieutenant governor presented the press with a packet full of news releases and newspaper stories demonstrating the work Fogarty had accomplished on matters ranging from promoting literacy and healthcare to supporting efforts against societal violence.[17]

When not defending the job he sought against engineered attacks, Fogarty fired targeted strikes against Healey. Calling Healey a "a very colorful character," Fogargy said that eliminating the office of lieutenant governor "is not an issue on the minds of Rhode Islanders."[18] Perhaps calling attention to what he saw as Healey's questionable capabilities and lack of demonstrated commitment to the post he pursued, Fogarty stated, "I think people want an independent lieutenant governor who has proven his ability to lead and who is an advocate for them. I think people in Rhode Island take this job seriously, and they expect their elected officials to take their responsibility seriously...I have not seen from [Healey] a seriousness I would expect and which people would expect for the second-highest office in the state."[19]

While Fogarty took the lion's share of shots against his Cool Moose Party opponent, he did not stand out as the sole shooter. Republican candidate Pagliarini spearheaded some attacks against Healey's thinking as well. Pagliarini said the Cool Moose Party candidate's well-publicized intention to eliminate the office has "sizzle," especially amongst disgruntled voters. But he then added, "even a bad piece of meat sizzles."[20] That both Fogarty and Pagliarini took time to address Healey at all suggests they feared the Cool Moose Party's maverick message and its potential allure to Rhode Island voters.

For Healey's part, he couldn't let Fogarty's comments about his candidacy stand unchallenged. In a somewhat demeaning tone, Healey shot back, "I'm sure Charlie likes the office. Charlie likes the pay ($80,000 annually). Who wouldn't? And you get to campaign for four years. He has 10 people working for him who need work so he puts them on issues that will win him votes."[21]

His comical and cutting comments aside, Healey reinforced continually his campaign's core message. He wanted to save Rhode Islanders one million dollars annually. In 2002, the state had forecasted a 115 million dollar budget shortfall.[22] Healey offered a four-million-dollar savings over the next four years, and millions more over the coming decades. To further his point, with questionable tact, Healey looked to the voters and charged, "If the people of Rhode Island don't elect me, they're nuts. They get upset about the House Speaker [John Harwood] creating a job for Wendy Collins[23], but if you want to talk about creating jobs, look at the lieutenant governor's office."[24]

Apart from his campaign message and rhetoric, Healey's 2002 campaign loaded up on unusual campaign paraphernalia of one sort or another. The Cool Moose Party trinkets called attention to the unique option Healey offered Rhode Islanders. Such campaign giveaways included a coffee mug emblazoned with Healey's likeness. The caption read, "Have you seen this man?" A refrigerator magnet reminded, "If Nothing Is What You Want." Perhaps the most hair-raising campaign item in Healey's 2002 election campaign inventory were condoms with wrappers declaring, "Nothing Never Felt So Good."[25]

At some point in the campaign, Healey shared one of the condoms with his old friend, Rhode Island Representative Robert Craven. Before doing so, Healey said to his former law school peer, "I got something for you." Craven thought it was a button or an object of that nature. Craven recalled of the exchange with Healey:

Of all Bob Healey's campaign paraphernalia, his employment of a "NOTHING NEVER FELT SO GOOD!" condom might stand out as the most attention getting selection.

"He reaches into his pocket and he hands me a condom. And I say, 'Well, that's, ah, different. Ah, [that] could be offensive to some people.' He said, 'Well you don't need to take it if you take offense.' And I said, 'No, no. I, ah, I think I know what you are trying to say. But what do you think the message is?' Healey responded, 'Well I'll tell you. The voters are getting fucked. So I think they ought to wear a prophylactic.'

Craven explained of Healey, "If Bob walked into a campaign trinket store that had pens, balloons, or the kitchen magnet, he would pick out this thing. [Craven held up the condom Bob Healey had presented him years earlier.] He would walk by all the other things saying, 'That's normal. That's normal. Oh, that [condom] ain't normal. Let's go with that.' That's what he would do. He pushed the envelope. That's what he did. Always."

For all the novelle ideas introduced and the spirited exchanges had, the best "show in town," as one reporter referenced the 2002 lieutenant governor's race, suffered from low viewership.[26] Healey might have provided a performance for the ages, but his maverick stance, colorful commentaries, and entertaining campaign paraphernalia did not attract enough people to his political theater and underlying message. Maybe as a result, little changed from early 2002 to November 2002. Fogarty, who enjoyed a comfortable lead throughout the entire race, won easily. In fact, he more than doubled the voter percentage of his nearest vote getter, John Pagliarini. While arguably Bob Healey had brought the most attention to the campaign,[27] he secured only 19 percent of the vote, finishing ahead of only Gregg Stevens, who drew 2.9 percent of the vote.

Healey called his results "disappointing."[28] And they were. But they did not qualify as "awful." With an anemic source of campaign revenue (by choice), he had won over almost 20 percent of Rhode Islanders. He finished first in white-collar, Republican-leaning Barrington. He also won in blue-collar, Democratic-leaning Warren. And he finished ahead of the Democratic or Republican candidate in several other communities.[29] But all that positive figuring still added up to a loss.

On the night of his impressive election victory, the soon-to-be second term Rhode Island lt. governor delivered a victory speech in a somewhat uncharacteristic fashion. Translating a bit like a spiked football dance in the endzone at the feet of Bob Healey, the normally mild-mannered lt. governor exclaimed, "Bob [Healey] raised the question, and he got his answer, overwhelmingly. I think the people recognized the importance of the office, and the difference I have made to people."[30]

Perhaps bankrupt of smart comebacks, Healey resorted to a sour reflection of yet another political defeat: "It shows the people want to waste their money. It's fine with me. You can lead a horse to water but you can't make him drink."[31]

Healey had challenged the people with, "If nothing is what you want, Healey for Lt. Gov."[32] The people chose to go with *something*, for now.

THE 2006 CAMPAIGN

As the 2002 election got logged into Rhode Island campaign history lore, the issues Healey had raised did not disappear. In October

2005, Cranston Mayor and Republican US Senate candidate, Stephen P. Laffey, rejected the notion that he would pursue the lieutenant governor position. Laffey commented in a National Review article, "In Rhode Island, the job of lieutenant governor is to ride a bicycle around the state and wait for the governor to die." [33] Jeff Neal, spokesman for Republican Governor Donald Carcieri, agreed, saying the position amounted to "an inefficient use of state employees and taxpayer money." "In fact," he added, "Many taxpayers would be surprised to learn that the state spends almost $1 million a year to fund the lieutenant governor's office." [34] In delivering the *news*, the Carcieri office must have assumed, and perhaps correctly, that Rhode Island taxpayers hadn't listened to Healey in the prior election.

However, Carcieri fell short of proposing that Rhode Islanders rid of the office, instead suggesting that the state's voters change the Constitution to allow the governor and lieutenant governor to run as a duo on the same ticket. Carcieri explained, "This would enable the governor to entrust the lieutenant governor with more official duties, and to better share the burden of running the executive branch. [35]

Charlie Fogarty felt compelled to weigh-in on all the chatter about the office he held. Even though Republican Governor Carcieri had clarified that his comments did not target the Democrat who currently held the office, Fogarty reminded inquiring reporters that the people had already decided the lieutenant governor post had great purpose and function. In effect, Fogarty pegged the talk about his office as old news which the last election had already *proven* to be predicated on a faulty premise.

State Senator Elizabeth Roberts agreed so much with Fogarty that in December 2005 she indicated (though did not yet announce officially) her interest in serving as Rhode Island's next lieutenant governor. To that end, Roberts accepted gladly the endorsement of EMILY's List, a political action committee that backs pro-choice Democratic women, normally at the national level. [36] Bob Kearney, national director of the Political Opportunity Program, a subset of EMILY's List that focused on gettiing candidates at lower levels of government elected, said of Roberts, "Her work on healthcare is recognized by people outside of Rhode Island. She has truly been a leader on that issue beyond her state borders." Kearney went on, "Elizabeth Roberts is a rising star. She's a rising star in Rhode Island and we believe she's a rising star on the national scene."[37]

The endorsement provided Roberts a leg up on her competition in the upcoming 2006 election. The energized potential candidate for lt. governor exclaimed, "I look at the women who have been elected with the support of EMILY's List and I am very proud to be among that group. It's a great boost for my campaign."[38] Rhode Island had never elected a woman lieutenant governor or governor. Elizabeth Roberts positioned herself to change that.

In January 2006, Kernan "Kerry" King joined the race as the Republican's nominee for lieutenant governor. During his announcement, King shared his affinity for Governor Donald Carcieri. This he stressed repeatedly[39] and effusively. King proclaimed, "I'm running for lieutenant governor because I believe in Don Carcieri." King continued, "Behind that engaging and handsome smile, is a tough guy. He's strong. Not only does he have the courage to take on the tough issues but to face off against the agents of sleaze."[40] A *Providence Journal* reporter observed, "At times, King's rally sounded more like Carcieri's campaign kick-off than his own."[41] And it did almost seem that way when King declared, "Governor Carcieri and I are running as a team." Even though the Rhode Island Constitution did not allow for such an arrangement, King continued on as if he and Carcieri presented as a package deal. King counseled voters, "If you're not going to vote for Governor Carcieri, don't vote for me." One reporter asked King if he was riding Carcieri's coattails. King responded emphatically, "I am indeed."[42]

For King to support Carcieri, the Republican lt. governor candidate needed to reclaim Rhode Island as his official residence. He had not voted in Rhode Island since 1960, working as an insurance executive over the years and living in Massachusetts and Florida. Moving back to Rhode Island in 2005, he registered to vote in the state on

November 9, claiming residence at a Narragansett home he had owned for 25 years.[43] Despite his long absence from the state, King assured potential voters of his credentials as a "native" Rhode Islander who spoke the cultural lingo; "I like coffee milk, Awful Awfuls, New York system hot weiners...I like clamcakes and Del's Lemonade."[44]

Though state Democratic Party Chairman William J. Lynch "welcomed" King to the state via a news release, he stated, "Kernan King may think moving to Rhode Island and running for lieutenant governor is a good retirement hobby, but Rhode Islanders deserve a lieutenant governor who has made a full-time commitment to our state."[45]

A month and a half after King's announcement, Bob Healey proclaimed officially that he would make his second bid for Rhode Island's lieutenant governor. This should not have surprised anyone. Earlier, in December 2005, Healey made his intentions to run clear, referencing himself in a letter to the editor as "a past and present candidate for lieutenant governor."[46] Still, Healey wanted his official declaration to have an element of surprise. To realize this, Healey had another plan. Just prior to his announcement, he told Claire Boyes, "Watch me get their attention."[47] And he did. Healey made his official candidacy announcement for Rhode Island's lieutenant governor from a beach, in Uruguay. He explained his reasoning for doing so. "I have chosen this location because I think that it demonstrates that, no matter where you are in the world, and no matter what you are doing, you can also be serving as Rhode Island's lieutenant governor." Healey explained his reasoning further; "Waiting for the demise of the governor can be accomplished just about anywhere, [at] any time, and by just about anyone with a pulse. I probably would do it here, on the beach."[48] Healey emailed the announcement to reporters.[49]

Though Bob Healey still ran under the Cool Moose Party banner, since his party did not enter a candidate for governor in the last election, Healey had to run officially as an independent.[50] This presented a drawback he had not faced during his prior campaign. This time around, Healey would not qualify for the ballot-listing lottery that could have placed his name in the first column where studies suggested voters tended to look first, thereby heightening the said candidate's exposure.

Healey made no significant changes to his core platform from four years earlier. Again, he campaigned for ridding the office and saving Rhode Islanders the expense of a 10-person office staff, which amounted to approximately $1,000,000 annually. Healey knew that ridding of the state's second-in-command office required amending the Rhode Island Constitution. However, he may have underestimated the difficulty of accomplishing that feat. Regardless, Healey explained the reasoning for eliminating the office he sought in his typical edgy tone: "I could not justify such a boondoggle being hoisted upon the backs of the hard-working taxpayers of Rhode Island. If I wish to advance my political career, I will do it without using a taxpayer subsidized soapbox."[51]

While Healey's 2006 proposals read like those of his 2002 bid for the same office, he decided to alter his campaign strategy. Unlike the last election where he tried to "…reason away the office," this campaign he would "…try to abolish it through ridicule."[52] Healey rationalized, "If nothing else, the humor and lampooning will at least amuse my highly literate voting base."[53] In that spirit, Healey handed out bumper stickers that chimed, "Lt. Governor? Lt. Governor? We don't need no stinkin' Lt. Governor,"[54] and fake money printed with the motto, "Elect Healey lieutenant governor and save Rhode Island a million bucks!"[55] Healey contributed $1,200 to his campaign to fund these giveaways.[56]

In addition to the campaign's tone change, Healey made other adjustments to his approach. While he would use some leftover trinkets (mugs, magnets, condoms) from his last campaign, this "less than ambitious"[57] run would utilize the Internet more and increase his walks through neighborhoods. But an increased humorous approach did not mean a less serious intent. Even though Healey would continue to employ amusing theatrics to draw attention, this time around, he vowed "a serious campaign to eliminate a not-so-serious office."[58]

Substance, Healey promised, would trump gimmicks (though not humor), most of the time.

In an effort to convince the electorate of this campaign's more serious intent and message, Healey stressed, "I've been doing this for twenty-five years. If it were just a joke, then it would be done and over. Like any joke, it only plays well the first time. To expend my own time and energy over two-and-half decades is perseverance. As Michelangelo said, 'Genius is eternal patience.'"[59] Healey, now 49 years old, explained his philosophy in abbreviated fashion: "I'm fiscally conservative, socially liberal, with a libertarian streak and I believe in small, efficient, open government."[60]

Healey espoused his qualifications in economic development, the law, and education as reasons he stood out as the most qualified candidate for lt. governor. As proof of such a claim he touted his co-ownership of a successful liquor wholesale business, Global Horizon Inc (1995 to 2002), development of property in Uruguay, his 22-year law practice, and his chairmanship of the Warren School Committee. Beyond touting his credentials, the candidate upped his personal meetings with voters. In doing so, he hoped the voter could get beyond the hair and beard and hear his message. As Healey explained, "...when they listen to me, they realize they are wasting their tax dollars on this office."[61]

Of his credentials to be lieutenant governor and, by extension, governor, Healey said, "I honestly believe that the people know that I am fully capable of governing, should the need ever arise. In the meantime, I am offering them a rare opportunity to hire me as their no-cost lieutenant governor."[62] And if they weren't convinced of his capabilities and qualifications, they could read a 41-page platform document that specified Healey's approach to government should circumstances require him to serve as governor. (This document is the focus of Chapter 9, *What Healey Thought*.)

In 2006, Healey stressed his no-cost angle. Not only would he not accept a paycheck for his services as lieutenant governor, this election season, he would not accept any campaign contributions. Instead, he invited potential contributors to make donations to a charity of their choosing.[63] Healey explained, "Since I intend to abolish the office, I will have no political plums to put on the table. I won't be able to give someone's drunken, deadbeat brother-in-law a job or hire an idiot just because he or she is the son or daughter of some politically connected supporter."[64]

Elizabeth Roberts officially entered the race for lieutenant governor in late May 2006, over two months after Healey's more *serious* road show commenced. She stressed her qualifications for the office, including her work on a proposal for the Rhode Island Affordable Health Plan and Reinsurance Program with the current lieutenant governor. Looking to the future, Roberts pledged to "expand and improve healthcare for all of us, and to build a healthy and strong Rhode Island...I can promise you...I will never stand down from the fight for quality affordable healthcare for every family in Rhode Island. I will not stand down!"[65] At the notion she could become the state's first female lieutenant governor, Roberts smiled widely and said, "That would truly be an honor."[66]

At Roberts's announcement to run for lieutenant governor, Rhode Island Senator Jack Reed introduced her, saying, "She brings to the task of government great intelligence, great integrity, and a real passion to help people."[67] Charles Fogarty, the current lieutenant governor, stood beside her at the announcement in clear support of his fellow Democrat's decision. Charles Fogarty had already announced his candidacy for Rhode Island governor.

Despite Healey's creative announcement and more serious approach toward campaigning, in comparison to his Democratic and Republican challengers, the media still largely overlooked his candidacy. Healey knew it, and had something to say about it, specifically to M. Charles Bakst, the *Providence Journal's* "make you or break you" political columnist. On July 6, 2006, Healey's letter to the editor read:

"In M. Charles Bakst's May 25 column concerning a Democratic candidate entering the race for lieutenant governor ("Kickoff contrasts: Dennis Michaud, Elizabeth Roberts"), he mentioned her primary opponent and her Republican opponent. In typical Bakst style, he omits my candidacy, although in the last election I garnered almost one-fifth of the vote...

Now I am aware of Bakst's longstanding policy of ignoring third-party and independent candidates, and I am aware that as an opinion writer he protects himself from having to fairly report a story, but his myopic avoidance of my candidacy in the race for lieutenant governor, in which I am actually raising the key issue (whether the office is necessary or just a waste of public funds), speaks volumes about his bias.

My only comfort is that Rhode Islanders don't really need a weatherman to tell them which way the wind is blowing.[68]

While Healey's response to Bakst's article drew some attention, his decision not to seek political contributions hampered the circulation of his message amongst the public. Though Bob Healey applied for the matching-funds program, he did so not to secure the money. Rather, he intended to mount a court challenge on the basis the system discriminates against independent candidates.[69] Healey explained, "The two-party system is a means of keeping the form of government the way it is." To challenge such an operation, Healey added, "Sometimes you have to think outside the box."[70] Healey's comment referenced the fact that third-party candidates had to meet more qualifications to utilize the same funds more readily available to the leading two candidates. That disadvantage, on top of all the other challenges faced by independent candidates, effectively secured the election of either a Democrat or Republican to higher office.

While Healey continued to voice his points to those who bothered to listen, Elizabeth Roberts defeated her primary opponent, Spencer Dickinson. In the Republican primary, Major Gen. Reginald

Centracchio won out over his Republican challenger and Carcieri enthusiast, Kernan King. The three runners now readied themselves at the new starting line for a two-month sprint toward November's election day.

Centracchio had joined the race well positioned to challenge Roberts. He had served 48 years in the Rhode Island National Guard, 10 of those years as the state adjutant general. Over those years, Centracchio worked with eight Rhode Island governors, including Lincoln Almond and Donald Carcieri, and the 2006 Democratic Party governor candidate, Lt. Governor Charlie Fogarty. He had earned the respect of both Democrats and Republicans.

Centracchio supported the governor and lt. governor running on the same ticket. He made his reasoning clear during a radio debate: "I think that the lieutenant governor is obliged to work with the governor, not on a separate agenda."[71] If elected lt. governor, Centracchio wanted to focus on emergency management, and often stressed leadership and accountability. He felt good about his chances, offering, "I think I've put in more time in parades than anyone else in the state."[72] More importantly, with the state's matching funds program, he had over $250,000 in his campaign coffer to challenge his frontrunner opponent, Liz Roberts.

Bob Healey's message annoyed Centracchio. Healey continued to insist that the lt. governor serves no useful purpose for the state. Seeing the office as "essential," Centracchio charged that his Cool Moose opponent had made "a mockery out of the whole election process," adding, "I am serious about this candidacy, and when I take an oath of office, I take it seriously."[73]

Healey had more "annoying" things to say about the lt. governor position he sought. Comparing the state's number two position to the vice presidency, Healey quoted Will Rogers; "The man that has the best job in the country is the vice president. All he has to do is get up every morning and say, 'How's the president?'"[74] Building on Will Roger's point, Healey questioned Lieutenant Governor Roberts's campaign emphasis on healthcare, and former state Adjutant General Reginald A. Centracchio's underscoring of emergency management: "Where else could you get a job, with a $1-million budget for the office, where you say, 'I think I'm going to do this' instead of the boss telling you what responsibilities you are going to have? It's absurd."[75]

No doubt Healey's arguments and antics gained the attention of Rhode Island voters. However, his campaign never gained the traction necessary to challenge the other high-powered candidates' better-funded campaigns. As a result, outside a couple cursory looks over their shoulders, in the final days of the campaign season neither Centracchio nor Roberts broke a sweat worrying over Healey's approach, or lack thereof. Healey's campaign demonstrated no final lap kick.

In what proved to be a "near dead-on" predictor of the 2006 election results,[76] South Kingstown High School history teacher Doug Carr and the students in his American Government class ran a schoolwide election involving 1,350 students. The young voters chose Robert J. Healey Jr. to be the state's next lt. governor. Carr attributed the students' choice of Healey to the appeal of his political party's name.[77] That fascination would not carry over to the general election.

As they normally did, Rhode Island voters chose the Democratic Party candidate for lieutenant governor. Elizabeth Roberts beat Robert Healey by approximately a four to one margin.[78] To become Rhode Island's first female lt. governor, Elizabeth Roberts spent $588,000. Reginald A. Centracchio expended $363,000 to realize his runner up placement.[79] Bob Healey dispensed $1,120.06 to bankroll his distant, last place finish.[80]

Healey did not take the defeat well. Similar to statements made after his past election losses, Healey offered a biting commentary addressing the reasons he had lost by so much, again.

"Lest I be considered a piker, I need to set the record straight. The Journal reported on Dec. 6 ("Less spent on '06 contest") that I spent a mere $417 on this year's lieutenant governor's

run. Nothing could be further from the truth. In this day and age of gross and indiscriminate spending on political advertising, no one could consider running for statewide office on such a paltry amount as $417. I spent $1,120.06 of my own money and received around 51,000 votes. I probably would have won if only I had sold out, raised money from special interests and spent a few hundred thousand dollars more on convincing the voters to pay a million dollars a year to finance a worthless office.

Without a doubt, advertisement moves the under-educated masses.[81]

Over the next several months, Bob Healey continued to write letters to the editor, five in total. Most espoused the same general message: you should have elected me to be lieutenant governor. And maybe he was right. But saying so in echo fashion sounded bad, or worse. In one particularly nasty tirade, Healey paraded what appeared to be personal vanity and contempt for the same voters (minus 51,000) whose support he had earlier courted:

Tremendous state budget deficits do not occur overnight. They take decades to mature. Knowing this, I looked back over the last 20 years. In 1986, when I ran for governor, I told you about the need for smaller, more open government and the need to rein in public-sector unions. In 1994, when I ran for governor, I told you about the need to reduce state spending. In 1998, when I ran for governor, I told you about the need to improve our system of taxation. In 2002 and 2006, when I ran for lieutenant governor, I sought to minimize government waste. These are all positions that I had committed to paper during those campaigns.

Now the sky is falling. Good luck, Rhode Island. You got exactly what you voted for—respectable-looking office holders

who ran the state into the ground. The bright side is that you
will have something to cogitate upon while standing in the soup
lines—your voting acumen, or lack thereof.

Over the last two decades you, as a Rhode Island voter,
did have access to options in voting that would have changed
the way Rhode Island operated. You chose otherwise. It is not
the politicians who deserve the blame. You've brought it onto
yourself.

As for me you can say "sour grapes." Possibly, but sour
grapes are never sweet. I too live here and will pay for this
avoidable disaster.[82]

The above commentary suggests that by the end of 2006, the Cool Moose had tired of the campaign processes, the disappointing outcomes, and the complacent electorate. In his view, it all added up to a government that operated on a "go along as usual" inflection. While one could argue persuasively that Bob Healey had done more to promote meaningful change than any other Rhode Island politician over the past twenty years, undeniably, nothing had changed—at least, not along the lines he had envisioned and campaigned vigorously for since 1986. Making the situation bleaker, any significant hope for advancement, at least of the revolutionary sort, still hinged on the Cool Moose, who no longer led an official status party, and whose losing record encouraged little confidence. If in the future Healey hoped to be the harbinger of governmental innovation, he needed to do something different from past campaigns. Catchy phrases, colorful comments, and consistent defiance had come up short, and flat. Or, at least, they hadn't moved people to vote for the possibilities Healey espoused. To reform Rhode Island, Bob Healey needed to rethink his strategy. He needed another plan.

CHAPTER 12

SO CLOSE
THE 2010 LIEUTENANT GOVERNOR RACE

L ieutenant Governor Elizabeth Roberts had a plan. In late February 2009, she floated the idea of running for governor. Adding buoyancy to that possibility, at a fundraiser she announced, "It is no secret that I am seriously exploring running for governor in 2010."[1] Continuing her not-so-clandestine campaign exploration, throughout much of 2009, Roberts moved about the state hyping her "Buy Local RI" initiative.

Healey recognized Roberts's movements around Rhode Island as a thinly veiled effort to politick for future governor votes. He made that view known and charged that Roberts "...talks about all these things that are really nice: she's going to work on healthcare, she's going to work on small-business issues...She's really good at making promises, but the proof is in the pudding."[2] When the Roberts's Buy Local roadshow toured Warren, she didn't visit Bob Healey's local business, The Cheese Plate. When a reporter asked Roberts about Healey's criticism that she did not deliver on her promises, the incumbent lieutenant governor declined to offer comment.[3] Her silence brought about no political reprisals. Throughout much of the state her "Buy

Local RI" tour experienced a warm welcome. Even in Healey's hometown, Roberts enjoyed a polite, if not enthusiastic reception.

Clearly, by spring 2009, Bob Healey's exposure could not compare to that which Elizabeth Roberts had fostered and enjoyed. Still, quite a few North Kingstown High School students thought enough of the perennial candidate to once again invite him to speak at their graduation.[4] David Lopes, a North Kingstown High School social studies teacher and a class of 2009 advisor, recalled that the students had sought on their own fruition to seek Healey's participation in their graduation exercises and made the most of the arrangements to secure his involvement.[5] Since his 1994 campaign for governor, the former Cool Moose Party leader remained wildly popular with North Kingstown's largely upper middle class youth.

Healey's popularity did not foster punctuality. Within minutes of the 2009 North Kingstown High School graduation ceremony kickoff, the faculty organizers grew anxious. Their keynote speaker had yet to arrive. Then, within seconds of the graduation procession's launch, Bob Healey darted into the University of Rhode Island parking lot and veered his automobile to the front of the Ryan Center. As soon as his car came to a screeching halt, Thomas Doran, a North Kingstown High School science teacher and a graduation organizer, rushed out to meet Healey. When Doran came upon the graduation speaker, he detected a strong odor. Doran recalled, "It was like he [Healey] drove down with the windows up and no air-conditioning on, and smoked several cigars and ate three pounds of cheese. He reeked of both."[6] Doran also remembered Healey's outwardly enthusiastic demeanor. "He really wanted to speak before the students,"[7] most of whom eagerly looked forward to hearing "the Cool Moose guy."

Doran escorted the guest speaker to the front of the procession line, passing local dignitaries along the way. As usual, Healey drew looks, reactions, and fascination.[8] When Bob Healey spoke to the students, the guest speaker stressed pursuing that which they considered most important. He assured the graduates that no one wishes on their deathbed that they had worked one more day. As he had before at North Kingstown High School, the perennial candidate won over his audience.

After the speech at North Kingstown High School, Healey went back to work and, like Roberts, thought about running for governor or taking another shot at securing the lieutenant governor's post. He settled on the latter, and he had a lot of company. Owing to Roberts's earlier consideration to run for governor, many other candidates had jumped into the prospective lt. governor candidate pool. Those waters teemed with a host of characters not often directly associated with politics. The players included a "Red Sox adviser, a casino pit boss, and a real-estate agent."[9] If elected, any one of them would stand a breath away from assuming the Rhode Island governor's responsibilities.

Even if Roberts hadn't announced that she might run for governor, the lengthening line of Rhode Island lt. governor candidates would not have surprised Healey. He explained, "It's the easiest job in the world. You look up sinecure [any office or position providing an income or other advantage but requiring little or no work] in the dictionary, and it says 'Rhode Island's lieutenant governor.'" Healey then reflected, "I can't do a legislative function because I'm not good at scratching backs or kissing butt."[10] And, so, he opted to be Rhode Island's *last* lieutenant governor.[11] And to make that happen, once again, he promised that if elected he would dismantle the office he sought.

But what made Healey think that this run for lieutenant governor would conclude differently than his other two prior failed attempts? As others had noted, "It's the economy, stupid."[12] With people's concerns heightened by the latest economic downturn from which the United States had yet to fully recover, Healey thought that maybe this year's anti-incumbent sentiment would boost his money-saving campaign idea.[13]

In July, Elizabeth Roberts announced she would seek reelection for lieutenant governor instead of pursuing the governor's post. Despite her delayed announcement, she assumed immediate favored status. *The Providence Journal* predicted that any Republican candidate running for the state's second-highest office would be hard pressed to beat Roberts.[14] History supported their prediction. Rhode Islanders had opted for a non-Democratic Party lieutenant governor only once in the past 70 years.[15] Further, Roberts remained popular, politically well supported, and amply funded.

When sizing up Roberts's competition, *The Providence Journal* made no mention of Robert Healey. The omission spoke volumes about Healey's standing before the press. And at the outset of the 2010 campaign season, popular opinion aligned closely with the media's demonstrated assessment of the Cool Moose Party candidate.

While clearly Roberts stood as Healey's most formidable opponent in the 2010 race for lieutenant governor, initially the Republicans drew more of Healey's attention. Healey offered of the state's second most powerful party, "I can't fathom why Republicans would run a candidate for that office when their supposed philosophy is small government."[16] Redirecting his ire toward Rhode Island's most popular party, Healey charged, "The Democrats want to keep the position because of the eight plum jobs that go with the office."[17]

When Healey announced his candidacy for lieutenant governor in February 2010, his commentary went to the heart of why he thought this year his message might stick. In his news release, Healey informed, "Four years ago when I proposed saving Rhode Islanders $1 million a year just by getting me elected, people would say, 'It's only a million dollars.' Now, in these economic times, I hear, 'It's a million dollars.'"[18]

Though to one degree or another the times had changed, elements of Healey's message did not. Humor, much of it self-deprecating, continued to characterize his political commentaries and campaign paraphernalia. Of his campaign to destroy the office he sought, Healey offered that the effort to do so would probably be "...busier than the job itself."[19] And similar to his last run, Healey assured that his campaign would save, not spend.[20] To do just that, the perennial

Healey campaigned on ridding of the Rhode Island lieutenant governor office he sought. In 2002, 2006, and 2010, he communicated his stance in numerous comical campaign ads. (Photo courtesy of DeWolf Fulton)

candidate put in place a unique method of promoting his candidacy. Rather than his 2010 campaign financing and distributing free large cardboard posters, visitors to his website could reproduce their own online prints. The Cool Moose Party shopper could choose from an array of political campaign materials. For instance, a Healey enthusiast might choose an enlarged image of John Lennon's body with Bob Healey's face superimposed from the shoulders upward. Under the Lennon/Healey image read a caption that played on one of the former Beatle member's songs: "IMAGINE, No Lt. Governor—It's Easy If You Try."[21] In another offering on the website, Healey's familiar bearded face appeared next to orange Dunkin' Donuts-style lettering that spelled out: "Vote for Healey, I Will Work for the Donut."[22] In addition to new campaign prints, Healey supporters could rehang Cool Moose Party posters from the past two lieutenant governor races. One particularly popular political advertisement of that genre included a black and white poster with five shrinking caricatures of Healey with the caption, "THERE HE WAS...GONE."

While Healey's ideas for change presented more substantive than his campaign gimmicks, his promotional strategies and messages continued to exhale an air of humor. In one such amusing example, Healey's 2010 campaign introduced an "e-mail this to your friends" approach. He termed the idea, "Just pick two." He explained of the concept, "I cringe when people say, 'vote out all the incumbents'... [because] there are, believe it or not, some good people in government and they should not be [thrown out like] the proverbial baby with the bath water."[23] Healey further explained, "I actually have a few incumbent officials I think worthy of re-election. I know that if pushed, I could whittle this down to two. That done, I could feel comfortable in voting for the two incumbents while voting out the rest of the dead wood."[24] In a related expressed point of view, but of a more serious overtone, Healey explained that he did not support term limits because "the voting public should be allowed to be as idiotic as they choose to be. The continual election of the same people is a self-created problem that needs to be solved by thinking minds in an election booth. To tell people they cannot vote for a person's re-election smacks of elitism."[25]

As in the past, Healey had a blueprint to obliterate the office he sought. First, he would take no salary for *upholding* the position. Second, he would not maintain a staff. Third, he would pressure the General Assembly to place a constitutional amendment on the ballot to either transform the office "into something that actually does something," or get rid of it entirely.[26] He preferred the latter. Fourth, during the interim he would remain in office in case the governor could not continue to serve.

A situation involving Elizabeth Roberts in 2007 may have helped Healey make a case that the Rhode Island lieutenant governor's office serves no relevant purpose, or at least that governors underutilize the office. In December 2007, Rhode Island Governor Donald Carcieri took a trip to Iraq. He did not bother to notify his lieutenant governor when he departed.[27] In fact, even after Carcieri's departure, Roberts had "no idea" the governor had exited the country.[28] As the fates would have it, during the governor's absence, a snowstorm hit the Ocean State with greater force than expected, and at the most inopportune time: rush hour. School buses got stuck. Traffic jams lengthened. Tempers rose. Everybody, including nervous mothers waiting for their young children to return from school and infuriated radio talk show hosts stuck in traffic, clamored for the government to step up and address the calamity. With the Republican governor several thousand miles away and the situation worsening, the predicament presented an opportune time to transfer command of the storm response to the Democratic lieutenant governor. Governor Carcieri chose to do otherwise. Even when an unusual circumstance made a case for the lt. governor's purpose, Roberts languished in dormancy—though not of her own choosing.

At some level, even Elizabeth Roberts might have realized Healey's point about her office. One year during her tenure as lieutenant governor, she submitted a humorous self-deprecating ad in the Providence Newspaper Guild Follies. The Follies offered a reprieve from serious politics for a night of jokes and laughter amongst politicians and the press. In an undeniable reference to Governor Carcieri and the lack of communication between his and her office, the ad taken out by Roberts portrayed her sitting by a telephone, with a caption that read, "He never calls."[29]

Many other state lieutenant governors shared Roberts's frustration, if not her wit. At a 2010 national lieutenant governors' conference, several second-in-command state office holders commented on their limited role in governing. An Illinois lt. governor revealed, that "boredom" accounted for her resignation from the office, while a New York lt. governor referenced "irrelevance" for the reason he left office.[30] Other lt. governors reflected on the divide with their state's sitting governor. When pressed by a reporter, one such lt. governor described her relationship with the state's governor as "polite."[31]

As Healey readied for his third pursuance of (and attack on) the Rhode Island lieutenant governor's position, Republican candidates seeking the same office battled it out for their party's nomination. The aspirants included Raymond X. Murray of Pawtucket, Heidi W. Rogers of Foster, Kara D. Russo of Providence, and Robert G. Tingle of Westerly.[32] Tingle had run before as a Republican candidate for the United States House of Representatives and Senate. In both runs, Tingle (and the Republican Party) failed to raise enough money to fund a substantial campaign, which in part lead to Tingle's resounding defeats.[33]

Tingle's past lack of political successes probably influenced the judgments of Giovanni Cicione, the Rhode Island Republican Party Chairman. Cicione's forthcoming declarations proved a game changer for Robert Healey's political fortunes. When Tingle first indicated an interest in running for lieutenant governor in 2010, Cicione declared, "I believe that the feeling among the grassroots GOP members is that supporting Bob Healey is the way to go for 2010. I'm going to withhold my personal opinion until the convention, but I will say that I'm supportive of the ongoing consideration of Healey as an option."[34] And Bob Healey had entertained the same notion. Heidi Rogers, the Republican competing for her party's lieutenant governor nomination, said that before the primary "Bob Healey had requested the [GOP] endorsement, then he withdrew his request."[35]

In the Democratic Party, Jeremy A. Kapstein, Boston Red Sox senior adviser, stepped up to challenge Elizabeth Roberts. In addition, Robert P. Venturini of Pawtucket entered the race as an independent. Venturini hosted a local cable TV show, "An Hour with Bob." He had joined the race declaring, "This is the time to run. This is the year to get rid of all the incumbents. People are just mad."[36] Bob Healey agreed with his independent competitor on that much, but obviously toward a different endgame.

Healey also agreed with the developments within the Republican Party. Days after defeating Kara Russo, Heidi Rogers (who wanted to get rid of the lt. governor position) dropped out of the general election—hours shy of the deadline for doing so. Rogers made that decision because she questioned the rationale for her and Healey running against one another when they shared the same goal. The continuation of that arrangement risked splitting their support base to the benefit of Elizabeth Roberts, who stood in opposition to the Republican and Cool Moose Parties' shared objective.[37]

Rogers, an early supporter of Healey, explained that she had entered the primary when other members of her party considered running for lt. governor and "...maintaining it in its current wasteful form."[38] When Rogers won the Republican primary, she met with the Republican state leadership and Bob Healey to talk about which candidate had the best chance of winning the election, she or Healey. Russo reported, "I had to concede that Mr. Healey has a long history of advocating for this position, and that he has a following of supporters who identify him with this cause."[39]

Regarding the fairness of the above arrangement to Kara Russo, Rogers offered: "She's very passionate about her issues. She's a very nice person. [But] I don't think that the issues that Kara was bringing forward were what's on the voters' minds right now...And the people that voted for me, I thank them, and I really hope that they'll stand behind Bob Healey as well."[40]

Russo saw something more sinister than political logic in Rogers's decision. Russo accused Rogers and the Rhode Island GOP of having "lied to the public." She went on angrily, "The will of the people—of the voters—was subverted. The people who voted for Heidi Rogers were under the impression that Heidi Rogers wanted to become the next Lieutenant Governor of Rhode Island. As she clearly did not, her entire 'candidacy' was deceptive, to say the least."[41]

Chairman Giovanni Cicione had a different take on developments within the state Republican Party. Rather than directing Kara Russo's concerns directly, he instead focused more on Heidi Rogers's reasons for opting out of the race. He offered, "I respect Heidi's decision to withdraw her candidacy and I applaud her willingness to stand by her convictions." Cicione added, "I understand the reasoning that went into this decision and I join my fellow members of the RI Republican Party and its leadership who are in support of Heidi's decision." Focusing on his candidate of choice, Cicione continued, "Bob Healey's commitment to end the abuse of taxpayer dollars for personal political gain through this office—to the tune of $1 million per year—is entirely consistent with the principles of the RI Republican Party and we understand that all Rhode Islanders will benefit, regardless of which individual saves that money for the taxpayers."[42]

Fellow Republican Kara Russo couldn't let Cicione's "understanding" go without a challenge. She took her concerns to the state board of elections and argued that the Republican Party's decision had disenfranchised the voters. However, she did not succeed in convincing the board to support her position. Soon after, the Rhode Island Supreme Court decided not to hear Russo's appeal. While frustrated, at that point Russo discontinued her efforts to challenge the state of affairs within the Rhode Island Republican Party.

With the Republican Party turmoil settled, the three remaining candidates, Elizabeth Roberts, Robert Healey, and Bob Venturini, readied themselves for a spirited race. (Roberts had defeated Kapstein in the Democratic Party primary.) Unlike the last election for lieutenant governor, the press, the people, and the three political participants anticipated an all-out run to the finish. And for the first time in recent memory, the Republicans would play the role of audience, cheering on the Cool Moose Party candidate.

While upbeat about the Republican Party's support of his candidacy, Healey remained cautiously optimistic about his improved chances. He offered, in a controlled and comical manner, "We have to wait and see what the people think. I mean I am not the prettiest candidate, and I know people have some sort of inbred animosity." He further processed, "It's odd to me. I mean the long hair and the beard certainly is a recognizable persona; on the other hand, I know it works against me in many ways." Then, comparing himself to Jesus Christ, if only in appearance, he reasoned; "I know people go to church every

Sunday and worship someone with long hair, and yet can't see that their elected officials could potentially have the same appearance."[43]

With the Republicans' endorsement of the Cool Moose candidate, Kara Russo's subsequent challenge of her party's decision, Elizabeth Robert's continued popularity, and the colorful candidacy of Robert Venturini, the 2010 lieutenant governor race drew hyped attention. Robert Weygand, a former lieutenant governor, took notice: "There hasn't been this much activity and comment about the lieutenant governor's race in 20 years."[44] Edward Fitzpatrick published an article on the race, entitled, "Grandmother wouldn't believe this circus." In that article, Fitzpatrick shared, "...the lieutenant governor's race—a guaranteed snoozer in most states—now has more twists and turns than Snake Hill Road."[45] He pointed out that Healey "usually can make a race interesting on his own."[46] This year he had help from Heidi Rogers, Kara Russo, and Bob Venturini, a celebrated customer of Leonard Hair Transplant Associates.[47]

Despite the Republican Party's decision to support the Cool Moose candidate for lieutenant governor, into October 2010 Elizabeth Roberts maintained a comfortable lead over Robert Healey. Early in that month, Roberts polled at 35.8 percent, followed by Robert Healey and Robert Venturini, who weighed in at 22.5 percent and 7.4 percent support respectively. Though the October numbers suggested a comfortable future win for Roberts, Healey had polled significantly better than the end results of his past runs. Also, he knew a lot could change in a month. And it did.

In October, Bob Healey continued to take the fight to his opposition, in all its forms, and at every opportunity. When the four major gubernatorial candidates—Frank T. Caprio, Lincoln D. Chaffee, John F. Robataille, and Kenneth J. Block—made a strong case for the lieutenant governor's office to remain in place, Healey leapt at their political jugulars. He charged that their support of the lieutenant governor's position discredited "...their own claims of seeking to control waste and unnecessary spending..." He continued, "It's just downright illogical to believe that these candidates are even remotely sincere in their positions related to fiscal control. Here is the lowest-hanging fruit to cut from the budget and yet these candidates cannot come out in support of the elimination. I don't think it reflects on the positive nature of the lieutenant governor's office, but instead works to undermine their positions that they will look high and low to eliminate waste."[48] Healey finished, "I leave people with the question, 'Can you believe these candidates on the issue of fiscal reform when you hear that they are okay with the status quo of keeping the waste of $1 million each and every year spent on an office of lieutenant governor?'"[49]

Healey's perseverance paid dividends. In mid-October, a poll, conducted by retired Rhode Island College political science professor Victor Profughi, reported that Healey stood within striking distance of Elizabeth Roberts. Her earlier double-digit lead had shrunk to five percentage points, with a nine-point margin of error. Though no one could account fully for the change in fortunes, approximately two weeks prior to the November election, the two frontrunners found themselves in a dead heat.[50] Interestingly, the poll reported Healey ahead in several districts, but behind in the East Bay, a traditional Healey stronghold. Regardless, Healey had gained ground on the incumbent, creating a nose-to-nose horse race. And Healey continued to pick up the pace.

On October 18, 2010, *The Providence Journal* published Robert Healey's 760-word commentary. Healey hit Roberts hard in the piece, unloading every one of his campaign speaking points. Making a fervent case for his cause, he made sure to hold nothing back. Like a runner in the last leg of a marathon race, he saw no reason to reserve energy for another lap. He wanted to reveal, reiterate, and repeat each relevant fact, opinion and argument his campaign espoused. The prospective voter needed to know, wholly and succinctly, why they should choose Robert Healey over Elizabeth Roberts. In pursuit of that feat, he had to leave everything on the campaign trail via his *Providence Journal* opinion piece. And he did just that:

One million dollars. What would you do?

No, this is not a lottery ad, it's the annual budget for the lieutenant governor's office. Okay, you say, it's only a million a year and we need a lieutenant governor. But do we?

The sole constitutional function of that office is embodied in Article 9 Section 9 of the Rhode Island Constitution. It requires that the lieutenant governor await the governor's demise. Our New England neighbors New Hampshire and Maine do not have a lieutenant governor. Nor does progressive Oregon. They all seem to survive quite well. And, of the states that have a lieutenant governor, many (Illinois, Louisiana, Utah, Florida, Massachusetts, Connecticut and California, to name a few) are currently discussing the need for such an obsolete office.

With the possible exception of Minnesota, no state with a lieutenant governor has an undefined role for the office. Lieutenant governors in those states are typically constitutionally required to act in various capacities, from presiding over the Senate, casting tie-breaking votes, serving as governor when the governor is beyond the state boundaries, or being assigned a legislative or executive portfolio.

Not so in Rhode Island. Having stripped the office of constitutionally mandated function, we let our lieutenant governors create their own agenda. So we get a political parking space that hires cronies to work on a publicly financed lobbying effort for the lieutenant governor's pet project. Further, with no constitutional authority to do so, the General Assembly had assigned various tasks and powerless "advisory" committee assignments to the office to create a public perception that there is work being done. And, even then, a majority of the appointments are either to defunct committees, or not made.

Meanwhile, the typical Rhode Island family of four earns about $52,000 a year (a decrease of $1,400 in the last 10 years). Yet the lieutenant governor's chief of staff alone is *earning over $156,000 a year, without counting the health benefits, pension costs, FICA and retiree health. There are seven people on a paid staff to do nothing at taxpayer expense.*

So, you ask, what would I do differently? I would serve as lieutenant governor, but I would do so without compensation and without hiring a staff, effectively shutting down the office, and immediately saving Rhode Island $1 million a year—$4 million during my entire term in office. I would assume all constitutionally required duties of the office. If called to serve as governor, I bring a far greater skill set to the office than just health care. My background spans the three major areas of state governance: law and general welfare, education, and economic development....

In short, I am not looking for a job... I cannot, in all good conscience, indulge myself in what I see as greed by demanding the people of Rhode Island pay me to speak out on my personal agenda while waiting for the governor to die.

As lieutenant governor, I would suspend my legal practice for my term in office... Like my opponent, Lt. Gov. Elizabeth Roberts, I am a millionaire, but my opponent wants to take the pay, and I don't. As my old Italian grandmother would say, "You can only eat so many hamburgers."

While I am known for my creatively thinking outside the box, for my accepting projects based on the challenge over the financial gain, for my stubborn perseverance to achieve a just end, and for my appearance, which keeps me on the outside of the political mainstream, I have always taken government service seriously and have dedicated myself to the role.

I seek the office of lieutenant governor to eliminate a wasteful office and to save the taxpayers millions without any loss of services or functions. A well-run business would not tolerate such a waste; why should you?

One million dollars a year. What would you do?[51]

Healey's editorial stripped down the lieutenant's office to its bare essence. He compared Rhode Island to other states that functioned "quite well" without a lieutenant governor's position, provided a cost analysis for not continuing the status quo, and perhaps most importantly, laid out his credentials favorably against Roberts's qualifications to be governor, should a circumstance necessitate assumption of such duties. He communicated the pointed list in a serious, and at times signature sarcastic, voice. And he had hammered home his positions within three weeks of election day. Propelled by a competitor's stride in sight of an unsnapped finish line tape, Healey had broken into a sprint toward the November 2 date.

If anyone in October 2012 still questioned Healey's arrival as a major political force, Elizabeth Roberts removed any lingering doubt. In past elections, Healey's opponents ignored him as much as possible. Acknowledging the Cool Moose in the room offered little potential gain for his opponent, but could provide increased exposure, and potentially political momentum, for the third-party candidate. Best to let a sleeping moose lie. Even during debates (when Healey *qualified* for such forums), opposing candidates within touching distance of his physical presence would rarely venture a glance in his direction. The avoidance communicated to the general public that Bob Healey didn't matter. But by late October 2010, clearly Healey did matter, and Roberts's campaign knew it. With days remaining in the campaign, the incumbent had no choice but to turn the klieg lights directly on the charging Cool Moose Party founder.

In addition to increasing unflattering interview mentions of Healey, the Roberts's campaign released a $200,000 anti-Healey television spot. In that political television commercial, a narrator stressed the following message in a deliberate, eerily haunting, deep voice:

> *Twenty times in the last decade lieutenant governors around the country have become governor. [Pause] It could happen here in Rhode Island. [Pause] So what do we really know*

about Bob Healey? We know he doesn't even have a plan for
jobs. We know he says he'll do absolutely nothing. No plan for
jobs? Nothing — with all the problems we face? Bob Healey
has failed the test. It's time to say no to Bob Healey."[52]

Roberts's campaign ad focused solely on the Cool Moose candidate, making no mention of the incumbent lieutenant governor. The Democrats' political ad sought a singular goal: raise doubts about Healey's fitness to govern. Roberts's campaign portrayed Healey as a mad recluse with no real-world solutions for the problems faced by serious government leaders, like Elizabeth Roberts. The ad enlisted a masterful, time-tested political campaign formula: instill fear, add unflattering images, throw fair play to the wind, and pipe in a Boris Karloff-like voiced narrator with chilling background music. The ad had an unnerving effect, as Ed Fitzpatrick of *The Providence Journal* picked up on, sort of. Fitzpatrick presented the "Scariest and Most Effective Campaign Ad Award" to Democratic Lt. Gov. Elizabeth H. Roberts. He wrote, "After seeing it, I locked the doors. Then I reviewed what I know about Healey: For instance, he used to run a wine and cheese shop, so I guess that could be scary if you're lactose intolerant."[53] Scary or not, the ad added up to political gold.

And for insurance purposes, the Roberts's campaign had capitalized on the element of surprise. Elizabeth Roberts stood as the female version of prior lieutenant governor Charlie Fogarty: polite, friendly, and just enough "golly gee" factor to lower the political opponents' guard. Healey probably never saw Roberts's stealthy attack ad coming. And she had released the high-profile offensive at the perfect time. There remained enough days in the campaign for the electorate to consider the message. Compounding the advantage for Roberts, there remained little opportunity for Healey to deflate the claims or counterattack. Further, in addition to the elapsing time, Healey's anemic campaign budget prevented him from funding an effective wide-ranging response.

Soon after airing the ad, and shortly before Election Day,

Elizabeth Roberts, Robert Healey, and Robert Venturini participated in a WPRO radio debate. Station news director Bill Haberman
moderated the debate. Local news reporter Jim Hummel and former
Lieutenant Governor Arlene Violet asked questions of the three candidates. The airwaves that Thursday filled with charges of "gimmicks,"
and "insider deals."[54] When not attacking one another, they bragged
about past accomplishments or made promises of future achievements. Unlike any other debate Healey had participated in before, he
served as the primary target of his opponents' attacks. In an unmis-
takable reference to Healey, the current lieutenant governor charged,
"We need a lieutenant governor who is serious, who has a deep understanding of how things run—not someone who's interested in creating more slogans, more gimmicks, and more self-promotion."[55] For
Healey's part, he made clear once again that the office he sought "is
powerless, needs to be eliminated, and wastes a million dollars" annually.[56] And in case someone hadn't already heard, Healey explained
that the lieutenant governor's job, as presently explained in the Rhode
Island Constitution, "is to wait for death, incapacity, or removal of the
governor."[57] Healey then laid out his plan for the office's demolition.

In the debate, Venturini played the part normally expected of
Healey: colorful commentator. The cable television host reduced the
choice for lieutenant governor to a race between "a ghost" (Roberts), "a
gimmick" (Healey), and Venturini, "the guy who spent 19 years pro-
ducing shows featuring Rhode Islanders" and who would transform
the lieutenant governor's position into "a bully pulpit" to take on crucial issues, such as rooting out corruption.[58]

At one point in the debate, Healey took umbrage with the $200,000
TV commercial recently released by the Roberts's campaign. Healey
questioned the ad's implications: "The candidate of nothing? The candidate of nowhere? I think the issue is really a negative ad proffered
by my opponent...the real issue is, should this person be your governor if the worst happens?"[59] Healey then ran through his credentials:
advanced degrees, established law practice, educational experience,

and business world success. He stood ready, he assured, to step in as governor, if a circumstance warranted.

For her part, Roberts brought up the Republican primary, intent on reminding the public of Healey's alleged sordid part in the episode. Of that prior bizarre development, Roberts charged, "It reeks of the kind of insider deal we see too often in Rhode Island, and I think Mr. Healey owes an apology to the people who voted in that primary."[60] Healey responded that the issue amounted to "a tempest in a teapot."[61]

The WPRO debate had continued the ongoing spirited back and forth confrontation between Roberts and Healey that had revved up in early October and would continue right up to Election Day, November 2. In an interview just prior to Election Day, over a breakfast of French fries and coffee at Rod's Grill in Warren, Healey remarked of Roberts that, "She thought she was going to have a cakewalk, and now she has a race." And in that same interview, Healey reiterated, yet again, that the lieutenant governor's office "is all pet projects that you make up yourself. People use it to push their [way to] higher elective office."[62]

During a Channel 10 political roundtable with Roberts, Healey, and Venturini, Healey dismissed Roberts's brag sheet of accomplishments and said, "It's all talk, talk, talk. The office has no power."[63] When responding to accusations of a backroom deal with Republicans right after their primary, Healey retorted, "I reject that emphatically. Because I know what happened. It was done in public and on the radio and at the [GOP] convention. It came down to, I had a better shot."[64]

In the home stretch, Roberts's referenced the lieutenant governor's office as "a clearinghouse" for Rhode Islanders' concerns.[65] Of Healey's competitive status in the race, Roberts claimed not to be surprised. She assured, "I take [Healey] very seriously."[66] Roberts hadn't complimented her opponent. Referring to the Republican primary as "rigged from the beginning," Roberts added, "I've been aware, particularly after they engineered the Republican departing the race—I knew this was going to be a more competitive race…" Then she put Healey's surprising high poll numbers in a wider negative context: "…Throughout the country you see people who are normally not credible candidates who have run multiple times, who are more competitive in this election."[67] (Roberts may have intended to reference the likes of Jimmy McMillan who ran for governor of New York that same year, repeatedly emphasizing the retort, "The rent is too damn high.")

Roberts's attacks may have hurt Healey's standing before Rhode Islanders, but probably not as much as two other developments in the final days of the campaign. With the race coming down to the wire, Healey did himself no favors when he released a low budget YouTube video four days prior to election day. In the video, Healey sat around flashing a wide grin, donned in a white robe, listening to a spoof on the Beatles' popular song, "All You Need is Love." The song's remake included lyrics such as, "All You Need is Gov," and "Nothing to be done and then you're done."[68] While entertaining, and vintage Bob Healey, the video, released at a critical point in the campaign, may have helped the current lieutenant governor question her opponent's standing as a serious candidate.

If the above video release didn't cause the public to question Healey's readiness for office, a PolitiFact report published three days prior to Election Day most certainly harmed his credibility. PolitiFact investigated comments Bob Healey had made about the irrelevance of the lieutenant governor's office. Referencing a recent Healey commentary piece in *The Providence Journal* (printed almost entirely earlier in this chapter), in which he stated that "... the states that have a lieutenant governor, many ... are currently discussing the need for such an obsolete office."[69] According to PolitiFact, "Healey sent more than a dozen citations of newspaper and magazine articles to support his statement that there is much buzz about eliminating the office."[70] But PolitiFact pointed out that the supplied sources amounted to little more than opinion pieces, "with no evidence of current wider discussion, broad-based movements or any legislative action."[71] Where drives to remove the office of lieutenant governor did occur, all had failed. The articles Healey provided "preceded the failed attempts."[72] When

PolitiFact approached Healey with their findings, he responded, "When people are talking about it in editorials or newspapers, people are talking about the issue. That's pretty much about the issue."[73] The PolitiFact researchers pretty much disagreed, and printed that determination for Rhode Islanders to read. PolitiFact concluded that Healey's reference to other states "currently discussing" the removal of their lieutenant governor position inferred "substantially more" than opinion pieces. They ruled Healey's statement, "Barely True."[74]

On election night, Lieutenant Governor Elizabeth Roberts arrived at the Biltmore Hotel in Providence, welcomed by faithful Democratic voters. After spending over a half million dollars for her re-election bid,[75] she now waited for the precincts to report their tallies. Bob Healey, after spending $3,600 to abolish the office he sought, sat in the WPRI studios in East Providence with a single reporter waiting for the same results that interested the current lt. governor. When Channel 12 reporter Erin Kennedy asked Healey where he would watch the results that night (an interesting question considering he was sitting in the Channel 12 studio as the results started to come in,) Healey responded in a very subdued manner, "Well, a variety of places. Rather than having a party of one [location] we decided to let our people go wherever they wish to go and see what happens."[76]

Just prior to news stations reporting the night's first results, Kennedy asked Healey about his anticipation of the election outcome: "It's very close. You can probably almost taste it, right?" Healey responded dryly, "Well, it's close. We knew it was going to be a horse race all the way so it's kind of interesting to see where it's all going to turn out." Kennedy then shared the first reporting of the night. Those numbers increased confidence, for a short while, in a Healey upset victory. She announced, "Less than one percent of precincts in, but we do have you at 51 percent versus Elizabeth Roberts at 42 percent." Healey did not show any outward excitement about the first incoming tallies. Instead, he cautioned that depending where those early precinct reports emanated determined the degree to which they indicated good news. And within a minute, the results changed dramatically, though again they reflected only a small percentage of the state's precinct results. Healey had fallen behind Roberts. In a somewhat dampening fashion, Healey reflected, "A win tonight would be very nice, but a loss tonight is probably my retirement from political careers."[77]

As the results continued to pour in, it became starkly clear that the night belonged to Roberts, once again. Taking 55 percent of the vote compared to Healey's 39 percent, Roberts got to ask and answer the question many had queried repeatedly: "So, do you think Bob Healey's right? Do you think the office should be eliminated?" She responded gleefully that the voters had spoken, and they had said, "No."[78]

Healey offered of his third loss in a lt. governor race, "I've lived in some very interesting times and had a great ride, and I really don't think the stars would align to make an independent grass-roots campaign work again." He added, "It shows that money wins elections."[79] As he had suggested earlier if he lost the election, he reiterated that maybe the time had arrived to retire from political life.

As he readied for his retirement from active campaigning, Healey continued to write letters to the editor on subjects he thought a need for his expressed opinion existed. As had become familiar in past post-election periods, most of his written contributions had a sarcastic, bitter overtone.

In one stark departure from the negative, Healey served as the incognito surprise guest at the 2011 Providence Newspaper Guild Follies. One thousand politicians, reporters, businessmen, and associated professionals attended the annual dinner. Dressed as the son God, Healey thanked everyone for partaking in his "retirement from politics party."[80] Giggling his way through much of his farewell address, Healey threw light political jabs at politicians, all in fun. He finished his retirement announcement by singing to the melody of *Feelings*: "All my life I'm losing. I'll never run again."[81] And this time he seemed to mean it.

The next statewide election was almost four years away.

CHAPTER 13

THE FINAL CAMPAIGN

Almost four years after his disappointing 2010 lieutenant governor race loss and three years after his political "retirement party" at the 2011 Providence Newspaper Guild Follies, Bob Healey sprang back into the political arena in headline-making fashion. This time he would run for governor. And how could he not? The Rhode Island Moderate Party had made him an offer too good to pass up.

The Moderate Party's proposal drew up everything to Healey's liking. William Gilbert, the party's chairman, offered Healey a short 2014 campaign season, with no primary battle. As the Moderate Party's candidate, Bob would assume immediately the status of a major party candidate and secure invites to all governor debates. And most importantly, he had carte blanche to say what he felt. The Moderate Party would not micromanage its candidate. Caging the Cool Moose Party founder would have served as a deal breaker.

Earlier in 2014, Healey had considered running for the lieutenant governor's office, yet again, as an independent. However, he did not secure enough signatures to qualify for the race.[1] As such, it appeared that Healey would not participate as a candidate for anything in the

2014 political season. However, developments in the state's *third* officially recognized political party changed the fates. In September 2014, James Spooner, the Moderate Party's original candidate for governor, withdrew from the race. Spooner, the former chair of the Rhode Island Democratic Party and a past candidate for local and state offices, dropped out of the contest due to ailing health. Spooner's removal created a crisis for the Moderate Party. In short order, the party needed to fill Spooner's spot. Of that process, William Gilbert explained, "We looked at the people that were available. We felt that Robert, Mr. Healey, actually aligned pretty significantly with the party, being for very centrist views" and "limited government."[2]

The Moderate Party's chairman had another reason for approaching Healey to run as their governor nominee, and this reasoning likely accounted as the chief motive for pursuing Healey's participation in the race. In 2010, Ken Block ran as the Moderate Party candidate for governor and earned 6.5 percent of the vote. Those results qualified the party to appear in one of the three more high profile positions on the Rhode Island 2014 ballot. Via a lottery, they might even qualify to appear first on the ballot, thereby drawing the potential favor of Rhode Island voters. In order for the Moderate Party to maintain their coveted spot on the 2018 ballot, they needed to secure at least 5 percent of the overall vote for governor in 2014. Ken Block had run unsuccessfully in the Republican primary to serve as that party's 2014 governor nominee. Therefore, with a narrowed field of available and viable political aspirants from which to choose, the Moderate Party figured rightly that naming Bob Healey as their candidate for governor significantly increased their chances of reaching the desired 5 percent vote threshold.

While the Moderates rolled out the former Cool Moose as a near perfect candidate to represent their party, in truth, Healey did not line up all that well with the Moderate Party—or, for that matter, any other party. Healey never tried to fit in or follow a prescribed path. Instead, he blazed trails for others to follow. In that sense, 2014 would not differ from his previous campaigns. While Moderate Party candidates accepted money to promote their message, Healey rarely did. To stress that point, Healey explained early on in his 2014 campaign, "To accept money and expect that that there's not going to be a call on that cash is just a ridiculous way of approaching politics."[3] Further demonstrating that Healey existed outside the Moderate Party realm, the former Cool Moose candidate pointed out, "Even though the Moderate Party has a candidate for lieutenant governor, I still want to get rid of the office."[4]

So, while the union between the Moderates and the former Cool Moose Party candidate did not meet the criteria of a partisan marriage made in political heaven, for the good of the order the Moderate Party leadership agreed to rally around their new candidate's central message. Healey called for a "cerebral revolution" that would inspire Rhode Islanders "to think differently."[5] He explained, "They have to think in terms of austerity, and they have to think in terms of consolidation, they have to think in terms of getting what they're paying for. Waste in government needs to be stopped. There have always been more efficient, more effective ways of providing services."[6]

Before Healey could get people to think differently, he first had to fend off a Republican Party challenge regarding the Moderate Party's eleventh-hour governor candidate appointment. Brandon Bell, Republican Party's lawyer, questioned whether Gilbert even had the authority to name Spooner's replacement. According to a recent filing with the secretary of state's office, Ken Block, the Moderate Party's creator, still served as the party's chair. But Healey pointed out that the Moderate Party had updated its organization papers with the Board of Elections a day prior to empowering their new chairman to make decisions, such as replacing a candidate who resigns for reasons such as ill health.[7]

Another point of contention over Healey's appointment involved the amount of time he had been a Moderate Party member prior to the organization naming him their governor candidate. This challenge led to a spirited exchange between Elections Board member Richard Dubois and Bob Healey:

Dubois: Mr. Healey, such an important office as governor and…
   they just picked you out of the sky. Do you know these people?
Healey: I know Mr. Gilbert and Mr. Spooner.
Dubois: Do you know their philosophy?"
Healey: I know of the philosophy of the party, but I don't know
   where the relevance is to the matter at hand.[8]

To this line of questioning, Healey wrote in his own filing to
the Election Board, "As an unaffiliated voter, both at the time of the
replacement and 90 days prior to the final day of declaration of candidacy, the issue is moot."[9]

Perhaps Healey's most persuasive argument defending his candidacy as the Moderate Party's governor nominee exists in his following
commentary: "It would be [a] miscarriage of justice to allow the election ballot to reflect a candidate who has withdrawn under a disability
[rather] than to have the electors choose a real and viable candidate."[10]
The Election Board agreed with Healey, deciding in a 4 to 1 vote to
support his nomination as the Moderate Party's governor candidate.[11]
After the board rendered its decision, Republican Party chairman
Mark Smiley reflected, "It's a hard issue to deal with. There was a
long, drawn-out primary battle, and there was a lot of work done by
those candidates that survived the primary…We just needed to make
sure that all the people on the ballot were properly qualified."[12] Smiley
pursued no further challenge in court. Healey stood as the Moderate
Party's 2014 candidate for governor.

With the Republican Party's challenge settled, Healey had less
than two months to make his case to Rhode Islanders. Though Healey
preferred sprint-like campaigns to marathon contests, winning over
Rhode Island voters within 60 days presented a most arduous assignment. Adding to those challenges, the two frontrunner candidates for
governor, Democrat Gina Raimondo—the state's general treasurer—
and Republican Allan Fung—Cranston's mayor—enjoyed wide name
recognition throughout Rhode Island. Raimondo had even garnered

significant national exposure, most notably for reforming the Rhode Island pension fund while state treasurer.[13] Fung focused his general election campaign on lowering taxes. Raimondo's message circulated around investing in infrastructure. Both campaigners drew the attention of Rhode Island's potential voters.

Neither of his high-profile political contenders phased Healey in the least. As such, he wasted no time taking on his two powerhouse opponents. When asked how he would single himself out from Allan Fung and Gina Raimondo, he replied, "I'm nicer."[14] In a more direct and serious commentary, Healey targeted Raimondo where she lived: in the land of promised economic growth. Healey professed, "I certainly don't believe in Gina's policies of growing success. I find it hard to believe that a venture capitalist would go into a business, see it failing, and say, 'What we need to do is give it more money to fail more.' What we need to do is actually restructure the business, the business of state...."[15] Of Fung, Healey commented, "He understands the problems of government, especially at a local level. I just haven't seen him really push forth on issues."[16] Healey said both his rivals were "cut of the same cloth."[17] He charged that they looked to government programs to fix problems rather than considering changes to the actual structure of the government.

Regardless of whether Fung and Raimondo were actually cut from the same cloth, Healey needed to separate himself discernibly from the candidate pack. In an attempt to do so, Healey called for a transformation in the Rhode Island government.[18] He charged that, "You can't just continue as Gina or Allan want to do. You can't just say you want to grow your way out. It's putting new tires on a vehicle that needs a new engine."[19] Healey added, "It's my job to convince people to think in a different way." Hearkening back to a famous line from President Kennedy's 1961 inaugural address, Healey elucidated further, "It's not what my state can do for me, it's what I can do for my state."[20]

While few questioned that Healey had a message to deliver, they did wonder whether he had enough money to take on two very well-financed campaigns. He did not, but that didn't concern Healey either.

He didn't need money, or hardly any. Healey had no paid staff. He planned no media blitz on television, radio, or in the newspapers. His volunteer supporters downloaded public-domain images of Healey "so anybody could produce anything."[21] Healey supporters printed their own signs, as they had in a past race when the then-Cool Moose candidate ran for lt. governor. A local sign maker did print larger signs for public dissemination, but he sold them to interested parties at cost.[22] If that proved unaffordable, people could get their hands on recycled signs from past elections for free. And while that practice seemed problematic to some, as most of Healey's old campaign signs referenced his run for the lieutenant governor position, Healey laughed off such concerns. He instructed his campaign volunteers to cross out "Lieutenant" on the old posters and give them out to all interested parties.[23] Healey liked that idea so much that he elected to expand the practice. He explained, "We recycled everything—anything I could cross out the word 'lieutenant.' We recycled buttons. We had some old bumper stickers from when I ran for governor in '98. In the attic, I found a case of Cool Moose combs, which I had in '86. Yardsticks."[24] But Healey didn't actually recycle *everything*. When asked whether he had any condoms leftover from his lt. governor campaigns, he admitted, "We did, but they all expired in 2003. We didn't want to be giving out expired condoms."[25]

Healey's campaign invented endless ways to save money. In one example of extreme frugality, Healey painted a campaign message on a building wall with old black paint. This proved more difficult than he first anticipated. Healey struggled to open old cans of Rust-Oleum. They had rusted shut. Healey jested, "I found that rather ironic. They should make [Rust-Oleum] cans that don't rust."[26]

Healey's campaign could not afford to print out promotional shirts to be distributed for free. Again, that presented no serious hurdle. Supporters of the Healey 2014 campaign *purchased* a "ton" of "Healey for governor" shirts.[27] In essence, Healey supporters paid to advertise their candidate.

Some questioned the exceptionally low expense report Healey provided at the end of the race. However, PolitiFact found his claims to be "true."[28] The Healey campaign expenditures stood in stark contrast with the high-powered Raimondo and Fung operations.

The 2014 political season qualified as the attention-grabbing headline variety. And even though Healey's campaign spent almost no money, Bob Healey earned his fair share of mentions in the press. Setting the stage for the new Rhode Island election season, *Providence Journal* reporter Edward Fitzpatrick wrote:

> "… the 2014 campaign season has had just about everything. Everything, that is, except another third-party candidacy by the founder of the Cool Moose Party.
>
> Well now, ladies and gentlemen, we have a full Rhode Island on our hands. On Thursday, the Cool Moose himself, Robert J. Healey Jr., jumped into the governor's race under the banner of the Moderate Party—which was founded by Ken Block, who abandoned that party to run for governor as a Republican but lost to Cranston Mayor Allan W. Fung, who will face General Treasurer Gina M. Raimondo, a Democrat, in the race to succeed Governor Chafee, a Republican-turned-independent-turned-Democrat who didn't seek reelection and ended up voting for former U.S. Sen. Claiborne Pell's grandson, Clay Pell, who, by the way, is married to Olympic figure skater Michelle Kwan.
>
> Got that?"[29]

Framing the governor's race specifically, Fitzpatrick wrote in the same article, "No matter who wins, the result is bound to be historic. Raimondo would be the state's first female governor. Fung would be the state's first Asian-American governor. And Healey would be the state's first Cool Moose/Moderate (Moderately Cool Moose?) governor."[30]

Early on in the election, General Treasurer Raimondo's Rhode

Island governor candidacy attracted national attention, not all of which her campaign welcomed. In one positive opinion *Washington Post* piece, Matt Miller penned that a Raimondo primary win "could transform the broader national conversation about how to achieve progressive goals in an aging America." He went on, "If Raimondo can lead a small state to rethink liberal reflexes on pensions in order to sustain progressive goals, there's no telling what she might yet do for the nation."[31] Offsetting the good feeling established in Miller's piece, David Sirota, of the *International Business Times*, wrote a scathing article on Raimondo's decision to transfer the state's pension money into hedge funds. Under the headline, "Rhode Island has lost $372 million as state shifted pension cash to Wall Street," Sirota wrote, "The pension investment strategy that Raimondo began putting in place in 2011 has delivered big fees to Wall Street firms. The one-two punch of below-median returns and higher fees has cost Rhode Island taxpayers hundreds of millions of dollars, according to pension analysts."[32] Just in case potential voters did not read the *International Business Times* piece, former Providence mayor, Buddy Cianci, amplified repeatedly Sirota's message on his widely listened-to WPRO radio talk show.

While Fung did not draw much (if any) national attention, he did defeat Ken Block's primary challenge soundly in Cranston by a 74.8 percent to 25.2 percent spread. While the statewide primary race proved much closer, the win in Cranston gave the city's mayor bragging rights. And gloat he did. "The people that know my record, that know my leadership abilities through my three terms as mayor, ignored the rhetoric that Ken was trying to sell, and they showed their trust in me with their vote."[33]

Though Healey did not attain anything close to frontrunner status in 2014, his candidacy did draw the ire of his major competitors' campaigns. This proved particularly true of Robert Coupe, a Fung campaign spokesman. Coupe charged that when the former Cool Moose candidate couldn't get enough signatures to run for lieutenant governor, he then dove into the race for governor as a Moderate Party candidate, giving "the impression that he doesn't have a real clear commitment to what he's doing."[34] While during Healey's last three runs for governor his competitors rarely addressed Healey and, in general, made it a point to not acknowledge the *moose* in the room, 2014 proved a little different. Coupe's comment suggests that he worried about Healey's impact on Fung's candidacy. And as developments suggested, Coupe had good reason for such apprehension.

In mid-October, Fleming & Associates released poll results that garnered the attention of CBS, *The New York Times*, and YouGov.com. The poll had Raimondo ahead of Fung by 6 percentage points. Healey drew 8.1 percent of potential votes. Independents, Kate L. Fletcher and Leon M. Kayarian accounted for less than 1 percent of the vote. The poll's rankings did not attract pollster Joseph Fleming's attention as much as did another interesting observation. According to Fleming, the polls showed "...that Fung is being hurt by Healey."[35] Fleming explained that voters from the Democratic union ranks "...are saying they cannot vote for Gina, but they don't want to vote for a Republican, so they are voting for Healey. Now if Healey wasn't in the race, and they don't want to vote for Gina, they would have no choice but to vote for Allan Fung."[36] According to Fleming, Healey played the part of spoiler. Raimondo benefitted from his role.

In October, four entities invited the three highest polling candidates for governor to face off against one another. While Healey had not received invitations to most past governor election debates, and once experienced an uninvite, this year, within just days of entering the race, he received invitations to every major forum. These opportunities provided Healey with more exposure than any of his previous six runs for higher state office.

On October 21, Raimondo, Fung, and Healey met for their first debate at the Providence Performing Arts Center, sponsored by *The Providence Journal* and WPRI (Channel 12) television. While Healey might have felt that politically he had arrived, the media panelists did not demonstrate a similar judgment. They asked Healey relatively few questions at the debate and focused most of their attention on back-and-forth exchanges between Raimondo and Fung. Still, Healey managed to make his presence felt at several junctures during the night.

Before the debate, Healey had clearly thought about his introductory speech—maybe too much so. Appearing a bit nervous (he hesitated, looked down at his paper, and spoke in a parched voice that begged for a drink of water), Healey hunched over the podium, and sputtered out his remarks with detectable conviction: "I need you to look at me. [Pause] And the reason for that is you probably won't see much of me over the next two weeks. I didn't get any campaign donations from Wall Street insiders or city union contractors. I'm only relying on the people and free media to get my message out. The only good thing about that is as governor, I would only answer to one boss and that boss being the people." Healey then addressed the hesitancy he knew many people harbored about filling in the ballot line beside his name. "You may say you are wasting your vote if you vote for me, but if you don't vote for the person who best represents you, you are wasting your vote then. If you want to pick winners, I say go to the track. If you want to pick a leader, you have to think wisely when you go to the polls." [37]

Healey's rival candidates referenced him only once during the debate, and then only indirectly because of a question that brought up an opinion Healey had earlier espoused. In that instance, *Providence Journal* reporter Edward Fitzpatrick inquired of Treasurer Raimondo whether or not she agreed with Healey's comments regarding the Health Exchange. Healey had argued Rhode Island should give back the grant money to the Federal Government because he felt that accepting the funds encumbered Rhode Island financially in the future. Raimondo responded in a blunt tone, "No, I don't agree." [38] She then went on to explain her thinking on the issue without a single mention of Healey, and without undertaking as much a glance in his direction.

Though Raimondo did not take observable notice of Healey, she most certainly heard his critical statement later in the debate when he referenced her position on the now defunct 38 Studios.[39] Raimondo argued that Rhode Island had a "moral obligation" to pay back the $75 million worth of state-backed bonds used to finance 38 Studios video game company.[40] Healey saw the matter differently. Referencing her controversial reform of the state pension fund, Healey insisted that Raimondo confused where the moral obligation lay. He corrected, "There is a moral obligation to our own people, not the people on Wall Street. And I think that is most important. To take care of our own, first."[41] Later, he added that the state needed to look after the "people who actually work for our state, taught our children."[42] Both comments drew audible support from the assemblage.

While the audience seemed to approve of Healey's comments, Tim White (Channel 12 investigative reporter) immediately challenged Healey's above response.

White: "Mr. Healey you said in your economic plan the key thing is that the state pays its economic debts. But here you are on the stage talking about the possibility that ..."

Healey: "I'm saying I don't recognize that as a moral obligation. ....

Is certainly not an obligation to the state of Rhode Island.

White: Is it a debt?

Healey: "It is a promise to pay for something the state did not engage in."[43]

Soon after the White-Healey exchange, one of the panelists asked about the repeal of the state's voter ID law. Fung said he would keep it, and Raimondo said she would sign repeal legislation if it reached her desk. Healey shared a different thought process. He revealed, "I think it's functioning well and I think I'm probably going to vote without an ID to see if it works."[44] While both of Healey's rival candidates laughed at his comment, Raimondo experienced more difficulty reeling herself in. As Raimondo continued to laugh, Tim White asked Healey, "Let us know how that works out." Healey responded, "I will." Treasurer Raimondo continued visible efforts to hold back her laughter as she received the next question.[45] Whether she had laughed because she thought Healey's response sounded funny or foolish, one could not readily determine. Either way, *The Providence Journal* apparently did not think enough of the exchange to mention the incident in their next issue's reporting of the debate.

In the debate's rapid-fire session, Tim White asked Healey whether he opposed any of the four bond referendums on the ballot.

Healey responded, "No, I do not."

Apparently seeking clarification, White asked, "You support all the bond referendums?"

"I didn't say that, either."

Raimondo laughed spontaneously. Again, she worked to compose herself while Healey took a short pause and then continued, "Some of the issues raised may be of interest to the state. I could support some of them. I'm willing to take a wait and see attitude as it develops."[46] Raimondo and Fung responded "No" to the same question.

At one point in the debate, Fitzpatrick seemed to target Healey over a 2006 Cool Moose Platform document (see Chapter 9, *What Healey Thought*) he had provided the press, instructing them, "If you read nothing else, read this." Fitzpatrick offered, "Well, I read it... [In that document] you said you believe that the large-scale entry of women into the workforce has caused detriment to the society that may be beyond repair. That's a provocative statement. Can you explain what you meant?"[47] Without hesitation Healey replied:

> *"Sure. It sounds masochist on its surface but the reality is the supply and demand of labor. What we forgot to do when we allowed women to enter into the workforce, we forgot to say that, hey, there are more extra laborers coming in. In that same document, as you will note, I think that the best person should*

be working for the same amount of wages. If you dilute the work force you drive down the cost of labor. Two people have to work ... when only one had in the past."

Then in an apparent push back to Fitzpatrick, Healey charged:

"If you read the document, you would know that is not a statement against women entering into the workplace. I think ... what would have happened if we had merged the workforce, instead of throwing everyone into it, labor could have stayed high and the parent best able to take care of the children would be home and we would still have a vibrant economy. To add people into the labor force pushes the price of labor lower. And in doing that it forces everyone to have two working parents and then we lose our home life."[48]

Though the above exchange marked one of the longest in the debate, the media did not report on that segment the next day.

After extended back-and-forths between Mayor Fung and Treasurer Raimondo about topics ranging from a ticketing scandal in Cranston, Rhode Island Housing, and leadership in government, the panelists afforded Healey another opportunity to speak. Healey used the occasion to mount an offensive.

"I think it's interesting that both of these people are speaking about transparency and getting all the facts out to the public and in one case one is not putting out enough fact and in the other case not showing enough transparency regarding investors. And it's all being played out on a stage where campaign funding is forcing these issues. We are not talking about the future of Rhode Island. We are bickering between people with one another about management. This is exactly what is happening in Rhode Island that gets us wound up in the whole situation of not advancing

because we like to blame each other instead of working together. It keeps money flowing from different sources to keep people apart by dividing rather than consolidation. I think if we really want to solve problems we really need to work together. We have to have the most transparency in government, and we have to be able to access documents and our leaders and in a way that makes the people in charge of this state."[49]

Neither Fung nor Raimondo responded to Healey's charges. The moderators asked for no rebuttal[1].

Healey used his closing remarks to address Treasure Raimondo's "Building Rhode Island" theme, which she had stressed throughout the debate and reiterated in her closing remarks. Healey concluded the night with the following statement:

"I'm looking to rebuild Rhode Island, but I'm looking to build Rhode Island from its foundation. We've gone too far in building and the structure is not stable. What we have to do is return, return to that point where we actually have a society that encourages jobs, that works for the education of our children, that has a reasonable tax system. In doing this we can bring ourselves into a competitive state with others. And also, in doing that we can keep our children here in the state by providing them employment opportunities. If we think that we are going to build our way out of everything, this is just not going to happen. It's fantasy. And what we have to do is look at what we have, go to our basic structure, and restore freedom and liberty to the people in the meantime. And that's why I'm running for governor."[50]

Though the panelists had not given as much attention to Healey as they afforded the two frontrunners, the Moderate Party candidate had made his presence known. He had stirred the crowd to laughter and applause more than either of his two opponents. And with three more debate opportunities awaiting, the perennial third-party candidate had to be optimistic about the prospects to improve his political lot.

Shortly after the Providence Performing Arts Center debate, the candidates met at the North Kingstown High School Candidates Day forum in front of 700 students and approximately 40 faculty members. A few candidates from the forum's other sessions stayed behind or arrived early to witness the Raimondo-Fung-Healey interchange. Under the oversight of a school faculty member, students produced and moderated the program. The only forum of its kind in the state, 95 percent of the candidates (local, state, and national) on the North Kingstown ballot participated in the event every election year.

Healey looked forward to the debate at North Kingstown High School. In his view, their format served democracy better than most other programs that he felt rolled out like a "dog and pony" show. At North Kingstown, the organizer permitted students to ask unscreened questions. This raised the likelihood of both awkward moments and raw exchanges. Sometimes students made inquiries better suited for a candidate seeking another office. At other times, a student's offering sounded more like a complaint or charge rather than a question. While reporters could ask very penetrating questions, most often candidates foresaw the inquiry. Nothing foreseeable comes from providing a 17-year-old high school student a microphone with a license to share what is on their mind. All this suited Healey well. In truth, if Healey had it his way, the political affair would look more like the wild west than a well-structured event. Healey would have favored a forum that permitted candidates to sit at a round table (or roam around the stage, if they wished) and have it out with almost no guidelines, few governing rules, and a moderator who factored little in the debate.[51]

Most politicians would have none of that. They preferred orderly settings and produced programs over gun-slinging style affairs. The former provided probable questions that could be handled skillfully by ultra-polished politicians. The latter led to an uncontrolled setting and threw candidates off their game. That state of affairs made politicians uncomfortable. This cautionary mindset describes well the thinking of Treasurer Gina Raimondo's campaign handlers as the North Kingstown High School event approached.

Raimondo's campaign did not commit to the North Kingstown High School Candidates Day 2014 forum until hours before the scheduled session.[52] And when they did commit, they did so under strict conditions. The Raimondo campaign insisted that the original planned debate style format be changed to allow each candidate a designated separate time with the students. In order for Treasurer Raimondo to participate, there could be no semblance of real-time exchanges between the candidates. In the interest of securing the top three candidates for governor (all five candidates for governor had been invited), the school's faculty organizer agreed to the Raimondo campaign's wishes. These parameters differed from those to which the other governor candidates had agreed. While Mayor Fung received the change in stride, Healey did not. And he had much to say about the program's alterations.

On the day of the forum, Healey expressed his outrage to the Candidates Day organizer. Healey wanted to know how a single candidate could dictate the running of the forum. Further, he wanted to know how the announced format changes benefited the students participating. While he never raised his voice, his demeanor and tone communicated disappointment and discontent. The organizer explained that the Raimondo campaign had forced him to choose between maintaining a format or losing the frontrunner's participation. With some reluctance, he chose in favor of the latter.

Healey spoke first at the forum's governor session. While clearly frustrated by the late-hour format change, counterintuitively, the modifications served Healey well. Fueling his ascendance to the auditorium stage, he seemed to cut any strings that might have otherwise constrained him in front of a high school audience. It seemed as if he didn't think about what he had to say, but rather pushed his views

Robert Healey directs students' questions at North Kingstown High School's 2014 Candidates Day. Students at that high school received Healey enthusiastically over the years. The student body invited him to be their commencement speaker twice. Healey accepted both invitations. (Photo courtesy of Robert Silveira)

forward in raw form for the students, faculty members, and other assembled candidates to make of as they would.

While the unflappable Healey remained composed during his session, he had turned angry. This change of mood manifested itself in crisper statements and short to the point responses to student questions. He came across clear and easy to understand. As usual, he did not speak down to his younger audience. He complimented students who asked good questions, and moved briskly onto the next inquiry. He wanted to address as many student questions as possible during his allotted time. And the students lined up enthusiastically to ask the Moderate Party candidate about what concerned them.

Gina Raimondo and Alan Fung took the stage after Bob Healey. Poised and on point, the students received them well. But in the end, any comparison between Healey and his rivals amounted to comparing homeruns to singles. The day belonged to Healey.

Healey's reach extended beyond the students. After the session many attending teachers commented on how much sense Healey had made. Based on what they had witnessed that afternoon, many teachers said they would consider voting for Healey. Prior to hearing him speak at the forum, most would not have voted for the long-haired candidate they had heard so much about over the years but had never seriously contemplated putting into the office he sought.

The day after the North Kingstown High School session (October 24,) Brown University released the result of their Rhode Island Governor's race poll. They reported that Gina Raimondo's lead over Allan Fung had jumped to eleven percent. Fung's campaign manager, Patrick Sweeney, protested. He charged, "It is malpractice for Brown to release this poll. The methodology and weighting are absurd."[53] Sweeney claimed that the poll had "over-sampled" certain groups, most notably Providence voters, a Democratic Party enclave.[54] The Raimondo camp seemed to support the Brown Poll findings. Nicole Kayner, a Raimondo campaign spokeswoman, offered, "After weeks of false attacks against Gina, it's encouraging to see Rhode Islanders rejecting these misleading ads by Allan Fung and his national Republican allies."[55] According to the same poll, Healey's numbers had changed little from earlier reporting's. He registered still in single digits.

The day after the release of the Brown Poll, Gina Raimondo got another boost when Secretary of State Hillary Rodham Clinton swooped into Rhode Island to tout the state's Democratic Party governor nominee. Clinton counseled the citizens of Rhode Island, "You deserve a governor who is focused like a laser on jobs." Clinton added in front of approximately 1,000 people who gathered that Friday at Rhode Island College. "...You deserve a governor who will fight for everyone."[56] Of Raimondo specifically, Clinton shared, "I really think that Rhode Island will be so well served by having this extraordinary woman take responsibility for your state. She knows how to get results by finding common ground, but she sure knows how to stand her ground."[57] When Clinton spoke of Raimondo's opposition, she referenced the Republican Party candidate, Mayor Fung. She did not acknowledge the Moderate Party candidate, Robert Healey.

Fresh off his impressive performance at the North Kingstown High School political forum, on October 28 Healey strided into the Roger Williams University field house in Bristol for a Channel Six ABC sponsored debate. However, the man who stole the show in North Kingstown showed up at Roger Williams University in person only. Somewhere along the three-bridge journey from North Kingstown to Bristol, Healey had lost his vigor, and voice. The former Cool Moose Party founder did not come across well. Healey delivered a lackluster performance. And, perhaps to his benefit at this particular event, in comparison to Raimondo and Fung, the panel afforded Healey even fewer opportunities to speak than other panelists had at the earlier televised Providence Performing Arts Center debate.

During the Raimondo and Fung slugfest at Roger Williams, the press seemed to relegate Healey to the role of spectator. And Healey knew it. At one point in the debate Healey got a word in edgewise and let it be known that he didn't relish his "cameo" appearance in "the Allan & Gina show."[58]

While Fung and Raimondo rehashed old speaking points throughout most of the debate, the Providence Journal printed several of those comments. However, they published only Healey's questions of Raimondo and Fung. He offered those questions during his introduction and closing remarks.[59] Healey asked Raimondo why neither she nor Governor Chafee had requested an advisory opinion from the Rhode Island Supreme Court when they considered pension reform. Healey wanted to know from Fung whether or not he had negotiated the Cranston pension deal with contributors to his mayor campaign.[60] Neither question led to a memorable response. Though not all the blame lied with Healey, overall, his performance proved disappointing.

On the eve of their next debate, Brown's Taubman Center for Public Policy & American Institutions released the results of a poll that showed a much closer race for Rhode Island Governor than had

Bob Healey and his campaign manager, Grant Garvin, enjoy a lighter moment during the 2014 political season. (Photo courtesy of Kris Craig)

been previously reported. In the new poll, Raimondo led Fung, but barely—38 percent to 37.4 percent. Though no one made much of it, Healey had upped his percentage from earlier poll reports to 11.8 percent. In an apparent attempt to put the poll results in a less damaging context, Nicole Kayner of the Raimondo campaign commented on the new numbers, "We expect this to be a close race and the stakes couldn't be higher with the economy as tough as it is. Gina is going to be working hard to earn every single vote."[61] Robert Coupe, spokesman for the Fung campaign, said that there is "...danger in putting too much emphasis on polling in general, but certainly on a single poll."[62] Still, no doubt Mr. Coupe enjoyed a little *told you so* mantra after challenging the prior poll results that the Raimondo campaign had heralded.

In the last gubernatorial debate, sponsored by Channel 10 (WJAR-TV) and Rhode Island Public Radio, the Raimondo-Fung road show rolled on. In reporting the debate, *The Providence Journal* saw fit to quote Healey only twice, and to no real distinguishing purpose. In one of the quotes the *Journal* reported, "And while they [Raimondo and Fung] jabbed at each other, Moderate Party candidate Robert J. Healey Jr. urged voters to take back control of their government, by voting for him over the two major party candidates with hundreds of thousands of dollars of special-interest money backing their TV attack ads."[63] *The Journal's* only other mention of Healey concerned his grading of current Governor Chafee as a "D." Raimondo assessed the governor's performance a "C." Fung graded him an "F."[64]

On the morning after the Channel 10 and Rhode Island Public Radio debate, the Greater Providence Chamber of Commerce held a breakfast forum for governor candidates Fung, Healey, and Raimondo. Fung opened the forum breakfast with, "Thank you to the Chamber of Commerce for hosting our final debate...thank God."[65] Little doubt, all three candidates agreed on that sentiment.

While the Greater Providence Chamber of Commerce forum churned out nothing new, Healey did manage to get in one more humorous and pointed remark. He explained that the state could resolve all its budget problems by levying a 50-percent tax on campaign contributions.[66] Considering that Raimondo alone would spend 5.4 million dollars before her campaign finished,[67] Healey's *tax plan* would have generated considerable economic relief.

At one point during the forum, the candidates asked questions of each other. Healey liked this format. But by this point, all three candidates had punched themselves out. A humorous exchange reported in the *Providence Journal* bore this out:

Raimondo: "My question is for Mayor Fung,"
Fung: [laughing]"Surprise, surprise."
Healey: I'm surprised no one would ask him when he was dropping out of the race.[68]

By the end of the Greater Providence Chamber of Commerce forum, the candidates had offered nothing that made any measurable difference to the voters. And what more could have been said? It now only mattered what the electorate thought. It was time to vote.

In the last days before the campaign season, most of the media talk centered around Fung and Raimondo. Newspaper columns, television clips, and radio commentaries referenced Healey as a footnote (if at all) to conversations about the two frontrunners. But the Healey campaign picked up on signals that suggested their candidate had gained significant ground against his two main competitors.[69] Activity on their web page jumped, and the talk on the street suggested a growing amount of people might vote for Healey. One radio and television commentator would later reference the uptick in Healey's campaign support as "palpable." [70]

Palpable or not, the late-stage surge in support did not grow solely from organic origins outside the campaign. Earlier on, the Healey campaign had strategized a last-hour message bombardment over the internet and on the streets.[71] To do so earlier risked a late campaign attack ad along the lines his lieutenant governor campaign had experienced in 2010. And even more so than the last campaign, Healey knew he lacked the funding to respond adequately and timely to such a political assault.

Though the surmised last-minute rise in Healey's support would prove real, the press turned a deaf ear to late campaign chatter interest in the Moderate Party's candidate. Whether or not Healey's sudden rise in popularity stemmed from years of exposure, a public discontent with his rivals, or some other factor, one cannot determine definitively. But clearly, by November 1, Democrats, Republicans, Moderates, and other unaffiliated voters had tired from the barrage of political advertisements, surface speeches, and all-too-familiar photo opportunities. In that sense, Healey stood apart from his two chief rivals. And yet, at the same time, the Moderate Party candidate benefitted from a considerable exposure boost over most prior years' campaigns. Regardless of the exact reason for his gains, with days remaining in the contest, Healey found himself in a semblance of a race (though still in third place) rather than a romp.

However, before Healey could pick up enough ground to challenge the lead candidates, the voters declared the race's winner. They elected Gina Raimondo. She took 40.7 percent of the vote, which made her Rhode Island's first female governor. Mayor Allan W. Fung secured 36.2 percent of the vote.[72] Normally, the third-place finisher's numbers garner no interest. But in 2014, the opposite proved true. Healey's third-place finish seemed to capture the wonderment of the state, and beyond. Bob Healey had run three times before for governor and lost by a landslide each time. In one of those races, he received just under 2 percent of the vote. And as late as September 2014, things didn't seem to shape up much differently than past runs for office. Healey had filed to run as an 11th-hour candidate, and that candidacy came under serious challenge right out of the gate. He signed on with a political party that differed with some of his views. He campaigned for less than two months and spent a total of $36.28[73] to get his word out. He did not run a single television ad or radio spot and polled most of the time in single digits. His opponents spent millions on their campaigns. But on Election Day, 2014, Healey captured over 21 percent of the vote, winning in two towns and finishing second in several others. The fascination over the results crystallized into two primary questions:

1. How did this happen?
2. What did it mean?

Answers varied. Healey offered his reasoning. "I think I was being used to send a message to the Democratic Party: that you can't play around with people's lives and pensions. Public employees who retired wanted to show their disgust with Gina."[74] On that singular point, most agreed. But some analysts thought that the "disgust with Gina" vote actually took from Fung's numbers. Healey disagreed. The "beautiful coalition," as he called it, consisted of "Democrats, *not* so many Republicans, just a lot of people who felt disenfranchised."[75] Keeping with the broader interpretation of his performance, Healey stressed, "My 22 percent [just shy of that number] shows people are dissatisfied with government, with negative ads, with the 24-hour bombardment."[76] Healey joked, "It's amazing what $35 can do…if we only spent $75, $80, we might've won the race."[77]

While Healey celebrated his relative success in the 2014 governor's race, and no doubt read the headlines that reinforced his merriment, others reached unflattering conclusions about his performance and results. Some thought Healey's message had sounded like little more than a rework of Republican speaking points, with a Libertarian twist. Justin Haskins, former field director of the Rhode Island Republican Party, hammered this notion home. Haskins charged of Healey's run, "... his platform is virtually identical to that held by many Republicans in the state, so Healey's efforts do nothing more than siphon away votes from candidates who otherwise have the support, funding, and reputation to win."[78] Again, Healey thought otherwise.[79] He argued that Fung had lost because he did not run an effective campaign. Dan Yorke of WPRO radio agreed, referencing Fung as a "nice guy" but a "B player."[80]

Raimondo did not want such above commentaries to diminish her achievement. She made no mention of Bob Healey as a possible factor in her win. Even though she had secured far less than a majority victory, Raimondo processed, "I don't think it's realistic to think you would get 50 percent in a three-way race. I was delighted: over 40 percent, winning by 5 points, in a midterm when Democrats got clobbered all over the country."[81]

While Raimondo had won fair and square, she did so by attracting only 18 percent of Rhode Island's eligible voters.[82] One has to wonder what the results would have been had the voters who stayed home in that election (approximately 50 percent of the electorate) had cast a ballot. If these potential voters made up a significant portion of the so-called disgruntled population who despised Raimondo and/or had given up on the two-party system, might their votes have propelled Bob Healey to challenge for the second spot in the race—or better, yet? With an eye to the 2018 election, many wondered the same.[83]

CHAPTER 14

THE WILL

Robert J. Healey Jr. died a failure. At least, *he* appraised his life's work as such. A mass card, which he designed,[1] addressed his legacy in four short sentences: "I am ready to board the last flight even though I have no idea where it goes. I spent my life trying to change the world, but alas, I failed. Few regrets. I leave my unfinished work to others."[2]

The media processed Healey's March 16, 2016 death within a 24-hour news cycle. The state did not order Rhode Island flags to half-mast. Governor Raimondo's office released a statement that kept with her role as the state's top official but lacked a genuine sense of loss. In her short press release, she stated that Healey's death "saddened" her, and added, "My thoughts and prayers are with his family and friends. I will miss his passion and willingness to engage in spirited debate."[3] When a reporter's microphone caught up with the governor shortly after Healey's passing, she referenced her deceased, low-polling political opponent as "quite a character."[4]

Healey's obituary ran in papers across the country, including *The New York Times*. *The Providence Journal* and *Warren Times Gazette* ran front page stories chronicling his political life and abrupt passing.

On March 17, 2016, Rhode Island's ABC, NBC, and CBS television stations led off their morning news with the shocking bulletin that Robert J. Healey Jr. had died at age 58. Healey's long-term political supporters probably noticed and anguished that their leader's death, at least in the immediate sense, commanded more media attention than did his three decades of political campaigning.

Well known political and media personalities weighed in on the loss of Bob Healey. Scott McKay (political analyst) said of the perennial candidate, "He was a very interesting guy. He was both a man of what I call studied eccentricity and also unvarnished candor. And he had a great sense of humor." Tim White (Channel 12 WPRI investigative reporter) shared of Healey, "[he] showed you didn't have to dress the part to be effective. He had a knack for shaking up campaign season and…having everyone look at it very differently. I think people saw a caricature of a guy if they were just watching the newscast, but when you talked to him, when you interviewed him, he was super smart and that is exactly how I am going to remember him. I loved bumping into him in the sandbox of Rhode Island. He was very smart. A great guy."[5]

John Loughlin, former Rhode Island State Representative, Republican congressional candidate, and current WPRO talk show host, offered one of the more personal reflections about Healey's passing. Referencing Bob as "Maybe…ahead of his time," he shared a humbling story from his daughter's perspective:

> "When I was running for office in 2010, I took my ten your old daughter along with me that summer— I called it 'political camp.' We got booked with Healey a lot, and he took a shine to my daughter. She thought the sun rose and set around him. She said, 'You know dad, Bob Healey is the smartest guy in politics. On Election night, when I was making the call to concede the race to [Cicilline], I saw that my daughter was crying on the bed. I thought I'd tell her we tried and we did our best, but she looked up to me and said, 'Dad, Bob lost — that's why I'm crying!"[6]

Bob Healey's death affected one man so much that he wrote a song in his memory. Mark Stoutzenberger performed the melody, "Cool Moose," on Dan Yorke's March 30, 2016 *State of Mind* television show:

First time I saw you I was a kid and didn't know a thing.
Your beard, your hair, and the clothes that you wear seemed a bit strange.
A lot of folks thought that you were a joke, but you never seemed that way to me.
Well, they can judge a book by its cover, but not with Bob Healey.
I was born in 81, and that's the last time you won.
Did you do it for me?
Did you do it for fun?
Did you do it for daughters and the sons of our island, Rhode Island?
Mr. Healey, I'm so sad that you're gone.
I have a picture of you on my fridge with Gina and Alan Fung.
And there will always be a spot for you beside the campfire.
You had a whole lotta moose in you.
You are so honest in a world filled with liars.
You were born in 57. You always been a friend to me.
You may not have been our governor, but you gave me faith in democracy. Maybe it was the way that you looked that kept you from getting there.
It's really too bad so many folks judged you by your beard and your hair.
Mr. Healey, I'm so sad that you're gone, and there will always be a place for you by the fire.[7]

Like many young men, Stoutzenberger credited Healey for his interest in politics at an early age. While Stoutzenberger had tried to write a song about the passing of Providence Mayor Buddy Cianci months before Healey's death, he lacked the inspiration to carry it through. The loss of Robert Healey compelled Stoutzenberger to put his thoughts to verse and melody.

Soon after March 17, 2016, the talk about Healey centered almost exclusively around his contested will. Healey had drawn up his final wishes many years prior and had updated the document periodically, most recently four months before he passed.[8] Once one got by Healey's wish to have his body stuffed, stored, and showcased one year after his dying day at a "death anniversary party,"[9] his will read in fairly standard fashion. Bob divvied up his $1.5 million worth of assets amongst those closest to him. He left Claire Boyes, his longtime companion and executor of his will, one million dollars in cash and property. He willed to Jade Gotauco, his close friend and companion over the last seven years of his life, a life estate interest in the Warren property or the purchase thereof for $35,000 by the trust. Healey left Natalia Machado-Lemos, an old friend from South America, $50,000 and land Healey owned in Uruguay. Healey distributed other belongings and lesser cash amounts amongst friends and family. He left Bob Mello, a long-time *Providence Journal* reporter, $500 for "one great day at a racetrack."[10]

All the above directions seemed clear enough. Then came the challenges to the will. A growing line of ardent creditors, friends, and family battled over what Bob Healey's will *meant*, and for good reason. Serious questions arose about Healey's movement of funds. Plus, Bob had left less-than-thorough instructions about how to process the will, especially given the forthcoming claims. Initially, the most serious inquiry involved the Correia Family Trust. According to the charge, Healey had withdrawn over $130,000 out of their family trust and transferred the money into two or more separate accounts. Why did he do that? Answering such questions required explanations that Healey did not write into his four-page will. Reinforcing this notion, Ralph Kinder, Jade Gotauco's attorney, commented about Healey's will: "It's hard to say what his intent was. We don't know."[11]

Jade Gotauco offered a most optimistic take on the otherwise sorry situation. She suggested Bob Healey purposely put in motion the mayhem surrounding his will to "see what people were made of." Gotauco added that doing so "would be just like Bob. He loved to challenge people."[12] Maybe. But over six years after his death, many of those he cared most about still had yet to tease out the particulars of his plan, at that point well-hidden by a maze of legal entanglements and competing assertions. Healey's business associate and friend, Gavin Hunter, might have come closest to the truth when he said of Bob and the arguments surrounding his will, "This isn't what he wanted or wished for."[13]

If Gavin Hunter is correct, later challenges to the will must have tormented, posthumously, the Cool Moose Party founder. In particular, a charge brought forward by his lifelong friend, Gregory Rufo, ranks most troubling. Greg Rufo had shared a paper route with Bob in younger days. Over the years the two enjoyed competing in Scrabble contests. The childhood friends remained close through March 16, 2016.

Healey had planned to meet up with Rufo on the night he died. The next day, after Bob did not return phone calls, Rufo worried and ventured to search Healey's residence. Shortly after his arrival, he discovered his old friend in bed, lifeless.

Months after Healey's death, Rufo reported that his life savings ($291,463[14]) had gone missing, at least partially. In 2014 Rufo had withdrawn the funds from his bank account to be deposited into Bob Healey's IOLTA for "safekeeping."[15] Why he thought the money would be any more protected in Healey's possession than his own makes for interesting contemplation.[16] Did another undisclosed reason account for the transfer of funds between friends, besides security? After that fund transmission, Healey paid the rent on a workplace space that Rufo occupied.

Rufo charged that in 2014 he had entrusted Healey to manage those transferred funds. Rufo said he had planned to use that money for future business endeavors. To maintain that option, Rufo needed to determine those assets' whereabouts and secure their return. That pursuit required legal assistance.

To represent the case against his longtime friend's estate, Greg Rufo hired lawyer Richard Boren. Boren's investigation unearthed bank records that indicated Healey shifted monies from his IOLTA (interest on lawyer trust account) to the Zultan International business account, a Rhode Island corporation for international trade and consulting. Healey oversaw the dealings of that company as president, treasurer, and secretary. Of that activity, Attorney Richard Boren charged, "There's quite a bit of money that's not accounted for."[17] Boren said an examination of Healey's IOLTA account revealed a $147,739 shortfall.[18]

According to Boren, determining exactly where all the money ended up presents considerable challenges. He explained, "To give you an example, in February of 2016, which was a typical month, there were eight cash withdrawals and four checks. And the four checks were to his own credit cards."[19] Boren surmised of the missing funds' whereabouts, "There's some question whether the cash went to Uruguay, or some other country in South America for purchase of wine, purchase of ceramics."[20]

Even though on its face the missing IOLTA money does not involve Healey's estate directly, Boren saw a strong connection between the two entities. Because Claire Boyes, executor of Healey's estate, serves as President of Zultan International (and, prior to Healey's passing, served as vice president), Boren charged a conflict of interest and, on those grounds, entered a motion in Barrington Probate Court to remove Boyes as executor.[21]

Adding to the spectacle that surrounded Healey's will, at the request of attorney Richard Boren, Probate Judge Marvin Homonoff recused himself as judge overseeing Healey's estate case. Homonoff had an indirect connection to the case. In the proceedings that some lawyers referenced as a "mess," Homonoff realized that as counsel to a Dorothy Spencer, he might have received monies from the Healey estate.[22] While no one charged Homonoff with wrongdoing in the case, Boren said given the circumstances he might have to call for Homonoff's deposition.[23]

Beyond Richard Boren, other lawyers expressed serious concerns about Healey's alleged dealings with his clients' money. Timothy Dodd, a frequent legal analyst for Providence's NBC channel 10, represented the Correia Family case. According to Dodd, Healey used money from the Correia Family trust ($115,00) for his personal business. Dodd contends that Healey "...was kiting the money back and forth. The money would move out of the escrow account. He'd put it back in. He'd take it out again."[24] Dodd said Healey shifted much of this money during his 2014 run for governor.

Several lawyers offered a variety of verdicts directing Healey's alleged intentions and actions for everyone to contemplate after his death. Attorney Dodd charged that Healey's activities with the Correia family accounts were "absolutely wrong" and "improper." He added, "You can't do it ethically."[25] Attorney Boren surmised about the consequences for Healey had he lived: "He'd probably be suspended from the practice of law at a bare minimum, and he would likely be looking at criminal charges—unless he had an extraordinary explanation."[26] Tucker Wright, a Warren attorney and friend of Robert Healey, offered of Healey's handling of accounts, "I don't think he ever intended to steal anything." However, he shared that his lawyer friend, Healey "...was very sloppy with his work, very sloppy."[27]

Though there might not exist an explanation that fully resolves Healey's handling of the two accounts discussed above, a comment he made prior to his death may help clarify his reasoning during these most concerning episodes. In February 2016, Bob Healey met up with his first serious girlfriend, Katherine Kittell. During their ensuing conversation, which would prove to be their last, Bob referenced the need to sell his Metacom Avenue property to address a cash flow problem. Bob talked of using the proceeds to pay for property taxes and other expenses.[28] The sale of that property would generate a significant amount of revenue. Might Bob Healey have figured to use those monies to plug cash flow issues that had *caused* him to move funds about in the first place? Investigative reporter and persecuting attorney Timothy Dodd claimed that Bob Healey transferred monies from his clients' escrow accounts and then later returned those monies to their rightful place of origin, at least partially. Healey's return of funds suggests he did not intend to keep the money. It is plausible that he shifted funds to manage short-term deficits and figured wrongly that such activity caused little and/or only temporary harm. Though Healey knew of his compromised health, he might have counted on more time to settle pending matters satisfactorily.

Several other considerations support Healey's above conceivable intentions and thinking. First, in the case involving Greg Rufo, as mentioned earlier, the transfer of money between the old friends might have resulted from another prior arrangement. Even if that proved not to be the case, it is difficult to fathom that Bob Healey would seek to confiscate money from one of his oldest and most cherished friends. Second, regardless of any prior arrangements, apparently Rufo did not require the subject funds in the short run, as Bob would have known. Therefore, shifting the money temporarily would impact Rufo little (if at all) in the long run. Third, Healey's day-to-day behaviors do not suggest a man in search of great wealth for personal use. He certainly did not require large sums of money to support his lifestyle. His car purchases, upkeep of his living quarters, and maintenance of wardrobe necessitated minimal funding. Evidently, he did not long for the lifestyle trappings of big money. Fourth, those who knew Bob best vouch unwaveringly for his honesty, commitment to friends and the needy, and his generous overall spirit. Many speak to Bob's tendency to help people financially. One source went so far as to reference this tendency as something problematic.[29] Healey thought of others' needs first, and his own financial well-being second. That *problem* may have had a hand in causing a temporary shortage of ready cash, providing an impetus for Bob Healey to seek a short-term remedy to manage his financial affairs until funds from other sources (lawyer fees, land sales, etc.) came forward. Fifth, Bob could have made large sums of money as a lawyer, but instead often chose to represent parties for little or no money. In so doing, he fulfilled his stated intentions upon entering law school: to provide legal services for people who couldn't afford such representation. Again, this long-lived practice reinforces his disinterest in amassing excessive wealth. And sixth, how could Bob think he would get away with any of the alleged activities and intentions? He knew full well that if he did not rectify the subject situations, he would face legal consequences.

If the above considerations hold as evidence suggests they could, then Bob Healey carried out the reported undertakings for temporary economic fixes rather than for long-term personal monetary gains. While the above explanations do not spare Bob Healey from serious questioning—and, had he lived, possible subsequent litigation—those contemplations may at least clarify the context of the alleged acts. As such, the discoveries since Healey's passing may very well reveal a flawed man who made questionable judgments, but not a fraudulent lawyer intent on stealing money. His reported actions demonstrate a man who intended on returning all the moved funds to their rightful accounts. Certainly, Robert Healey's alleged attorney dealings during his last year(s) are inconsistent with other established behaviors and actions undertaken during his life as a political force, practicing lawyer, and generous local philanthropist.

CHAPTER 15

WHAT WAS IT ALL ABOUT?

Robert Healey wanted his unfinished political work to continue. However, despite numerous writings describing the Cool Moose Party's political manifesto, discerning exactly what his ultimate goal entailed requires significant questioning and exploration, including determining what motivated Robert Healey to persevere through David-and-Goliath political struggles and inevitable resounding defeats. The answers to such inquiries do not avail themselves as readily as some pontificators might suggest.

Though many spent time with Bob Healey, truth be told, few knew him very well. Like a moose in the wild, one could spot him easily when out in the open, but most often he proved elusive, and to a degree, unattached. Bob had no siblings. He never married. He fathered no children. And though his campaigns drew attention, some people who spent significant time in his company found him to be "a low-key kind of guy," perfectly content to go unnoticed by others.[1] While friendly to all, caring of most, and engaging with almost everyone he came in contact, he opened up personally to only a select few individuals. Bob maintained an intimate circle, within a tightly contracting circumference.

And perhaps by design, Bob did not present to everyone in the same way. Even his closest friends and innermost political advocates saw only what Bob offered them.[2] Family, friends, and affiliates' commentaries do not suggest he hid information or deceived anyone, but rather that he shared what the person before him needed to know, and little more.[3] Certain people knew of his health issues, and/or his political views, and/or his personal trappings, but to varying degrees. With perhaps one or two exceptions, no one seemed to know everything about Bob Healey.

Because the perennial candidate shared predominately an outward jovial presence, one could conclude logically that he harnessed an eternally optimistic mindset. He did not. People often frustrated Bob, causing him at times to lose faith in the possibilities he promoted. At such times his commentary about the Rhode Island electorate could turn offensive and borderline belligerent. His optimism would spike after an election where he exceeded pundits' expectations, renewing his belief that change along the lines he had talked about for years could take hold. He would think, maybe, finally, people had listened, had understood, and were ready to pull the *right* voting lever. However, especially as he aged, his hope for change declined. Some of his closest friends saw this darker Healey. The rest of us saw only glimpses into this part of his persona when he wrote editorials that lashed out at voters who, on Election Day, had decided to support his opponents, and thereby the status quo.

Healey's ride of "interval" political optimism spouted sporadically, not consistently. He experienced highs and lows. Many closest to him speak to this observance. After losing campaigns, he sometimes lost his drive and languished in neutral—but not for long. Eventually, seemingly in abrupt fashion, a thought or observance inspired him to re-engage. At such times, he would separate himself from people for an extended period so he could think, write, and plan his next mission.[4] At such junctures, he would sleep little.[5] While his social hibernation might last hours or days, he would reemerge, ready to renew his cause. The energy he harnessed at such moments fueled him through campaigns, and sometimes beyond. But eventually, impatience and discouragement would get the best of him, again.

At other times, the onset of boredom hindered his political pursuits (and drew on his long-term business endeavors.) He dreaded the part of politics that requires the successful candidate and government official to take part in the trappings and banalities of office holding. Healey found political promotions, pomp, and peddling distasteful, and lacking of any real purpose. He lived in the world of pondering, possibilities, preparation, and implementation. He wanted the people to choose a like passageway. But in large numbers, they chose to pursue other paths.

Certain personal traits might have contributed to Bob Healey's political defeats. If the art of compromise contributes to a politician's successes, then Healey may have harbored a disadvantage. Healey possessed a domineering spirit in his personal life[6] that could manifest itself in his political dealings as well. Oftentimes, ideas and plans had to unfold as he intended. He had heart, but did not always demonstrate a conciliatory spirit. Complementing this spirit, his mother had taught him to argue relentlessly. His training as a lawyer had further honed that inclination and skill. Even parties with considerable debating capabilities acknowledged Healey's superiority in that realm. While a dominant presence and argumentation competencies can serve the politician well, the knack for assuaging differences of opinion serve at least on par in the successful political figure. Perhaps that aspect of Healey's political being needed more development. And he might very well have agreed. Within days of his passing, his communications to Jade Gotauco suggest a man willing and intent on becoming a better and more positive person.[7]

Even if one opts to ignore the personal and psychosomatic elements of Bob's being, gaining an understanding of his political self presents a more complex challenge than one might surmise. Because he lost every statewide political contest he entered, usually by mammoth proportions, the reviewer, relegated to reading his campaign statements, gets to consider only what Healey intended to do. Healey never governed at the state level. We heard the promises every two to four years, but they never matured to birth. This fact matters. In 1982, a young Bob Healey won election to the Warren School Committee seeking to improve communication within the Warren School Department and with other governing bodies. He promised that. But he didn't do that.

And while Healey's governing experience as the Warren School Committee Chairman does provide a four-year study of his leadership substance and style, any determinations based solely on those years can only rise to the level of contemplation of future governance. In 1982, when Healey first took the helm as School Committee Chairman, his prefrontal cortex may not have fully developed. At age 26, he remained a work in progress. With age, Healey became more "amenable."[8] He matured, and mellowed, at least marginally. One can reason credibly that Governor Healey would differ from Chairman Healey.

Though Bob Healey never governed at the state level, some thought they could peg his political essence. Justin Haskins, as shared in Chapter 12, had Healey pinned as a "rehashed Republican."[9] While certainly Healey's economic views veered more conservative than liberal, by his own account Healey defied a standard-bearer Republican characterization. As one writer referenced him, Healey existed as an "island."[10] Yes, he shared a significant number of views with rank-and-file Republicans, but Healey stated that the Republican Party did the bidding for the rich and powerful. The Cool Moose Party founder had no intention of expanding that penchant.

Others saw Healey as a Libertarian, and reasonably so. On more than one occasion Healey described himself as a minimalist who espoused libertarian views. But just as he had with the Republican Party, he also expressed views incompatible with the Libertarian Party philosophy.[11] Healey's writings and platforms demonstrate a larger role for government in his prospective administration than a Libertarian would espouse or even tolerate.

Still others questioned whether Bob Healey's political ambitions extended beyond establishing himself as a perennial third-party candidate. Such individuals thought that maybe he only intended to represent a pet issue or ruffle his competition's political feathers every two to four years. Adding credibility to this notion, in 2002 Healey offered, "Third-party politics is fraught with delusions of grandeur. As long as you can put that into perspective, you understand what third-party politics is all about. It's about being outside the mainstream, being able to challenge the status quo. As one person said to me, `You can't beat City Hall, but you can piss on the steps.'"[12] Clearly, Healey knew well the common role third parties played throughout American history. Also, he initiated campaigns that he knew had little chance of winning. In such contests he aspired primarily to improve his lot in the next election. So, by design, did most of his runs for state office amount to campaigns of interesting considerations rather than crusades committed to significant outcomes? Did Healey have any intention of winning election to Rhode Island's top executive offices?

On at least one occasion, WPRO radio talk show host, Dan Yorke, wondered the same about Healey. True to his established style, the popular radio commentator wasted little time putting the question before his studio guest. On the air, he asked Healey directly and vociferously if he truly wanted to win election to higher office. Healey assured Yorke that he did. His response apparently convinced the conservative-leaning host. Yorke then took considerable time to offer Healey an on the air advisory session on how to win an election or at least more seriously challenge his political opponents.

Those closest to Bob Healey vouched for the perennial candidate's earnest pursuit of the offices for which he campaigned. Claire Boyes, who often heard Healey air out his reasoning for running prior to declaring his candidacy for state office, stressed the conviction with which Bob pursued the prize. Everyone in Healey's inner circle agreed with Boyes. And Bob Healey reiterated repeatedly his willingness and readiness to govern. The number of times he sought state office reinforces his stated intentions.

His ambitions and plans aside, considering Healey lost every race he undertook for Rhode Island lt. governor and governor, how does one gain an understanding of Bob Healey's unfinished work? The answer lies within the *reasons* he lost so often, and by so much. But once again, determining such is not as simple as it might first appear. While theories abound about why Healey lost elections, in and of themselves they do not explain fully why victory eluded the perennial candidate. And, most of those proposed reasons for defeat contribute nothing to realizing the larger purpose of his ongoing political pursuits.

Many attribute Bob Healey's political race losses to his hairstyle and beard. The renowned *Providence Journal* political columnist, Charles Bakst, elevated that theory to gospel. After one of the governor debates in the 1990s, Bakst wrote that Healey was "a haircut and shave away from being governor."[13] And certainly, some voters shied from voting for Healey because of such superficial reasons. A father to one of his high school friends, who liked and respected Bob enough to hire him for legal work, could not bring himself to vote for his highly regarded lawyer. He expressed discomfort with Healey's outward appearance representing Rhode Island to the nation.[14] No doubt, many others felt the same.

Though most think Healey's appearance contributed toward his political detriment, in many respects his exterior look served as an asset. While voters usually can't discern one candidate from another running for the same office, citizens of all political persuasions recognized Healey instantly. A verbal reference to "that bearded guy" separated him from the pack of other prototypical-looking candidates. Most candidates would pay handsomely for such recognition. For Healey, the swift identification came free of charge.

Not only did his appearance make him more detectable, his

unconventional look heightened a concealed advantage. In an indirect reference to his guise, Healey said, "My greatest asset is that people underestimate me."[15] Many voters could not help but arrive quickly at a premature judgment of the man they often recognized, but rarely contemplated. People assumed Healey's long hair and beard communicated a flower child aura and an accompanying thinking pattern from decades past. But when prospective voters listened to him speak, they quickly realized the inaccuracy of their preconceived notions. The contrast between visual stereotypical perceptions and actual substantive realizations presented starkly to most, and almost always to Bob's benefit. His appearance piqued curiosity. In-person meetings sold the inquisitive voter on Healey's remarkably well-developed arguments and considerable capabilities. Because the voter, sometimes uninformed, expected otherwise, the surprise discovery increased Healey's impact and served to loosen (though not defeat) his political challengers' hold on the electorate.

Some point out that if Healey had raised more money for his campaign, he would have increased his exposure and thereby have won over more voters. A television ad with the pro-bono lawyer delivering his "power to the people" message and attacking his opponent's alleged cronyism could have gone a long way toward convincing Rhode Islanders that Healey stood ready to lead. Throw in the right background music and some properly angled vignettes, and the campaign could produce a made-over candidate ready for prime time. But had Healey given over to well-financed, staged productions, he would diminish his core appeal. He might have gained a few votes, but he could have lost just as many. Healey had no stomach for a machine-like political operation. Even if more publicity helped Healey's political chances, this potential fix for what ailed his campaigns overrates the potential benefits and overlooks the probable downsides. By the mid-1990s, most Rhode Islanders knew of Bob Healey. A high-profile media production would have widened his exposure little, and likely ruined the Cool Moose brand. Any such overhaul would appear forced and fake, because it would have been forced and fake. Healey just couldn't pull that off, and that pleased most of his supporters.

An impromptu meeting Healey had during one of his campaigns illustrates the above point. State Representative Rob Craven once saw Healey painting a caricature of himself on the side of a building in Providence and decided to check in on him. After Healey explained what he was doing, the two old law school buddies talked. Craven had many questions.

> **Craven:** "I know what you're doing … But I want to know why you don't have someone else doing it."
>
> **Healey:** "What do you mean? I don't want to spend a lot of money."
>
> **Craven:** "I can't help but think you could be doing something else like campaigning somewhere as opposed to painting your own mural sign on the side of this building."
>
> **Healey:** "Well, I'd rather be doing this than go around shaking hands and kissing babies."
>
> **Craven:** "Yah, I think that's the kind of thing you have to do in order to gain publicity."

Craven stated that Healey would "have none…of conventional campaigns." He further explained, "[Healey] wasn't much for retail politics…where you find the festival…or the religious organization having a parade. That's the place you wear out a pair of shoes…But he didn't feel comfortable with…that typical politician setting."[16] In the same vein, Jade Gotauco, Healey's friend and companion, explained, "Bob was just Bob. He couldn't understand how he could be any different than he was."[17] Healey would rather paint than shake hands. And so, he painted.

One factor that contributed to Healey's defeats gets overlooked often: while many reference Bob Healey's considerable debate skills, a review of his taped forums suggests an inconsistent performer, at best. While he could deliver a position clearly and passionately in a one-to-one meeting, in public forums, he most often did not. In key debates, he came across nervous. Worse yet, at other times he seemed disengaged, distracted, and even disgusted with the whole affair. With a couple of exceptions, he didn't take the fight to his political opponents. And he needed to do that. As the underdog, he had to promote his ideas and take the opposition down a peg, or two, or three. However, despite his developed intellect, argumentation skills, and reported unflappable nature, he never scored a knockout blow in a widely publicized debate forum. His political "handlers" never knew which type of Healey might show up at the debate.[18] More often, a nebulous Healey made his way to the debate floor.

So, admittedly, while appearance, finances, and performances present as plausible sources for Bob Healey's numerous losing campaigns, those considerations do not divulge a conclusive reason for his continuous and crushing defeats. To determine such a root source, one needs to look deeper than surface contemplations. Specifically, they must revisit Healey's core message and ethos. Scrutiny of both clarifies not only why he lost so many political contests, but also unearths the blueprint for carrying on his work.

Healey didn't merely direct voters to select the best representative of the people—he asked them to represent themselves. He cautioned that even the most well-intended political officials could lose their way and serve selfish ends instead of the people entrusted to them. He worried of that potential shortcoming in himself, as well.[19] And so, he called upon the people to lead. He meant for the masses to inform themselves, march to public meetings, determine necessary changes, demand that change, follow up on that change, and never abandon their cause. If the people decided the status quo served their interests better, then defend that, but never become a passive, uninformed bystander. According to Bryan Rodrigues, his longtime friend and political advocate, Healey "...believed in grassroots democracy with the will of the people being expressed as directly and robustly as possible."[20] That to which Rodrigues speaks emanated from Healey's bone marrow. He wanted the electorate to shut down the overuse of closed political sessions and bring the people's business out into the open for all to witness and affect. The concept, apparently before its time, urged the voter to get "in the room where it happens,"[21] where the important decisions are made. Better yet, Healey would argue, blow up that room and replace it with an outdoor arena, where the citizenry could, should, and would gather, speak their minds, demand referendums, and initiate change. In short, his core message summoned people to pay attention, root out problems, and devise solutions.

Healey's message resonated well, at least for surface contemplation, but pointed toward a path too steep for most voters to climb. Even when Bob won and governed (Warren School Committee, 1982), his followers would march only so far with him, at least on their own fruition. In 1986, when the Warren voters heard and believed in *his* referendum call to reject the arbitrator's award that otherwise would have ended the contentious stalemate between Warren teachers and the town's School Committee (see Chapter 6—*The Year It All Hit the Fan*), Healey had to produce the message, promote the cause, and prod the people to engage.[22] Aside from considerations of the cause's merit, he could make all that happen in a small town. He could not pull that off statewide, even in the smallest state in the union.

In 1994, Healey surprised pollsters by convincing over 9 percent of Rhode Islanders to support his bid for governor. Soon afterwards, trying to capitalize on his party's newly achieved official status, and the momentum generated from the 32,822 votes recently cast in his favor, Healey organized the Cool Moose Party's first convention. Only weeks after his impressive showing in the 1994 race, few Cool Moose supporters made the tract to the party's inaugural convention. Again, despite evidence demonstrating growing support for Bob Healey, the voters' necessary active engagement did not materialize.

Undertaking the actions Healey called his followers to champion requires, well, a lot of work. It's easier to let representatives exert that effort, quietly, even secretly, if need be. And while that comes at a potential cost, including maintenance of the status-quo, even some of the Cool Moose's disciples lacked the motivation to take on the burdens of a Healey win.[23] Choosing Healey meant the voter had signed up for an active role in the governing process. The common voter had no intention of taking on such a responsibility. Healey asked much of his potential constituents, and so does his legacy.

Bob Healey's unfinished work does not circulate around Bob Healey. The inherited goal does not beckon one to emulate, resurrect, or wait for the next Cool Moose. Bob Healey did not hope for a sequel, nor a remake.[24] And he would have counseled against the lure of apparent clones. As James Safford, a writer at irrelevant.com, wrote of Healey wannabes, "How then could anyone expect to be a clone of another individual and still themselves be their own person? They can't."[25] Healey wanted people to be themselves, even though that expectation sometimes disheartened and often disappointed him.

In the end, Healey could make people think, but not act—at least not on the scale necessary to formulate a consequential movement. He saw that reality as proof of his own failure. But did the shortcoming lie with Bob Healey? In Healey, the people got what they had long sought. The electorate *wanted* a leader who spoke from the mind and heart and presented their findings and fixes without any outside strings controlling the message. Healey came before the people informed, caring, unbought, and true to principle. He delivered a consistent, sound, and purposeful message. He appeared before them in a natural and genuine state of being. However, a disconnect existed. Either the voter did not truly want that which they asked for, or they initially underestimated their necessary role in Healey's campaign movement. Either way, Healey had done his part, and pledged to do more. The audience for whom he advocated did not.

So, where does all this leave us with Bob Healey's unfinished work? He left that determination to others. He did not seek hero worshiping, nor want to be remembered as the "father figure" of a future Cool Moose Party.[26] Though many saw his Moderate Party 2014 election results as an opportunity to reinvigorate The Cool Moose Party to greater heights, Healey worried about efforts to "pervert" the party's message into something foreign from its core mission.[27] To avoid that, as his health spiraled downward in 2015, he entrusted the party leadership over to Gloria Garvin, a longtime advocate and mother to Grant Garvin (who had run Healey's impressive 2014 campaign for governor).

In 1995, Bob Healey said the following at a North Kingstown High School graduation to voters in the best position to determine the extended future of their town, state, and nation: "Be yourself. If you're not yourself, you're only acting in front of others."[28] For the purpose of the further defining of his unfinished work, he might have added, "And in the process of finding yourself, engage vigorously in the opportunity to govern yourself." That message would serve well the extended working-class neighborhood where Bob Healey grew up. And from the outset, that connection and commitment may very well capture what Bob Healey, the Cool Moose, was all about.

EPILOGUE

Some felt Bob Healey would posthumously affect the 2018 governor's race.[1] Such expectations had Governor Gina Raimondo, Mayor Allan Fung, Representative Joe Trillo, Moderate Party candidate Bill Gilbert, and other political contenders vying for the effectually disenfranchised Robert Healey voters. Healey had left the 2018 aspirants a road map to do just that. After the 2014 election, Healey outlined four chief causes moving forward.[2]

- Statewide teacher contract
- State bank
- State monopoly over marijuana sales
- A revision of the election process

Healey welcomed all interested parties to make these ideas their own. He offered, "Even though these ideas were based on my campaign, I freely encourage all to take them and implement them in a way that is responsive to the needs and the people of Rhode Island."[3] In doing so, Healey flung the barn door open for any candidate to pick-up and run with the Cool Moose speaking points. In effect, he had left his ideas on the side of the road for anyone to gather up and make their own. Certainly, a 2018 Cool Moose Party candidate for governor would have been in the best position to seize on the momentum of the 2014 election results and evoke Healey's memory and message. However, in 2018 the Cool Moose Party did not put forth a candidate for governor.

In fact, no one in 2018 ran with the Healey banner. Governor Raimondo and Mayor Fung, both established candidates with earlier prepared stances, did not entice Cool Moose Party followers. Gilbert or Trillo, both third-party candidates, did not capture Healey's spirit or speaking points in 2018. Other lesser-known third-party candidates, such as an engaging Dr. Luis Munoz, could have picked up the Cool Moose mantra. They did not. If Healey hovered over the 2018 election in any form, even a hawkeyed Cool Moose search party would have been hard pressed to report as much as a ghost-like sighting of the former perennial candidate.

In March 2019, a candidate for state representative tried to catch the back winds of Healey's legacy. In a special election for the Rhode Island District 68 representative seat,[4] the Gaspee Project (a conservative political advocacy group) supported William Hunt, an endorsed Libertarian. The Gaspee Project *"employed"* Bob Healey's black-and-white facial caricature below Hunt's image on their Facebook Page.[5] The caption beside Healey's image read, "THE HEALEY VISION LIVES ON." Under the image, the Gaspee Project added, "Like Bob Healey, Billy Hunt stands for libertarian American values, such as empowering parents with more educational choices! He needs your support; every vote counts!"[6] The same image and caption appeared on the Hunt for RI District 68 campaign Facebook feed.[7]

The above activity might insinuate to some that the Cool Moose Party endorsed Hunt's candidacy. However, the Cool Moose Party offered no such support and made that stance clear. Instead, Cool Moose Party advocates stressed in a most spirited fashion the differences between Bob Healey and William Hunt and insisted that Hunt remove Healey's caricature from his Facebook page. As of the publication of this book, neither the Hunt campaign nor the Gaspee Project had removed the past subject reference from their feeds.[8]

The Rhode Island lieutenant governor's office continued to draw attention during the post Healey years. From 2014 through the early part of 2021, Dan McKee held the post of lieutenant governor in Rhode Island. By most accounts, the relationship between McKee and Governor Raimondo remained distant. When the COVID-19 pandemic gripped Rhode Island starting in 2020, communications between the two leaders persisted in a strained fashion. At one news conference, a reporter questioned Raimondo about the working relationship between her and the lieutenant governor. The governor replied that the reporter should tell McKee to give her a call. Before the lieutenant governor had much of a chance to phone the governor, in early 2021, President Joe Biden offered Governor Gina Raimondo the Secretary of Commerce position in his cabinet. Though she had played down such ambitions earlier, without hesitation, Raimondo accepted the President's invitation. Raimondo's departure from the Rhode Island political scene provided cause for Lieutenant Governor Dan McKee to assume the Rhode Island governor post.

Though McKee's ascendance to the lieutenant governor post might reinforce the need for the office in Rhode Island, in 2022, former state representative Larry Valencia announced that he would run for the second highest state office so that he could eliminate the position. Crediting Bob Healey with motivating him to do so, like the former Cool Moose candidate, Valencia said that if elected, he would accept no payment for his services as lieutenant governor.

The vacuum left by Bob Healey's passing can be felt to varying degrees, both intellectually and psychologically, in every town throughout Rhode Island, and to a lesser degree, beyond the state's borders. On the streets of Warren, the loss rises to a tangible level. Warren no longer presents as it did in Healey's heyday. Warren High School now stands as Kickemuit Middle School, and Warren's ninth through twelfth graders attend Mt. Hope High School, the former Bristol High School. The working-class town now sports many trendy bars and highly touted restaurants. Warren's real estate market thrives and its art community flourishes on Water Street, along Main Street, up Child Street, and beyond. And by design, the colonial feel remains a part of the town's attractive character. In the same vein, the community's fisherman, small business owners, farmers, and hourly wage workers maintain Warren's connection to its core character and cherished past. And yet, for all these positive developments and the purposeful maintenance of a bygone era, the aura and atmosphere bolstered by Healey's frequent appearances and orations throughout the town goes missing. Today a Warren resident or passerby would be hard pressed to encounter a bold visionary and persistent campaigner, long haired or otherwise, who challenges them to think differently. The man they called the Cool Moose engaged the youngest citizens and the eldest members of the electorate to amplify their voices. And he always had a plan to help them do just that.

Those bothered by Healey's resolve and reformist (sometimes radical) thinking currently have little cause for worry. Over six years after his death, scant evidence suggest that the political experiment left unfinished by Robert Healey's departure marches on. Instead, the substance of his life's work moderates amongst conflicting claims over his will, occasional political references in newspaper articles, and monthly remembrances and treatments on the Fed up in RI website. Healey transferred the leadership of the Cool Moose Party to an invested and passionate leader. However, realizing the political transformation the party's founder envisioned requires more than one steward, no matter how charismatic and capable they may be. To grow the movement Healey invoked in 1986 and lead through 2016 calls for the masses to rise up in unison and march onward together, and at least partly on their own fruition. For the time being, public activism of that order remains dormant

ACKNOWLEDGEMENTS

As I looked through Robert Healey's personal and political writings, I wondered often what the subject of this book would think of my efforts to tell his story and determine his life's meaning. While from the outset I committed to let the historical record guide my work, frequent discussions with personal friends of Robert Healey affected my thinking and writing just as much. I hope my offering in the following pages does justice to both information sources.

From the very outset, Claire Boyes, Robert Healey's faithful friend, longtime companion, and staunch political ally, informed my work in a most open and honest fashion. I communicated with her often at every phase of this work. I will always appreciate her reception of my many requests.

Numerous friends of Robert Healey shared their memories of him with the author. They include Gary Lavey, his close friend from sixth grade onward; Brian Fortin, his childhood friend and future political campaign manager; Tom Tracy, his high school acquaintance and future campfire confidant; Joe Moniz, Bob's early life acquaintance turned future business partner; and Joseph A. DePasquale and Adam Tracy, Bob's young friends and mentees. Their stories added insights into Bob's personality that only a close friend could depart.

If not for Jade Gotauco, Bob's friend and companion during the later years of his life, this book would lack critical understandings of Bob Healey's inner thought processes. Her contribution to this work via reflective assessments and clear articulation cannot be overstated.

Members of the Cool Moose Party, including Bryan Rodrigues (campaign artist and political contributor), Viki White (Cool Moose Party Secretary), Grant Garvin (who ran Robert Healey's impressive 2014 campaign), and Gloria Quaranta Garvin (who Healey entrusted with the Cool Moose Party leadership just prior to his passing) helped the author appreciate the challenges inherent in running a third-party campaign in Rhode Island. Their commitment to the Cool Moose Party's perennial candidate surpasses even the most enthusiastic Cool Moose Party supporter.

Kathy Kittel, Robert Healey's first serious girlfriend and lifelong friend, provided valuable perspectives on Rob's life journey. Her memories of the Healey family homestead in the early 1970s proved particularly important to this work.

Robert Craven, North Kingstown's Rhode Island state representative, attended New England Law School with Robert Healey. They became friends in school and maintained contact throughout the years. Craven's well-crafted stories of his fellow practicing lawyer provided numerous humorous anecdotes and serious contemplations addressed throughout this work.

In preparation of the photographs used to help illustrate points raised in the book, I thank Kim Ries at Imagn, USA Today Network, Janet Moscarello at Janet Moscarello Photography, and Robert Silviera, North Kingstown High School photography teacher.

Ruth Ellen Stone Seymour (of the Martinelli family) and James Healey (of the Healey side), provided the author with most insightful reflections of growing up with their cousin Robert Healey, Jr., and visiting with his parents and extended family.

Thank you to the staff at the Warren Town LIbrary and the

Rhode Island Historical Society for their support and efforts during the research phase of this project.

I owe much to Steven and Dawn Porter, and the dedicated staff at Stillwater River Publications. Special thanks go out to Christina Bagni, copy editor, Matt St. Jean for the cover design, Elisha Gillette for the interior design, and Dawn Porter for her work (and patience) with the copy-edited manuscript.

Simone Verria, at Diversified Communications, developed a promotional strategy for sharing this work with the world. While I am not sure at what point she took over directing her father instead of the reverse, I know that the development served this undertaking most productively.

As is the case with every challenge I take on that commands much of my attention, overwhelms my capabilities, and exhausts my patience, I am grateful for my wife, Celeste Verria, for knowing when to let me be, when to cheer me on, and, at critical points, when to remind me to breathe.

ENDNOTES

CHAPTER 1

1 Named after the former editor and publisher of the East Bay Newspapers, The Roswell S. Bosworth, Jr. Lecture Series offers presentations on topics of general interest to Rhode Island audiences.

2 The panelists included former Bristol Town Administrator Diane Medeiros, former RI Republican Committee Delegate Virginia Butterworth, Roger Williams University Political Science professor June Speakman, and Roger Williams University history professor Debra Mulligan.

3 DeWolf Fulton (former reporter and longtime acquaintance of Robert J. Healey Jr.) in discussion with the author, July 18, 2019.

4 Ibid.

5 Ibid.

6 Ibid.

7 Claire Boyes (longtime close companion of Robert J. Healey Jr.) in discussion with the author, July 26, 2019.

8 Gloria Garvin (political organizer for the Cool Moose Party) in discussion with the author, January 4, 2021.

9 Ruth Ellen Stone Seymour (first cousin to Robert J. Healey Jr.) in discussion with the author, July 30, 2019.

10 Ibid.

11 Tom Tracy (close friend to Robert J. Healey Jr.) in discussion with the author, March 1, 2020.

12 Ibid.

13 Ibid.

14 Joe DePascuale (close friend to Robert J. Healey Jr.) in discussion with the author,

August 8, 2020.

15 Ibid.

16 Ibid.

17 Kathy Kittell (close friend to Robert J. Healey Jr.) in discussion with the author, July 27, 2019.

18 Ruth Ellen Stone Seymour (first cousin to Robert J. Healey Jr.) in discussion with the author, July 30, 2019.

19 Jade Gotauco (close friend to Robert J. Healey Jr.) in discussion with the author, July 25, 2019.

20 Ibid.

21 Brian Fortin (close friend and political advisor to Robert J. Healey Jr.) in discussion with the author, July 28, 2020.

22 Ibid.

23 Ibid.

24 Jacqueline Tempera, "Passages: Robert Healey—A cool passion for R.I. politics—Cool Moose Party founder discovered dead Sunday," Providence Journal, March 22, 2016, p. 1.

25 Robert Craven (fellow law student and New England Law School with Robert J. Healey Jr.) in discussion with the author, August 20, 2019.

26 Joe Moniz (close friend to Robert J. Healey Jr.) in discussion with the author, January 11, 2020.

27 Jade Gotauco (close friend to Robert J. Healey Jr.) in discussion with the author, July 25, 2019.

28 Bryan Rodrigues, (close friend of Robert J. Healey Jr.) in discussion with the author, December 8, 2020.

29 Ibid.

30 Katherine Kittell (close friend to Robert J. Healey Jr.) in discussion with the

author, July 27, 2019.

31　Jade Gotauco (close friend to Robert J. Healey Jr.) in discussion with the author, July 25, 2019.

32　Gloria Garvin (political organizer for the Cool Moose Party) in discussion with the author, January 4, 2021.

33　Grant Garvin (2014 campaign manager for the Cool Moose Party) in discussion with the author, January 9, 2021.

34　Brian Fortin (close friend and political advisor to Robert J. Healey Jr.) in discussion with the author, July 28, 2020.

35　Ibid.

36　Ibid.

37　Ibid.

38　Bryan Rodrigues (close friend of Robert J. Healey Jr.) in discussion with the author, December 8, 2020.

39　Kathy Kittell (close friend to Robert J. Healey Jr.) in discussion with the author, July 27, 2019.

40　Ibid.

41　Jade Gotauco (close friend to Robert J. Healey Jr.) in discussion with the author, July 25, 2019.

42　Jade Gotauco (close friend to Robert J. Healey Jr.) in discussion with the author, July 25, 2019.

43　Ibid.

44　Adam Tracy (close friend to Robert J. Healey Jr.) in discussion with the author, January 21, 2020.

45　Joe Moniz (close friend to Robert J. Healey Jr.) in discussion with the author, January 11, 2020.

46　Jacqueline Tempera, "Passages: Robert Healey—A cool passion for R.I. politics—Cool Moose Party founder discovered dead Sunday," Providence Journal, March 22, 2016, p. 1.

47　Ibid.

CHAPTER 2

1　"Warren MARY J. HEALEY," The Providence Journal obituary, June 23, 1998, p. C-04.

2　Robert J. Healey Sr., Obituary, The Providence Journal, February 27, 1990, p. E-02.

3　Gary Lavey (longtime friend of Robert J. Healey Jr.) in discussion with the author, July 21, 2019.

4　Scott MacKay, "One strange man Barefoot Bob Healey," The Providence Journal, June 23, 1985, p. M-04.

5　Kathy Kittell (longtime friend of Robert J. Healey Jr.) in discussion with the author, July 27, 2019.

6　Gary Lavey (longtime friend of Robert J. Healey Jr.) in discussion with the author, July 21, 2019.

7　Ibid.

8　Ibid.

9　Jody McPhillips, "'98 Election This may be the last run for Cool Moose leader," The Providence Journal, October 25, 1998, p. A-19.

10　Ibid.

11　Kathy Kittell (longtime friend of Robert J. Healey Jr.), in discussion with the author, July 27, 2019.

12　Robert Healey, "What I Have Stolen from Others," circa 1987, p. 2.

13　Ibid.

14　Claire Boyes (longtime Robert Healey Jr. girlfriend) in discussion with the author, July 26, 2019.

15　Kathy Kittell (longtime friend of Robert J. Healey Jr.) in discussion with the author, July 27, 2019.

16　Ibid.

17　Ibid.

18　Ibid.

19　Robert Healey, "What I Have Stolen

from Others," circa 1987, p. 2.

20 Ruth Ellen Stone (cousin to Robert J. Healey Jr.) in discussion with the author, July 30, 2019.

21 Ibid.

22 Ibid.

23 Kathy Kittell (longtime friend of Robert J. Healey Jr.) in discussion with the author, July 27, 2019.

24 Robert Healey, "What I Have Stolen from Others," circa 1987, p. 2.

25 Ibid., 6.

26 Ibid

27 Ibid., 7.

28 Ibid

29 Ibid., 2.

30 Robert Healey, "What I Have Stolen from Others," circa 1987, p. 7.

31 Kathy Kittel (longtime friend of Robert J. Healey Jr.) in discussion with the author, July 27, 2019.

32 Robert Healey, "What I Have Stolen from Others," circa 1987, p. 11.

33 Ibid.

34 Ibid.

35 Ibid.

36 Gary Lavey (longtime friend of Robert J. Healey Jr.) in discussion with the author, July 21, 2019.

37 Lavey would go on to be captain of the Warren Redskins football team and play at Boston University.

38 Gary Lavey (longtime friend of Robert J. Healey Jr.) in discussion with the author, July 21, 2019.

39 Ibid.

40 Scott MacKay, "One strange man Barefoot Bob Healey," The Providence Journal, June 23, 1985, p. M-04.

41 Karen Lee Ziner, "CAMPAIGN 2010-LIEUTENANT GOVERNOR-Healey gets traction in quest to abolish the office he seeks," Providence Journal, October 23, 2010, p. A8.

42 Robert Healey, "What I Have Stolen from Others," circa 1987, p. 1.

43 Gary Lavey (longtime friend of Robert J. Healey Jr.) in discussion with the author, July 21, 2019.

44 Ibid.

45 Ibid.

46 Ibid.

47 Ibid.

48 Kathy Kittel (longtime friend of Robert J. Healey Jr.) in discussion with the author, July 27, 2019.

49 Gary Lavey (longtime friend of Robert J. Healey Jr.) in discussion with the author, July 21, 2019.

50 Joe Marques, (veteran Warren School Department teacher) in discussion with author, July 22, 2020.

51 Gary Lavey (longtime friend of Robert J. Healey Jr.) in discussion with the author, July 21, 2019.

52 Ibid.

53 Ibid.

54 Kathy Kittell (longtime friend of Robert J. Healey Jr.) in discussion with the author, July 27, 2019.

55 Ibid.

56 Ibid.

57 Ibid.

58 Ibid.

59 Ibid.

60 Ibid.

61 Gary Lavey (longtime friend of Robert J. Healey Jr.) in discussion with the author, July 21, 2019.

62 Kathy Kittell (longtime friend of Robert J. Healey Jr.) in discussion with the author, July 27, 2019.

63 Gary Lavey (longtime friend of Robert J. Healey Jr.) in discussion with the author, July 21, 2019.

64 Kathy Kittell (longtime friend of

Robert J. Healey Jr.) in discussion with the author, July 27, 2019.

65   Ibid.

66   Robert Healey, "What I Have Stolen from Others," circa 1987, p. 11.

67   Ibid.

68   Scott MacKay, "One strange man Barefoot Bob Healey," The Providence Journal, June 23, 1985, p. M-04.

69   Kathy Kittell (longtime friend of Robert J. Healey Jr.) in discussion with the author, July 27, 2019.

70   Robert Craven (fellow law school student in the early 1980s) in discussion with the author, August 20, 2019.

71   Tom Tracy (longtime friend of Robert J. Healey Jr.) in discussion with the author, March 1, 2020.

72   Kathy Kittell (longtime friend of Robert J. Healey Jr.) in discussion with the author, July 27, 2019.

73   Ibid.

74   Ibid.

75   Scott MacKay, "One strange man Barefoot Bob Healey," The Providence Journal, June 23, 1985, p. M-04.

76   Ibid.

77   Robert Healey, "What I Have Stolen from Others," circa 1987, p. 12.

78   Kathy Kittell (longtime friend of Robert J. Healey Jr.) in discussion with the author, July 27, 2019.

79   Ibid.

80   Scott MacKay, "One strange man Barefoot Bob Healey," The Providence Journal, June 23, 1985, p. M-04.

81   Robert Healey, "What I Have Stolen from Others," circa 1987, p. 12.

82   Joe Marques, (veteran Warren School Department teacher), In discussion with author, July 22, 2020.

83   Scott MacKay, "One strange man Barefoot Bob Healey," The Providence Journal,

June 23, 1985, p. M-04.

84   Ibid.

85   Robert Healey, "What I Have Stolen from Others," circa 1987, p. 12.

86   Ibid.

87   Karen Lee Ziner, "CAMPAIGN 2010—LIEUTENANT GOVERNOR—Healey gets traction in quest to abolish the office he seeks," The Providence Journal, October 23, 2010, p. A8.

88   Brian Fortin (longtime friend and political manager of Robert J. Healey Jr.) in discussion with the author, July 28, 2020.

89   Brain and Debbie Fortin had christened the mountain, which was more of a large hill, "Freak Mountain."

90   Obituary https://www.dignitymemorial.com/obituaries/warren-ri/bob-healey-6857377 (accessed 12/29/2019 Wilbur-Romano Funeral Home / 615 Main Street, Warren, RI

91   "History of Trilium Farm, Soil and Sky, https://soilandskycenter.wixsite.com/soil-and-sky/history-of-the-trillium-farm, accessed June 15, 2020.

92   Scott MacKay, "One strange man Barefoot Bob Healey," The Providence Journal, June 23, 1985, p. M-04.

93   Ibid.

94   Ibid.

95   Brian Fortin (longtime friend and political manager of Robert J. Healey Jr.) in discussion with the author, July 28, 2020.

96   Robert Healey, "What I Have Stolen from Others," circa 1987, p. 3.

97   Ibid., 13.

CHAPTER 3

1   Robert Craven (fellow law school student in the early 1980's) in discussion with the author, August 20, 2019.

2   Dave McCarthy, "Credibility a top issue in school board race," The Providence Journal, October 22, 1982, C-01

3   John Killion, "Killion says do best to upgrade schools for children," Warren Times Gazette, October 27, 1982, p.18.

4   Spencer Hackley, "Time for change on Committee, Hackley Says, Warren Times Gazette, October 27, 1982, p.18.

5   Dave McCarthy, "Credibility a top issue in school board race," The Providence Journal, October 22, 1982, C-01

6   Scott MacKay, "One strange man Barefoot Bob Healey," The Providence Journal, June 23, 1985, p. M-04.

7   Ibid.

8   Ibid.

9   Ibid.

10   Ibid.

11   Ibid.

12   Ibid.

13   Ibid.

14   Ibid.

15   "Teachers reach accord in contract with committee," Warren Times Gazette, May 19, 1982, p. 5.

16   "Communication will make school 'cool'—Healey," Warren Times Gazette, November 10, 1982, p. 13.

17   Ibid.

18   "Sunday Advance Hold for Silverman Dubious Achievement Awards '82," The Providence Journal. January 2, 1983. p. C-01.

19   "Healey named head of School Committee," Warren Times Gazette, November 23, 1982, p. 15.

CHAPTER 4

1   "Secretaries," Warren Times Gazette, November 23, 1982, p. 3.

2   Robert Healey, "Surplus might not be enough for funding," Warren Times Gazette, December 1, 1982, p. 11.

3   Ibid., 14.

4   "More money needed for schools—Healey," Warren Times Gazette, January 19, 1983, p. 3.

5   To Healey's warnings, the Warren Times Gazette clarified, "While voters have the option of refusing to allocate the $100,000 [for the nurse settlement], they do not have the authority to refuse to pay the settlements. They must be paid whether or not the special appropriations is passed… Under state law, a special appropriation, such as that for sports, cannot be earmarked specifically. While the committee most likely would use the money for sports, it is not legally bound to do so and could use the $25,000 to the settlement fees if necessary… Thus, putting the two items on special resolutions to be approved or rejected doesn't necessarily mean the decision rendered by the voters will be the end of the committee's problems." (Resolutions aren't necessarily the easy way out, Warren Times Gazette, February 2, 1983, p. 4.)

6   Lauren Brannan, "Sports program left for voters to decide," Warren Times Gazette, February 2, 1983, p. 1.

7   Robert Healey, "Committee wont use sports as leverage to get budget passed, Warren Times-Gazette, April 13, 1983, p. 15.

8   Lauren Brannan, Sports program left for voters to decide, Warren Times Gazette, February 2, 1983, p. 1.

9   Robert Healey, "Budget hike necessary to avoid cuts," Warren Times Gazette, February 2, 1983, p. 5.

10   Ibid., 13.

11   "School Committee will ask teachers' union to renegotiate raises," Warren Times

Gazette, March 3, 2020, p. 1 / p. 3

12   Robert Healey, Committee, council share ideas, avoid 'horror stories' of past, "Warren Times Gazette, March 9, 1983, p. 13.

13   "School Committee will ask teachers' union to renegotiate raises," Warren Times Gazette, March 3, 2020, p. 1 / p. 3

14   Lauren Brannan, "Sports program left for voters to decide," Warren Times Gazette, February 2, 1983, p. 1.

15   Robert Healey, "All town unions should consider reopening contracts," Warren Times-Gazette, March 16, 1983, p. 15.

16   Editorial, Warren Times-Gazette, April 13, 1983, p. 4.

17   Robert Healey, It's a 'grim' tale when taxpayers don't fund school budget," Warren Times Gazette, March 30, 1983, p. 13.

18   Bob Mello, "Schools, union reach tentative agreement,' Providence Journal, April 18, 1983, P. B-01.

19   Ibid.

20   Ibid.

21   Ibid.

22   Robert Healey, "Teachers are easy target in fight against budget," Warren Times-Gazette, April 27, 1983, p. 18.

23   "Tax rate jumps $7.74," Warren Times-Gazette, May 18, 1983, p. 15.

24   Ibid.

25   Robert Healey, "Renegotiating Contract still beneficial," Warren Times Gazette, May 18, 1983, p.20.

26   "Teachers should consider renegotiating contract," Warren Times-Gazette, March 9, 1983, p. 4.

27   Robert Healey, "Committee seeks contract talks; teachers don't see much to gain," Warren Times-Gazette, June 2, 1983.

28   "Committee," Warren Times-Gazette, June 29, 1983, p. 1.

29   Robert Healey, "Communications breakdown with the union," Warren Times-Gazette, August 31, 1983, p. 6.

30   Ibid.

31   Ibid

32   Robert Healey, "Putting the fist behind a velvet glove," Warren Times-Gazette, September 28, 1983, p. 17.

33   Robert Healey, "Basic Education should not be mandated," Warren Times-Gazette, November 30, 1983, P. 17.

34   Dave McCarthy, "School board head determined to speak out despite criticism," Providence Journal, December 15, 1983, p. C-01.

35   Robert Healey, "Basic Education should not be mandated," Warren Times-Gazette, November 30, 1983, P. 17.

36   Ibid., 14.

37   Anthony Mogayzel's daughter was also a Warren teacher.

38   Dave McCarthy, "Board chairman upset by benefit vote Calls Killion's explanation for approval 'limp,"' Providence Journal, April 4, 1984, p. C-01.

39   Ibid.

40   The Providence Journal reported that John Killion was given a clean bill of health by the state Conflict of Interest Commission, because he voted that he could vote on the subject budget item that "affected this wife, a school teacher, because she was part of a group that benefited as a whole." (Robert Healey, "Real conflict is with conflict commission," Providence Journal, August 1, 1984, p. 5.) Bob Healey disagreed. See Chapter 8, Not Business as Usual; Healey out of Politics.

41   Dave McCarthy, "Board chairman upset by benefit vote Calls Killion's explanation for approval 'limp,"' Providence Journal, April 4, 1984, p. C-01.

42   Robert Healey, Healey will continue

to talk to the press, Warren Times-Gazette, December 21, 1983, p.14.

43   Dave McCarthy, "Healey hits legislators for not helping school boards," Providence Journal, January 25,1984, p. C-01.

44   Robert Healey, "Committee's hands tied: state can help," Warren Times Gazette, January 25, 1984, p. 11.

45   Robert Mello, "Rep. Urban 'shocked' by Healey's criticism of local legislators," Providence Journal, January 27, 1984, p. C-01.

46   Bob Mello, "Councilmen criticize school board head for statements to the press Comments on legislators called 'backstabbing'," Providence Journal, January 30, 1984, p. B-01.

47   "Healey, Urban clash over role of legislators," Warren Times-Gazette, February 1, 1984, p. 4.

48   "Harvey objects to appointments; Healey 'either right or crazy," Warren Times-Gazette, February 29, 1984, p. 3.

49   "Committee supports sports—Healey," Providence Journal, February 8, 1984, p. 14.

50   "Healey's newsletter 'hits the fan,'" Warren Times-Gazette, February 22, 1984, p. 4.

51   Robert Healey, "Healey responds to Duperron's comments," Warren Times-Gazette, February 29, 1984, p. 6.

52   Paul Newman, in the movie "Cool Hand Luke" said to authorities, "What we have here is a failure to communicate." Authorities shot him shortly afterward.

53   "Healey 'in trenches,' but not in proper dress," Warren Times-Gazette, March 7, 1984, p. 2-3.

54   Ibid.

55   Robert Healey, "Healey clarifies his job role, projections," Warren Times-Gazette, March 14, 1984, p. 11.

56   "Sick Days: Teachers behind

union—Healey Union Can't police abuse—Dupperon," Warren Times-Gazette, March 14, 1984, p. 1.

57   Bob Mello, "Sick leave by teachers could lead to $44,000 deficit, officials project," Providence Journal, March 26, 1984, Page: B-01.

58   Ibid.

59   Robert Healey, Public scrutiny affects teachers' absences, Warren Times-Gazette, April 18, 1984, p. 17.

60   Bob Mello, "Brule criticizes Killion for voting on tax issue that affects his wife," The Providence Journal, March 27, 1984, p. C-01.

61   Ibid.

62   John J. Killion III, "Killion: Healey doesn't speak for him," Warren Times-Gazette, April 11, 1984, p. 5.

63   Dave McCarthy, "Healey says it's his job to keep voters informed," Providence Journal, April 11, 1984, B-03.

64   Ibid.

65   William Daponte, "Political quarrels could hurt quality of education," Warren Times-Gazette, March 21, 1984.

66   Phyllis Manchester-Masteka, "The question is: 'Just what is conflict?'" April 18, 1984, p. 6.

67   "Committee stretches to trim," Warren Times-Gazette," May 23, 1984, p. 1.

68   Robert Healey, "Is council's budget 'hypocrisy at its best?," Warren Times-Gazette, April 25, 1984, p. 15.

69   Ibid.

70   Ibid.

71   Bob Mello, "Budget cover letter by Healey rejected," Providence Journal, April 24, 1984, p. C201.

72   Ibid.

73   "Healey to speak for committee," Warren Times-Gazette, May 16,1984, p. 4.

74   Robert Healey, "Council uses school

budget as smokescreen," Warren Times-Gazette, May 16, 1984, p. 17.

75 Ibid.

76 "School board budget folder to include 2 cover letters from feuding factions," Providence Journal," May 16, 1984, p. C-01.

77 "Committee stretches to trim," Warren Times-Gazette," May 23, 1984, p. 1.

78 "School board budget folder to include 2 cover letters from feuding factions," Providence Journal," May 16, 1984, p. C-01.

79 "Healey, Nunes clash over letter, sarcasm," Warren Times-Gazette, November 28, 1984, p. 3.

80 Robert Healey, "Actions show Nunes attitude toward committee," Warren Times-Gazette, November 28, 1984, p. 22.

81 Dave McCarthy, "Warren Year in Review Revaluation contributed to Democratic defeats in '84," Providence Journal, January 2, 1985. P. C-01.

82 "Healey says 'don't celebrate' yet," Warren Times-Gazette, October 14, 1984, p. 21.

CHAPTER 5

1 "Smoking at home is parents' responsibility," Warren Times Gazette, January 19, 1983, p. 1.

2 "Communication will make school 'cool'—Healey," Warren Times Gazette, November 10, 1982, p. 13.

3 Bob Mello, "Police checking buses for pot," The Providence Journal, January 12, 1983, B-01.

4 Scott MacKay, "One strange man Barefoot Bob Healey," The Providence Journal, June 23, 1985, p. M-04.

5 Bob Mello, Police checking buses for pot, The Providence Journal, January 12, 1983, B-01.

6 "Smoking at home is parents' responsibility, not schools," January 19, 1983, Warren Times Gazette, P. 1.

7 Robert Healey Jr, "Smoking at home is parents' responsibility—Healey," January 19, 1983, Warren Times Gazette, P. 11.

8 Robert Healey, Pot smoking at home is parents' responsibility—Healey," Warren Times Gazette, January 19, 1983, p. 11.

9 "Days of prejudice over one's appearance should be at end," Warren Times Gazette, January 19, 1983, p. 4.

10 Bob Mello, "Healey: nab pot smokers at home," Providence Journal, January 13, 1983, C-01.

11 Bob Mello, "Chairman Healey is barefoot again," Providence Journal, July 26, 1983, p. C-03.

12 Ibid.

13 "Barefoot season ends when it starts," Warren Times-Gazette, August 3, 1983, p. 2.

14 Robert Healey, "He takes a firm stand—on bare feet," August 10, 1983, p. 6.

15 "In step to meet," Providence Journal, August 12, 1983, p.C-01.

16 Lauren Brannan, "Healey urges residents to demand better water," Warren Times-Gazette, July 27, 1983, p. 2.

17 "Healey will take water campaign to Barrington and Bristol," Warren Times-Gazette, August 3, 1983, p. 3.

18 Ibid.

19 Ibid., 4.

20 Robert Healey, "Healey updates water situation," Warren Times-Gazette, October 12, 1983, p. 5.

21 "Healey Walks to Reservoir," Warren Times-Gazette, November 9, 1983, p. 17.

22 Ibid.

23 Dave McCarthy, "Rep. Urban to join Healey's fight for warning signal in front of school," Providence Journal, September 24, 1984, p. C-01.

24   Ibid.

25   Robert Healey, "Why should committee pay for the state's error," Warren Times-Gazette, August 1, 984, p. 22.

26   Dave McCarthy, "Healey continues crusade for warning signs at Quirk despite promise from state Newspaper," September 25, 1984, p. C-01.

27   Ibid.

28   "If they won't do it…" Warren Times-Gazette, October 17, 1984, p. 3.

29   Bob Mello, "Healey hopes drivers will see the light, go slow near school, Providence Journal, October 18, 1984, p. C-01.

30   Bob Mello, "Radar convinces chief that speeders pose hazard to Quirk School children,' Providence Journal, October 19, 1984, p. C-01.

31   Dave McCarthy, "A walking Christmas tree blinks warning to drivers: Slow down near school," Providence Journal, December 21, 1984, P. C-01.

32   Ibid.

33   Ibid.

34   Ibid.

35   Robert Healey, "Taxpayers pay for contract, have right to know," February 20, 1985, p. 18.

36   "Warren's shows beat networks hands down," Warren Times-Gazette editorial, September 6, 1984, p. 4.

CHAPTER 6

1   NEA-Warren President Andrew Duperron, teachers Manuel Barboza, Jack Syrette, and Mary Ann Pallazzio, and National Education Association Rhode Island (NEARI) associate Jeanette Wooley) and the School Committee's two-man team negotiating (Committeemen Paul E. Brule and Chairman Robert J. Healey Jr.,)

2   Dave McCarthy, "Teacher 'wish-list' is 10 pages long, the school board is 35," Providence Journal, January 11, 1985, p. C-01.

3   "Negotiations off to a shaky start," Warren Times-Gazette, January 16, 1985, p. 3, 21.

4   Ibid.

5   Ibid.

6   Ibid.

7   Ibid.

8   Robert Healey, "Teacher wages stay same in budget proposal," Warren Times Gazette, January 16,1985, p. 22.

9   Like Robert Healey, Jeanette Wooley came to negotiations with little prior experience. She had served as a NEA negotiator for less than six months.

10   "School budget starts smoothly, Warren Times-Gazette, January 1, 1985, p. 22.

11   "Contract party delayed for now," Warren Times-Gazette, February 27, 1985 p. 21.

12   Ibid.

13   Ibid..

14   "School appointment: Healey's letter criticized," Warren Times-Gazette, March 13, 1985 p.1, 24.

15   Ibid..

16   Robert Healey, "Road to open meetings paved with intentions," Warren Times-Gazette, March 20, 1985 p. 22.

17   "Council backs school budget," Warren Times-Gazette, March 27, 1985, p. 3.

18   Paul Brule (Warren School Committeeman from 1982 – 1986), in discussion with the author, October 10, 2020.

19   Jeanette Wooley, (Rhode Island National Education Association negotiator) in discussion with the author, August 14, 2021.

20   Paul Brule (Warren School Committeeman from 1982 – 1986), in discussion

with the author, October 10, 2020.

21   Joe Marques, (veteran teacher at Warren High School), in discussion with the author, July 22, 2020.

22   Scott MacKay, "One strange man Barefoot Bob Healey," Providence Journal, June 23, 1985, p. M-04.

23   Ibid.

24   "Committee promises teachers clarity, courtesy in the future," Warren Times Gazette, March 27, 1985, p. 8.

25   Robert Healey, "Let us know if teachers should get a raise," Warren Times-Gazette, March 27, 1985, p. 26.

26   Ibid.

27   Ibid.

28   "Healey hits the pavement—and the teacher salaries," Warren Times-Gazette, April 10, 1985, p. 7.

29   Ibid.

30   Bob Mello, "Teachers file complaint on Healey's sign, flyers Newspaper," Providence Journal, April 16, 1985, p. C-01.

31   Ibid.

32   Ibid.

33   Robert Healey, "Will hand out salaries until ordered to stop," Warren Times-Gazette, April 1, 1985 p. 22.

34   The Warren Times posed the question, "Should teachers get a raise?" and recorded responses that suggested the local electorate was of mixed opinions. ("Should teachers get a raise?" Warren Times-Gazette, May 1, 1985, p. 1.)

35   Robert Healey, "Will hand out salaries until ordered to stop," Warren Times-Gazette, April 1, 1985 p. 22.

36   Scott MacKay, "Town to publish teacher salaries Board votes to list school workers' names, pay at annual meeting," Providence Journal, April 23, 1985, D-01.

37   Ibid.

38   Robert Healey, "He says teachers'

union is crying wolf," Warren Times-Gazette, May 1, 1985, p. 26.

39   "School budget surplus more than $134,000." Warren Times-Gazette, 5/15/1985 p. 31

40   Scott MacKay, "One strange man Barefoot Bob Healey," Providence Journal, June 23, 1985, p. M-04.

41   Bob Mello, "Teachers' union requests arbitration for settlement Newspaper," Providence Journal, May 28, 1985, p. C-01.

42   Ibid.

43   Ibid.

44   Ibid.

45   Scott MacKay, "One strange man Barefoot Bob Healey," Providence Journal, June 23, 1985, p. M-04.

46   Scott MacKay, "One strange man Barefoot Bob Healey," Providence Journal, June 23, 1985, p. Ibid.

47   Ibid.

48   Ibid.

49   "Doors Shut on teacher-student hearing," Warren Times-Gazette, June 26, 1985, p. 16.

50   Robert Healey, "The Class of 1985 is exceptional," Warren Times-Gazette, May 12, 1985, p. 31.

51   Robert Healey, "More money spent on student supplies," Warren Times-Gazette, June 6, 1985, p. 2.

52   Robert Healey, "Duperron calls for Killion resignation," Warren Times-Gazette, July 17, 1985 p. 5.

53   Ibid.

54   Pat Leduc, "Killion will not vote on teacher contracts," Warren Times-Gazette June 17, 1985. p. 18.

55   "Negotiations stalled," Warren Times-Gazette, July 31, 1985, p. 15.

56   Robert Healey, "Healey opposes union binding arbitration bid," July 31, 1985, p. 16.

57   Robert Healey, "If teachers strike, sports will not be affected," Warren Times-Gazette, August 21, 1985, p. 2.
58   Ibid.
59   Ibid.
60   Ibid.
61   Scott MacKay, "Committeeman Anthony S. Nunes was the lone member to call for reopening negotiation," August 27, 1985, p. D-01.
62   Ibid.
63   John Philip Schuyler, letter to the editor, "No explanations given at school board meeting," Warren Times-Gazette, August 28, 1985, p. 4.
64   Robert Healey, "Who should cast the first stone," Warren Times-Gazette, September 4, 1985, p. 21.
65   Robert Healey, "Schools open Sept. 4, Warren Gazette-Times, August 28, 1985, p. 27.
66   "Teachers deserve credit for going back to school without contract," Editorial, Warren Times-Gazette, September 11, 1985, p. 4.
67   Scott MacKay, "Teachers go to work, still without contract," Providence Journal, September 4, 1985, p. C-01.
68   "Teachers deserve credit for going back to school without contract," Editorial, Warren Times-Gazette, September 11, 1985, p. 4.
69   Scott MacKay, "Teachers go to work, still without contract," Providence Journal, September 4, 1985, p. C-01.
70   Bruce Landis, "Warren teachers vote to report; Newport, Pawtucket in doubt," Providence Journal, September 3, 1985, p. 1.
71   Robert Healey, "Schools open Sept 4," Warren Times-Gazette, August 28, 1985, p. 27.
72   Ibid.

73   Robert Healey, "Who should cast the first stone," Warren Times-Gazette, September 4, 1985, p. 21.
74   Ibid.
75   Ibid.
76   Ibid.
77   Ronald L. DiOrio, "president NEA Rhode Island, letter to the editor," Warren Times-Gazette, September 11, 1985, p. 29.
78   Ibid.
79   Scott MacKay, "Negotiators criticized by DiOrio Former NEA head raps 'delay' by school board," Providence Journal, September 12, 1985, p. C-01.
80   Robert Healey, "Alternatives to the fall ritual of teacher strikes," Providence Journal, September 21, 1985, p. A 21.
81   Ibid.
82   Many of Robert Healey's friends and associates reference him as "unflappable."
83   Scott MacKay, "Students urge contract compromise Leaders of student council and senior class say they fear that a strike will interrupt school year," Providence Journal, September 25, 1985, p. C-01
84   Denise MacDougall, Rosalie Walsh, "Students want to lose contract naïveté," Warren Times Gazette, October 21, 1985, p. 4.
85   Ibid.
86   Ibid.
87   Robert Healey, "Healey wants to lead arbitration battle," Warren Times-Gazette, October 9, 1985, p. 25.
88   Scott MacKay, "AG's office won't rule on teacher contract talks Board sought ruling on keeping negotiations open," Providence Journal, October 17, 1985, p. C-03.
89   Ibid.
90   Robert Healey, "Sellout of local school boards," Providence Journal, November 21, 1985, p. A-21.
91   Ibid.

92 "The matter is in arbitration and the final arbitration session is scheduled for Jan. 2 in Providence. The arbitrator is Milton J. Nadworny, a University of Vermont economics professor." (Scott MacKay, "Killion gets right to vote on binding arbitration May break impasse between teachers, school committee," Providence Journal, December 17, 1985, p. D-01.

93 Scott MacKay, "Killion gets right to vote on binding arbitration May break impasse between teachers, school committee," Providence Journal, December 17, 1985, p. D-01.

94 Ibid.

95 Barbara Polichetti, "Labor panel orders School Committee to stop publishing data on teachers Report accuses school officials of unfair bargaining practice," Providence Journal, December 24, p. C-01.

96 Ibid.

97 Ibid.

98 Robert Healey, "Labor Board rules against Bob Healey," Warren Times-Gazette, December 30, 1985, p. 2.

99 Ibid.

100 Barbara Polichetti, "Labor panel orders School Committee to stop publishing data on teachers Report accuses school officials of unfair bargaining practice," Providence Journal, December 24, p. C-01.

101 Robert Healey, "Labor Board rules against Bob Healey," Warren Times-Gazette, December 30, 1985, p. 2.

102 Peter F. Gray, "Healey should take pink flamingos and sandwich board to Washington," Warren Times-Gazette, September 18, 1985, p.4.

103 Robert Evans, "A teacher writes to Bob Healey," Warren Times-Gazette, October 9, 1985, p. 24.

104 Don Stevens, "Read feels like cork in bottle," Warren Times-Gazette, January 8,

1986, p. 3.

105 Ibid.

106 Ibid.

107 Scott MacKay, "Healey threatens to quit as chairman; calls for committee vote of confidence," Providence Journal, January 15, 1986, p. C-01.

108 Ibid.

109 Ibid.

110 Patricia Read said, "I reserve the right to disagree with you [Healey]. I reserve the right to disagree with anybody." (Scott MacKay, "Healey gets 2-1 vote of confidence from board, will continue as chairman Says tally means majority is 'moving in same direction,'" Providence Journal, January 28, 1986, p. B-01.)

111 Scott MacKay, "Healey gets 2-1 vote of confidence from board, will continue as chairman Says tally means majority is 'moving in same direction,'" Providence Journal, January 28, 1986, p. B-01.

112 Ibid.

113 Don Stevens, "DeLeo makes impassioned speech to School Committee," Warren Times-Gazette, January 29,1986, p. 2 / 3.

114 Scott MacKay, "Healey gets 2-1 vote of confidence from board, will continue as chairman Says tally means majority is 'moving in same direction,'" Providence Journal, January 28, 1986, p. B-01.

115 Ibid.

116 Ibid.

117 Robert Healey, "Healey says; I'll take Main Street," Warren Times-Gazette, January 29, 1986, p. 4.

118 Healey abstained, and Paul Brule voted against the motion introduced by Patricia Read.

119 "School board: Healey doesn't speak for us," Providence Journal, February 12, 1986, p. D-01.

120 Ibid.

121 Ibid.

122 Robert Healey, "Healey will sit down, but won't shut up," Warren Times-Gazette, February 12, 1986, p. 27.

123 Don Stevens, "Is Healey chairman or isn't he? That is the question," Warren Times Gazette, February 12, 1986, p. NEED TO CHECK THIS ARTICLE

124 "Time for a school settlement is now," Editorial Warren Times-Gazette, March 19, 1986, p. 4.

125 Ibid.

126 Ibid.

127 "D-Day is coming for Warren schools," Warren Times-Gazette, April 9, 1986, p.13.

128 Robert Healey, "Machine vote in June would avoid strike now," Warren Times Gazette, April 9, 1986, p. 27.

129 Ibid.

130 "Strike Day 3: No concessions, No injunction, nowhere to go," Warren Times-Gazette, April 23, 1986, p. 1,3.

131 Claire Frye, "WHS faculty Letter to the Editor "Parents share blame for situation," Warren Times Gazette, April 23, 1986, p. 4.

132 Ibid.

133 "'Illegal' education for Warren pupils." Warren Times-Gazette editorial, April 23, 1984, p. 4.

134 Joe Marques (Veteran Warren School Department teacher), in discussion with the author, July 22, 2020.

135 Don Stevens, "School Committee attends to business,' Warren Times Gazette, April 30, 1986, p. 3.

136 Ibid.

137 Herman Grabert, "Feels teachers should be supported," Warren Times-Gazette, April 30, 1986, p. 11.

138 Don Stevens, "Talks but no listening; talks stall,' Warren Times Gazette, April 30, 1986, p. 1.

139 Don Stevens, "JAIL THE TEACHERS THEY ARE NOT ABOVE THE LAW," Photo 4/23/1986 p. 15.

140 Joe Marques, (veteran Warren School Department teacher), in discussion with author, July 22, 2020.

141 Ken Mingis, "Warren teachers give Friday contract deadline for extracurricular activities," Providence Journal, April 29, 1986, p. A-03.

142 Ibid.

143 Ibid.

144 Robert J. Healey Jr., Letter to the Editor "Vote 'no,'" Warren Times Gazette, April 30, 1986, p. 26.

145 Jody McPhillips, "Union weighing new offer in Warren teachers strike," Providence Journal, April 27, 1986, p. A-03.

146 Ibid.

147 Ibid.

148 Jody McPhillips, "Man in the news Robert J. Healey Jr.: The strange man who thrives in public eye," Providence Journal, April 22, 1986, p. A-06.

149 Ibid.

150 Tiny Tim, a comical singer, played a ukulele and had gained a cultish following. Like Bob Healey, he sported shoulder length hair, but did not sport a beard.

151 Jody McPhillips, "Man in the news Robert J. Healey Jr.: The strange man who thrives in public eye," Providence Journal, April 22, 1986, p. A-06.

152 Ibid.

153 Ibid.

154 Ibid.

155 Ibid.

156 Ken Mingis, "Warren teachers reject offer School head to seek injunction against union," Providence Journal, May 2, 1986, p. A-01.

157 Ibid.

158 Ibid.

159 Ibid.

160 Ibid.

161 Ibid.

162 Ibid.

163 Ibid.

164 Jody McPhillips, "Judge to weigh the issue of harm to children as Warren board calls for teachers' return," Providence Journal, p. A-03.

165 Ibid.

166 Don Stevens, "Teachers return to class on negotiators' advice," Warren Times Gazette, May 7, 1986 p. 1, 3.

167 Jody McPhillips, "Warren back in class we can't defy court, union president says," Providence Journal, May 7, 1986, p. A-01.

168 Ibid.

169 Joe Marques, (veteran Warren School Department teacher), in discussion with author, July 22, 2020.

170 Jody McPhillips, with reports from Judy Rakowsky and Bob Mello, "Special master' enters strike Warren teachers, committee ordered to start talking," Providence Journal, May 9, 1986, p. A-01.

171 Judy Rakowsky, "Warren teachers ratify contract, will return to classroom today," Providence Journal, May 12, 1986, p. A-01.

172 Ibid.

173 Ibid.

174 Ibid.

175 Jeanette Wooley, "Wooley responds to Braun letter," Warren Times-Gazette, 5/28/1986, p. 4.

176 Jeanette Wooley, (Rhode Island National Education Association negotiator) in discussion with the author, August 14, 2021.

177 In the 1987-88 negotiations, the Warren teachers fared better than they had in 1986. After November 1986, Healey no longer served as the town's School

Committee Chairman.

178 Judy Rakowsky, "Warren teachers ratify contract, will return to classroom today," Providence Journal, May 12, 1986, p. A-01.

179 Karen Perry, "Contract settled; healing wounds will take longer," Providence Journal, May 14 1986, p. 1.

180 Robert J. Healey Jr., "All's quiet in school; tentative union pact," Warren Times-Gazette, June 4, 1986, p. 31.

181 Glenice G. Sousa, "Teachers keep faith: justice to be done," Warren Times-Gazette, May 21, 1986, p. 4.

182 Glenice G. Sousa, "Letter stated facts, time to cut losses," Warren Times-Gazette, June 4, 1986, p. 31.

183 Robert Healey, "Who are these Warren taxpayers?" Providence Journal, July 29, 1986, A-13.

184 Ibid.

185 Paul Brule (Warren School Committeeman from 1982 – 1986), in discussion with the author, October 10, 2020.

CHAPTER 7

1   "R.I.'s moose takes a holiday," Providence Journal, October 15, 1985. P. A-03.

2   Peter Lord, "Moose in Rhode Island Moose captured", Providence Journal, October 6, 1985, p. A-01.

3   Ibid.

4   James A. Merolla, "CAMPAIGN 2002—Fogarty enjoys fundraising edge," The Providence Journal East Bay Window, Section B, p. 1, April 20, 1994.

5   Claire Boyes, (longtime Robert Healey Jr. girlfriend) in discussion with the author, July 26, 2019.

6   Jody McPhillips, "'Cool Moose' party founded to bring town politics new faces", Providence Journal, June 4, 1986, p. C-01.

7   According to Bob Healey's longtime girlfriend, Claire Boyes, Rhode Island's roaming moose captivated Bob during the Fall of 1985. So much so was this the case, he named his newly formed party after the celebrated and tragic figure.

8   Jody McPhillips, "'Cool Moose' party founded to bring town politics new faces", Providence Journal, June 4, 1986, p. C-01.

9   Ibid.

10 Ibid.

11 Ibid.

12 Ibid.

13 Healey once suggested he wouldn't run for higher office unless selected for Rhode Island commissioner of education. Most assumed he offered the comment in jest.

14 "Campaign '86 Healey campaigning more for Cool Moose Party than for himself," Providence Journal, October 31, 1986, p. A-06.

15 Ibid.

16 John Kiffney, "Campaign '86 3 independents challenge parties in races for governor, treasurer," Providence Journal, September 13, 1986, p. A-04.

17 Ibid.

18 "Fund-raiser set for Cool Moose Party candidate," Providence Journal, August 20, 1986, p. C-03.

19 Ibid.

20 John Kiffney, "Campaign '86 3 independents challenge parties in races for governor, treasurer," Providence Journal, September 13, 1986, p. A-04.

21 Brian Jones, "Two of four gubernatorial candidates invited to join in debates on public TV," Providence Journal, September 29, 1986, p. A-03.

22 Ibid.

23 Ibid.

24 Ibid.

25 Ibid.

26 Ibid.

27 Brian C. Jones. "Independent candidate to ask DiPrete to debate," Providence Journal, October 13, 1986, p. A-07.

28 Ibid.

29 Ibid.

30 Ibid.

31 Ibid 7.

32 Brian C. Jones, "CAMPAIGN '86 2 independents rejected for TV debates in governor race," Providence Journal, October 6, 1986, p. A-17.

33 Ibid.

34 Ibid.

35 Brian Jones, "Two of four gubernatorial candidates invited to join in debates on public TV," Providence Journal, September 29, 1986, p. A-03.

36 Deborah Fortin, "For governor," Providence Journal, October 3, 1986, p. A-21.

37 Jody McPhillips, "'Cool Moose' party founded to bring town politics new faces", Providence Journal, June 4, 1986, p. C-01.

38 Gary Lavey (Longtime friend of Bob Healey), In discussion with the author, July 21, 2019.

39 "Campaign '86 Healey campaigning more for Cool Moose Party than for himself," Providence Journal, October 31, 1986, p. A-06.

40 Ibid.

41 Jody McPhillips, "'Cool Moose' party founded to bring town politics new faces", Providence Journal, June 4, 1986, p. C-01.

42 Ibid.

43 "Campaign '86 Healey campaigning more for Cool Moose Party than for himself," Providence Journal, October 31, 1986, p. A-06

44 Ibid.

45 Ibid.

46 Ibid.

47 Channing Gray, "THE

GOVERNOR'S RACE A vote for the ARTS Here's how the candidates stand on support," Providence Journal, November 2, 1986, p.H-01.

48   Charles Bakst, "CAMPAIGN '86 Women's Caucus rates the candidates," Providence Journal, November 1, 1986, p. B-28.

49   Ibid 8.

50   "Students mock vote foretells results," Providence Journal, November 7, 1986, p. C-03.

51   Claire Boyes, (long time Robert Healey Jr. girlfriend) in discussion with the author, July 26, 2019.

CHAPTER 8

1   Robert Craven (Healey's law school peer and long-time friend) in discussion with the author, August 20, 2019.

2   Ibid.

3   Ibid.

4   Ibid.

5   Ibid.

6   Ibid.

7   Ibid.

8   Ibid.

9   Ibid.

10   G. Wayne Miller, "THE DECADE IN REVIEW: LOCAL HEADLINERS," The Providence Journal, December 31, 1989, p. A-19.

11   Robert Healey, "Real conflict is with conflict commission," The Providence Journal, August 1, 1984, p. 5.

12   Ibid.

13   Ibid.

14   "Attorney general probes closed committee meeting," The Providence Journal," July 6, 1984, p. C-01.

15   Ibid.

16   Ibid.

17   Bob Mello, "Attorney general tells school board its closed meeting violated state law," The Providence Journal, August 17, 1984, C-01.

18   John Hill, "Central Falls board rules against City Council candidate," The Providence Journal, September 15, 2009, p. A-09.

19   Robert Craven, (Healey's law school peer and longtime friend), in discussion with the author, August 20, 2019.

20   John Hill, "Central Falls board rules against City Council candidate," The Providence Journal, September 15, 2009, p. A-09.

21   Ibid.

22   Ibid.

23   Tracy Breton, "Candidate sues over straight-party voting option on R.I. ballot," The Providence Journal, July 28, 2010.

24   Ibid.

25   Ibid.

26   "U.S. judge rejects challenge to R.I.'s party-line voting," The Providence Journal, September 1, 2010.

27   Cool Moose Party v. State of RI, 6 F. Supp. 2d 116 (D.R.I. 1998), JUSTIA US Law, https://law.justia.com/cases/federal/district-courts/FSupp2/6/116/2347646/, May 27, 1998 (accessed 11/29/2021.)

28   Ibid.

29   Ibid.

30   Ibid

31   Arlene Violet, "Robert Healey: A true patriot." https://www.valleybreeze.com/2016-04-05/north-providence/arlene-violet-robert-healey-true-patriot#.XgpYaC-MrLJw, 4/5/201, (accessed 12/29/2019)

32   Robert Craven (Healey's law school peer and longtime friend) in discussion with the author, August 20, 2019.

33   Ibid.

34   Vickie White (Healey client, and later secretary for the Cool Moose Party) in discussion with the author September 19, 2019.

35   Claire Boyes (Bob Healey's longtime companion) in discussion with the author, December 5, 2020.

36   Joe Moniz (Bob Healey's friend and business partner) in discussion with the author, January 11, 2020.

37   Ibid.

38   According to friend Joe Moniz, while in Uruguay Bob Healey abandoned for a short while his vegetarian lifestyle.

39   Joe Moniz (Bob Healey's friend and business partner) In discussion with the author, January 11, 2020.

40   Claire Boyes (Bob Healey's longtime companion) in discussion with the author, December 5, 2020.

41   Joe Moniz (Bob Healey's friend and business partner) in discussion with the author, January 11, 2020.

42   Ibid.

43   Ibid.

44   Ibid.

45   Ibid.

46   Ibid.

47   Ibid.

48   Karen Lee Ziner, "CAMPAIGN 2010—LIEUTENANT GOVERNOR— Healey gets traction in quest to abolish the office he seeks," The Providence Journal, October 23, 2010, p. A8.

49   Joe Moniz (Bob Healey's friend and business partner) in discussion with the author, January 11, 2020.

50   Bob Healey referenced in writing that Joe Moniz was the greatest influence of his life in learning the ins and outs of the business world.

51   Jade Gotauco, email to the author, July 25, 2019.

52   Healey's ice cream business was the first of others, including a California "Cool Moose Red" wine, planned to fall under the Cool Moose line of Zultan International Ltd., of which Healey assumed the corporation's presidency.

53   Gail Ciampa, "Cool Moose still wacky, now frozen," The Providence Journal, September 15, 2004, Lifebeat / Food, p. G-01.

54   Rudy Cheeks, "Rest in Peace, Bob Healey," http://www.rifuture.org/rest-in-peace-bob-healey/, March 21, 2016, Accessed August 3, 2019.

55   Gary Lavey (longtime friend of Robert J. Healey Jr.) in discussion with the author, July 21, 2019.

56   As of the publication date of this book, rights to Robert Healey's book are contested in the will.

57   In reference to Frank McCourt's published book, Teacher Man. McCourt self-described teaching methods and philosophy matched-up relatively well to Robert Healey's.

58   Gavin Garvin, (longtime friend of Robert J. Healey Jr. and Cool Moose Party officer) in discussion with the author, January 8, 2021.

59   Joseph DePascuale (longtime friend of Robert J. Healey Jr. and Warren Town Council President 2002- 2010 and 2012 to 2024) in discussion with the author, October 12, 2020.

60   Bryan Rodrigues (longtime friend of Robert J. Healey Jr.) in discussion with the author, December 8, 2020.

61   Ibid.

62   Ibid.

63   Ibid.

64   Ibid.

65   Ibid.

66   Ibid.

67   Gloria Garvin (longtime friend of

Robert J. Healey Jr. and Cool Moose Party officer) in discussion with the author, January 4, 2020.

CHAPTER 9

1   2014 Rhode Island Governor Debate, https://www.youtube.com/watch?v=ziyM-vGUVVug, 10/21/2014, accessed 6-03-19.
2   In Rhode Island the lieutenant governor replaces the governor in cases of incapacitation, resignation, removal from office, death, or criminal conviction.
3   Robert J. Healey Jr., Guest MIND-SETTER™ "Candidate for Governor of Rhode Island twitter sharing button," https://www.golocalprov.com/politics/guest-mindsetter-robert-j.-healey-jr.-candidate-for-governor-of-rhode-islan, GoLocal-Prov, September 20, 2014, accessed July 24, 2020.
4   Robert Healey, "The Platform Document of Robert J. Healey, Jr., Candidate for Lieutenant Governor of the State Rhode Island 2006, p. 8, http://files.golocalprov.com.s3.amazonaws.com/GOVER-NOR%20-%202006%20LT%20GOV%20PLATFORM.pdf accessed July 20, 2020.
5   Ibid.
6   Ibid.
7   Ibid.
8   Ibid.
9   Ibid.
10 Ibid.
11 Ibid.
12 Ibid.
13 Ibid.
14 Ibid.
15 Ibid.
16 Ibid.
17 Ibid.
18 Ibid.
19 Ibid.
20 Ibid.

21 Ibid.
22 Ibid.
23 Ibid.
24 Ibid.
25 Ibid.
26 Ibid.
27 Ibid.
28 Ibid.
29 Ibid.
30 Ibid.
31 Ibid.
32 Ibid.
33 Ibid.
34 Ibid.
35 Ibid.
36 Ibid.
37 Ibid.
38 Ibid.
39 Ibid.
40 Ibid.
41 Ibid.
42 Ibid.
43 Ibid.
44 Ibid.
45 Ibid.
46 Ibid.
47 Ibid.
48 Ibid
49 Ibid.
50 Ibid.
51 Ibid.
52 Ibid.
53 Ibid.
54 Ibid.
55 Ibid.
56 Ibid.
57 Ibid.
58 Ibid.
59 Ibid.
60 Ibid.

CHAPTER 10

1   Robert Healey, "Eligible for matching

funds?", The Providence Journal, May 28, 1987, p. A-19.

2   Wayne Miller, "THE DECADE IN REVIEW: LOCAL HEADLINERS," The Providence Journal, December 31, 1989, p. A-19.

3   Ibid.

4   Jonathan Karp, "Healey challenges hiring lawmaker as teacher," The Providence Journal, February 16, 1988, p. C-01.

5   Ibid.

6   Ibid.

7   Ibid.

8   Claire Boyes (longtime Robert Healey Jr. girlfriend) in discussion with the author, July 26, 2019.

9   Ibid.

10   Ibid.

11   Bob Mello, "Healey, Cool Moose candidate, announces 2nd run for governor," The Providence Journal, February 2, 1994, p. B-05.

12   Ibid.

13   Ibid.

14   Wayne Miller, "THE DECADE IN REVIEW: LOCAL HEADLINERS," The Providence Journal, December 31, 1989, p. A-19.

15   Bob Mello, "Healey, Cool Moose candidate, announces 2nd run for governor," The Providence Journal, February 2, 1994, p. B-05.

16   Claire Boyes (longtime Robert Healey Jr. girlfriend) in discussion with the author, July 26, 2019.

17   Joe Moniz (Bob Healey's friend and business partner) in discussion with the author, January 11, 2020.

18   Ibid.

19   While there is no official figure to support this claim, several sources support this notion.

20   Bob Mello, "Healey, Cool Moose candidate, announces 2nd run for governor," The Providence Journal, February 2, 1994, p. B-05.

21   Ross Perot had polled very well going into the summer of 1992. However, in July he dropped out of the race reportedly because he thought political operatives were aiming to disrupt his daughter's wedding. When he rejoined the race several weeks later, some voters questioned his commitment and general mindset.

22   James Stockdale, an aviator in the Vietnam War, partook in the two 1964 US responses to the Gulf of Tonkin Incident. He rightly questioned the reason for the second US counterattack. Shortly afterward, Stockdale parachuted from his plane after the North Vietnamese shot it down. He spent the rest of the war in the infamous Hanoi Hilton prisoner of war camp. While highly decorated and an American hero to many, his poor performance in the 1992 vice presidential debate may have contributed measurably to Ross Perot's loss in the general election.

23   Bob Mello, "Healey, Cool Moose candidate, announces 2nd run for governor," The Providence Journal, February 2, 1994, p. B-05.

24   Ibid.

25   Ibid.

26   Ibid.

27   Ibid.

28   Grant Garvin (Robert J. Healey Jr.'s longtime time political advocate and campaign director in the 2014 governor's race) in discussion with the author, January 8, 2021.

29   Bob Mello, "Healey, Cool Moose candidate, announces 2nd run for governor," Providence Journal, February 2, 1994, p. B-05.

30   Scott MacKay, "York, Almond assail

Machtley tax vow," The Providence Journal, March 16, 1994, p.A-01.

31 John Castellucci, "Sundlun assailed on DEM record," The Providence Journal, March 20, 1994 p. B-01.

32 Ibid.

33 Scott MacKay, "Lottery to determine ballot placement," The Providence Journal, April 20, 1994 p. B-06.

34 "The placement of all individual independent candidates will be decided by lottery, Leonard said. In a July 1993 ruling, Senior U.S. District Judge Raymond J. Pettine cited 'incredible' errors by the state during preparation of the 1992 ballot and ordered that the secretary of state be 'permanently enjoined from utilizing this configuration in future statewide elections.' Pettine's ruling came in response to a lawsuit by several independent candidates upset that they were listed in sample ballots mailed to more than 400,000 voters under a column for independent presidential candidate Lyndon LaRouche, a convicted felon. The placement gave the impression, the candidates argued, that the independent candidates for state offices were aligned with LaRouche." Scott MacKay, "Lottery to determine ballot placement," The Providence Journal, April 20, 1994 p. B-06.

35 "Healey urges lower campaign spending," The Providence Journal, May 31, 1994, p. D-04.

36 Ibid., 8.

37 Ibid.

38 "Healey urges lower campaign spending," The Providence Journal, May 31, 1994, p. D-04.

39 Ibid.

40 Ibid.

41 Ibid.

42 Ibid.

43 Ibid.

44 Scott MacKay, "Sundlun isn't apologizing for physique remark about Quinn," The Providence Journal, June 9, 1994, p. D-15.

45 Ibid.

46 Ibid.

47 Ibid.

48 Ibid.

49 Ibid.

50 Ibid.

51 "Cool Moose Party candidate supports Mayer and reform," The Providence Journal, June 14, 1994, p. C-04.

52 Ibid.

53 Ibid.

54 Ibid.

55 Elizabeth Rau, "Candidates for governor pitch their economic plans," The Providence Journal, June 24, 1994, p. A-04.

56 Ibid.

57 Ibid.

58 Ibid.

59 Ibid.

60 "CAMPAIGN BRIEFS Almond: Overhaul state personnel system," The Providence Journal, August 3, 1994, p. D-09.

61 Ibid.

62 Ibid.

63 CAMPAIGN BRIEFS Almond urges overhaul of real estate policy," Newspaper August 25, 1994, p. D-17.

64 "CAMPAIGN BRIEFS Almond seeks probe of Port Authority," The Providence Journal, September 30, 1994, p. C-06.

65 Ibid 6.

66 Ibid.

67 CAMPAIGN BRIEFS Almond urges overhaul of real estate policy," Newspaper August 25, 1994, p. D-17.

68 "CAMPAIGN BRIEFS Weygand aide attacks Driver TV commercial," The Providence Journal, September 7, 1994, p. D-10.

69 "CAMPAIGN BRIEFS Weygand aide attacks Driver TV commercial," The Providence Journal, September 7, 1994, p. D-10.

70 "CAMPAIGN BRIEFS York says she'll close ethics loophole on aides," The Providence Journal, September 6, 1994, p. D-06.

71 Russell Garland, "This could be a close one Brown poll finds Almond, York neck and neck," The Providence Journal, September 27, 1994, p. A-01.

72 "CAMPAIGN BRIEFS Almond seeks probe of Port Authority," The Providence Journal, September 30, 1994, p. C-06.

73 Ibid.

74 Ibid.

75 John Martine, "Healey protests Ch. 10's dis-invitation," The Providence Journal, October 3, 1994, p. C-05.

76 Katherine Gregg, "Almond, vs. York—face to face," The Providence Journal, October 13, 1994, p. D-12.

77 Claire Boyes, (Longtime Healey companion in discussion with the author) July 2019.

78 Katherine Gregg, "Almond, vs. York—face to face," The Providence Journal, October 13, 1994, p. D-12.

79 "CAMPAIGN BRIEFS Healey criticizes York, Almond for 'baggage,'" The Providence Journal, October 22, 1994, p. A-04.

80 Jerry O'Brien, "Cool Moose Healey: The governed should govern," The Providence Journal, October 16, 1994, p. A-18.

81 "CAMPAIGN BRIEFS Healey criticizes York, Almond for 'baggage,'" The Providence Journal, October 22, 1994, p. A-04.

82 Ibid

83 Jerry O'Brien, "Cool Moose Healey: The governed should govern," The Providence Journal, October 16, 1994, p. A-18.

84 "CAMPAIGN '94 CAMPAIGN BRIEFS Realtors give Almond their first endorsement," The Providence Journal, October 18, 1994, p. B-04.

85 President Coolidge proclaimed, "The business of America is business."

86 Jerry O'Brien, "Cool Moose Healey: The governed should govern," The Providence Journal, October 16, 1994, p. A-18.

87 Some have argued that President Coolidge did promote change in the 1920s by halting progressive legislation forwarded by those who continued to push for a pre-World War I Progressive era Agenda.

88 Jerry O'Brien, "Cool Moose Healey: The governed should govern," The Providence Journal, October 16, 1994, p. A-18.

89 Ibid.

90 "CAMPAIGN BRIEFS URI's faculty union endorses York, Pine," The Providence Journal, October 26, 1994, p. D-07.

91 Ibid.

92 Chris Poon, "Cool Moose's Healey wins high school's mock election," The Providence Journal, October 27, 1994, p. D-01.

93 Katherine Gregg, "Almond leads York by 12 points in poll," The Providence Journal, October 29, 1994, p. A-05.

94 James M. O'Neill, "CAMPAIGN '94 Almond's absence from forum scored by moderator Fowlkes," November 1, 1994, p. C-07.

95 Ibid.

96 James M. O'Neill, "CAMPAIGN '94 Almond's absence from forum scored by moderator Fowlkes," November 1, 1994, p. C-07.

97 Katherine Gregg, "Candidates go all out in TV finale," The Providence Journal, November 7, 1994, p. A-01.

98 Ibid.

99 Ibid.

100 Ibid.

101 Ibid.

102 "Almond squeaks past York Narrow victory climaxes no-holds-barred campaign," The Providence Journal, November 9, 1994, p. A-01.

103 "Official Election Day tallies offer no surprises in top races, The Providence Journal, November 23, 1994, p. B-05.

104 Toni De Paul, "Cool Moose Party seeks toehold," The Providence Journal, February 19, 1995, p. B-01.

105 Ibid.

106 Ibid.

107 Ibid.

108 Ibid.

109 Ibid.

110 Ibid.

111 Ibid.

112 Michael Maynard, "Providence holds parade in honor of St. Patrick," The Providence Journal, March 19, 1995, p. B-01.

113 Robert Healey, "Muddle by moose?" The Providence Journal, April 14, 1995, p. A-13.

114 Scott MacKay, "Business can get tax breaks under bill passed by House," The Providence Journal, May 11, 1995, p. D-16.

115 Ibid.

116 Algernon D'Ammassa, "The Cool Moose deserves a voice," Providence Journal, May 23, 1995, p. A-11.

117 Chris Poon, "GRADUATION DAY Cool Moose candidate: 'Be yourself' *Unsuccessful gubernatorial candidate Robert Healey Jr. implores graduates to think big, take chances and follow their instincts," The Providence Journal, June 13, 1995, p. C-01.

118 Ibid.

119 Ibid.

120 Ibid.

121 Robert Craven (law school student with Bob Healey) in discussion with the author, August 20, 2019.

122 Ibid.

123 Ibid.

124 Ibid.

125 Jerry O'Brien, "Party tells the council it's time to appoint a member of his party to the town Board of Canvassers," The Providence Journal, November 7, 1995, p. C-01.

126 Ibid.

127 Ibid.

128 Scott MacKay, "POLITICAL SCENE Buchanan battling to get on primary ballot," The Providence Journal, January 8, 1996, p. B-01.

129 Eugene Emery Jr., "In 2nd mayoral try, this dark horse is Cool Moose," The Providence Journal, May 10, 1996, p. C-01.

130 Ibid.

131 Ibid.

132 Russell Garland, "Parties join to promote campaign changes," The Providence Journal, June 19, 1996, p. B-04.

133 Ibid.

134 Jody McPhillips, "Journal-Bulletin's Town Meeting '96 Third parties proliferate, gain respectability," The Providence Journal, September 1, 1996, p. A-01.

135 Ibid.

136 Art Turgeon, "Cool Moose primary looms on horizon," The Providence Journal, June 27, 1996, p. C-01.

137 Ibid.

138 Ibid.

139 Ibid.

140 Scott MacKay, "Cool Moose Party files challenge to primary law *Robert J. Healey Jr., chairman of the Cool Moose Party, wants the state's primary election law declared unconstitutional," Providence

Journal, September 10, 1996, p. B-05.

141 Ibid.

142 Art Turgeon, "COOL MOOSE CONTEST Oops? Healey wins House primary," The Providence Journal, September 11, 1996, p. C-01.

143 Ibid.

144 Ibid

145 Ibid.

146 Ibid.

147 Ibid.

148 Ibid.

149 Ibid.

150 Ibid.

151 Jody McPhillips, "Cool Moose Party wins second spot on ballot," The Providence Journal, September 17, 1996, p. B-03.

152 Ibid.

153 "CAMPAIGN '96 Political Journal Cool Moose Party backs voter initiative," The Providence Journal, October 7, 1996, p. C-02.

154 Ibid.

155 Ibid.

156 Ibid.

157 "CAMPAIGN NOTES," The Providence Journal, October 14, 1996, p. B-02.

158 Ibid.

159 Ibid.

160 Robert Healey, "Letters to the Editor Cool Moose candidate vows to limit campaign spending," The Providence Journal, November 7, 1997, p. C-04.

161 Ibid.

162 Ibid.

163 Robert Healey, "Cool Moose candidate vows to limit campaign spending," The Providence Journal, November 7, 1997, p. C-04.

164 Russell Garland, "Never say die: Cool Moose back in '98 *With his 9 percent showing in the 1994 race for governor, Robert Healey qualifies for equal footing on the ballot and in public campaign funds," The Providence Journal, April 10, 1998, p. A-01.

165 Ibid.

166 Ibid.

167 Ibid.

168 Ibid.

169 Ibid.

170 Ibid.

171 Ibid.

172 Jody McPhillips, "Area politicians, analysts say Clinton speech went halfway," The Providence Journal, August 19, 1998, p. A-09.

173 Ibid.

174 Ibid.

175 Ibid.

176 Scott MacKay, Jonathan Saltzman, "POLITICAL SCENE Only the boss knows about those bonuses," The Providence Journal, October 12, 1998, p. B-01.

177 Ibid.

178 Ibid.

179 "CAMPAIGN NOTEBOOK," The Providence Journal, October 21, 1998, p. A-19.

180 Ibid.

181 Jody McPhillips, "'98 Election This may be last run for Cool Moose leader," The Providence Journal, October 25, 1998, p. A-19.

182 Ibid.

183 Ibid.

184 Ibid.

185 Ibid.

186 Ibid.

187 https://www.c-span.org/video/?113012-1/rhode-island-gubernatorial-debate C-Span October 5, 1998, accessed Jan 27, 2022

188 "Katherine Gregg and Jody McPhillips, "'98 Election The race for governor As candidates outline views on the issues,

differences are clear," The Providence Journal, October 28, 1998, p. A-01.

189 Ibid.

190 Ibid.

191 Claire Boyes (Bob Healey's longtime companion) in discussion with the author, July 26, 2019.

192 Ibid.

193 Ibid.

194 Christopher Rowland, "Familiar barbs mark final forum *Governor Almond questions how Myrth York plans to finance her education plan; York chides Almond over traffic jams and traffic court," The Providence Journal, October 31, 1998, p. A-01.

195 Ibid

196 Jonathan Saltzman and Scott MacKay, "York, Almond bring in the heavy hitters," The Providence Journal, October 31, 1998, p. A-01.

197 Katherin Gregg, "ALMOND 51%— YORK 42% Almond outruns polls, cruises to 2nd term as governor," The Providence Journal, November 4, 1998, p. A-01.

198 Ibid.

199 Scott MacKay, "How the suburbs elected almond Older urban areas losing political clout," The Providence Journal, November 5, 1998, p. A-17.

200 Ibid.

CHAPTER 11

1 Liz Anderson, "Fogarty announces reelection bid," The Providence Journal, March 19, 2002, p. B-01.

2 Ibid.

3 Ibid.

4 Ibid.

5 Ibid.

6 Ibid.

7 Ibid.

8 Katherine Gregg, "Lynch out front in fundraising for AG race," The Providence Journal, February 9, 2002, p. A-08.

9 Liz Anderson, "CAMPAIGN 2002— Fogarty enjoys fundraising edge," The Providence Journal, August 2, 2002, p. B-01.

10 Tom Mooney, "CAMPAIGN 2002— Seriously: Running for lieutenant governor," The Providence Journal, October 31, 2002, p. A-01.

11 Scott Mayerowitz, Katherine Gregg, Edward Fitzpatrick, and Scott MacKay, "POLITICAL SCENE—Laffey not alone in suggesting the job of the lieutenant governor is a waste," The Providence Journal, October 24, 2005, p. C-01.

12 Tom Mooney, "CAMPAIGN 2002— Seriously: Running for lieutenant governor," The Providence Journal, October 31, 2002, p. A-01.

13 Arlene Violet, "Robert Healey: A true patriot," https://www.valleybreeze.com/2016-04-05/north-providence/arlene-violet-robert-healey-true-patriot#.XgpYaC-MrLJw, 4/5/201, (accessed 12/29/2019

14 Tom Mooney, "CAMPAIGN 2002— Seriously: Running for lieutenant governor," The Providence Journal, October 31, 2002, p. A-01.

15 Ibid.

16 Ibid.

17 Ibid.

18 Ibid.

19 Ibid.

20 Ibid.

21 Ibid.

22 Ibid.

23 Speaker John Harwood hired Wendy Collins, reportedly with few qualifications, to conduct legislative research. She later alleged sexual harassment against the speaker. The scandalous story received a lot of attention, especially on talk radio.

24 Tom Mooney, "CAMPAIGN 2002—Seriously: Running for lieutenant governor," The Providence Journal, October 31, 2002, p. A-01.

25 Scott Mayerowitz, "A long-distance runner for lieutenant governor," The Providence Journal, March 17, 2006, p. A-01.

26 Tom Mooney, "CAMPAIGN 2002—Seriously: Running for lieutenant governor," The Providence Journal, October 31, 2002, p. A-01.

27 Tom Mooney, "ELECTION 2002—Fogarty easily wins, turning back challenge to need for lt. Gov.," The Providence Journal, November 6, 2002, p. A-16.

28 Ibid.

29 Robert Healey, Letter to the editor, "Bakst omits the one with best plank," The Providence Journal, July 6, 2006, p. B-05.

30 Tom Mooney, "ELECTION 2002—Fogarty easily wins, turning back challenge to need for lt. Gov.," The Providence Journal, November 6, 2002, p. A-16.

31 Ibid.

32 Scott Mayerowitz, Katherine Gregg, Edward Fitzpatrick, and Scott MacKay, "POLITICAL SCENE—Laffey not alone in suggesting the job of the lieutenant governor is a waste," The Providence Journal, October 24, 2005, p. C-01.

33 Ibid.

34 Ibid.

35 Ibid.

36 "Pro-choice group supports Roberts," The Providence Journal, December 8, 2005, p. B-06.

37 Ibid.

38 Ibid.

39 Scott Mayerowitz, "Ocean State native King returns to run for office," The Providence Journal, January 31, 2006, p. A-01.

40 Ibid.

41 Ibid.

42 Ibid.

43 Ibid.

44 Ibid.

45 Ibid.

46 "Pro-choice group supports Roberts," The Providence Journal, December 8, 2005, p. B-06.

47 Claire Boyes (Bob Healey's Llongtime companion) in discussion with the author, December 5, 2020.

48 Scott Mayerowitz, "A long-distance runner for lieutenant governor," The Providence Journal, March 17, 2006, p. A-01.

49 Ibid.

50 Elizabeth Gudrais, "Campaign matches may cost public $3 million," The Providence Journal, August 6, 2006, p. B-01.

51 Scott Mayerowitz, "A long-distance runner for lieutenant governor," The Providence Journal, March 17, 2006, p. A-01.

52 Ibid.

53 Ibid.

54 Edward Fitzpatrick, "Healey serious about eliminating job he's running for," The Providence Journal, October 30, 2006, p. A-02.

55 Ibid.

56 Edward Fitzpatrick, "Healey serious about eliminating job he's running for," The Providence Journal, October 30, 20Edward Fitzpatrick, "Healey serious about eliminating job he's running for," The Providence Journal, October 30, 2006, p. A-02.06, p. A-02.

57 Scott Mayerowitz, "A long-distance runner for lieutenant governor," The Providence Journal, March 17, 2006, p. A-01.

58 Ibid.

59 Edward Fitzpatrick, "Healey serious about eliminating job he's running for," The Providence Journal, October 30, 2006, p. A-02.

60 Ibid.

61   Ibid.

62   Scott Mayerowitz, "A long-distance runner for lieutenant governor," The Providence Journal, March 17, 2006, p. A-01.

63   Katherine Gregg, "POLITICAL SCENE—DMV newsletter aimed for 'giggle' but got controversy," The Providence Journal, April 24, 2006, C-01.

64   Ibid.

65   Elizabeth Gudrais, "State senator enters race for lieutenant governor," The Providence Journal, May 23, 2006, p. A-01.

66   Ibid.

67   Ibid.

68   Robert Healey, Letter to the editor, "Bakst omits the one with best plank," Providence Journal, July 6, 2006, p. B-05.

69   Elizabeth Gudrais, "Campaign matches may cost public $3 million," The Providence Journal, August 6, 2006, p. B-01.

70   Ibid.

71   Elizabeth Gudrais, "Lieutenant Governor's Race—Roberts vs. Centracchio—Longtime military officer serious about new mission," The Providence Journal October 30, 2006, p. A-01.

72   Ibid.

73   Ibid.

74   Edward Fitzpatrick, "Healey serious about eliminating job he's running for," The Providence Journal, October 30, 2006, p. A-02.

75   Ibid.

76   Katie Mulvaney, "ELECTION FALL-OUT—SKHS students are close to perfect on election poll," The Providence Journal, November 9, 2006, p. D-01.

77   Ibid.

78   Tracy Breton, "ELECTION 2006: Roberts is new lt. Governor," The Providence Journal, November 8, 2006, p. A-13.

79   Elizabeth Gudrais and Scott Mayerowitz, "Less spent on '06 contest," The Providence Journal, December 6, 2006, p. A-01.

80   Ibid.

81   Robert Healey, "Advertising elects our officials," Providence Journal, December 10, 2006, p. D-07.

82   Robert Healey, "LETTERS—Ocean Staters got what they voted for," Providence Journal, November 18, 2007, p. D-07.

CHAPTER 12

1   Edward Fitzpatrick, "Roberts looks to 2010 race," The Providence Journal, March 1, 2009, Providence Journal, p. C-01.

2   Ibid.

3   Ibid.

4   Robert Healey became the only person to serve as the graduation speaker on two separate occasions at North Kingstown High School, doing so in 1995 and 2009.

5   David Lopes, (North Kingstown High School Class of 2009 co-advisor) in discussion with the author, July 2008.

6   Thomas Doran, (North Kingstown High School graduation committee) in discussion with author, June 17, 2020.

7   Ibid.

8   Ibid.

9   Lynn Arditi, "Incumbent sees host of challengers for Lt. Governor," The Providence Journal, July 1, 2010, p. A8.

10   Edward Fitzpatrick, "Cool Moose prepares to charge again," The Providence Journal, August 13, 2009, A-04.

11   Ibid.

12   This phrase was used by the Bill Clinton campaign when he ran for president in 1996. The phrase ran on a banner that hung in his campaign headquarters.

13   Katherine Gregg, "Cool Moose Healey launches 'just pick two' campaign," The

Providence Journal, February 19, 2010, PROJO POLITICS BLOG.

14 The Providence Journal referenced Healey as a "big underdog." Edward Fitzpatrick, "Cool Moose prepares to charge again," The Providence Journal, August 13, 2009, A-04.

15 Katherine Gregg, "Update: GOP primary winner drops out of RI lt. gov. Race," The Providence Journal, September 17, 2010, Section: breaking news.

16 Edward Fitzpatrick, "Cool Moose prepares to charge again," The Providence Journal, August 13, 2009, A-04.

17 Ibid.

18 Randal Edgar, "Healey announces run for lieutenant governor," The Providence Journal, February 8, 2010, Section: breaking news.

19 Lynn Ariditi, "Running for office to abolish it," The Providence Journal, February 10, 2010, p. A6.

20 Ibid.

21 Ibid.

22 Edward Fitzpatrick, "Grandmother wouldn't believe this circus," The Providence Journal, October 5, 2010, p. A4.

23 Katherine Gregg, "Cool Moose Healey launches 'just pick two' campaign," The Providence Journal, February 19, 2010, PROJO POLITICS BLOG.

24 Ibid.

25 Ibid.

26 Lynn Arditi, "Running for office to abolish it," The Providence Journal, February 10, 2010, p. A6.

27 Scott MacKay, "R.I. Politics: No Women Need Apply," wrnipolitcs blog, https://wrnipoliticsblog.wordpress.com/2010/09/18/r-i-politics-no-women-need-apply/, September 18, 2010, accessed August 27, 2020.

28 Beth Comery, "You Know He's Right,"

Providence Daily Dose, https://providencedailydose.com/2008/01/13/you-know-hes-right/, June 13, 2008, Accessed August 15, 2021.

29 Scott MacKay, "R.I. Politics: No Women Need Apply," wrnipolitcs blog, https://wrnipoliticsblog.wordpress.com/2010/09/18/r-i-politics-no-women-need-apply/, September 18, 2010, accessed August 27, 2020.

30 A.G. Sulzeberger, "Jokes and Secret Hopes for Lieutenant Governors," The New York Times, https://www.nytimes.com/2010/12/04/us/04lieutenant.html?pagewanted=all&_r=0, December 3, 2010.

31 Ibid.

32 Lynn Arditi, "Incumbent sees host of challengers for Lt. Governor," The Providence Journal, July 1, 2010, p. A8.

33 PROJO POLITICS BLOG, The Providence Journal, Section: WEBLOG, June 21, 2010.

34 Ibid.

35 Ibid.

36 Lynn Arditi, "Incumbent sees host of challengers for Lt. Governor," The Providence Journal, July 1, 2010, p. A8.

37 Katherine Gregg, "Update: GOP primary winner drops out of RI lt. gov. Race," The Providence Journal, September 17, 2010, Section: breaking news.

38 Ibid.

39 Ibid.

40 Ibid.

41 Ibid.

42 Ibid.

43 Katherine Gregg, "Campaign 2010—Lt. Governor—Rogers nods to Healey, withdraws from race," The Providence Journal, September 18, 2010, p. A1.

44 Karen Lee Ziner, "CAMPAIGN 2010—THE LIEUTENANT

GOVERNOR—Should office even exist?" The Providence Journal, September 24, 2010, p. A1.

45 Edward Fitzpatrick, "Grandmother wouldn't believe this circus," The Providence Journal, October 5, 2010, p. A4.

46 Ibid.

47 Ibid.

48 "Healey says Rhode Island gubernatorial candidates hypocritical," The Providence Journal, October 7, 2010, Section: WEBLOG.

49 Ibid.

50 Kareen Lee Ziner, "Campaign 2010— Lieutenant governor candidates have a lively debate," The Providence Journal, October 22, 2010, p. A7.

51 Robert J. Healey Jr., "COMMENTARY—Time for R.I. to stop funding useless office of lt. Gov.," Providence Journal, October 18, 2010, p. B7.

52 "Twenty," RINPR, October 19, 2010, https://wrnipoliticsblog.wordpress.com/2010/10/19/roberts-dropping-200k-tv-bomb-on-healey/ accessed July 9, 2020.

53 Edward Fitzpatrick, "This was the race Lincoln D. Chafee wanted," The Providence Journal, November 3, 2010, p. A8.

54 Kareen Lee Ziner, "Campaign 2010— Lieutenant governor candidates have a lively debate," The Providence Journal, October 22, 2010, p. A7.

55 Ibid.

56 Ibid.

57 Ibid.

58 Ibid.

59 Ibid.

60 Ibid.

61 Ibid.

62 Karen Lee Ziner, "CAMPAIGN 2010—LIEUTENANT

GOVERNOR—Healey gets traction in quest to abolish the office he seeks," The Providence Journal, October 23, 2010, p. A8.

63 Ibid.

64 Ibid.

65 Ibid.

66 Ibid.

67 Ibid.

68 Karen Lee Ziner, "ELECTION 2010—LT. Governor—Incumbent Roberts fends off challenge," The Providence Journal, November 3, 2010, p. A10.

69 Cynthia Needham and Karen Lee Ziner, "projo PolitiFact—Politics |-Healey's claim is off the mark," Providence Journal, October 30, 2010, p. A5.

70 Ibid.

71 Ibid.

72 Ibid.

73 Ibid.

74 Ibid.

75 Ibid.

76 "Bob Healey talks elections, future," https://www.youtube.com/watch?v=6X-Uqqd-9cV8, November 2, 2010, Assessed July 9, 2020.

77 Ibid.

78 Karen Lee Ziner, "ELECTION 2010—LT. Governor—Incumbent Roberts fends off challenge," The Providence Journal, November 3, 2010, p. A10.

79 Ibid.

80 Amanda Mikovits, "Healey plays giggly Son of God at Newspaper Guild Follies," The Providence Journal, February 25, 2011, Section: breaking news.

81 Ibid.

CHAPTER 13

1 Healey had said he would run for the

lieutenant governor's position for a fourth time if he had the signatures in place to do so. According to Clara Boyes, Healey left that matter mainly to other parties who did not follow through with securing the required signatures.

2   Randall Edgar an Katherine Gregg, "campaign 2014 | Cool Moose will carry the Moderate banner," The Providence Journal, September 12, 2014, p. 1.

3   Ibid.

4   Edward Fitzpatrick, "Politics | We now have a 'full Rhode Island' election this year," The Providence Journal, September 14, 2014, p. 05.

5   Randall Edgar an Katherine Gregg, "campaign 2014 | Cool Moose will carry the Moderate banner," The Providence Journal, September 12, 2014, p. 1.

6   Ibid.

7   Katherine Gregg, "campaign 2014 | Healey gets OK to run for governor," The Providence Journal, September 18, 2014, p. 01.

8   Ibid.

9   Ibid.

10   Ibid.

11   Ibid.

12   Ibid.

13   While Treasurer Raimondo had won over many Rhode Islanders for reforming the state's pension fund, she had also alienated a significant core of police officers, fireman, teachers, and state workers who felt strongly that the "reforms" broke long-standing implied contracts.

14   Katherine Gregg, "campaign 2014 | Healey gets OK to run for governor," The Providence Journal, September 18, 2014, p. 01.

15   Ibid.

16   Ibid.

17   Ibid.

18   Randall Edgar and Katherine Gregg, "campaign 2014 | Cool Moose will carry the Moderate banner," The Providence Journal, September 12, 2014, p. 1.

19   Ibid.

20   Ibid.

21   C. Eugene Emery Jr, "Politics | Healey stayed true to budget in governor's race," The Providence Journal, November 9, 2014, p. 10.

22   Ibid.

23   Ibid.

24   Ibid.

25   Ibid.

26   Ibid.

27   Ibid.

28   Ibid.

29   Edward Fitzpatrick, "Politics | We now have a 'full Rhode Island' election this year," Providence Journal, September 14, 2014, p. 05.

30   Ibid.

31   Ibid.

32   Ibid.

33   Ibid.

34   Ibid.

35   Ibid.

36   Katherine Gregg, "campaign 2014 | Raimondo keeps lead," The Providence Journal, October 15, 2014, p. 01.

37   2014 Rhode Island Governor Debate, https://www.youtube.com/watch?v=ziyM-vGUVVug, 10/21/2014, accessed 6-03-19.

38   Ibid.

39   In 2010, former Red Sox pitcher, Curt Schilling, secured a $75 million loan guarantee from the Rhode Island Economic Development Corporation to move his company, 38 Studios, to Rhode Island. In 2012, 38 Studios went bankrupt, setting off an intense debate over the state's responsibility to make on the outstanding loan payments.

40 Ibid.

41 Ibid.

42 Katherine Gregg, "Campaign 2014, A question of leadership," The Providence Journal, October 22, 2014, p. 01.

43 2014 Rhode Island Governor Debate, https://www.youtube.com/watch?v=ziyM-vGUVVug, 10/21/2014, accessed 6-03-19.

44 Ibid.

45 Ibid.

46 Ibid.

47 Ibid.

48 Ibid.

49 Ibid.

50 Ibid.

51 Claire Boyes (longtime friend and companion of Bob Healey) in discussion with the author, July 26, 2019.

52 The Raimondo campaign had been offered any time slot of their choosing from 7:15 A.M. to 2:00 P.M over a two-day period. Every other schedule commitment to candidates (95 percent of those appearing on the North Kingstown ballot) remained tentative based on the treasurer's schedule.

53 Katherine Gregg, "Campaign 2014 The race for governor | Fung challenges methodology of Brown poll," Providence Journal, October 25, 2014, p. 03.

54 Ibid.

55 Ibid.

56 Alisha A. Pina, "Clinton stumps for Raimondo | Campaign 2014," Providence Journal, October 25, 2014, p. 01.

57 Ibid.

58 Katherine Gregg, "Campaign 2014 governor's race | Verbal clash erupts over candidates' qualifications," Providence Journal, October 29, 2014, p. 01.

59 Ibid.

60 Ibid.

61 Ibid.

62 Katherine Gregg, "In turnaround, Brown poll shows Raimondo, Fung neck and neck," The Providence Journal, October 29, 2014, p. 01.

63 Katherine Gregg, "Last gubernatorial debate contentious," The Providence Journal, October 31, 2014, p. 01.

64 Ibid.

65 Paul Grimaldi, "Governor's race | Candidates face off for final time," The Providence Journal, November 1, 2014, P. WPG_H, Section: News.

66 Ibid.

67 "Getting down to business | Election 2014 The transition," The Providence Journal, November 9, 2014, p. 01.

68 Paul Grimaldi, "Governor's race | Candidates face off for final time," Providence Journal, November 1, 2014, P. WPG_H, Section: News.

69 Robert Healey, Lively Experiment, https://www.youtube.com/watch?v=YrdCB1T6-9Q&feature=youtu.be, November 21, 2014, accessed July 21, 2014.

70 Dan Yorke, Dan Yorke's State of Mind, https://www.youtube.com/watch?v=XzVzrWQDlzk, November 7, 2014, accessed January 28, 2022.

71 Robert J. Healey, Jr., Dan Yorke's State of Mind, https://www.youtube.com/watch?v=XzVzrWQDlzk, November 7, 2014, accessed January 28, 2022.

72 Edward Fitzpatrick, "Getting down to business | Election 2014 The transition," The Providence Journal, November 9, 2014, p. 1.

73 C. Eugene Emery Jr, "Politics | Healey stayed true to budget in governor's race," The Providence Journal, November 9, p. 10.

74 Edward Fitzpatrick, "How did Healey get 22 percent of governor's vote with $36?" The Providence Journal, November 6, 2014, p. RICOVER_01 | Section: News.

75   Ibid.

76   Ibid.

77   "This Rhode Island governor candidate won 22 percent of the vote. He only spent $35, Washington Post, https://www.washingtonpost.com/news/the-fix/wp/2014/11/05/this-rhode-island-governor-candidate-won-22-percent-of-the-vote-he-only-spent-35/?arc404=true, accessed June 13 2020.

78   Justin Haskins, "The infuriating case of Robert Healey," http://www.providencejournal.com/opinion/commentary/20141113-justin-haskins-the-infuriating-case-of-robert-healey.ece?start=2, November 13, 2014, Accessed June 15, 2020.

79   Robert Healey argued vehemently that Fung's fizzling campaign produced the Cranston mayor's disappointing election results.

80   Dan Yorke, Dan Yorke's State of Mind, https://www.youtube.com/watch?v=Xz-VzrWQDlzk, November 7, 2014, accessed January 28, 2022.

81   Edward Fitzpatrick, "Getting down to business | Election 2014 The transition," The Providence Journal, November 9, 2014, p. 1.

82   Scott MacKay, Lively Experiment, https://www.youtube.com/watch?v=Yrd-CB1T6-9Q&feature=youtu.be, November 21, 2014, accessed July 21, 2020.

83   Several friends and political cohorts reported that the 2014 governor race results rejuvenated Bob Healey, for the short term.

CHAPTER 14

1   Claire Boyes (longtime close companion of Robert J. Healey Jr.) in discussion with the author, July 26, 2019.

2   Robert J. Healey, Jr., funeral card, Wilbur-Romano Funeral Home, March 16, 2016.

3   Jacqueline Tempera, "Passages: Robert Healey—A cool passion for R.I. politics—Cool Moose Party founder discovered dead Sunday," The Providence Journal, March 22, 2016, p. 1.

4   "Cool Moose Party founder Robert Healey dead at 58." https://www.youtube.com/watch?v=pcINSBIu8Bw channel 12, WPRI, Providence, accessed October 12, 2019, March 21, 2016.

5   Political Round Table, https://thepublicsradio.org/article/political-roundtable-pagliarini-guns-tolls-robert-cool-moose-healey March 26, 2016 / Accessed July 25, 2019.

6   Katie Nagle, "Robert Healey, 1957-2016: Rhode Island Leaders React," GoLocalProv, https://www.golocalprov.com/politics/robert-cool-moose-healey-1957-2016-rhode-island-leaders-react, March 22, 2016, accessed July 17, 2020.

7   Dan Yorke's State of Mind, https://www.youtube.com/watch?v=DjQ07zs-12Rc&t=967s, March 30, 2016, accessed January 28, 2022.

8   Claire Boyes (longtime close companion of Robert J. Healey Jr.) in discussion with the author, July 26, 2019.

9   Ted Hayes, "Three years after his death, Bob Healey's estate is far from settled Cool Moose founder's will, conflicts and claims bog down probate process," https://www.eastbayri.com/seekonk/stories/three-years-after-his-death-bob-healeys-estate-has-yet-to-be-settled,64051, East Bay RI, accessed May 8, 2020, April 9, 2019.

10   Ibid.

11   Ted Hayes, "Three years after his death, Bob Healey's estate is far from settled Cool Moose founder's will, conflicts and

claims bog down probate process," East Bay RI, April 10, 2019, p. 9.

12 Ibid.

13 Ibid.

14 Parker Gavigan, "Missing money grows, involving deceased political candidate Bob Healey," https://turnto10.com/news/local/nbc-10-i-team-large-amounts-of-money-missing-from-bob-healey-estate, NBC 10 News, April 30, 2021, Accessed May 5, 2021.

15 Linda Horowitz (lawyer representing Clara Boyes) in discussion with the author, May 23, 2022.

16 Ibid.

17 Parker Gavigan, "Missing money grows, involving deceased political candidate Bob Healey," https://turnto10.com/news/local/nbc-10-i-team-large-amounts-of-money-missing-from-bob-healey-estate, NBC 10 News, April 30, 2021, Accessed May 5, 2021.

18 Ibid.

19 Ibid.

20 Ibid.

21 Ibid.

22 Ibid.

23 Ibid.

24 Ibid.

25 Ibid.

26 Ibid.

27 Ted Hayes, "Three years after his death, Bob Healey's estate is far from settled Cool Moose founder's will, conflicts and claims bog down probate process," https://www.eastbayri.com/seekonk/stories/three-years-after-his-death-bob-healeys-estate-has-yet-to-be-settled,64051, East Bay RI, accessed May 8, 2020, April 9, 2019.

28 Katherine Kittell (close friend to Robert J. Healey Jr.) in discussion with the author, July 27, 2019.

29 Jade Gotauco (close friend and companion to Robert J. Healey Jr.) in discussion with the author, July 25, 2019.

CHAPTER 15

1 Jacqueline Tempera, "Passages: Robert Healey—A cool passion for R.I. politics— Cool Moose Party founder discovered dead Sunday," The Providence Journal, March 22, 2016, p. 1.

2 Gloria Garvin (Robert J. Healey Jr.'s longtime time political advocate) in discussion with the author, January 5, 2021.

3 Ibid.

4 Claire Boyes (longtime friend and companion to Robert J. Healey Jr.) in discussion with the author, July 26, 2020.

5 Grant Garvin (Robert J. Healey Jr.'s longtime political advocate and campaign director in the 2014 governor's race) in discussion with the author, January 8, 2021.

6 Jade Gotauco (close friend to Robert J. Healey Jr.) in discussion with the author, July 25, 2019.

7 Ibid

8 Bryan Rodrigues (Robert J. Healey Jr.'s longtime friend and political advocate) in discussion with the author, March 1, 2020.

9 Justin Haskins, "The infuriating case of Robert Healey," http://www.providencejournal.com/opinion/commentary/20141113-justin-haskins-the-infuriating-case-of-robert-healey.ece?start=2, November 13, 2014, Accessed June 15, 2020.

10 James Safford, "Bob Healey Showed One Man Can Be an Island," http://www.rirelevant.com/politics/safford-bob-healey-showed-one-man-can-island/?fbclid=IwAR1gSQFC-CP6T0AiayRv1cCP3C7BkRY4EjaPle_L2OP_nbKtW8tZ3Vy6ZY5o, riRelent.

com, January 21, 2018, accessed 7/18/19.

11   Claire Boyes (longtime friend and companion to Robert J. Healey Jr.) in discussion with the author, July 26, 2020.

12   Ian Donnis, "Narrow Choice," The Providence Phoenix, http://www.providencephoenix.com/archive/features/02/10/03/THIRD.html October 4, 2002, accessed June 12, 2019.

13   Katie Nagle, "Robert Healey, 1957-2016: Rhode Island Leaders React," GoLocalProv, https://www.golocalprov.com/politics/robert-cool-moose-healey-1957-2016-rhode-island-leaders-react, March 22, 2016, accessed July 17, 2020.

14   Thomas Tracy (longtime friend of Robert J. Healey Jr.) in discussion with the author, January 20, 2020.

15   Jacqueline Tempera, "Passages: Robert Healey—A cool passion for R.I. politics—Cool Moose Party founder discovered dead Sunday," The Providence Journal, March 22, 2016, p. 1.

16   Robert Craven (longtime friend and law school peer of Robert J. Healey Jr.) in discussion with the author, August 19, 2019.

17   Ted Hayes, "Three years after his death, Bob Healey's estate is far from settled Cool Moose founder's will, conflicts and claims bog down probate process," East Bay RI, May 8, 2020, p.?

18   Gavin Garvin (longtime friend of Robert J. Healey Jr. and Cool Moose Party officer) in discussion with the author, January 8, 2021.

19   Jade Gotauco (close friend to Robert J. Healey Jr.) in discussion with the author, July 25, 2019.

20   Bryan Rodrigues (Robert J. Healey Jr.'s longtime friend and political advocate) in discussion with the author, December 8, 2020.

21   The line references the song, "The Room Where It Happens," from Lin-Manuel Miranda's play, Hamilton.

22   Fellow School Committeeman Paul Brule worked just as hard toward the same end but did so more behind the scenes.

23   Even when the Cool Moose Party earned on official party status (owing to an impressive 1994 governor's race showing), the following year only a handful of party members participated in the first Cool Moose Party convention.

24   Bryan Rodrigues, (Robert J. Healey Jr.'s longtime friend and political advocate) in discussion with the author, December 8, 2020.

25   James Safford, "Bob Healey Showed One Man Can Be an Island," http://www.rirelevant.com/politics/safford-bob-healey-showed-one-man-can-island/?fbclid=IwAR1gSQFC-CP6T0AiayRv1cCP3C7BkRY4EjaPle_L2OP_nbKtW8tZ3Vy6ZY5o, riRelent.com, January 21, 2018, accessed 7/18/19.

26   Gloria Garvin, (Robert J. Healey Jr.'s longtime time political advocate) in discussion with the author, January 5, 2021.

27   Ibid.

28   Jacqueline Tempera, "Passages: Robert Healey—A cool passion for R.I. politics—Cool Moose Party founder discovered dead Sunday," The Providence Journal, March 22, 2016, p. 1.

EPILOGUE

1   Bob Plain, "Can Cool Moose's ghost posthumously swing RI governor's election?" RIFuture.org, https://www.rifuture.org/ghost-of-the-cool-moose/ March 6, 2018, accessed July 24, 2020.

2   Robert Healey, "Four ideas that will improve Rhode Island, RI Future, http://www.rifuture.org/four-ideas-that-will-improve-rhode-island/, November 10, 2014, Accessed July 29, 2020.

3   Ibid

4   Laufton Ascencao had secured that seat in the November 2018 election, but due to serious ethical and legal questions decided to vacate the position to which he was elected.

5   William Hunt referenced Robert Healey's example as a reason he decided, initially, to enter politics.

6   The Gaspee Project, https://www.facebook.com/GaspeeProjectRI/, February 19, 2019, accessed July 30, 2020.

7   William Hunt for District 68, https://www.facebook.com/HopeWithHunt/, February 19, 2019, accessed July 30, 2020.

8   William Hunt lost the elections of 2019 and 2021 to June Speakman. Speakman, widely viewed a liberal candidate, had invited Healey to speak at her Roger Williams law class several times.

BIBLIOGRAPHY

NEWSPAPER ARTICLES

"Almond squeaks past York Narrow victory climaxes no-holds-barred campaign," *The Providence Journal*, November 9, 1994.

Anderson, Liz. "CAMPAIGN 2002— Fogarty enjoys fundraising edge," *The Providence Journal*, Section B, August 2, 2002.

Anderson, Liz. "Fogarty announces reelection bid," *The Providence Journal*, Section B, March 19, 2002.

"Attorney general probes closed committee meeting," *The Providence Journal*, Section C, July 6, 1984.

Arditi, Lynn. "Incumbent sees host of challengers for Lt. Governor," *The Providence Journal*, July 1, 2010.

Arditi, Lynn. "Running for office to abolish it," *The Providence Journal*, February 10, 2010.

"Barefoot season ends when it starts," *Warren Times-Gazette*, August 3, 1983.

Bakst, Charles. "CAMPAIGN '86 Women's Caucus rates the candidates," *The Providence Journal*, Section B, November 1, 1986.

Brannan, Lauren, "Healey urges residents to demand better water," *Warren Times-Gazette*, July 27, 1983.

Brannan, Lauren, "Sports program left for voters to decide," *Warren Times Gazette*, February 2, 1983.

Breton, Tracy. "Candidate sues over straight-party voting option on R.I. ballot," *The Providence Journal*, July 28, 2010.

Breton, Tracy. "ELECTION 2006: Roberts is new lt. Governor," *The Providence Journal*, November 8, 2006.

"CAMPAIGN BRIEFS Almond seeks probe of Port Authority," *The Providence Journal*, Section C, September 30, 1994.

"CAMPAIGN BRIEFS Almond: Overhaul state personnel system," *The Providence Journal*, Section D, August 3, 1994.

CAMPAIGN BRIEFS Almond urges overhaul of real estate policy," *The Providence Journal*, Section D, August 25, 1994.

"CAMPAIGN BRIEFS Healey criticizes York, Almond for 'baggage,'" *The Providence Journal*, October 22, 1994.

"CAMPAIGN BRIEFS Realtors give Almond their first endorsement," *The Providence Journal*, Section B, October 18, 1994.

"CAMPAIGN BRIEFS Weygand aide

attacks Driver TV commercial," *The Providence Journal*, September 7, 1994.

"CAMPAIGN '96 Political Journal Cool Moose Party backs voter initiative," *The Providence Journal*, Section C, October 7, 1996.

"CAMPAIGN BRIEFS URI's faculty union endorses York, Pine," *The Providence Journal*, Section D, October 26, 1994.

"CAMPAIGN BRIEFS York says she'll close ethics loophole on aides," *The Providence Journal*, Section D, September 6, 1994.

"CAMPAIGN NOTEBOOK," *The Providence Journal*, October 21, 1998.

"CAMPAIGN NOTES," *The Providence Journal*, Section B, October 14, 1996.

"Campaign '86 Healey campaigning more for Cool Moose Party than for himself," *The Providence Journal*, October 31, 1986.

Castellucci, John. "Sundlun assailed on DEM record," *The Providence Journal*, Section B, March 20, 1994.

Cheeks, Rudy. "Rest in Peace, Bob Healey," http://www.rifuture.org/rest-in-peace-bob-healey/, March 21, 2016, Accessed August 3, 2019.

Ciampa, Gail. "Cool Moose still wacky, now frozen," *The Providence Journal*, Section G, September 15, 2004.

"Committee promises teachers clarity, courtesy in the future," *Warren Times Gazette*, March 27, 1985.

"Committee stretches to trim," *Warren Times-Gazette*," May 23, 1984.

"Committee supports sports—Healey," *The Providence Journal*, February 8, 1984.

"Communication will make school 'cool'—Healey," *Warren Times Gazette*, November 10, 1982.

"Contract party delayed for now," *Warren Times-Gazette*, February 27, 1985.

"Cool Moose Party candidate supports Mayer and reform," *The Providence Journal*, Section C, June 14, 1994.

"Council backs school budget," *Warren Times-Gazette*, March 27, 1985.

D'Ammassa, Algernon. "The Cool Moose deserves a voice," *The Providence Journal*, May 23, 1995.

Daponte, William. "Political quarrels could hurt quality of education," *Warren Times-Gazette*, March 21, 1984.

"D-Day is coming for Warren schools," *Warren Times-Gazette*, April 9, 1986.

De Paul, Toni. "Cool Moose Party seeks toehold," *The Providence Journal*, Section B, February 19, 1995.

DiOrio, Ronald L. "president NEA Rhode Island, letter to the editor," *Warren Times-Gazette*, September 11, 1985.

"Days of prejudice over one's appearance should be at end," *Warren Times Gazette*, January 19, 1983.

"Doors Shut on teacher-student hearing," *Warren Times-Gazette*, June 26, 1985.

Editorial, *Warren Times-Gazette*, April 13, 1983.

Edgar, Randal. "Healey announces run for lieutenant governor," *The Providence Journal*, Breaking News, February 8, 2010.

Edgar, Randall, and Katherine Gregg, "campaign 2014 | Cool Moose will carry the Moderate banner," *The Providence Journal*, September 12, 2014.

Emery, Eugene Jr. "In 2nd mayoral try, this dark horse is Cool Moose," *The*

Providence Journal, Section C, May 10, 1996.

Emery, C. Eugene Jr, "Politics | Healey stayed true to budget in governor's race," *The Providence Journal*, November 9, 2014.

Evans, Robert. "A teacher writes to Bob Healey," *Warren Times-Gazette*, October 9, 1985, p. 24.

Fitzpatrick, Edward. "Cool Moose prepares to charge again," *The Providence Journal*, August 13, 2009.

Fitzpatrick, Edward. "Getting down to business | Election 2014 The transition," *The Providence Journal*, November 9, 2014.

Fitzpatrick, Edward, "Grandmother wouldn't believe this circus," *The Providence Journal*, October 5, 2010.

Fitzpatrick, Edward. "Healey serious about eliminating job he's running for," *The Providence Journal*, October 30, 2006.

Fitzpatrick, Edward. "How did Healey get 22 percent of governor's vote with $36?" *The Providence Journal*, Section: News, November 6, 2014.

Fitzpatrick, Edward. "Politics | We now have a 'full Rhode Island' election this year," *The Providence Journal*, September 14, 2014.

Fitzpatrick, Edward. "Roberts looks to 2010 race," *The Providence Journal*, Section C, March 1, 2009.

Fitzpatrick, Edward. "This was the race Lincoln D. Chafee wanted," *The Providence Journal*, November 3, 2010.

Fitzpatrick, Edward. "Politics | We now have a 'full Rhode Island' election this year," *The Providence Journal*, September 14, 2014.

Fortin, Deborah. "For governor," *The Providence Journal*, October 3, 1986.

Frye, Claire. "WHS faculty Letter to the Editor "Parents share blame for situation," *Warren Times Gazette*, April 23, 1986.

"Fund-raiser set for Cool Moose Party candidate," *The Providence Journal*, August 20, 1986.

Garland, Russell. "Never say die: Cool Moose back in '98 *With his 9 percent showing in the1994 race for governor, Robert Healey qualifies for equal footing on the ballot and in public campaign funds," *The Providence Journal*, April 10, 1998.

Garland, Russell. "Parties join to promote campaign changes," *The Providence Journal*, Section B, June 19, 1996.

Garland, Russell. "This could be a close one Brown poll finds Almond, York neck and neck," *The Providence Journal*, September 27, 1994.

"Getting down to business | Election 2014 The transition," *The Providence Journal*, November 9, 2014.

Gray, Channing. "THE GOVERNOR'S RACE A vote for the ARTS Here's how the candidates stand on support," *The Providence Journal*, Section H, November 2, 1986.

Gray, Peter F. "Healey should take pink flamingos and sandwich board to Washington,", *Warren Times-Gazette*, September 18, 1985, p.4.

Grabert, Herman. "Feels teachers should be supported," *Warren Times-Gazette*, April 30, 1986, p. 11.

Gregg, Katherine. "ALMOND 51%— YORK 42% Almond outruns polls, cruises to 2nd term as governor," *The Providence Journal*, November 4, 1998.

Gregg, Katherine. "Almond, vs. York—face to face," *The Providence Journal*, Section D, October 13, 1994.

Gregg, Katherine. "Campaign 2010—Lt. Governor—Rogers nods to Healey, withdraws from race," *The Providence Journal*, September 18, 2010.

Gregg, Katherine. "Campaign 2014, A question of leadership," *The Providence Journal*, October 22, 2014.

Gregg, Katherine. "Campaign 2014 governor's race | Verbal clash erupts over candidates' qualifications," *The Providence Journal*, October 29, 2014.

Gregg, Katherine. "Campaign 2014 | Healey gets OK to run for governor," *The Providence Journal*, September 18, 2014.

Gregg, Katherine. "Campaign 2014 The race for governor | Fung challenges methodology of Brown poll," *The Providence Journal*, October 25, 2014.

Gregg, Katherine. "Candidates go all out in TV finale," *The Providence Journal*, November 7, 1994.

Gregg, Katherine. "Cool Moose Healey launches 'just pick two' campaign," *The Providence Journal*, PROJO POLITICS BLOG, February 19, 2010.

Gregg, Katherine. "In turnaround, Brown poll shows Raimondo, Fung neck and neck," *The Providence Journal*, October 29, 2014.

Gregg, Katherine. "Last gubernatorial debate contentious," *The Providence Journal*, October 31, 2014.

Gregg, Katherine. "Lynch out front in fundraising for AG race," *The Providence*

Journal, February 9, 2002.

Gregg, Katherine, and Jody McPhillips. "'98 Election The race for governor as candidates outline views on the issues, differences are clear," *The Providence Journal*, October 28, 1998.

Gregg, Katherine, "POLITICAL SCENE—DMV newsletter aimed for 'giggle' but got controversy," *The Providence Journal*, Section C, April 24, 2006.

Gregg, Katherine. "Update: GOP primary winner drops out of RI lt. gov. Race," *The Providence Journal*, Breaking News, September 17, 2010.

Grimaldi, Paul. "Governor's race | Candidates face off for final time," *The Providence Journal*, Section: News, November 1, 2014.

Gudrais, Elizabeth. "Campaign matches may cost public $3 million," *The Providence Journal*, Section B, August 6, 2006.

Gudrais, Elizabeth, and Scott Mayerowitz, "Less spent on '06 contest," *The Providence Journal*, December 6, 2006.

Gudrais, Elizabeth, "Lieutenant Governor's Race—Roberts vs. Centracchio—Longtime military officer serious about new mission," *The Providence Journal*, October 30, 2006.

Gudrais, Elizabeth, "State senator enters race for lieutenant governor," *The Providence Journal*, May 23, 2006.

Hackley, Spencer. "Time for change on Committee, Hackley Says," *Warren Times Gazette*, October 27, 1982.

"Harvey objects to appointments; Healey 'either right or crazy,'" *Warren Times-Gazette*, February 29, 1984.

"'Illegal' education for Warren pupils," *Warren Times-Gazette*, April 23, 1984.

"Healey charges 'censorship' by school groups," *The Providence Journal*, Section D, May 4 1994.

"Healey continues 'better water' campaign with Ciallella, group," *Warren Times-Gazette*, August 10, 1983.

"Healey 'in trenches,' but not in proper dress," *Warren Times-Gazette*, March 7, 1984.

"Healey hits the pavement—and the teacher salaries," *Warren Times-Gazette*, April 10, 1985

"Healey named head of School Committee," *Warren Times Gazette*, November 23, 1982.

"Healey's newsletter 'hits the fan,'" *Warren Times-Gazette*, February 22, 1984.

"Healey, Nunes clash over letter, sarcasm," *Warren Times-Gazette*, November 28, 1984.

Healey, Robert J. Jr. "Actions show Nunes attitude toward committee," *Warren Times-Gazette*, November 28, 1984.

Healey, Robert J. Jr. "Advertising elects our officials," *The Providence Journal*, Section D, December 10, 2006.

Healey, Robert J. Jr. "All's quiet in school; tentative union pact," *Warren Times-Gazette*, June 4, 1986.

Healey, Robert J. Jr., "Alternatives to the fall ritual of teacher strikes," *The Providence Journal*, September 21, 1985.

Healey, Robert J. Jr. "All town unions should consider reopening contracts," *Warren Times-Gazette*, March 16, 1983.

Healey, Robert J. Jr. "Bakst omits the one with best plank," *The Providence Journal*, Section B, July 6, 2006.

Healey, Robert J. Jr. "Basic Education should not be mandated," *Warren Times-Gazette*, November 30, 1983.

Healey, Robert J. Jr. "Budget hike necessary to avoid cuts," *Warren Times Gazette*, February 2, 1983.

Healey, Robert J. Jr. "Committee, council share ideas, avoid 'horror stories' of past," *Warren Times Gazette*, March 9, 1983.

Healey, Robert J. Jr. "Committee's hands tied: state can help," *Warren Times Gazette*, January 25, 1984.

Healey, Robert J. Jr. "Committee seeks contract talks; teachers don't see much to gain," *Warren Times-Gazette*, June 2, 1983.

Healey, Robert J. Jr. "Committee won't use sports as leverage to get budget passed," *Warren Times-Gazette*, April 13, 1983.

Healey, Robert J. Jr. "Communications breakdown with the union," *Warren Times-Gazette*, August 31, 1983.

Healey, Robert J. Jr. "Cool Moose candidate vows to limit campaign spending," *The Providence Journal*, Section C, November 7, 1997.

Healey, Robert J. Jr. "Council uses school budget as smokescreen," *Warren Times-Gazette*, May 16, 1984.

Healey, Robert J. Jr. "Eligible for matching funds?" *The Providence Journal*, May 28, 1987.

Healey, Robert J. Jr. "Duperron calls for Killion resignation," *Warren Times-Gazette*, July 17, 1985.

Healey, Robert J. Jr., funeral card, Wilbur-Romano Funeral Home, March 16, 2016.

Healey, Robert J. Jr. "Healey clarifies his job

role, projections," *Warren Times-Ga-zette*, March 14, 1984.

Healey, Robert J. Jr. "He says teachers' union is crying wolf," *Warren Times-Ga-zette*, May 1, 1985.

Healey, Robert J. Jr. "He takes a firm stand—on bare feet," *Warren Times-Ga-zette*, August 10, 1983.

Healey, Robert J. Jr. "Healey updates water situation," *Warren Times-Gazette*, October 12, 1983, p. 5.

Healey, Robert J. Jr. "Let us know if teachers should get a raise," *Warren Times-Gazette*, March 27, 1985.

Healey, Robert J. Jr. "Healey wants to lead arbitration battle," *Warren Times-Ga-zette*, October 9, 1985.

Healey, Robert J. Jr. "Healey responds to Duperron's comments," *Warren Times-Gazette,* February 29, 1984.

Healey, Robert J. Jr. "Healey will continue to talk to the press," *Warren Times-Ga-zette*, December 21, 1983.

Healey, Robert J. Jr. "If teachers strike, sports will not be affected," *Warren Times-Gazette*, August 21, 1985.

Healey, Robert J. Jr. "Is council's budget 'hypocrisy at its best?" *Warren Times-Gazette*, April 25, 1984.

Healey, Robert J., Jr. "It's a 'grim' tale when taxpayers don't fund school budget," *Warren Times Gazette*, March 30, 1983.

Healey, Robert J. Jr. "Legal Matters facing committee explained," *Warren Times Gazette*, December 8, 1982.

Healey, Robert J. Jr. "Machine vote in June would avoid strike now," *Warren Times Gazette*, April 9, 1986, p. 27.

Healey, Robert J. Jr. "More money spent on student supplies," *Warren*

Times-Gazette, June 6, 1985.

Healey, Robert J. Jr. "Muddle by moose?" *The Providence Journal*, April 14, 1995.

Healey, Robert J. Jr. "Healey opposes union binding arbitration bid," *Warren Times-Gazette*, July 31, 1985.

Healey, Robert J. Jr. "Healey says; I'll take Main Street," *Warren Times-Gazette*, January 29, 1986.

Healey, Robert J. Jr. "Healey will sit down, but won't shut up," *Warren Times-Ga-zette*, February 12, 1986.

Healey, Robert J. Jr. "Labor Board rules against Bob Healey," *Warren Times-Ga-zette*, December 30, 1985.

Healey, Robert J. Jr. "LETTERS—Ocean Staters got what they voted for," *The Providence Journal*, Section D, November 18, 2007.

Healey, Robert J. Jr. "Public scrutiny affects teachers' absences," *Warren Times-Ga-zette*, April 18, 1984.

Healey, Robert J. Jr. "Putting the fist behind a velvet glove," *Warren Times-Gazette*, September 28, 1983.

Healey, Robert J. Jr. "Real conflict is with conflict commission," *The Providence Journal*, August 1, 1984.

Healey, Robert J. Jr. "Renegotiating Contract still beneficial," *Warren Times Gazette*, May 18, 1983.

Healey, Robert J. Jr. "Road to open meetings paved with intentions," *Warren Times-Gazette*, March 20, 1985.

Healey, Robert J. Jr. "Schools open Sept. 4, *Warren Gazette-Times*, August 28, 1985.

Healey, Robert J. Jr. "Surplus might not be enough for funding," *Warren Times Gazette*, December 1, 1982.

Healey, Robert J. Jr. "Taxpayers pay for contract, have right to know," *Warren Times Gazette*, February 20, 1985.

Healey, Robert J. Jr. "Sellout of local school boards," *The Providence Journal*, November 21, 1985.

Healey, Robert J. Jr. "The Class of 1985 is exceptional," *Warren Times-Gazette*, May 12, 1985.

Healey, Robert J. Jr. "Teachers are easy target in fight against budget," *Warren Times-Gazette*, April 27, 1983.

Healey, Robert J. Jr. "Teacher wages stay same in budget proposal," *Warren Times Gazette*, January 16, 1985.

Healey, Robert J. Jr. "Time for R.I. to stop funding useless office of lt. Gov.," *The Providence Journal*, Section B Commentary, October 18, 2010.

Healey, Robert, J. Jr. "Vote 'no,'" *Warren Times Gazette*, April 30, 1986.

Healey, Robert, J. Jr. "Who are these Warren taxpayers?" *The Providence Journal*, July 29, 1986.

Healey, Robert J. Jr. "Who should cast the first stone," *Warren Times-Gazette*, September 4, 1985.

Healey, Robert J. Jr. "Why should committee pay for the state's error," *Warren Times-Gazette*, August 1, 984.

Healey, Robert J. Jr. "Will hand out salaries until ordered to stop," *Warren Times-Gazette*, April 1, 1985.

"Healey says 'don't celebrate' yet," *Warren Times-Gazette*, October 14, 1984.

"Healey to speak for committee," *Warren Times-Gazette*, May 16,1984.

"Healey, Urban clash over role of legislators," *Warren Times-Gazette*, February 1, 1984.

"Healey urges lower campaign spending," *The Providence Journal*, Section D, May 31, 1994.

"Healey Walks to Reservoir," *Warren Times-Gazette*, November 9, 1983.

"Healey says Rhode Island gubernatorial candidates hypocritical," *The Providence Journal*, Section WEBLOG, October 7, 2010.

"Healey will take water campaign to Barrington and Bristol," *Warren Times-Gazette*, August 3, 1983, p. 3.

Hill, John. "Central Falls board rules against City Council candidate," *The Providence Journal*, September 15, 2009.

"If they won't do it…" *Warren Times-Gazette*, October 17, 1984.

"In step to meet," *The Providence Journal*, Section C, August 12, 1983.

Jones, Brian. "Independent candidate to ask DiPrete to debate," *The Providence Journal*, October 13, 1986.

Jones, Brian. "Two of four gubernatorial candidates invited to join in debates on public TV," *The Providence Journal*, September 29, 1986.

Jones, Brain. "CAMPAIGN '86 2 independents rejected for TV debates in governor race," *The Providence Journal*, October 6, 1986.

Karp, Jonathan. "Healey challenges hiring lawmaker as teacher," *The Providence Journal*, Section C, February 16, 1988.

Kiffney, John. "Campaign '86 3 independents challenge parties in races for governor, treasurer," *The Providence Journal*, September 13, 1986.

Killion John. "Killion: Healey doesn't speak for him," *Warren Times-Gazette*, April 11, 1984.

Killion, John. "Killion says do best to upgrade schools for children," *Warren Times Gazette*, October 27, 1982.

Landis, Bruce. "Warren teachers vote to report; Newport, Pawtucket in doubt," *The Providence Journal*, September 3, 1985.

Leduc, Pat. "Killion will not vote on teacher contracts," *Warren Times-Gazette*, June 17, 1985.

Lord, Peter. "Moose in Rhode Island Moose captured," *The Providence Journal*, October 6, 1985.

MacDougall, Denise, and Rosalie Walsh, "Students want to lose contract naïveté," *Warren Times Gazette*, October 21, 1985.

Manchester-Masteka, Phyllis. "The question is: 'Just what is conflict?'" *Warren Times Gazette*, April 18, 1984.

"Mary J. Healey, Obituary," *The Providence Journal*, June 23, 1998.

MacKay, Scott. "AG's office won't rule on teacher contract talks Board sought ruling on keeping negotiations open," *The Providence Journal*, Section C, October 17, 1985.

MacKay, Scott. "Business can get tax breaks under bill passed by House," *The Providence Journal*, Section D, May 11, 1995.

MacKay, Scott. "Committeeman Anthony S. Nunes was the lone member to call for reopening negotiation," The Providence Journal, Section D, August 27, 1985.

MacKay, Scott. "Cool Moose Party files challenge to primary law *Robert J. Healey Jr., chairman of the Cool Moose Party, wants the state's primary election law declared unconstitutional," *The Providence Journal*, Section B, September 10, 1996.

MacKay, Scott. "Healey gets 2-1 vote of confidence from board, will continue as chairman says tally means majority is 'moving in same direction,'" *The Providence Journal*, Section B, January 28, 1986.

MacKay, Scott. "Healey threatens to quit as chairman; calls for committee vote of confidence," *The Providence Journal*, Section C, January 15, 1986.

MacKay, Scott. "How the suburbs elected almond Older urban areas losing political clout," *The Providence Journal*, November 5, 1998.

MacKay, Scott. "Killion gets right to vote on binding arbitration May break impasse between teachers, school committee," *The Providence Journal*, Section D, December 17, 1985.

MacKay, Scott. "Lottery to determine ballot placement," *The Providence Journal*, Section B, April 20, 1994.

MacKay, Scott. "Negotiators criticized by DiOrio Former NEA head raps 'delay' by school board," Providence Journal, September 12, 1985, p. C-01.

MacKay, Scott. "POLITICAL SCENE Buchanan battling to get on primary ballot," *The Providence Journal*, Section B, January 8, 1996.

MacKay, Scott, and Jonathan Saltzman, "POLITICAL SCENE Only the boss knows about those bonuses," *The Providence Journal*, Section B, October 12, 1998.

MacKay, Scott, "School board promises teachers courtesy," *The Providence Journal*, Section C, March 26, 1985.

MacKay, Scott. "Students urge contract compromise Leaders of student council and senior class say they fear that a strike will interrupt school year," *The Providence Journal*, Section C, September 25, 1985.

MacKay, Scott. "Sundlun isn't apologizing for physique remark about Quinn," *The Providence Journal*, Section D, June 9, 1994.

MacKay, Scott. "One strange man Barefoot Bob Healey," *The Providence Journal*, Section M, June 23, 1985.

MacKay, Scott. "Teachers go to work, still without contract," *The Providence Journal*, Section C, September 4, 1985.

MacKay, Scott. "Town to publish teacher salaries Board votes to list school workers' names, pay at annual meeting," *The Providence Journal*, Section D, April 23, 1985.

MacKay, Scott. "York, Almond assail Machtley tax vow," *The Providence Journal*, March 16, 1994.

Martine, John. "Healey protests Ch. 10's dis-invitation," *The Providence Journal*, Section C, October 3, 1994.

Maynard, Michael. "Providence holds parade in honor of St. Patrick," *The Providence Journal*, Section B, March 19, 1995.

Mayerowitz, Scott. "A long-distance runner for lieutenant governor," *The Providence Journal*, March 17, 2006.

Mayerowitz, Scott. "Ocean State native King returns to run for office," *The Providence Journal*, January 31, 2006.

Mayerowitz, Scott, and Katherine Gregg, Edward Fitzpatrick, and Scott MacKay, "POLITICAL SCENE—Laffey not alone in suggesting the job of the lieutenant governor is a waste," *The Providence Journal*, Section C, October 24, 2005.

McCarthy, Dave. "A walking Christmas tree blinks warning to drivers: Slow down near school," *The Providence Journal*, Section C, December 21, 1984.

McCarthy, Dave. "Board chairman upset by benefit vote Calls Killion's explanation for approval 'limp'," *The Providence Journal*, Section C, April 4, 1984.

McCarthy, Dave. "Credibility a top issue in school board race," *The Providence Journal*, Section C, October 22, 1982.

McCarthy, Dave. "Healey continues crusade for warning signs at Quirk despite promise from state, *The Providence Journal*, Section C, September 25, 1984.

McCarthy, Dave. "Healey hits legislators for not helping school boards," *The Providence Journal*, Section C, January 25, 1984.

McCarthy, Dave. "Teacher 'wish-list' is 10 pages long, the school board is 35," *The Providence Journal*, Section C, January 11, 1985.

McCarthy, David. "Rep. Urban to join Healey's fight for warning signal in front of school," *The Providence Journal*, Section C, September 24, 1984.

McCarthy, Dave. "School board head determined to speak out despite criticism," *The Providence Journal*, Section C, December 15, 1983.

McCarthy, Dave. "Warren Year in Review Revaluation contributed to Democratic defeats in '84," *The Providence Journal*, January 2, 1985. P. C-01.

McPhillips, Jody. "Area politicians, analysts

say Clinton speech went halfway," *The Providence Journal*, August 19, 1998.

McPhillips, Jody. "'Cool Moose' party founded to bring town politics new faces", *The Providence Journal*, Section C, June 4, 1986.

McPhillips, Jody. "Cool Moose Party wins second spot on ballot," *The Providence Journal*, Section B, September 17, 1996.

McPhillips, Jody. "Journal-Bulletin's Town Meeting '96 Third parties proliferate, gain respectability," *The Providence Journal*, September 1, 1996.

McPhillips, Jody. "'98 Election This may be the last run for Cool Moose leader," *The Providence Journal*, October 25, 1998.

McPhillips, Jody. "Judge to weigh the issue of harm to children as Warren board calls for teachers' return," *The Providence Journal*.

McPhillips, Jody. "Man in the news Robert J. Healey Jr.: The strange man who thrives in public eye," *The Providence Journal*, April 22, 1986.

McPhillips, Jody. "'98 Election This may be last run for Cool Moose leader," *The Providence Journal*, October 25, 1998.

McPhillips, Jody. "Union weighing new offer in Warren teachers strike," *The Providence Journal*, April 27, 1986.

McPhillips, Jody. "Warren back in class we can't defy court, union president says," *The Providence Journal*, May 7, 1986.

McPhillips, Jody, with reports from Judy Rakowsky and Bob Mello. "Special master' enters strike Warren teachers, committee ordered to start talking," *The Providence Journal*, May 9, 1986.

Mello, Bob. "Attorney general tells school board its closed meeting violated state law," *The Providence Journal*, Section C, August 17, 1984.

Mello, Bob. "Brule criticizes Killion for voting on tax issue that affects his wife," *The Providence Journal*, Section C, March 27, 1984.

Mello, Bob. "Budget cover letter by Healey rejected," *The Providence Journal*, Section C, April 24, 1984.

Mello, Bob. "Chairman Healey is barefoot again," *The Providence Journal*, Section C, July 26, 1983.

Mello, Bob. "Councilmen criticize school board head for statements to the press Comments on legislators called 'backstabbing'," *The Providence Journal*, Section B, January 30, 1984.

Mello, Bob. "Healey, Cool Moose candidate, announces 2nd run for governor," *The Providence Journal*, Section B, February 2, 1994.

Mello, Bob. "Healey hopes drivers will see the light, go slow near school, *The Providence Journal*, Section C, October 18, 1984.

Mello, Bob. "Healey: nab pot smokers at home," *The Providence Journal*, Section C, January 13, 1983.

Mello, Bob. "Police checking buses for pot," *The Providence Journal*, Section B, January 12, 1983.

Mello, Bob. "Radar convinces chief that speeders pose hazard to Quirk School children," *The Providence Journal*, Section C, October 19, 1984.

Mello, Bob. "Sick leave by teachers could lead to $44,000 deficit, officials project," *The Providence Journal*, Section B, March 26, 1984.

Mello, Bob. "Schools, union reach tentative

agreement," *The Providence Journal*, Section B, April 18, 1983.

Mello, Bob. "Rep. Urban 'shocked' by Healey's criticism of local legislators," *The Providence Journal*, Section C, January 27, 1984.

Mello, Bob. "Teachers file complaint on Healey's sign, flyers Newspaper," *The Providence Journal*, Section C, April 16, 1985.

Mello, Bob. "Teachers' union requests arbitration for settlement Newspaper," *The Providence Journal*, Section C, May 28, 1985.

Merolla, James A. "CAMPAIGN 2002—Fogarty enjoys fundraising edge," *The Providence Journal*, East Bay Window, Section B, April 20, 1994.

Mikovits, Amanda. "Healey plays giggly Son of God at Newspaper Guild Follies," *The Providence Journal*, Section: breaking news, February 25, 2011.

Miller, Wayne G. "THE DECADE IN REVIEW: LOCAL HEADLINERS," *The Providence Journal*, December 31, 1989.

Mingis, Ken. "Warren teachers give Friday contract deadline for extracurricular activities," *The Providence Journal*, April 29, 1986.

Mingis, Ken. "Warren teachers reject offer School head to seek injunction against union," *The Providence Journal*, May 2, 1986.

Mooney, Tom. "CAMPAIGN 2002—Seriously: Running for lieutenant governor," *The Providence Journal*, October 31, 2002.

Mooney, Tom. "ELECTION 2002—Fogarty easily wins, turning back challenge to need for lt. Gov.," *The Providence Journal*, November 6, 2002.

"More money needed for schools—Healey," *Warren Times Gazette*, January 19, 1983.

Mulvaney, Katie. "ELECTION FALLOUT—SKHS students are close to perfect on election poll," *The Providence Journal*, Section D, November 9, 2006.

Needman, Cynthia, and Karen Lee Ziner. "projo PolitiFact—Politics |-Healey's claim is off the mark," *The Providence Journal*, October 30, 2010.

"Negotiations off to a shaky start," *Warren Times-Gazette*, January 16, 1985.

"Negotiations stalled," *Warren Times-Gazette*, July 31, 1985.

O'Brien, Jerry. "Cool Moose candidate backed for board," *The Providence Journal*, Section C, November 13, 1995.

O'Brien, Jerry. "Cool Moose Healey: The governed should govern," *The Providence Journal*, October 16, 1994.

O'Brien, Jerry. "Cool Moose Healey: The governed should govern," *The Providence Journal*, October 16, 1994.

O'Brien, Jerry. "Party tells the council it's time to appoint a member of his party to the town Board of Canvassers," *The Providence Journal*, Section C, November 7, 1995.

"Official Election Day tallies offer no surprises in top races, *The Providence Journal*, Section B, November 23, 1994.

O'Neill, James M. "CAMPAIGN '94 Almond's absence from forum scored by moderator Fowlkes," *The Providence Journal*, Section C, November 1, 1994.

Perry, Karen. "Contract settled; healing wounds will take longer," *The Providence*

Journal, May 14 1986.

Pina, Alisha A. "Clinton stumps for Raimondo | Campaign 2014," *The Providence Journal*, October 25, 2014.

Polichetti, Barbara. "Labor panel orders School Committee to stop publishing data on teachers Report accuses school officials of unfair bargaining practice," *The Providence Journal*, Section C, December 24, 1985.

Poon, Chris. "Cool Moose's Healey wins high school's mock election," *The Providence Journal*, Section D, October 27, 1994.

Poon, Chris. "GRADUATION DAY Cool Moose candidate: 'Be yourself' *Unsuccessful gubernatorial candidate Robert Healey Jr. implores graduates to think big, take chances and follow their instincts," *The Providence Journal*, Section C, June 13, 1995.

"Pro-choice group supports Roberts," The Providence Journal, Section B, December 8, 2005.

"PROJO POLITICS BLOG," *The Providence Journal*, Section: WEBLOG, June 21, 2010.

Rakowsky, Judy. "Warren teachers ratify contract, will return to classroom today," *The Providence Journal*, May 12, 1986.

Edgar, Randall, and Katherine Gregg. "campaign 2014 | Cool Moose will carry the Moderate banner," *The Providence Journal*, September 12, 2014.

Rau, Elizabeth. "Candidates for governor pitch their economic plans," *The Providence Journal*, June 24, 1994.

"R.I.'s moose takes a holiday," *The Providence Journal*, October 15, 1985.

"Robert Healey, Committee, council share ideas, avoid 'horror stories' of past," *Warren Times Gazette*, March 9, 1983.

"Robert J. Healey Sr., Obituary," *The Providence Journal*, February 27, 1990.

Rowland, Christopher. "Familiar barbs mark final forum *Governor Almond questions how Myrth York plans to finance her education plan; York chides Almond over traffic jams and traffic court," *The Providence Journal*, October 31, 1998.

Saltzman, Saltzman, and Scott MacKay. "York, Almond bring in the heavy hitters," *The Providence Journal*, October 31, 1998.

"School appointment: Healey's letter criticized," *Warren Times-Gazette*, March 13, 1985.

"School board budget folder to include 2 cover letters from feuding factions," *The Providence Journal*, Section C, May 16, 1984.

"School board: Healey doesn't speak for us," *The Providence Journal*, Section D, February 12, 1986.

"School budget starts smoothly, *Warren Times-Gazette*, January 1, 1985.

"School budget surplus more than $134,000." *Warren Times-Gazette*, May 15,1985.

"School Committee will ask teachers' union to renegotiate raises," *Warren Times Gazette*, March 3, 2020.

Schuyler, John Philip. "No explanations given at school board meeting," *Warren Times-Gazette*, August 28, 1985.

"Secretaries," *Warren Times Gazette*, November 23, 1982.

"Sick Days: Teachers behind union— Healey Union Can't police abuse

– Duperron," *Warren Times-Gazette*, March 14, 1984.

"Smoking at home is parents' responsibility," *Warren Times Gazette*, January 19, 1983.

Sousa, Glenice G. "Letter stated facts, time to cut losses," *Warren Times-Gazette*, June 4, 1986, p. 31.

Sousa, Glenice G. "Teachers keep faith: justice to be done," *Warren Times-Gazette*, May 21, 1986.

Stevens, Don. "DeLeo makes impassioned speech to School Committee," *Warren Times-Gazette*, January 29,1986.

Stevens, Don. "Is Healey chairman or isn't he? That is the question," *Warren Times Gazette*, February 12, 1986.

Stevens, Don. "Read feels like cork in bottle," *Warren Times-Gazette*, January 8, 1986.

Stevens, Don. "School Committee attends to business," *Warren Times Gazette*, April 30, 1986.

Stevens, Don. "Teachers return to class on negotiators' advice," *Warren Times Gazette*, May 7,1986.

"Strike Day 3: No concessions, No injunction, nowhere to go," *Warren Times-Gazette*, April 23, 1986.

"Students mock vote foretells results," *The Providence Journal*, Section C, November 7, 1986.

"Sunday Advance Hold for Silverman Dubious Achievement Awards '82,'" *The Providence Journal*. Section C, January 2, 1983.

"Tax rate jumps $7.74," *Warren Times-Gazette*, May 18, 1983.

"Teachers deserve credit for going back to school without contract," *Warren Times-Gazette*, September 11, 1985.

"Teachers reach accord in contract with committee," *Warren Times-Gazette*, May 19, 1982.

"Teachers should consider renegotiating contract," *Warren Times-Gazette*, March 9, 1983.

Tempera, Jacqueline. "Passages: Robert Healey—A cool passion for R.I. politics—Cool Moose Party founder discovered dead Sunday," *The Providence Journal*, 22 March 2016, p. 1.

"Time for a school settlement is now," *Warren Times-Gazette*, March 19, 1986, p. 4.

Turgeon, Art. "COOL MOOSE CONTEST Oops? Healey wins House primary," *The Providence Journal*, Section C, September 11, 1996.

Turgeon, Art. "Cool Moose primary looms on horizon," *The Providence Journal*, Section C, June 27, 1996.

Turgeon, Art. "PRIMARY '96 Healey seeks recount of votes," *The Providence Journal*, Section C, September 13, 1996.

"U.S. judge rejects challenge to R.I.'s party-line voting," *The Providence Journal*, September 1, 2010.

"Warren's shows beat networks hands down," *Warren Times-Gazette*, September 6, 1984.

Wooley, Jeanette. "Wooley responds to Braun letter," *Warren Times-Gazette*, 5/28/1986.

Ziner, Karen Lee. "CAMPAIGN 2010—LIEUTENANT GOVERNOR—Healey gets traction in quest to abolish the office he seeks," *The Providence Journal*, October 23, 2010.

Ziner, Kareen Lee. "Campaign 2010—Lieutenant governor candidates have a lively debate," The Providence Journal, October 22, 2010.

Ziner, Karen Lee. "ELECTION 2010—LT. Governor—Incumbent Roberts fends off challenge," *The Providence Journal*, November 3, 2010.

Ziner, Karen Lee. "CAMPAIGN 2010—THE LIEUTENANT GOVERNOR—Should office even exist?" *The Providence Journal*, September 24, 2010.

INTERVIEWS

Boyes, Claire. Interview by Lawrence Verria. Barrington, Rhode Island. July 26, 2019.

Brule, Paul. Interview by Lawrence Verria. Warren, Rhode Island. October 10, 2020.

Craven, Robert. Interview by Lawrence Verria. North Kingstown, Rhode Island. August 20, 2019.

DePascuale, Joe. Interview by Lawrence Verria. Bristol, Rhode Island. August 8, 2020.

Doran, Thomas. Interview by Lawrence Verria. Portsmouth, Rhode Island. June 17, 2020.

Fortin, Brian. Interview by Lawrence Verria. Bristol, Rhode Island. July 28, 2020.

Fulton, DeWolf. Interview by Lawrence Verria. Bristol, Rhode Island. July 18, 2019.

Garvin, Gloria. Phone interview by Lawrence Verria. January 4, 2021.

Garvin, Gavin. Phone interview by Lawrence Verria. January 8, 2021.

Gotauco, Jade. Email to the author, July 25, 2019.

Gotauco, Jade. Interview by Lawrence Verria. Warren, Rhode Island. July 25, 2019.

Healey, James. Phone interview by Lawrence Verria. Barrington, Rhode Island. July 28, 2022.

Kittell, Katherine. Interview by Lawrence Verria. Warren, Rhode Island. March 1, 2020.

Lavey, Gary. Interview by Lawrence Verria. Bristol, Rhode Island. July 21, 2019.

Lopes, David. Interview by Lawrence Verria. North Kingstown, Rhode Island. June 5, 2018.

Marques, Joe. Interview by Lawrence Verria. Warren, Rhode Island. July 22, 2020.

Moniz, Joe. Interview by Lawrence Verria. Swansea, Massachusetts. January 11, 2020.

Rodriguez, Brian. Phone interview by Lawrence Verria. March 1, 2020.

Seymour, Ruth Ellen Stone. Interview by Lawrence Verria. Bristol, Rhode Island. July 30, 2019.

Tracy, Adam. Phone interview by Lawrence Verria. January 21, 2020.

Tracy, Tom. Phone interview by Lawrence Verria. Warren, Rhode Island. March 1, 2020.

White, Vickie. Interview by Lawrence

Verria. Brisotl, Rhode Island. September 19, 2019.

Wooley, Jeanette. Phone interview by Lawrence Verria. August 14, 2021.

ONLINE AND MISCELLANEOUS SOURCES

"Bob Healey talks elections, future," https://www.youtube.com/watch?v=6XUqqd-9cV8, November 2, 2010, assessed July 9, 2020.

Cool Moose Party v. State of RI, 6 F. Supp. 2d 116 (D.R.I. 1998), JUSTIA US Law, https://law.justia.com/cases/federal/district-courts/FSupp2/6/116/2347646/, May 27,1998, accessed 11/29/2021.

Comery, Beth. "You Know He's Right," *Providence Daily Dose*, https://providencedailydose.com/2008/01/13/you-know-hes-right/, June 13, 2008.

"Cool Moose Party founder Robert Healey dead at 58." https://www.youtube.com/watch?v=pcINSBIu8Bw channel 12, WPRI, Providence, accessed October 12, 2019, March 21, 2016.

Donnis, Ian. "Narrow Choice," The Providence Phoenix, http://www.providencephoenix.com/archive/features/02/10/03/THIRD.htmlOctober 4, 2002, accessed June 12, 2019.

Gavigan, Parker. "Missing money grows, involving deceased political candidate Bob Healey," https://turnto10.com/news/local/nbc-10-i-team-large-amounts-of-money-missing-from-bob-healey-estate, NBC 10 News, April 30, 2021, Accessed May 5, 2021.

Haskins, Justin, "The infuriating case of Robert Healey," http://www.providencejournal.com/opinion/commentary/20141113-justin-haskins-the-infuriating-case-of-robert-healey.ece?start=2, November 13, 2014, Accessed June 15, 2020.

Hayes, Ted. "Three years after his death, Bob Healey's estate is far from settled Cool Moose founder's will, conflicts and claims bog down probate process," https://www.eastbayri.com/seekonk/stories/three-years-after-his-death-bob-healeys-estate-has-yet-to-be-settled,64051, East Bay RI, April 9, 2019. accessed May 8, 2020.

Healey, Robert J. Jr. Guest MINDSET-TER™ "Candidate for Governor of Rhode Island twitter sharing button," https://www.golocalprov.com/politics/guest-mindsetter-robert-j.-healey-jr.-candidate-for-governor-of-rhode-islan, GoLocalProv, September 20, 2014, accessed July 24, 2020.

Healey, Robert. Lively Experiment, https://www.youtube.com/watch?v=YrdCB1T6-9Q&feature=youtu.be, November 21, 2014, accessed July 21, 2014.

Healey, Robert J., Jr. "The Platform Document of Robert J. Healey, Jr., Candidate for Lieutenant Governor of the State Rhode Island 2006." http://files.golocalprov.com.s3.amazonaws.com/GOVERNOR%20-%202006%20LT%20GOV%20PLATFORM.pdf, accessed July 20, 2020.

Healey, Robert J. Jr. "What I Have Learned from Others," Circa 1987. "Robert J. Healey Obituary," https://www.dignitymemorial.com/obituaries/warren-ri/bob-healey-6857377, accessed December 29, 2019.

"History of Trilium Farm, Soil and Sky, https://soilandskycenter.wixsite.com/soil-and-sky/history-of-the-trillium-farm, accessed June 15, 2020.

MacKay, Scott. *Lively Experiment*, https://www.youtube.com/watch?v=YrdCB1T6-9Q&feature=youtu.be, November 21, 2014, accessed July 21, 2014.

MacKay, Scott. "R.I. Politics: No Women Need Apply," *wrnipolitcs blog*, https://wrnipoliticsblog.wordpress.com/2010/09/18/r-i-politics-no-women-need-apply/, September 18, 2010, accessed August 27, 2020.

Nagle, Katie. "Robert Healey, 1957-2016: Rhode Island Leaders React," GoLocalProv, https://www.golocalprov.com/politics/robert-cool-moose-healey-1957-2016-rhode-island-leaders-react, March 22, 2016, accessed July 17, 2020.

Political Round Table, https://thepublicsradio.org/article/political-roundtable-pagliarini-guns-tolls-robert-cool-moose-healey March 26, 2016 / Accessed July 25, 2019.

"PROJO POLITICS BLOG," *The Providence Journal*, Section: WEBLOG, June 21, 2010.

"Twenty," https://wrnipoliticsblog.wordpress.com/2010/10/19/roberts-dropping-200k-tv-bomb-on-healey/, RINPR, October 19, 2010, accessed July 9, 2020.

Reach Out, https://www.youtube.com/watch?v=LAOKjcmFN20 March 4, 2011 / Accessed July 30, 2020.

Safford, James, "Bob Healey Showed One Man Can Be an Island," http://www.rirelevant.com/politics/safford-bob-healey-showed-one-man-can-island/?fbclid=IwAR1gSQFC-CP6T0AiayRv1cCP3C7BkRY4EjaPle_L2OP_nbKtW8tZ3Vy6ZY5o, riRelent.com, January 21, 2018, accessed July 18, 2019.

2014 Rhode Island Governor Debate, https://www.youtube.com/watch?v=ziyMvGUVVug, 10/21/2014, accessed 6-03-19.

Sulzeberger, A.G., "Jokes and Secret Hopes for Lieutenant Governors, *The New York Times*, https://www.nytimes.com/2010/12/04/us/04lieutenant.html?pagewanted=all&_r=0, December 3, 2010.

"This Rhode Island governor candidate won 22 percent of the vote. He only spent $35," Washington Post, https://www.washingtonpost.com/news/the-fix/wp/2014/11/05/this-rhode-island-governor-candidate-won-22-percent-of-the-vote-he-only-spent-35/?arc404=true, accessed June 13 2020.

Violet, Arlene. "Robert Healey: A true patriot." https://www.valleybreeze.com/2016-04-05/north-providence/arlene-violet-robert-healey-true-patriot#.XgpYaCMrLJw, April 5 2016, (accessed 12/29/2019.)

ABOUT THE AUTHOR

Lawrence W. Verria serves as the North Kingstown High School Social Studies Department Chair. His teaching career spans forty years. His professional recognitions include the 2000 Rhode Island Teacher of the Year, the 2008 Susan B. Wilson Civic Education Award, and the 2022 Gilder Lehrman Institute of American History Rhode Island Teaching Award. He and his wife, Celeste Verria, live in Bristol, Rhode Island where they raised their three daughters.

Made in United States
North Haven, CT
12 December 2022

28612303R00212